W9-AXJ-925

EMBATTLED NEIGHBORS

EMBATTLED NEIGHBORS

SYRIA, ISRAEL, AND LEBANON

ROBERT G. RABIL

LYNNE
RIENNER
PUBLISHERS

BOULDER
LONDON

Published in the United States of America in 2003 by
Lynne Rienner Publishers, Inc.
1800 30th Street, Boulder, Colorado 80301
www.rienner.com

and in the United Kingdom by
Lynne Rienner Publishers, Inc.
3 Henrietta Street, Covent Garden, London WC2E 8LU

Library of Congress Cataloging-in-Publication Data
Rabil, Robert G.
    Embattled neighbors : Syria, Israel, and Lebanon / Robert G. Rabil.
        p.   cm.
    Includes bibliographical references and index.
    ISBN 1-58826-149-2
    1. Arab-Israeli conflict.   2. Israel—Foreign relations—Syria.   3. Israel—Foreign
relations—Lebanon.   4. Syria—Foreign relations—Israel.   5. Lebanon—Foreign
relations—Israel.   6. Israel—Politics and government—20th century.   7. Syria—Politics and
government—1971–   8. Lebanon—Politics and government—1975–1990.   9. Arab-Israeli
conflict—1993—Peace.   I. Title.

DS119.7.R2199 2003
327'.09569—dc21

                                                                                    2002068271

British Cataloguing in Publication Data
A Cataloguing in Publication record for this book
is available from the British Library.

Printed and bound in the United States of America

The paper used in this publication meets the requirements
of the American National Standard for Permanence of
Paper for Printed Library Materials Z39.48-1984.

To Antoinette, my mother

Contents

A Note on Transliteration and Sources

The English transliteration from Arabic generally follows the rules of the *International Journal of Middle Eastern Studies.* Arabic names commonly used by the *New York Times* and whose spellings are thus becoming standard retain their original form as they appeared in that newspaper. For example, Farouk al-Shara has not been transliterated as Faruq al-Shar'.

Due to the contemporaneous and comprehensive nature of this work and the unavailability of Syrian archives, the primary sources of this study depended in no small measure on official documents and statements, personal interviews, and lectures. Being the mouthpieces of the Syrian government, Syrian newspapers were considered official documents. Arabic newspapers such as *Al-Hayat* and autobiographies and articles written by former and present state officials were pertinent to this study. Secondary sources were used where extensive research has been undertaken and where Arabic primary sources were either unavailable or nonexistent.

Acknowledgments

I am grateful for the financial support that I have received from the Department of Near Eastern and Judaic Studies at Brandeis University, the Tauber Institute for the Study of European Jewry at Brandeis University, and the Interuniversity Fellowship Program in Jewish Studies at Brooklyn College and the Hebrew University of Jerusalem. Special thanks go to Professor Asher Susser, Dr. Eyal Zisser, and Dr. Joshua Tietelbaum, whose assistance was paramount to my research. I thank Professor Moshe Ma'oz for his advice. I thank the faculty and staff of the Department of Near Eastern and Judaic Studies at Brandeis University for their moral, academic, and administrative support. I thank the faculty and staff of the Center for Middle Eastern Studies, and the directors of the Middle East Seminar, Harvard University, especially Professor Lenore Martin, for their support, advice, and friendship. My deep appreciation goes to all interviewees, Syrians, Israelis, and Lebanese whose insightful and instructive information proved time and again invaluable to my work.

I am grateful to all my colleagues at Harvard and Brandeis Universities, and friends, especially Terry Gaines, John Kingsley, Patrick Apel, Dr. Robert Allison, Franck Salameh, and Hasan Mneimneh, whose encouragement, support, and belief gave me the confidence to overcome all obstacles. Special thanks go to David Finnegan, whose support and generosity of heart overwhelmed me. I am grateful to Raymond Bandar and family, who embraced me with their friendship, love, and hospitality. I am grateful to Julie Ariagno for reading the first paper I wrote on the subject and for hardening my dedication to finish the job. I am thankful to Heidi Burns, who edited some of my work and provided instructive suggestions. I thank Kanan Makiya and Rend Rahim Francke for their support. I am deeply thankful to Dr. Olga Davidson for reading on short notice some of my work and for being my good and patient friend. Lynne Rienner and staff deserve my commendation for their professionalism and support.

I am largely indebted to Professors Sadek al-Azm, Antony Polonsky, and Avigdor Levy for their immense contribution to my work, ranging from academic advice to constructive criticism, let alone their friendship, which I cherish. Professor Levy deserves infinite gratitude for guiding me every step of the way, from the initial research to the final writing of the book, and encouraging me to rise above the level of my expectations.

I am deeply thankful to all my family, whose love gave me the will to survive the darkest hours, weather the vagaries of life, and appreciate and enjoy life. More specifically, I am eternally thankful to my mother, Antoinette, to whom this book is dedicated. I am blessed by her unbounded, unquestionable love and her belief in decency and seeking the truth. I thank her for inculcating in me the belief in awakening every day, rain or shine, with a smile on my face and a will to passionately, courageously, and decently hew the passage of a better life for all. I love you.

Introduction:
Embattled Neighbors

Negib Azoury, in his 1905 book *Le Reveil de la Nation Arabe dans l'Asie Turque,* prophesied that the future of the Near East would depend on the struggle between two rising, vigorous, and antagonistic nationalisms: Zionism and Arab nationalism. Azoury wrote:

> Two important phenomena, of the same nature but opposed, are emerging at this moment in Asiatic Turkey. They are the awakening of the Arab nation and the latent effort of the Jews to reconstitute on a very large scale the ancient kingdom of Israel. These two movements are destined to confront each other continuously, until one prevails over the other. The final outcome of this struggle, between two peoples that represent two contradictory principles, may shape the destiny of the whole world.[1]

Almost a century later Azoury's prophecy still rings true in the Middle East. Israel and Syria came to embody Zionism and Arab nationalism respectively, becoming embattled neighbors. Squeezed between the two countries and afflicted by sectarian strife, Lebanon was caught up in the Arab-Israeli conflict and became the focus of a fierce rivalry between Damascus and Tel Aviv. Syria won the struggle for Lebanon and transformed Beirut into a satellite capital. But during the last few years the Middle East has been affected by many changes: the eruption of the Palestinian intifada, the end of the Cold War, the disintegration of the Soviet Union, the emergence of the United States as the sole dominant superpower, and the success of the United States and its international and Arab allies in the Gulf War. Israel and Syria, as integral players in the Middle East and the Arab-Israeli conflict, could not escape the effects of this trend of change and development. Under the auspices of the United States, the two countries committed themselves to a peace process, based on UN Security Council Resolutions 242 and 338 and on the principle of "land for peace," launched in Madrid in 1991. The process has continued by fits and starts to the present moment.

Israel signed the Oslo Accords with the Palestinians in 1993 and a peace treaty with Jordan in 1994, but has failed to resolve its conflict with Syria. Despite a history of negotiations that made familiar the issues at hand, and despite U.S.-led efforts at mediation, Israel and Syria now seem both as close and as distant as ever from concluding a peace treaty. Questions linger as to why a breakthrough in Israeli-Syrian relations has not occurred yet. What are the internal and external constraints on the governments of both countries? What are the sensitive issues hamstringing the negotiations between them? How does Lebanon figure into Syria's domestic and foreign policies, especially with respect to peacemaking with Israel? Where does the United States stand in regard to the peace process and what are its real commitments to both Israel and Syria? What are the conditions and implications of the Egyptian, Jordanian, and Palestinian peace accords and treaties with Israel for Israeli-Syrian peace negotiations? What kind of post–Cold War political climate has dawned on the region and what are its implications for Israel and Syria? What are the peace perspectives of each country? Were there any "missed opportunities" for peace, and why has peace been elusive so far?

This book tries to answer these questions by attempting to chart the course of the Israeli-Syrian aspect of the Arab-Israeli conflict and to mark its phases from Israel's War of Independence to the present peace process and negotiations between the two states, with the focus from the struggle for Lebanon in 1975. The aim is to examine and analyze the subject comprehensively by covering its domestic, regional, and international dimensions, providing in the process a detailed and comparative analysis of both countries and their positions on the peace process. Following this integrated approach, I strive to discuss the recent history of the two countries, bearing in mind the difficulty of seeking to portray the complexities of this conflicted relationship by attempting to correlate the domestic, regional, and international problems and obstacles to peace. This forms the methodological basis of the book's systematic and comprehensive account of the Israeli-Syrian conflict. Beyond this, however, I strive to maintain a stance of considered objectivity as I investigate the fundamental issues making up the substance of the Israeli-Syrian conflict. Behind my objective of this detailed and systematic study is an attempt not only to analyze the experiences that have shaped the conflict, but also to present the obstacles and consequently draw the lessons that need to be projected into the present to help bring about peace.

Upon analysis, it becomes clear that although the two countries committed themselves to peace, they were neither prepared nor ready for it. The protracted nature of the Israeli-Syrian negotiations and their unwillingness to make territorial compromise show that both countries are having difficulty shedding their deep-seated anxieties, ingrained habits, and the traditional constraints of their domestic politics. In addition, contrary to expectations, the post–Cold War era did not lead to a lessening of tensions in the region. Peace has been elusive so far because of the cumulative effect of these problems and obstacles, which intensified Syria's and Israel's need respectively for a "dignified" and "secure" settlement.

In carrying out this project, I found it necessary and useful to devote the first chapter to a review and analysis of the origins and development of the contentious issues gripping the Israeli-Syrian conflict. Chapter 1 also delineates the course of the direct conflict between them and its consequences for the possibilities of peace. Chapter 2 examines the internal setting of Lebanon in relation to the configuration of the Arab-Israeli conflict. It also analyzes the proxy war waged by Israel and Syria in Lebanon and its ramifications for the three countries. Chapter 3 is dedicated to an examination of the triangular relationship that arose between the United States, Syria, and Israel, including the U.S. role in peacemaking and mediating. Chapters 4, 5, and 6 deal with the regional and domestic constraints as well as the security and water concerns that the governments of the two countries have encountered in their relations with each other. Chapter 7 treats the sequence of negotiations since the Madrid peace conference of 1991. Chapter 8 scrutinizes the peace perspectives of both antagonists, analyzes "missed opportunities," and evaluates why peace has been elusive so far. The book's conclusion surveys the smooth transition of power in Syria and the new configuration in the region following Israel's withdrawal from Lebanon. It discusses the challenges facing the new ruler of Damascus and how Syria and Israel emerged from a decade-long peace process, which had been anything but the "peace of the brave."

Note

1. Negib Azoury, *Le Reveil de la Nation Arabe dans l'Asie Turque* (Paris: Plon-Nourrit, 1905, microform at Harvard University), p. v.

1

Decades of Direct Conflict: 1948–1975

To understand why Syria and Israel have fulfilled Azoury's prophecy by becoming such embattled neighbors, it is necessary to start with a review of the origins and developments of the contentious issues that have shaped the Israeli-Syrian conflict. The newly born state of Israel quickly came to embody Jewish nationalism's achievements and to represent its defensive shield and striking arm. The immediate impact of this development was to push the no-less newly formed Syrian state to increasingly regard itself as the embodiment of Arab nationalist aspirations and as the vanguard of Arabism's forward march. This set the stage not only for important political transformations and upheavals inside Syria, but also for the coming decades of direct conflicts and confrontations between the two new neighboring countries.

As a consequence, this chapter is devoted to a review and analysis of these decades of conflict from the 1948 war and its aftermath to the disengagement agreement signed by the two antagonists in 1974; the relevant shifts, changes, and alignments inside Syria and Israel that exacerbated the confrontations leading to the June war of 1967; the efforts of the United States to manage, contain, and mediate the conflicts and confrontations against a background of superpower rivalry and a raging Cold War threatening nuclear annihilation; and the two countries' perceptions of each other and of the Golan Heights.

The 1948 War: Implications and Consequences

During the second phase of Israel's War of Independence, referred to by the Palestinians as Al-Nakba, or "The Catastrophe," which lasted from May 1948 to January 1949, Israel's forces were able to repel the Arab armies of Transjordan, Egypt, Syria, Lebanon, and Iraq, with the result that Israel expanded its boundaries beyond those demarcated by the 1947 UN partition resolution. By the end of the 1948 war, the Lebanese army stood within its international boundary with Israel; the Iraqi army occupied the northern part of the West Bank; the Transjordanian army—the Arab Legion—occupied most of the central and all of the southern part of the West Bank; and the Egyptian army occupied the Gaza Strip, although the Israeli army had encircled an entire Egyptian brigade at Al-Faluja. Whereas all these Arab forces occupied areas outside Palestine's territory awarded to Israel by the 1947 UN resolution, Syria had succeeded in capturing three small areas west of its international boundary with Palestine, falling within the Palestine territory awarded to Israel by the UN. These areas, as we shall see, became the focus of the conflict.

As Israel gained the upper hand in the war and pressured the Arab armies into inactivity, all antagonists agreed to opening armistice talks mediated by the UN. By January 1949 the UN had established two frameworks for promoting a peaceful resolution of the Palestine conflict. The first, based upon UN Security Council (UNSC) Resolution 62 of November 16, 1948, called upon the parties "to seek agreement forthwith, by negotiations conducted either directly or through the acting mediator, with a view to the immediate establishment of [an] armistice."[1] The other based its starting points on UN General Assembly (UNGA) Resolution 194 (Article III) of December 11, 1948, which dealt with key issues such as the Palestine refugee problem created by the war and the future of Jerusalem. The latter resolution also established the Conciliation Commission for Palestine (PCC) to, among other things, "take steps to assist the governments and authorities concerned to achieve a final settlement of all questions outstanding between them."[2]

On January 13, 1949, the parties to the conflict began their official armistice talks at the Hotel des Roses on the island of Rhodes, under the chairmanship of UN acting mediator Ralph Bunche. The negotiations involved direct formal and informal Arab-Israeli meetings. The United States and Great Britain exerted much positive influence on the dynamics of the negotiations, as all delegates, including those from the UN, appealed to them. The Rhodes negotiations resulted in armistice agreements between Israel and each of Egypt, Lebanon, Jordan, and Syria, signed respectively on February 24, March 23, April 3, and July 20, 1949. The agreements with Egypt, Jordan, and Lebanon drew armistice lines largely in conformity with the military situation on the ground, reflecting Israel's gain of territory in the war. But in the negotiations between Israel and Syria, Israel faced the reverse situation, with Syria controlling areas awarded to Israel by the 1947 UN partition resolution. Whereas Syria argued that the armistice line should conform to the war's outcome and as such to the cease-fire line, Israel adamantly insisted that the armistice line should correspond to the international boundary.

During the mandate of Britain over Palestine and France over Lebanon, the two mandatory powers reached an agreement in March 1923 over the international boundary between Syria, Lebanon, and Palestine. The demarca-

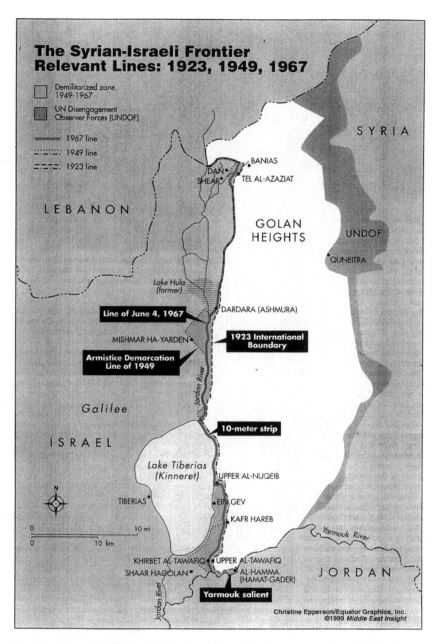

The Syrian-Israeli Frontier
Relevant Lines: 1923, 1949, 1967

Demilitarized zone,
1949-1967

UN Disengagement
Observer Forces (UNDOF)

1967 line
1949 line
1923 line

SYRIA

BANIAS

DAN
SHEAR
TEL AL-AZAZIAT

LEBANON

GOLAN
HEIGHTS

UNDOF

QUNEITRA

Lake Hula
(former)

Line of June 4, 1967

DARDARA (ASHMURA)

MISHMAR HA-YARDEN

1923 International
Boundary

Armistice Demarcation
Line of 1949

Jordan River

Galilee

ISRAEL

10-meter strip

Lake Tiberias
(Kinneret)

UPPER AL-NUQEIB

N

TIBERIAS

EIN GEV

KAFR HAREB

0   10 mi
0   10 km

Yarmouk River

KHIRBET AL-TAWAFIQ UPPER AL-TAWAFIQ
SHAAR HAGOLAN   AL-HAMMA
                    (HAMAT-GADER)

JORDAN

Jordan River

Yarmouk salient

Christine Epperson/Equator Graphics, Inc.
©1999 *Middle East Insight*

Reprinted from *Middle East Insight,* September–October 1999, © 1999 *Middle East Insight.* Used with permission of the publisher.

tion line incorporated in Palestine the Dan River (the main source of the Jordan River), the Jordan River, Lake Huleh, and Lake Tiberias. In the north-east and the north, the Banias River and its springs, and the Hasbani River, both sources of the Jordan River, remained respectively in Syrian and Lebanese territory. The boundary along the entire eastern side of the Huleh Valley was agreed to be 100 meters above the water level of Lake Huleh, leaving the entire lake and valley in Palestine. From Lake Huleh down to Lake Tiberias (the Sea of Galilee), the boundary line ran 50–400 meters to the east of the Jordan River, placing it and its east bank in Palestine. The boundary from Lake Tiberias ran 10 meters to its northeastern part, widening further to the east while moving south, thus leaving the entire lake in Palestine. The agreement, however, gave the Syrians certain fishing and navigation rights in Lake Huleh and Lake Tiberias, and in the section of the Jordan River between the two lakes. The government of Palestine was responsible for policing the lakes.[3]

Israel was in an advantageous position while negotiating with Syria, since all the other Arab states had already signed their armistice agreements and as a result had forsaken the military option. In addition, Syria's military was handicapped by a shortage of ammunition and arms. Equally significant, Syria was gripped by fractious domestic politics exacerbated by years of French colonial rule. At the time the French took control over Syria (1920), Sunni Muslims constituted 69 percent of the population, heterodox Muslims 16 percent (Alawis, Druzes, Ismailis), and Christians 14 percent (Catholics, Uniates, Greek Orthodox).[4] Socioeconomic and cultural differences were inseparable from religious and urban-rural divisions. The mountains and hill districts harbored compact minorities. The Druzes had concentrated southeast of Damascus in Jabal al-Druze, and the Alawis in the mountains northwest of Latakia. In the northeast, the Jazira province contained significant communities of Christians and Kurds. Rural-urban and class contrasts more often than not coincided with sectarian differences between urban Sunni Muslims and rural confessional minorities. The French exploited the ethnic and religious differences in order to contain the spread of Arab nationalism and favored the military recruitment of Alawis, Druzes, and other minorities in the Troupes Speciales du Levant, which subsequently constituted the embryo of the Syrian national army.[5]

A compromise was eventually reached whereby Syria would withdraw from the areas it had captured, which would then be demilitarized. But no agreement between the two countries was reached over sovereignty in the Demilitarized Zone (DMZ). The Israeli-Syrian General Armistice Agreement was finally signed on July 20, 1949. The preamble of the agreement stated that the parties, "in order to facilitate the transition from the present truce to permanent peace in Palestine, to negotiate an armistice, . . . have agreed upon the following provisions":

The injunction of the Security Council [of November 1948] against resort to military force in the settlement of the Palestine question shall henceforth be scrupulously respected by both Parties. . . . No aggressive action by the armed forces—land, sea or air—of either Party shall be undertaken, planned or threatened, against the people or the armed forces of the other (Article I).

No element of the land, sea or air, military or para-military forces of either Party, including non-regular forces, shall commit any warlike or hostile act against the military or para-military forces of the other Party, or against civilians in territory under the control of that Party, or shall advance beyond or pass over for any purpose whatsoever the Armistice Demarcation Line (Article III).

The Armistice Demarcation Line shall follow a line midway between the existing truce lines, as certified by the United Nations Truce Supervision Organisation for the Israeli and Syrian forces. Where the existing truce lines run along the international boundary between Syria and Palestine, the Armistice Demarcation shall follow that boundary line. . . . Where the Armistice Demarcation Line does not correspond to the international boundary between Syria and Palestine, the area between the Armistice Demarcation Line and the boundary, pending final territorial settlements between the Parties, shall be established as a Demilitarised Zone from which the armed forces of both Parties shall be totally excluded, and in which no activities by military or para-military forces shall be permitted. This provision applies to the Ein Gev and Dardara sectors which shall form part of the Demilitarised Zone (Article V).

The execution of the provisions of this Agreement shall be supervised by a Mixed Armistice Commission . . . whose Chairman shall be the United Nations Chief of Staff of the Truce Supervision Organisation (Article VII).[6]

The DMZ (an area less than 100 square miles) comprised the three areas captured by the Syrians: one in the north next to Tel Dan, the second south of Lake Huleh lying on both banks of the Jordan River, the third running from the northeastern bank of Lake Tiberias to its southeastern bank, extending to the boundary line (importantly, the Syrians controlled the ten-meter strip of beach and the east bank of the Jordan River, as well as Arab villages east of Lake Tiberias, such as Al-Hamma and Khirbet al-Tawafiq).[7] Despite the agreement's call for nonaggressive action, the impasse over the question of sovereignty in the DMZ gradually heightened the tension between the two countries. Here, one may surmise that the decades of direct conflict began at this point. For example, until early 1951, Israel kept trying to establish settlements in the DMZ manned by farmer-soldiers. This elicited condemnation from Syria. Too weak to resist Israeli actions, Syria complained to the Mixed Armistice Commission (MAC) and mimicked Israel by sending its own soldiers, disguised as civilians, into other parts of the DMZ. In early 1951, Israel raised the stakes when it went ahead with a development project to drain Lake Huleh in order to reclaim swaths of land for cultivation and to eliminate malaria from the region. Although Lake Huleh was outside the DMZ, Syria opposed the project on the grounds that it effected a topographical change giving Israel a military advantage, and that it involved work on Arab-owned lands. Israel adopted a tough stance, and armed clashes between the two countries erupted. The clashes, however, did not escalate into a war, as the two parties shucked this option. The upshot was the informal division of the DMZ:

> Southern Sector: Al-Hamma, [K]Hirbet Tawfiq, Nuqueib and the ascent to the Golan Heights were under Syrian control; the rest was in Israeli hands. Central Sector: The area east of the Jordan and the triangle west of the Jordan and north of the Jordan's entry to Lake Tiberias were under Syrian control; the area west of the Jordan was Israeli-controlled. Northern Sector: The majority was under Syrian control.[8]

Significantly enough, the Syrians exercised effective control over the northeastern shore of Lake Tiberias. Equally significant, although this partition would experience some alterations over the next sixteen years—all minor and at the expense of Syria—it would roughly define the line of June 4, 1967.

A Debate: Syria's Peace Offers to Israel

The Palestinian debacle, the indignant outlook of the urban notables toward the army, and factionalism among Syria's political elites prompted the army to mount a coup d'état on March 30, 1949. At the head of the coup was Colonel Husni al-Zaim, of Kurdish origin, who seized power by taking advantage of the rise of radical forces on the left and the resentment of a number of nationalist officers against the fresh Palestine experience. British scholar Patrick Seale remarked: "Zaim's successful putsch was the first intervention of the army in politics in the Middle East: it set a fashion which was to be widely followed."[9]

Zaim seized power after Egypt, Lebanon, and Jordan had signed their armistice agreements with Israel. Because of the coup, Syria's scheduled armistice talks were postponed until April. Zaim found it expedient to enlist Iraq's support in order to strengthen his negotiating position with Israel. But Syrian plans for alignment with Iraq triggered regional attempts to thwart them. Egypt and Saudi Arabia were wary of Hashimite (Iraqi and Jordanian) ambitions in the region, typified now by a Fertile Crescent scheme (union of Iraq, Syria, Lebanon, and Transjordan), and thus sought to win over Syria. Descendants of the prophet Muhammad and leaders of the Arab world, as well as allies of Britain during World War I, the Hashimites had been driven out of power from Saudi Arabia (Najd and Hijaz) as well as Syria, and thus contemplated plans to regain their regional leadership. At the time, they ruled Iraq and Transjordan thanks in large part to Britain. With Iraq slow and cautious in dealing with Zaim, who was the first Arab ruler to stage a coup d'état, and with Egypt and Saudi Arabia conveying their support to Zaim, which was conditional on Syria's continued independence, Zaim's interest in aligning Syria with Iraq waned. Conversely, his relations with the leadership in both Egypt and Saudi Arabia improved as he promised them to defend the independence of the Syrian state in the face of Hashimite ambitions.[10]

Zaim also tried to improve Syria's relations with France and the United States, which were in turn trying to attain leverage in Syrian politics. After granting Syria its independence, France was scrambling to improve its relations with Syria. The coming to power of Zaim was an opportune event to France, which recognized Zaim's regime, gave him its support, and made efforts to induce other countries to recognize his regime as well. U.S. interest in Syria stemmed from two factors: the United States was leading the PCC in Lausanne for promoting a peaceful resolution of the conflict, while at the same time probing Soviet intentions in the region. Contacts between Zaim and the United States had taken place before the coup. A Central Intelligence Agency (CIA) agent in the Middle East, Miles Copeland, reported in his book *The Game of Nations,* that Major Stephen Meade, the assistant military attaché of the U.S. legation in Damascus, had established contact with Husni Zaim, then chief of the general staff of the Syrian army, who brought up the idea of a coup.[11] According to Copeland, Zaim transmitted his program to the United States, which entailed, among other points, the institution of social and economic reforms and doing "something constructive about the Arab-Israel problem."[12] In his conversations with Meade, Zaim envisaged a plan of action in which technical and military aid to Syria figured substantially.

During the Lausanne conference of late April to early May 1949, meant to complement the Rhodes armistice agreements, Zaim conveyed to Israel, through informal channels, his "willingness to meet with Ben Gurion, to enter into peace negotiations with Israel, and to settle 250,000 or 300,000 Palestinian refugees in northeastern Syria."[13] Zaim offered Israel full peace and cooperation, including a common army, and resettlement of Palestinian refugees in exchange for an adjustment in the international border through the middle of Lake Tiberias.[14] The exchange of messages between Zaim's Syria and Ben Gurion's Israel lasted from April until early August 1949, but did not bear any fruit. Ben Gurion's refusal to meet Zaim and Israel's reaction to the Syrian initiative have been part of a historiographical debate that has been raging in Israel for some time.

During the 1980s, Israel, Britain, and the United States declassified documents and state papers, which have been examined by scholars, including a new generation of Israeli scholars (known as "new historians") who were not involved in the 1948 war but focused on its core and controversial questions: the origins of the war,[15] the birth of the Palestinian refugee problem,[16] the military balance, and the elusive peace.[17] Our concern is with the last question, which deals with the reasons why a peace treaty was not signed between Israel and Syria at the end of the war.

Avi Shlaim has criticized Israel's response to the Syrian offer as a "short-sighted" policy that maintained "that time was on Israel's side and that Israel could manage perfectly well without peace with the Arab states and without a solution to the Palestinian refugee problem,"[18] and has characterized Ben Gurion as having a "general preference for force over diplomacy as a means of resolving disputes between Israel and the Arabs."[19] Shlaim noted that Ben Gurion, as his diary reveals, "considered that the armistice agreements with the neighboring Arab states met Israel's essential needs for recognition, security, and stability."[20] Ben Gurion, according to Shlaim, "knew that for formal peace agreements Israel would have to pay by yielding substantial tracts of territory and by permitting the return of a substantial number of Palestinian refugees, and he did not consider this a price worth paying."[21] Shlaim also has criticized Itamar Rabinovich's book *The Road Not Taken: Early Arab-Israeli Negotiations,* which examined the controversy surrounding Zaim's offer. Shlaim remarked that the book "does not advance any thesis," and that "Rabinovich prefers to remain above the battle."[22]

Benny Morris, author of *The Birth of the Palestinian Refugee Problem, 1947–1949,* agreed with Shlaim's conclusion that Israeli leaders were satisfied with the armistice agreements and were "far from eager to pursue a peace process that would entail substantial Israeli concessions."[23] Morris quotes Abba Eban, Israel's ambassador to the UN at the time, and Moshe Sharett, Israel's foreign minister at the time, both considered conciliatory Zionist officials, as being content with the armistice agreements as well.[24] Morris also criticized Rabinovich's book. He points out that Rabinovich expresses a contempt for Zaim similar to Ben Gurion's admonishment, calling him a power-hungry, corrupt megalomaniac and other names in order to justify Ben Gurion's negative response to the Syrian overture.[25]

Morris concluded that Ben Gurion's "rejectionism was anchored in something far more solid than real or feigned suspicions regarding Zaim's personality. And that something was territory and water resources."[26] To bolster his argument, Morris quoted Sharett: "In negotiations with Syria, any promise or hint of possible promise on our part of a change in the border between Palestine and Syria and along the Jordan and the lakes should be avoided. On the contrary, it should be clear to the other side that under no circumstances can such a change be contemplated. On the other hand, the Syrian delegation should be encouraged to think about a large-scale absorption of refugees."[27]

Moshe Ma'oz, not considered a new historian, remarked that Ben Gurion's position "might have reflected his long-term strategic thinking and his deep convictions concerning Israeli-Syrian relations." Ma'oz explained that Ben Gurion "was not prepared to make important strategic concessions to Syria in return for a formal peace treaty signed by an unpredictable and corrupt Syrian dictator, who might not be willing or able to fulfill Syria's peace commitments to Israel in the future."[28]

Husni Zaim was overthrown and executed in a military coup led by Colonel Sami Hinnawi on August 14, 1949. Retrospectively, one could safely argue that Zaim's policies, which entailed social reforms, rapprochement with France and the United States, and disengagement from the possibility of union with Iraq, had alienated the same elements in Syrian society that brought him to power in the first place. After all, Hinnawi was his accomplice in the coup and had been pro-Iraqi; other radical nationalist forces had been critical not only of Zaim's rapprochement with the Western powers that helped create Israel, but also of Zaim's overtures to Israel. Zaim's peace offer to Israel could be looked upon as an attempt to neutralize the military power of Israel with the aim of strengthening his position at home. Accordingly, he could withdraw Syrian troops from the Israeli-Syrian front and foil any Hashimite plot against his regime, while at the same time working on his reforms at home with U.S. support. Israel, on the other hand, was not ready under any circumstances to adjust to new borders with Syria whereby Syria would share with Israel the waters of Lake Tiberias. Needless to say, this early Israeli rejectionism contributed in no small measure to the deepening and later intensification of the conflict with Syria.

On December 19, 1949, Colonel Adib Shishakli overthrew the short-lived Hinnawi regime, which seemed close to entering into a union with Baghdad. Shishakli, like Zaim before him, tried to strengthen his position at home and improve Syria's relations with the United States in the hope of receiving needed military and financial aid. He underscored the priority of building a strong army that would be instrumental in pushing his socioeconomic reforms, protecting his regime against internal and external (Hashimite) plots, and defending it against any Israeli attack. In May 1950 the big powers (the United States, France, and Britain) issued the tripartite declaration that opposed the use of force in the Middle East and rationed the arms supply. This big powers' policy ran counter to Shishakli's objective of building his army. Thereupon, the idea of neutralizing Israel through peace negotiations in order for the regime to attend to domestic priorities gained momentum. Formal and informal talks took place between the representatives of Israel and Syria to the Mixed Armistice Commission. In February 1951, Shishakli conveyed to Israel a compromise proposal regarding the DMZ. Direct negotiations followed in March, in which Shishakli participated. These negotiations came to naught also, as Israel rejected the Syrian proposal to divide the DMZ along the Jordan River and the eastern shores of Lake Tiberias.[29]

After the armed clashes between Israel and Syria in the DMZ over the drainage of Lake Huleh, informal meetings between the Israeli and Syrian delegates to the MAC began in November 1951. In these informal meetings, which took place over a period of three years, the delegates were able to conduct pragmatic talks whereby tension along the border was significantly reduced.[30] In May 1952, Shishakli made a peace offer to Israel similar in content to Zaim's proposal, which Israel, as before, did not accept. This offer was aimed more at improving Syria's relations with the United States than with Israel. Shishakli's main concern had been to consolidate his regime with U.S. help. The United States in turn believed that the consolidation of Shishakli's regime would sanction some sort of an agreement with Israel, thereby enhancing stability in the region.[31] In fact, Shishakli's offer was no more than a non-belligerency agreement that did not entail normalization of relations, but did provide for the absorption of half a million Palestinian refugees, "on [the] condition that Syria would receive $200 million for economic development."[32] The failure of these negotiations could to a certain extent be attributed to the inability of the United States and Syria to conclude an agreement. Syrian nationalist forces such as Akram Hawrani, which had helped Shishakli seize power, adamantly opposed any policy alignment with the United States, Israel's alleged creator. Before long, a large coalition of forces, which included both conservative and radical nationalist groups, minorities (particularly Druzes), and a number of independents, all united in an effort to dislodge the dictatorship of Shishakli's regime.[33] In February 1954 the dictator was overthrown, and all attempts to negotiate with Israel were put to rest. A new period of Israeli-Syrian relations had begun.

Tension Along the Border: Toward War

The armistice agreement between Israel and Syria did not resolve the issue of sovereignty in the DMZ. In the aftermath of the 1951 clashes, the UN passed Security Council Resolution S/2157 of May 18, 1951, following which Arabs were permitted to return to the DMZ (mainly those Arabs expelled by Israel from the central sector of the DMZ), and Israel stopped any work on Arab-owned lands.[34] But again the problems stemming from the DMZ were not resolved; rather they were sharpened, leading in large measure to the eruption of the June 1967 war. In fact, Israel's continuous annexation of the DMZ and Syria's determination to check Israeli advances dominated much of the history of the 1951–1967 period.

The problems in the DMZ were caused by three underlying but connected factors: the legal status of the DMZ, cultivation of land within the DMZ, and water resources. Israel contended that the armistice agreement dealt with military matters only, and that Israel had political and legal rights over the DMZ. Syria, on the other hand, contended that neither Israel nor Syria had sovereignty over the DMZ, and that the MAC had broad jurisdiction over the DMZ. Syria claimed a locus standis in the DMZ, a recognized authority for intervention. It maintained that neither party could undertake unilateral action in the DMZ such as drainage, water diversion, and other projects that might change the military status quo and affect Arab property in the zone.[35]

Underlying Israel's position was a strategy to claim sovereignty over the DMZ in order to assert that sovereignty all the way to the 1923 boundary, to reclaim the Huleh swamp, to win exclusive control over Lake Tiberias, and to complete the country's National Water Carrier to divert water from the Jordan River to the Negev desert. In fact, Israel's complaints centered not only on the DMZ, but also on Syria's de facto annexation of the ten-meter strip and direct access to Lake Tiberias.[36] Underlying Syria's position was an apparent strategy to frustrate Israel's plans to deny Damascus both the rights of a riparian state with respect to the Jordan River and direct access to Lake Tiberias. Syria was adamant about checking Israel's advances in the DMZ. Its determination was reinforced by domestic political considerations and by the competition for Arab leadership between Syrian leaders and Egyptian president Gamal Abdul Nasser.

UN officials found fault with the policies of both Israel and Syria and often accused the two countries of destabilizing the Israeli-Syrian border. However, UN opinions with regard to the status of the DMZ were closer to the Syrian view. Over the question of sovereignty, UN officials maintained that it was to be resolved within the context of a final peace treaty. They insisted that both parties observe Article V of the general armistice agreement, which provides for the exclusion of armed forces from the DMZ and the supervision of the DMZ by the chairman of the UN Truce Supervision Organization (UNTSO). They also perceived that no party could justify a violation of the cease-fire.[37]

Notwithstanding UN positions, thousands of violent incidents occurred on the Israeli-Syrian border and low-intensity conflicts soon turned into major confrontations. For example, tension rose sharply between the two countries in December 1955. Though both Lake Tiberias and Lake Huleh were wholly situated within Israel proper, inhabitants of Syria and Palestine had under mandatory agreements obtained fishing and navigation rights there. Syria and the UNTSO held that these agreements were still binding, while Israel contended that it had never accepted them. Israel argued that it might consider Arab rights only in the context of a permanent peace.[38] Israel demanded that the Arabs not use Lake Tiberias's waters without its prior permission, and it used patrol boats to monitor the lake against Arab violations as well as to protect Israeli fishermen. Asserting its fishing and navigation rights to the lake, Syria reacted by firing at Israeli vessels. On December 11, 1955, Israel launched a major attack on a Syrian position north of Lake Tiberias, in which fifty Syrian soldiers were killed. The UNTSO and then the UN Security Council condemned the Israeli raid.[39]

Other major incidents took place on December 4, 1962, and August 19, 1963. They followed to a great extent a pattern of action and reaction. Israel would move tractors and equipment, often guarded by police, into disputed areas of the DMZ. From its high ground positions, Syria would fire at those advancing, and would frequently shell Israeli settlements in the Huleh Valley. Israel would retaliate with excessive raids on Syrian positions, including the use of air power. But it was largely the dispute over Israel's water diversion schemes and the Ba'th Party's assumption of power in Syria that further heightened tensions along the border. The dispute over the use of the waters of the Jordan River and its tributaries greatly deepened after Israel neared the completion of its project to divert the Jordan's waters to the Negev.

In November 1964, Israel began construction works in the Ayn Tal al-Qadi, near a spring of the Jordan River. Syria saw this project not only as an Israeli encroachment over the armistice demarcation line, but also as a threat to its interests as a riparian state. The UNTSO asked Israel to postpone its works until an independent team of surveyors could inspect the area.[40] While Israel rejected the UNTSO's request, Syria ignored the supervisory organization's instructions and fired at an Israeli military patrol that had moved into disputed territory. Israel retaliated, and by the time a cease-fire could be effected, three Israelis and seven Syrians had been killed, with nine Israelis and twenty-six Syrians injured, let alone material damage inflicted on Israeli agricultural settlements and Syrian villages. This incident assumed gravitational significance, because the dispute over water weighed heavily on Israel's policy to assert its sovereignty over the DMZ and Syria's determination to oppose it.

Significantly enough, domestic considerations in Syria hardened its position. Following a bloodless coup d'état in March 1963, the Ba'th Party controlled the new regime in Syria, and under its revolutionary ideology the Syrian government stood in militant opposition to Israel. This stance, however, was fueled more by domestic considerations than by ideology. Upon assumption of power, the Ba'th Party increased its ranks in both the military and civilian sectors, following a recruitment policy that favored minorities, particularly Alawis. The Ba'thi regime also initiated agrarian reform in order to expand its political base of support to the rural classes, cutting across sectarian lines. This plan went hand in hand with the regime's policy of nationalizing key sectors of the Syrian economy, with the object of curbing the mercantilistic power of the urban class. In addition, the Ba'thi leadership suppressed their former Nasserite allies (supporters of union with Egypt) so as to be independent from any Egyptian influence. These policies incited the wrath of the Sunni urban middle and upper classes as well as the organization of the Muslim Brotherhood. In response, the regime conveniently began to emphasize the anti-Israeli aspect of its ideology, translating it into a militant opposition to Israel at all levels and thus enhancing its image domestically and putting its critics on the defensive.[41]

With the prospect that Israel's National Water Carrier would soon be operational, the Arab states called for a summit meeting to decide a plan of action. The Arabs considered this ambitious water project as key to Israel's capacity to absorb future immigrants and thus consolidate the Jewish state at the expense of the Palestinians. The summit convened in Cairo in January 1964, at which the Arab leaders devised a plan to preempt Israel's project. The Arab plan proposed erecting dams on the Hasbani and Banias Rivers, the two sources of the Jordan River rising outside Israel. From the dams, the headwaters of the Jordan River would be diverted southward and westward respectively through a canal and a tunnel to bypass Israel's Lake Tiberias. Other results of the Arab summit were, first, a call for the creation of a Palestinian organization that would fight for the rights of Palestinians to self-determination and for the liberation of Palestine, and second, a call to organize Palestinian guerrillas to sabotage Israeli water installations. The Palestine Liberation Organization (PLO) was founded, with much fanfare, in May 1964 in Jerusalem. With the blessing of Egypt, the PLO shortly thereafter set up a Palestine Liberation Army (PLA) in the Gaza Strip. But Egypt maintained virtual control over the PLA. Guerrilla groups were already appearing on the scene, among which was the Palestinian National Liberation Movement, known as Fatah, led by Yasser Arafat. Regarded as subversive by Arab governments, especially by Egypt and Jordan, Fatah had to operate in secret until 1962.

Israel's National Water Carrier began operation in summer 1964. The Arabs held another summit meeting in September and decided to press ahead with the project they had adopted in January. Israel warned that it would use whatever means necessary to stop the diversion project. Frustrated by the failure of Arab and UN efforts to halt Israel's diversionary works, Syria in fall 1964 moved heavy earth-moving equipment close to the Banias River and began its own diversionary works. Throughout 1965 and 1966, Israel carried out several ground and aerial strikes against Syrian diversionary works, reducing them to insignificance.[42]

As Syria was unable to single-handedly fight Israel, it needed Arab support, which really meant the military support of Egypt. Egypt, however, had realized that it was unprepared to enter prematurely into a war with Israel, especially over the waters of the Jordan River. Egypt had been restricting the movements of armed Palestinians along the Egyptian-Israeli border in the Gaza Strip to prevent Israel from using this as a pretext for attack. For Egypt at the time, "Palestinian nationalism could destabilize the cease-fire with Israel and jeopardize Egyptian security if left unchecked and uncontained."[43] Meanwhile, the Ba'th Party had adopted an aggressive strategy against Israel, laying strong emphasis on the Palestinian problem. In the Eighth All-Arab Ba'th Congress in spring 1965, the party issued its resolutions, two of which dealt with Palestine and Israel in the following terms:

(i)   Arab policy on the Palestine problem, whenever it has been expressed in the international arena in the shape of the demand for the implementation of the United Nations resolutions, implicitly based itself on the recognition of Israel's existence. However, the 8th all-Arab Congress

rejects this logic, regarding the refusal to resign themselves to Israel's very existence, which contradicts Arab existence, to be the strategic point of the (policy of the) Arab states.
(iii) The Arab Palestinian problem should be regarded as the first and basic instrument for the liberation of Palestine, and should be organized accordingly and all restrictions over the exercising of this task should be removed.[44]

The congress's resolutions expressed Syrian political preferences, which highlighted the political rift between Syria and Egypt. In contrast to the latter, Syria was not only willing to stand against Israel but also ready to engage in a "people's war of liberation" by sponsoring Palestinian guerrilla raids into Israel. In the meantime, the Ba'th Party was experiencing a power struggle between its military and civil wings. Led by Alawi officers, prominent among them Salah Jadid and Hafiz Asad, the military wing wielded real power in Syria. When the old-guard Ba'thi politicians attempted to recover their political power, the military staged a coup in February 1966 that removed them, including the founders of the Ba'th Party. Salah Jadid became the de facto ruler of Syria, exercising his power through the position of assistant secretary-general of the Syrian Ba'th Party.

The repercussions of the coup only reinforced the drift in the direction of a collision with Israel. Notwithstanding the Ba'th Party's secular and revolutionary ideology, the sectarian and radical nature of the new regime further alienated the majority Sunni population. Consequently, the neo-Ba'thists relied more heavily on an aggressive policy toward Israel in order to deflect domestic opposition. The attitude of the new regime to Israel was best described in the Extraordinary Regional Congress of March 10–27, 1966: "We have to risk the destruction of all we have built up in order to eliminate Israel."[45] The neo-Ba'thists actively abetted Palestinian guerrilla raids into Israel, giving their support to Fatah. This assistance served as an unequivocal testimony to Syria's call for a "people's war of liberation." It heightened Syria's revolutionary character in contrast to Egypt's timid stance, typified by its restriction of Palestinian activity in the Gaza Strip.[46]

Israel experienced economic and political problems that sharpened its policy of deterrence, contributing to the eruption of the June 1967 war. In the early 1960s, Israel's economic problems, stemming from overly rapid growth, precipitated a serious labor shortage, particularly in skilled labor, giving rise to high wages and inflation. In addition, a steadily growing trade imbalance exacerbated the economic conditions of the country, increasing its trade deficit. In response, Israel enacted various measures to reduce the deficit and inflation. These measures brought about an economic slowdown. By winter 1966–1967, in a dramatic reverse of the previous economic situation, recession set in, significantly raising unemployment. This condition cast a pall of gloom and uncertainty over the economic health of the country, negatively affecting the psychological mood of the nation.

Along with the economic situation, political problems further intensified the atmosphere of dissatisfaction and uncertainty. This increased the pressure on the government to improve its credibility by dealing more decisively with foreign challenges. After the resignation of Ben Gurion in January 1961, Levi Eshkol became the new prime minister. Unlike Ben Gurion, Eshkol had a reputation for moderation on Arab issues. In 1964, Ben Gurion, along with Shimon Peres, Moshe Dayan, and other followers, split from the leading Zionist party, Mapai, and founded the Israel Workers List, known as Rafi. Meanwhile, in 1965, the Herut Party, which had been founded by the Zionist revisionists, merged with the Liberal Party, the heir of General Zionism, forming the Herut-Liberal Bloc, known as Gahal.

Gahal, wearing the mantle of Vladimir Jabotinsky's revisionist Zionist ideology, embraced a militant attitude toward the Arabs and stood for territorial maximalism. Although the 1965 election confirmed Mapai's plurality (along with Ahdut Ha'avoda, a Zionist Labor Party) in the Israeli parliament (the Knesset), Gahal was able to form a sizable bloc on the right of Israel's political spectrum. Faced with the militant ideology of Gahal on the right and with Rafi's militant attitude toward the Arabs on the left (in addition to the economic crisis), Mapai's leadership was pressured to replace its image of moderation with one of control and determination. This had a direct impact on Israel's handling of Arab guerrilla infiltration into its territory, and of Syria's "people's war of liberation," leading to excessive punitive retaliations in response to Arab guerrilla raids.

Between Syria's extremism and Israel's excessiveness, a cycle of raids and retaliations pushed the region irrevocably toward the brink. The June 1967 war has already been the subject of many studies on both ends of the Arab-Israeli intellectual fence. Within the span of few days, Israel vanquished the Arab armies and occupied the Sinai Peninsula and Gaza Strip from Egypt, the West Bank including East Jerusalem from Jordan, and the Golan Heights from Syria. Significantly enough, by June 10, 1967, the line of June 4, 1967, which conceptually reflected the disposition of the Israeli and Syrian forces confronting each other in the DMZ, was well to the rear of Israeli forces.

When in August 1967 Israel formally adopted a resolution (decided in June) that it would return the captured territories to Egypt and Syria on the basis of the international boundary, provided peace was achieved, Syria refused to negotiate with Israel. Syria, unlike Egypt and Jordan, rejected any political settlement of all issues involved in the conflict. It boycotted the summit convened by the Arab states in Khartoum in September 1967, at which the Arab states agreed on uniting their political efforts to ensure inter alia the withdrawal of Israeli forces from occupied Arab lands, but insisted that their efforts must involve no negotiation with Israel, no peace, and no recognition of Israel. According to some analysts, by not ruling out political compromise since a military option was not considered, the summit contained a conciliatory aspect in that it legitimized the efforts of Arab leaders who sought a diplomatic solution.[47] In the meantime, the members of the UN Security Council diplomatically wrangled over the formulation of a resolution that would serve as a basis for resolving the Arab-Israeli conflict. After several drafts and arduous debates lasting several months, the council finally agreed on Resolution 242, adopted on November 22, 1967.

An outcome of compromise, accommodating both the Arab and Israeli positions, Resolution 242 was sufficiently ambiguous to allow the Arab states and Israel to read into it what they wanted. In the preamble, the resolution emphasized "the inadmissibility of the acquisition of territory by war and the need to work for a just and lasting peace in which every state in the area can live in security." It then affirmed:

> The fulfillment of Charter principles requires the establishment of a just and lasting peace in the Middle East which should include the application of both the following principles: (i) Withdrawal of Israeli armed forces from territories occupied in the recent conflict; (ii) Termination of all claims or states of belligerency and respect for acknowledgment of the sovereignty, territorial integrity and political independence of every state in the area and their right to live in peace within secure and recognized boundaries free from threats or acts of force.[48]

While Egypt and Jordan accepted the resolution, Syria rejected it. Israel's UN representative endorsed it but reserved the right to interpret it as the country saw fit. Israel stressed that only within the framework of a comprehensive peace treaty with secure and recognized boundaries would a withdrawal of Israeli forces from occupied territories take place. It also emphasized that its withdrawal would be from "territories occupied in the recent conflict," and not from "the territories," meaning that Israel expected an adjustment in the international boundary. Egypt interpreted the resolution as calling for Israel's withdrawal from all "the occupied territories," prior to any political settlement. Conversely, the resolution's ambivalence provided room for the parties concerned to change their attitudes in response to shifting political and military conditions while still agreeing on the resolution as a basis to enter into negotiations.

Toward Another War: The October
1973 War and Its Consequences

The June 1967 war redefined the contours of the Arab-Israeli conflict and the possible means to its settlement. The watershed was that Israel occupied Arab territories, and both Arab and Israeli parties entertained divergent ideas on the modalities of reaching a political settlement. By the time Resolution 242 was adopted, Syria had not only rejected it but had also reaffirmed its commitment to the "people's liberation war." The Ba'thi regime continued to glorify the

Palestinian guerrillas, whose reputation had been enhanced as a consequence of the regular Arab armies' defeat. Israel, on the other hand, due to the belligerent attitude of Syria and to its own domestic considerations (which stemmed from its perceived security needs on the Golan Heights, chiefly protecting the water sources of the Jordan River—the Banias River and its springs—and maintaining peace in the former DMZ), approved the creation of settlements on the Golan Heights, as well as keeping water sources under its control. It was against this background that new developments in the Ba'thi apparatus took place in Damascus, which had a direct impact on the course of events of the Arab-Israeli conflict.

Shortly after the defeat, two schools of thought within the Ba'thi Syrian state crystallized and provoked an intra-Ba'thi power struggle. One school, led by the assistant secretary-general of the Ba'th Party, Salah Jadid, advocated a transformative socialist policy that gave priority to socioeconomic reforms. It also wanted to commit Syria to the "people's liberation war" against Israel, thereby allowing Palestinian guerrillas to be in the vanguard of the fight, and denying any role to the Arab states in the military struggle on account of their allegedly reactionary regimes. The other school of thought, led by Defense Minister Asad, advocated a nationalist policy that gave priority to strengthening the Syrian defense establishment along with cooperation with other Arab countries, in the interest of the military struggle against Israel.[49] In addition, Asad had reservations about the role the Palestinian guerrillas could play in that struggle. He believed that irregulars could do little to change the outcome of a battle and were in fact a military liability, for they provided Israel with a pretext to strike against Syrian positions. So he wanted the guerrillas placed under strict army control.

Asad went on to consolidate his power in the military establishment and to purge it of all Jadid loyalists. Jadid reinforced his power in the civilian branch of government and the party apparatus while continuing to lead the radical Ba'thi regime. The regime pressed on with the program of the "socialist transformation" of Syrian society, which further alienated the urban classes. In addition to supporting the guerrilla organizations, notably the PLO, which came under the control of Fatah's leadership in 1968, led by Yasser Arafat, the Ba'thi regime established its own guerrilla organization, known as Al-Saiqa, in late 1968. But Jadid's regime failed catastrophically in its attempt to control the army, over which Asad had already tightened his grip.

The uneasy situation between the two Ba'thi factions intensified when, on February 24, 1969, Israeli air force planes attacked two guerrilla camps inside Syria, and shot down two Syrian planes (MiGs). Jadid's civilian wing exploited the incident to discredit Asad, criticizing the military for ineffectiveness against the enemy. Conversely, Asad's military wing accused the radicals of preparing to stage a coup. On the next day, he ordered his army units to seize key Ba'th Party offices in Damascus. From this point onward, Asad began to flex his muscles in the party, advancing his strategy of cooperation with Arab countries in the interest of confrontation with Israel. No longer did Asad countenance Jadid's policies.

Where Asad forced his decisions on the regime but refrained from ousting Jadid, Jadid constantly maneuvered to whittle away at Asad's power. This internal Ba'thi conflict soon led to a complete break of all relations between the Ba'thi regime's military and civilian wings. This conflict came to a head when the regime intervened in Jordan's civil war on the side of the Palestinians in September 1970. Supported by the United States and Israel, Jordan's king launched a counteroffensive that turned the tide of battle against the Syrian and Palestinian forces. As defense minister and air force commander, Asad decided against sending the air force to protect the Syrian army units, which turned on its tail back toward Damascus. This decision was a highly calculated strategic move on the part of Asad, who knew if Syria went far enough in Jordan to threaten King Hussein, Israel would intervene and defeat Syria on a huge scale. The civilian wing convened the Ba'th Party's Tenth Extraordinary National Congress in October–November 1970, and tried to push through a decision calling for the resignation of Defense Minister Asad.[50] In response, Asad carried out a bloodless coup d'état on November 13, 1970, that turned him formally into the strongman of the Ba'thi state.

Upon his assumption of power, Asad reaffirmed Syria's rejection of Resolution 242 and began in earnest preparing for battle with Israel. He appreciably improved Syria's relations with the Soviet Union in order to receive sufficient and better arms, but he refrained from concluding any treaty of friendship and cooperation with the Soviets, as they would have liked. He averted any ideological identification with the Soviet Union, opting instead to build a relationship of trust with a significant measure of coordination. Simultaneously, Asad looked at Egypt as the only credible ally. Jordan's recent cooperation with the United States and Israel in the Jordanian civil war had obviously made it a questionable partner. Meanwhile, Egypt's charismatic leader, Gamal Abdul Nasser, died in September 1970, and just a month before Asad seized power, Egyptian vice president Anwar Sadat, considered a weak figure at the time, became Egypt's president. The two leaders came into direct contact when Asad, breaking Syria out of its regional isolation, decided to join the proposed Federation of Arab Republics, comprising Egypt, Libya, and Sudan.

Asad found in Sadat's Egypt not only a credible ally but also a receptive one. According to Patrick Seale:

> At the start Asad's alliance was forged under the cover of the proposed Federation. . . . Although Sudan dropped out and the project withered to an empty husk, the frequent summits provided Asad and Sadat with occasions for secret meetings. By the end of 1971 the two leaders had taken soundings in Moscow, had appointed Egypt's war minister, General Muhammad Sadiq, supreme commander of both armies, and had reached agreement on broad strategy.[51]

Being the populous country with large resources, Egypt eventually became the senior partner in the alliance with Syria. Mohamed Heikal, the leading journalist and President Sadat's friend at the time, wrote that "planning for such an attack had started a long time ago—in one form or another from the immediate aftermath of the 1967 defeat. It had, inevitably, taken different forms according to the partner or partners with whom Egypt was expecting to operate, and this had only finally been determined with the setting up of the unified command of the armed forces of Egypt and Syria on 31 January 1973."[52] Significantly enough, earlier, in March 1972, President Asad had declared that Syria would accept Resolution 242, provided it would entail Israel's withdrawal from all Arab lands captured in 1967 and recognition of the rights of the Palestinians.[53]

Although Israel believed that war with Egypt and Syria was inevitable, it was not able to discern their planning for a surprise attack. Several considerations made Israel conclude that an attack was not in the immediate offing. Defense Minister Dayan, along with many Israeli military leaders, calculated during 1972 and 1973 that neither Egypt nor Syria would go into battle due to Israel's military superiority.[54] Israel's military establishment misread and misconstrued the mixed signals and events respectively that were unfolding in the region.

As the Arab deception plan was being prepared, President Sadat of Egypt repeated his promise of the "year of decision" regarding the conflict with Israel. As Egypt's frontier remained quiet, no one took his threat seriously. In addition, in March 1972, Sadat abruptly expelled Russian military personnel from Egypt on the grounds that the Soviet authorities were sacrificing Arab interests on the altar of détente with the United States.[55] Whether or not these signals were staged to camouflage Egypt's intentions, they nevertheless succeeded in conveying the impression to Israel that no war plans were being made. Even Dayan, on receiving credible intelligence information of an impending Egyptian attack on October 6, 1973, entertained the idea that President Sadat would probably cancel it. He recalled in his memoirs: "We had received similar messages in the past, and later, when no attack followed, came the explanation that President Sadat had changed his mind at the last moment. On this occasion, too, it was indicated that if Sadat discovered that the information was known to us and that he had lost the element of surprise, it was possible that he would cancel the attack, or at least postpone it."[56]

On October 6, Egypt and Syria launched their surprise attack with the objective of retaking their territories, the Golan Heights and Sinai Peninsula. For the first time since 1948 their armies broke through Israeli defense lines, inflicting heavy losses on Israeli troops. Egypt crossed the Suez Canal, and Syria stormed the Golan Heights, stopping a few miles away from the eastern shore of Lake Tiberias. During the first days of the battle, Israel seemed on the verge of defeat. However, Egypt's and Syria's divergent goals coupled with Israeli resolve turned the tide of battle in favor of Israel. All along,

President Sadat had regarded the war option as a means to break the stalemate of "no peace, no war" and thus revive peace diplomacy from a position of strength. He believed that a limited successful attack on Israel (smashing Israeli fortifications along the Suez canal and recapturing a strip of land on its eastern bank) would be enough to disrupt the balance of power and pressure Israel into peace negotiations. So he had a political objective behind his surprise attack. In contrast, President Asad had a purely military objective; he simply wanted to fight Israel and retake part or all of the Golan Heights. He did not believe that diplomacy with Israel, as a substitute for war, could advance a political settlement.

The Egyptians fed the Syrians spurious war plans.[57] Instead of pressing along deep into the Sinai Peninsula, Egypt had taken a defensive posture along the eastern bank of the Suez Canal. This Egyptian duplicity enabled the Israeli Defense Forces (IDF) to concentrate their military efforts on the Syrian front. By October 10, the IDF had regained almost all the territory lost in the first two days of fighting on the Golan Heights and subsequently advanced in the direction of Damascus. Angered and discomfited by Egyptian duplicity, Asad had no choice but to insist that Sadat come to his aid. As the IDF pressed forward inside Syrian territory, Sadat, on October 13, found it imperative to launch an attack into the Sinai Peninsula in order to relieve pressure on the Syrian forces and to prevent the IDF from launching a counteroffensive on the Egyptian front. Sadat's offensive was too late to stop the Israeli juggernaut. The IDF crossed the Suez Canal on October 15 and by October 22 was less than seventy miles west of Cairo; the IDF had almost fully encircled the Egyptian Third Army.

The Soviet Union and the United States were engaged in intense diplomacy. The Soviets were pushing for cease-fire proposals, which the United States held up until Israel recouped its losses. Only when Israel gained the upper hand on both the Egyptian and Syrian fronts did a cease-fire resolution go into effect, on October 22. Egypt and Israel accepted Security Council Resolution 338 of October 22, 1973, but this did not reflect the fact that the two Arab armies had been vanquished by Israel, nor that Israel had emerged as the victor. U.S. Secretary of State Henry Kissinger had already prefigured that neither total victory for Israel nor total defeat for the Arab armies was conducive to future peace negotiations. During the fighting, Israel was in dire need of military supplies, and Kissinger ordered a huge airlift for Israel from October 14 until October 21, without which Israel would have been at great risk. Conversely, Kissinger saved the Egyptian Third Army when its fate was endangered by the IDF. As a result, Kissinger was able not only to lay the groundwork against which he would work for the implementation of Security Council Resolution 338, but also to appear as a credible mediator to both Egypt and Israel. Resolution 338 states:

> The Security Council (1) calls upon all parties to the present fighting to cease all firing and terminate all military activity immediately, no later than

12 hours after the moment of the adoption of this decision, in the positions they now occupy; (2) calls upon the parties concerned to start immediately after the cease-fire the implementation of Security Council Resolution 242 (1967), in all of its parts; (3) decides that immediately and concurrently with the cease-fire, negotiations start between the parties concerned under appropriate auspices aimed at establishing a just and durable peace in the Middle East.[58]

At first Syria rejected the resolution, thus giving Israel a pretext to continue its operation launched on October 21 and recapture the strategic area of Mount Hermon on October 22. The following day, Syria accepted Resolution 338, interpreting it in the same manner as Resolution 242, that is, that Israel should withdraw from the occupied territories prior to any political settlement. Losing no time, Secretary of State Kissinger set about on his step-by-step diplomacy in the region, which emphasized working out a political agreement, even on minor matters, such that the vested interests of the concerned parties would not ruin it at any one stage of the negotiations. He worked out an interim "disengagement of forces agreement" (Sinai I) between Egypt and Israel in January 1974, and thereafter shifted his attention toward Syria to conclude a similar agreement. Unlike Egypt, Syria was a difficult party to negotiate with. Much acrimony and national interest dominated the Syrian attitude. Israel, on the other hand, was not only critical of Syria's attitude but also incensed with Syria's mistreatment of Israeli prisoners of war.[59] In addition, the two countries had emerged from the recent war in shambles.

Despite its pyrrhic victory, Israel's deterrence strategy and image of invulnerability had been shattered. Secretary of State Kissinger painted the picture perfectly: "Deep down, the Israelis knew that while they had won the last battle, they had lost the aura of invincibility. The Arab armies were not destroyed. The Arab nations had not won but no longer need they quail before Israeli might."[60] Following the war, other equally important issues tormented the Jewish state. Israel suffered 2,552 dead and over 3,000 wounded. This heavy toll in human lives and Israel's narrow escape from defeat provoked the Israeli public to demand accountability from their government, which in turn formed the Agranat Commission to investigate the mismanagement of the war and the issues underlying public dissent. The government was deeply shaken.

In contrast to Israel, Syria was defeated on the battlefield, but since the Syrian regime had made military struggle against Israel a national priority, it had to claim a certain victory for an otherwise flawed policy. Therefore the most militant state against Israel had to vindicate its claim of victory to justify domestically its negotiations with Israel. Vindicating a claim hard to prove put an onus on the negotiations. The 1973 fighting ended with Israel capturing Syrian territories beyond the 1967 cease-fire line (minor advances on the southern front and significant territory in the north, only twenty miles from Damascus), backed by the strategic area of Mount Hermon. Syria had no other option than to accept U.S. mediation with Israel in order to recover its newly occupied territory. But Syria was in a double bind: Inasmuch as it needed the withdrawal of Israel, it could not settle only for the restoration of the October 6 (prewar) line. It needed a symbolic gain of land captured by Israel in 1967 to safeguard the legitimacy of the regime, to rationalize domestically the negotiations with Israel, to keep pace with Egypt, which had recovered a piece of the Sinai Peninsula, and to justify the October war itself. It was against this background that Secretary of State Kissinger began his shuttle diplomacy between Tel Aviv and Damascus to conclude a disengagement of forces agreement.

Whether the origins of the 1973 war lay in the ideology of the Ba'th Party or in the stigma of defeat and treason, President Asad, like President Sadat, primarily wanted to change the balance of power. Syria's and Egypt's defeat in the 1967 war was humiliating and domestically untenable. In a society that applauds pride and strength, humiliation and weakness are perceived as mortal enemies, more so than the enemy (Israel) itself. The 1973 war broke the stalemate of "no peace, no war" and restored some equilibrium to the balance of power in the region, which had tipped completely in Israel's favor after the 1967 war.

On May 31, 1974, Syrian and Israeli military representatives signed the Israeli-Syrian Disengagement Agreement in Geneva. Israel and Syria were to scrupulously observe the cease-fire and refrain from all military actions against each other, in implementation of UN Security Council Resolution 338. The agreement was not a peace treaty. It was a step toward a "just and durable peace on the basis of Security Council Resolution 338."[61] Israel was to withdraw from all land captured in the October war and the few strips of territory conquered in 1967, including the city of Quneitra. The disengagement agreement defined three areas of security provisions in order to uphold the scrupulous observance of the cease-fire: the area of separation under the UN Disengagement Observers Force (1,250 men), which included Quneitra; a second area of equal length (10 kilometers) to both parties from the area of separation, limited to 75 tanks, 36 short-range guns, and 6,000 soldiers for each; a third area, also of equal length (10 kilometers), from the second area, limited to 450 tanks and less than 200 short-range guns. In addition, surface-to-air missiles could be deployed not less than 25 kilometers from the area of separation. Equally significant, Asad gave Kissinger his oral commitment that he would not allow the Golan Heights to become a source of guerrilla attacks against Israel.[62] The agreement was simple and reciprocative for both parties.

This agreement is important because it was the first one to be signed by Israel and Syria under the auspices of the United States. In addition, it has been scrupulously observed by both parties since its inception. Three main factors were responsible for its success. First, Secretary of State Kissinger was backed by President Nixon, and he increased U.S. input into the negotiations. The United States played not only the role of moderator but also that of mediator that advanced its own positions. The United States enlisted Arab support for its negotiations with Syria and used a carrot-and-stick approach with Israel, in that the United States compensated Israel for the concessions it was pressured into making. Second, the United States kept the Soviet Union at a distance from the negotiations, allowing for a symbolic Soviet role only. This is important because it conveyed to Arab leaders and particularly to Asad that without U.S. support there is no return to the status quo ante. This complemented the overall strategy of the Nixon administration in the Middle East, which set out to demonstrate that the Soviet Union's capacity to foment crises was not matched by its ability to resolve them.[63] The underlying implications of the U.S. strategy were to prod the Arab leaders to approach Washington for assistance in the peace process and to make manifest the Arabs' anachronistic concept of an all-or-nothing approach toward Israel. Finally, while the personality of Secretary of State Kissinger was a crucial factor in furthering the negotiations, the singular ingredient of success was the ability of the United States to convey to the Arab negotiator that it was able to pressure Israel, but that this pressure could not come cheap. This approach softened Syrian intractability.

The Ba'thi State and Israel

In order to better understand the conflicted Israeli-Syrian relationship, this and the next section deal with the impact of ideology on the behavior of the parties and their perceptions of each other and of the Golan Heights. Two Sorbonne-educated teachers, primarily Michel Aflaq, a Greek Orthodox, and Salah al-Din Bitar, a Sunni Muslim, formulated the doctrine of the Ba'th Party, emphasizing three tenets—Arab unity, freedom, and socialism. Aflaq's formulation was heavily couched in metaphysical terms. His message centered fundamentally on Arab nationalism, which is the essential instrument for achieving his primary goal, namely Arab unity. Aflaq wrote in 1940: "The nationalism for which we call . . . is the same sentiment that binds the individual to his family, because the fatherland is only a large household and the nation a large family."[64] This belief in Arab nationalism as the means to Arab unity is expressed in the opening article of the Ba'th Party's constitution of 1947: "The Arabs form one nation. This nation has the natural right to live in a single state and to be free to direct its own destiny."[65] In addition, the Ba'th Party (Article 7 of its constitution) defined the boundaries of the Arab nation in the following manner: "The Arab fatherland is that part of the globe inhabited by the Arab nation which stretches from the Taurus Mountain, the Pocht-i-Kouh Mountains, the Gulf of Basra, the Arab Ocean, the Ethiopian Mountains, the Sahara, the Atlantic Ocean, and the Mediterranean."[66]

However, the struggle for Arab unity is not conceived only in pan-Arab nationalistic terms. It is seen also as a regenerative process leading to the reform of Arab character and society. The revitalization of the Arab society is at the heart of the Ba'th Party's nationalist doctrine. This is the essence of the eternal mission of the party *(Risallah Khalida)*.[67]

Freedom, the second tenet of Ba'thi doctrine, comprises personal freedom and national independence, whereby the Arab has the freedom of speech,
assembly, and belief and is liberated from colonialism, as well as freed from
foreign control.[68] Socialism, the third tenet, takes on a distinct interpretation.
In Europe, socialism was internationalist. The nationalist movements of the
day (Ba'thism, Zionism) wanted a socialism that would serve their nationalism, so they came up with formulas of "nationalist socialisms." This is the
Ba'thi kind of socialism. In Aflaq's words, socialism, unlike in the West, is not
an internationalist movement claiming a materialistic philosophy in order to
stand against the Western practice of exploitation, tyranny, and reaction. Arab
socialism needs not a materialistic philosophy, for the Arab spirit has no blem-
ish of tyranny. Socialism for the Arab is a part and consequence of the national condition. The Arab nationalist understands that socialism is the best means
for the rebirth (renaissance) of the nation and of its nationalism. The Arab
struggle rests on Arab unity, which requires socialism. Socialism is a necessity emanating from the heart of Arab nationalism, which guarantees justice,
equality, and generous living for all. In this abstract formulation of socialism,
Aflaq tends to subordinate socialism to Arab nationalism in order to make
political unity a condition for a socialist society.

Aflaq believed that the party's three objectives were fused in such a manner that one could not be achieved without the other. So, Arab unity, freedom,
and socialism, when subsumed under the motto of the Ba'th Party—one Arab
nation with an eternal mission—can be interpreted to mean a revolution
against "reactionary" forces at home and colonialism. The novelty of
Ba'thism was that it emerged as an effective organized political movement to
preach total Arab unity. Ideas of Arab nationalism and unity were not new at
the time. The belief that the Arabs constituted a culturally and politically united nation had been gaining acceptance in intellectual nationalist circles for
many years thanks to the movements of the day, mainly the Arab Nationalist
Movement (ANM).[69] But it was the Ba'th Party that was able to crystallize the
notion that the artificial division of the Arab world by the colonialists, along
with the corrupt present political order, were at the root of the backward political, social, and economic condition of the Arabs. This led to a political program that found its expression in an anticolonial form of nationalism. Nearly
a decade before the appearance of Gamal Abdul Nasser in Egypt, the Ba'thi
leaders emerged as the most stringent anticolonialists in the Arab world.

Political Zionism (the movement to create a Jewish state in Palestine)
was ideologically and in every other way incompatible with the Ba'thists,
whose party preached Arab nationalism and unity. However, political Zionism
did not figure prominently in early Ba'thi writing. Once events in Palestine in
1947 and 1948 began to concern its party leaders, the Ba'th Party turned its
attention south and featured several articles in its mouthpiece newspaper, *Al-
Ba'th*. The general theme of the articles revolved around the notion that the
colonialists were conspiring with the Zionists against the Arabs and that the

time had come for the Arabs to unite and save Palestine. At the same time, the party attacked all "reactionary" regimes in the Arab world, especially the one in Syria, for their bankrupt handling of Palestine over the years. Although one article ended with a note calling for the death of the Zionists, the party seemingly saw in the situation in Palestine at the time an opportunity to advance its political program. The literature of the party consistently emphasized saving Palestine by strengthening the Arab nation through unification.[70] Israel gradually began to figure prominently in Ba'thi doctrine as the party went through a process of ideological and structural transformation concomitant with both the rising tension between Israel and Syria and the rivalry between Egypt and Syria over Arab leadership.

During the 1950s, the Ba'th Party maintained its depiction of Israel as a colonialist creation. The party attacked Israel in anticolonial terms, emphasizing Arab unity. In an October 1956 speech, Aflaq stated:

> For decades the colonial powers have striven to delay the resurrection [renaissance] of the Arab nation by impoverishing it, dividing it, and chaining it with many shackles. Then Israel was founded as the last efficacious means to occupy the Arabs, squander their efforts and strength, and cut off the path toward their liberty and unity.[71]

On another occasion Aflaq denounced the creation of Israel:

> In Palestine the colonialists cooperated with the Zionists to evict our people from their land, saying and affirming that Israel was created to stay. Not even a decade had passed since the catastrophe, before the Arab people in Palestine, Egypt, Syria, and every other Arab country answered: Israel was created to vanish and colonialism to vanish with it as well.[72]

Meanwhile, Nasser was emerging as the champion of Arab nationalism and attracting the attention of the Ba'thi leaders. The Suez crisis and war of 1956 substantially boosted the cause of Arab unity, making Nasser's role in bringing it about essential. The Ba'th Party sought the unity of Syria and Egypt. In 1958, the much drummed up goal of Arab unity was partially achieved when Egypt and Syria merged under the name of the United Arab Republic. But Egypt's assent to the union came only after it secured Syria's political subordination and the dismantling of all political parties, including the Ba'th. During the union, many Ba'thi officers became disgruntled with the way the Egyptians treated them. As if it were not enough that the Egyptians had brought about the dissolution of the Ba'th Party, they eyed the Ba'thi officers with suspicion (supposedly the partners in undertaking the unity) and sent scores of them to Cairo.[73] With no party apparatus to sustain them, many Ba'thi officers became directly involved in politics. Around this time, in 1960, Salah Jadid, Hafiz al-Asad, and Muhammad Umran founded the secret Ba'thi military organization known as the Military Committee. Meanwhile, chafing under Egyptian lordship, a group of Damascene officers staged a coup d'état and broke up the union in 1961. In this interim period, the Ba'th Party was able to reorganize itself again to become a significant force in Syrian political life. In March 1963 the party and its allies (Nasserite and independent officers) were able to seize power following an Iraqi Ba'th takeover of Iraq in February 1963.

The breakup of the United Arab Republic significantly undermined the ideological foundation of the Ba'th Party. Members with a Marxist inclination were disappointed with the party's past performances and sought to reformulate the Ba'thi ideology. Those party members were also encouraged by the contemporaneous ideological developments in the revolutionary Arab regimes (and in the communist world), which to some varying extent emphasized socialist commitments in their nationalism.[74]

Before the 1963 coup, literature critical of Ba'thi ideology circulated in Damascus. Prominent among the Ba'thi contributors were Jamal Atasi, Ilyas Murqus, and significantly, Yasin al-Hafiz. Atasi, a veteran Ba'thi official, criticized bourgeois (political) democracy and emphasized an economic (socialist) democracy that returns national wealth to all the people.[75] Atasi's philosophy revolved around a Marxist concept of socialism that called for the revolutionary forces to change the old system and end exploitation.[76] Murqus attacked the parliamentary system in Syria. Unlike in the West, where parliamentary government is associated with the rise of the bourgeoisie, in Syria the leaders of the ancien régime continued to wield power and influence and to hold sway in parliament.[77] Hafiz, a former communist, criticized Ba'thi ideology especially concerning the question of liberty. He condemned parliamentary government, declaring it a cover for capitalist control. He called for a popular (revolutionary socialist) democracy that would curtail reactionary groups and give the chance to the toiling masses to enjoy complete freedom. Only then could "liberty" be achieved. Hafiz also emphasized keeping the army out of politics.[78]

This ideological ferment formed the basis of a document adopted at the Sixth National Congress in October 1963. The document, called "Some Theoretical Propositions," reformulated the doctrine of the Ba'th Party. The parliamentary system was no longer accepted as a basis for political action. Power should rest with the toiling classes. And following Hafiz's line of thought, the document affirmed that liberty would require a popular democracy, led by a vanguard party, which would limit the political freedom of the bourgeoisie.[79] The congress decided to proceed with the socialist transformation of society. But it rejected the proposition advanced by Hafiz that the army should be kept out of politics. Instead, the congress emphasized the military's involvement in politics to bring about popular democracy, stressing the ideological indoctrination of the armed forces.[80] This further politicized the Ba'thi military, which espoused the new ideology.

The new ideology of the Ba'th Party had a direct impact on Syria's attitude toward Israel. The Palestinian problem became entangled with the social and political problems of Syria, which the Ba'th Party wanted to solve. Whereas before, support for the Palestinians was formulated only within the context of Arab unity, now that support came to be formulated within the context of Arab unity and socialism. At the Sixth National Congress the ideological document emphasized that the liberation of Palestine depended on the unity and growth of Arab progressive forces.[81] The congress also advocated (Resolution 21) the creation of a Palestine liberation front whereby the Palestinians would become the vanguard for the liberation of Palestine.[82]

Against a background of rising tension along the Syria-Israeli border and Syrian and Arab impotence toward Israeli advances in the DMZ, the Marxist notion of "popular struggle" and, when referring to Israel, the "people's war of liberation," easily entered the lexicon of Ba'thi discourse. The radical Ba'thists (or the neo-Ba'thists) came to see "popular struggle" as the only means to combat Israel. At the same time, "popular struggle" served as a pretext to marshal support for the regime at a time when the Ba'th Party had embarked on a socialist course to transform Syrian society. "Popular struggle" became the all-inclusive slogan to silence opposition.[83] When the military wing of the Ba'th Party assumed power in 1966, the Ba'thi regime's attitude toward Israel grew more militant. The regime translated its espoused ideology into actions. It made good on its ideology of conducting a "people's liberation war" by actively abetting Palestinian guerrilla raids into Israel. In addition, the Ba'thi regime took the position that it was ready to incur huge sacrifices in order to defeat Israel.[84] The Palestine question had become central to the Ba'thi state.

The loss of Syrian territory in the 1967 war did not mitigate but rather sharpened the Ba'thi militant attitude toward Israel. The Ba'thi regime strengthened its commitment to the concept of "popular struggle." Not only did the regime continue to support Palestinian guerrilla raids into Israel, but also it established its own loyal Palestinian guerrilla organization, Al-Saiqa, which also functioned as a political arm of Syria within the PLO. In addition, the Ba'thi regime proceeded with its policy of transforming Syria's society, essentially nationalizing the Syrian economy and curbing the mercantilistic power of the bourgeoisie. This radical orientation reached its climax and logical conclusion when the Syrian army intervened in Jordan's civil war in 1970 on the side of the Palestinians. The intervention failed as Jordan subdued the Palestinians and defeated the Syrian army, leading to the ouster of the radical Ba'thi regime of Salah Jadid by then–defense minister Hafiz al-Asad.

Israel figured prominently in Asad's ideology. In central disagreement with Jadid, Asad advocated a strategy of cooperation with the Arab countries in the interest of confronting Israel. Asad had a Ba'thi nationalist upbringing and was among the politicized army officers who espoused the radical ideology of the Ba'th Party. As a Ba'thist, Arab nationalism always weighed heavily in Asad's ideology. This was reinforced by his being a minority member of the Alawi sect. On the one hand, pan-Arabism mitigated the contradictions between what constitutes an Alawi, a Syrian, and an Arab, and allowed, especially an Alawi, to be a Muslim by religion, a Syrian by identification, and an Arab by conviction. On the other hand, it seems natural that a minority member would aggressively embrace pan-Arabism in order to dispel any doubts regarding his loyalty entertained by the majority (Sunni) that belonging to a minority group makes one ready to compromise pan-Arab national interests. After all, it was mainly the secular doctrine of the Ba'thi ideology that attracted many members of minority groups.

Asad, like all Ba'thi cadres, believed that Israel not only was an imperialist creation but also was an expansionist state seeking to dominate the region. He was convinced that Zionism's goal was to create a "Greater Israel" extending from the Nile to the Euphrates, with the objective of imposing Zionist hegemony over the Arabs, thus threatening the present and future existence of the Arabs.[85] Israel's 1956 invasion of Egypt (along with Great Britain and France), continuous aggression against the Palestinians and Syrians, and acquisition of nuclear weapons were incontrovertible testimonials to Tel Aviv's hegemonic nature. The course of events of the Arab-Israeli struggle during the 1970s and 1980s (the invasion of Lebanon) seemed to confirm this perception of Israel on the part of Asad. But at the same time, a more careful look at his position will also show how he slowly and gradually kept modifying and diluting in practice this initial ideological outlook under the pressure of the hard realities of the balance of military and political power between Israel and the Arabs. This forms the basis of Asad's famous pragmatism.

This pragmatism was manifested early on in his rule. He liquidated the extremists of the Ba'th Party, who espoused the concept of the popular struggle. He then strove to break Syria out of its regional and international isolation and, internally, to win the support of the bourgeoisie. But significantly enough, this pragmatism was evinced when Asad negotiated the May 1974 disengagement agreement with Israel through the United States. In an addendum to the agreement, Asad privately pledged to the U.S. Secretary of State Henry Kissinger to prevent Palestinian guerrillas from using Syrian territory to attack Israel.[86] This position has assumed great significance in view of the fact that the Golan front has been always quiet.

Asad's pragmatism has another significant dimension. There was in him a streak of taking bold moves at moments of crisis that go against the grains of Ba'thi ideology. Such moves on his part included the 1976 intervention in Lebanon against the Palestinians and the Lebanese progressive forces, the brutal suppression of the Muslim Brotherhood in Hama in the early 1980s, siding with Iran against Iraq in the first Gulf War (when all Arab countries supported Iraq), and finally, Syria's participation in the U.S.-led anti-Iraq coalition against Saddam Hussein in the second Gulf War. While these bold moves can be attributed to Asad's diligent readiness to adjust and readjust to the realities of balance of power, they lead inescapably to the subversion of all Ba'thi ideology.

However, the Ba'thi ideology, especially concerning Arab nationalism, had been already greatly weakened. This did not happen only on account of Asad's bold moves. In reality, his moves can be perceived as a consequence of Arab nationalism's weakness and not vice versa. Before Asad assumed power, the breakup of the United Arab Republic in 1961 and the defeat of the Arabs in the 1967 war had already dealt severe blows to Arab nationalism. This was followed by the Arab defeat in the 1973 war. So the point should be clear that when Asad undertook actions against the grain of Ba'thi ideology, the ideology itself was already in limbo. During the Gulf War (1990), this ideology reached its nadir when all pretense of Arab unity and nationalism was shed. What guided Asad in his policies was his awareness of the vulnerabilities of the Arab states, especially the vulnerabilities of his own country. Correspondingly, he paid great attention to his country's security imperatives. Herein lies the root of his diligent attempts to adjust to the military and political balance of power, which inadvertently went against the very concept of Arab nationalism. Therefore, a distinction must be drawn between Asad's ideology and his pragmatism. Asad's pragmatism took precedence over his ideology when Syria's national security was threatened, but this did not mean that he had completely forsaken his ideology, particularly when it came to Israel. This applied especially well to the Golan Heights.

The Heights were of no less great ideological significance than national interest to Asad. In fact, they typify the last symbol of Ba'thi ideology that has not been treaded upon. True, pan-Arabism played a major role throughout Asad's Ba'thi rule by being the only ideology capable of transcending tribal, regional, and sectarian differences in Syria. It has given the regime the ideological and inspirational legitimacy to win over the different segments of the population, especially the Sunnis, and to build a consensus on a political program revolving around confrontation with Israel. But after so many adjustments by Asad to the realities of power, coupled with a near bankrupt Arab nationalism, what remains of the ideology of the vanguard party—the Ba'th—in Arab society?

The Ba'th Party under Asad has been robbed of its ideological raison d'être: Arab unity and nationalism have been sacrificed at the expense of national security. All that remains are the Golan Heights as the last vestige and symbol of Ba'thi ideology in Syria. It is difficult to entertain the idea that Asad would have taken the final bold move of his rule and dealt the final blow to Ba'thi ideology, let alone undermine Syria's national interest, by compromising on the total return of the Golan Heights. From the 1974 disengagement agreement until his death in 2000, Asad remained adamant about the total return of the Golan Heights from Israel. This is reinforced by two important and interconnected reasons.

The first is the fact that Asad belonged to a minority group. Being an Alawi, Asad had a psychological need to reassert his Arab nationalism by taking a firm stand on nationalist issues. Being an issue of great national importance, the Golan Heights served Asad as a means to prove again his nationalist credentials. The second reason is the fact that Syria lost the Golan Heights to Israel when Asad was defense minister. It is well known that the opposition to Ba'thi rule in Syria, mainly the Muslim Brotherhood, trumpeted the charge that Asad was a traitor and the sectarian (Alawi) regime had colluded with Israel to surrender the Golan Heights. During the confrontation between the Asad regime and the Muslim Brotherhood in the late 1970s and early 1980s, the latter conducted a propaganda campaign that brought up the charge of treason against the Ba'thi regime and its leader.

In an article titled "The Treason of Asad in 5 June 1967," which appeared in the mouthpiece newspaper of the Syrian Muslim Brotherhood, *Al-Nadhir,* the sectarian Ba'thi regime was accused of collusion with Israel in the surrender of the Golan Heights. Among the evidence the article adduced to buttress its charge were the following points: (1) there was a consensus among the military to quickly finish the battle; (2) the governor of Quneitra, Abd al-Halim Khaddam, oversaw the evacuation of families with minority backgrounds; (3) after few sorties on the first day of the battle, the Syrian air force disappeared; (4) the commander in charge, General Ahmad Suweidani, ran away, leaving behind a state of confusion among his forces; (5) Rifa't al-Asad, the brother of then–defense minister Hafiz al-Asad, supported the decision taken by General Ezat Jadid to decline General Awwad Bagh's order to carry out a counteroffensive; and (6) the artillery units of the Seventieth Battalion were moved at night to Damascus in order not to face the enemy.[87] Other articles appearing in *Al-Nadhir* not only attacked Asad but also constantly described him with such epithets as "the professional spy," "Islam's number one enemy," and "the seller of the Golan."[88]

After Israel sacked Quneitra, the principal town in the Golan Heights, Patrick Seale remarked that the town "was thereafter to be the badge of Syria's defeat, an emblem of hatred between Syria and Israel and a cross Asad had to bear."[89] Admittedly, that reality was even more bitter to Asad, as he had to bear the stigma of treason as well, a cross far heavier to carry than that of defeat. These charges stigmatized Asad. The Golan Heights stand not only as an emblem of defeat for Asad, but also as the basis for the charge of treason. As a result, the cumulative effect of these two reasons not only hardened Asad's outlook regarding Israel, adding to it a personalized dimension mired in guilt and shame, but also made the return of the Golan Heights a matter of national honor. Recovering the entire Heights became a central component of Asad's strategy. Herein lay the reason behind Asad's intractable attitude concerning the Heights vis-à-vis his peace talks with Israel. Inasmuch as retrieving the Heights was important, compromising over their total return was unacceptable.

The Golan Heights in the Conceptual
Framework of the Zionist Ideology

As Israel defeated the Arab states and won its independence, Zionism and Arab nationalism, particularly as advocated by Syria, became highly antagonistic as the conflict metamorphosed from one between communities to one between states. From 1948 to 1967 various ideological currents within the two nationalist movements fueled the conflict. As we have seen, the Ba'th Party passed through phases of ideological fermentation that culminated in Syria's "people's war of liberation." During that period, Syria constructed military fortifications on the Golan Heights and abetted guerrilla infiltration inside Israel.

Following Israel's independence, the banner of Jabotinsky's revisionist form of nationalism was carried forward by Menachem Begin, who founded the Herut Party in 1948. The Herut emphasized territorial maximalism and called for Jewish sovereignty on both sides of the Jordan River. Although at the beginning the party had little impact on mainstream Zionist ideology, by 1966 its ideological weight assumed greater significance. In 1965, as noted earlier, the Herut merged with the Liberal Party, the heir of General Zionism. The merger brought about the Herut-Liberal Bloc, known as Gahal, representing an influential militant ideological current within Zionist ideology in general.[90] In 1955, the religious party Mizrahi (and its labor movement, Hapoel Hamizrahi) had evolved into the National Religious Party (Mafdal). In addition to becoming a political force in Israeli politics, Mafdal laid the ideological foundation for the settlers' movement, known as Gush Emunim. Many activists in the movement believed in Final Redemption and sought to expand Jewish presence into the biblical lands of Eretz Israel in order to hasten the coming of the Messiah.[91]

Immediately after the conquest of the Golan Heights by Israel, Gush Emunim and Gahal sought to establish Jewish settlements in the West Bank (Judea and Samaria) and the Gaza Strip with the objective of annexing them to Israel. The activities of Gush Emunim and Gahal had a direct impact on the Zionist ideology, for they helped to keep alive the pioneering spirit of Zionism nearly two decades after the Jewish state had been created. In this respect, these activities served not only to rekindle the spirit of Zionism but also to prod Labor Zionism to stay the course of its ideology.

Mainstream Labor Zionists had mixed feelings about expanding Jewish settlements into the West Bank and Gaza. They were concerned about the Jewish character of the state and were worried that an annexation of these territories along with their Arab majorities would dilute that character. On the other hand, they found it practical to build settlements there, as these would exemplify their dedication to the Zionist doctrine. In addition, the settlements would serve to enhance Israeli security and the economic foundations of the state, while at the same time developing the territories. In contrast to the other

Arab occupied territories, the Golan Heights have had a distinct position within the spectrum of the Zionist ideology.

Unlike the West Bank, the Golan Heights have no biblical significance. Their importance lies largely in the security and economic dimensions of the Zionist ideology. In fact, after World War I, the Zionist Organization had constructed a comprehensive framework for the future Jewish national home and submitted it as a memorandum to the Supreme Council at the Peace Conference. The Zionist Organization included most of the Golan Heights along with its central town of Quneitra in the memorandum of 1919, which proposed the boundary of the future Jewish state.[92] The inclusion of the Heights was based on providing the future state with a sound economic foundation, particularly with regard to conserving and controlling the water sources necessary for agricultural development and a thriving population. The Heights derive their importance from the access they give to the headwaters of the Jordan River, the main body of water in Israel (see Chapter 6 for details on the subject of water). Security considerations assumed greater significance when Syria used the strategic location of the Heights to pose a security threat to Israel. The Heights look down the Sea of Galilee (Lake Tiberias) and tower over northern Israel extending to the Lebanese border. In fact, during the 1967 war, senior Israeli military planners such as Yigal Allon and David Elazar argued for capturing the Golan Heights on account of their economic, security, and strategic significance.[93]

So although the Zionist ideology had no biblical claim to the Heights, still it applied the criteria of security and economic necessity to them. After Israel captured the Heights, Labor Zionist ideology facilitated the justification of building settlements there and controlling the land in terms of economic necessity and security for Israel. After all, the achievement of pioneering settlements had figured prominently in Labor Zionist ideology and had served as a basis for the Jewish claim to Palestine. Shortly after the capture, Yigal Allon, minister of labor in Israel's cabinet, argued that Israel's control of the Heights fitted Israel's overall strategy of mainly defending its water sources and the Israeli settlements next to the Syrian border (Huleh Valley).[94] This was reinforced by Syria's belligerent attitude toward Israel.

However, since the historical ideological component of the Jewish claim to the Heights was inapplicable, and since they were not considered a part of Eretz Israel, a certain ambivalence became evident in the Zionist ideology with regard to the Heights. This ambivalence revealed itself in the idea entertained by many Zionists at that time that Israel would return the Heights on condition that Syria sign a peace treaty, as well as in the slow pace of establishing settlements there. But as the possibility of a peace treaty with Syria seemed remote, this ambivalence receded to the background and settlement activities were gradually expanded.

In 1976 the right wing of Jewish nationalism, represented now by the Likud, which had been concentrating its efforts on settling the West Bank, established its first settlement (Shaal) on the Golan Heights. As the Likud came to power in Israel with Begin at its head in 1977, and as it embarked on peace negotiations with Egypt, the Heights began to figure prominently in the movement of the right-wing ideology. Following the Israeli-Egyptian peace treaty in 1979, Begin's government came under fire from Gush Emunim and other right-wing forces to renege on his promise to relinquish the Sinai Peninsula. Wanting to defuse the criticism, Begin extended Israeli law to the Heights in 1981 in a move to demonstrate his commitment to his party's platform of territorial maximalism, taking into consideration, of course, the Heights' strategic economic and security significance.

The extension of Israeli law to the Heights affected to some extent the Zionist perspective on the issue. Of great significance, the settlers could argue that the Heights were not open to compromise because they constituted the frontiers for the further realization of Zionism and were an integral part of Israel. This served to reinforce the security and economic dimensions of the Zionist ideology, as well as the general trend to retain the Heights, especially in light of Syria's belligerent attitude. In fact, Likud's argument (and that of a number of Labor hard-liners) to retain the Heights has been based on the assumption that Syria cannot be trusted because of the nature of its regime.[95] While Labor at first had encouraged settlement on the Heights, now Likud had made good on its advocacy of territorial maximalism and continued the same effort. Up until the peace process had begun in 1991, there was little ideological debate on the subject of the Heights.

But as Israel entered into peace negotiations with the Arabs, including the Syrians, the Zionist ideology suddenly arrived at a crossroads. It is the Zionist state that is negotiating the relinquishing of Arab occupied territories, territories that served to keep the Zionist spirit of settlement across the whole spectrum of Zionist ideology alive, in exchange for peace. The concept of return of territories, subject to Israeli conditions, went against the general grain of Zionist ideology. In addition, because the aims of the Zionist ideology had been largely accomplished, the critical question loomed as to what would become of the ideology itself, and how success would transform it. At this juncture, the issue of the Golan Heights not only brought to the surface the old ambivalence in the Zionist ideology regarding them, but also highlighted the necessity of reformulating the Zionist doctrine. On the one hand, the Zionist ideology was reduced to economic and security considerations concerning the Golan Heights. On the other hand, once those considerations are resolved with Syria there will remain no reasons to keep the settlements on the Heights, thereby bringing down Zionism's pioneering symbol. This has become all the more excruciating given the price the Zionist state is paying for its peace negotiations with the Palestinians.

Faced with such challenges, Israel began to oscillate and waver between its quest for peace and keeping the Golan Heights. Thus the Heights became a burning issue in Israeli politics. This explains, for example, why Israeli leaders, such as Yitzhak Rabin, made the return of the Heights to Syria conditional on a referendum. This way, Israel shifted the onus of swinging the pendulum between peace and the status quo to Syria. A show of goodwill on the part of Syria has become important to help alleviate Israeli fears and facilitate the decisionmaking process of Israeli leaders. Sammy Bar-Lev, mayor of the Golan Heights town of Katzrin, reflected the mood of the settlers concerning peace with Syria when he commented on Rabin's negotiations: "Rabin is just like Chamberlain, who believed he was bringing peace by signing a deal with a ruthless dictator. A deal that led to millions of deaths."[96]

All this is a reflection of the old conflict between two deeply rooted and powerful impulses within the Zionist project and ideology: the impulse to seek peace with and acceptance from the neighboring Arab world, against the impulse to acquire more land, settlements, and resources.

Notes

1. Neil Caplan, "A Tale of Two Cities: The Rhodes and Lausanne Conferences, 1949," *Journal of Palestine Studies* 21, no. 3 (Spring 1992), p. 6. For complete text of the resolution, see George J. Tomeh (ed.), *United Nations Resolutions on Palestine and the Arab-Israeli Conflict*, vol. 1, *1947–1974* (Washington, D.C.: Institute for Palestine Studies, 1975), pp. 130 ff.

2. Caplan, "Tale of Two Cities," p. 6.

3. See Fred J. Khouri, "Friction and Conflict on the Israeli-Syrian Front," *Middle East Journal* 17, nos. 1–2 (Winter–Spring 1963); Aryeh Shalev, *Israel and Syria: Peace and Security on the Golan* (Boulder: Westview Press, 1994), pp. 25–26; Leslie Susser, "Changing the Golan Map," *Jerusalem Report*, January 17, 2000, p. 16; and Frederic C. Hof, "Analysis: The Line of June 4, 1967," *Middle East Insight*, September–October 1999.

4. Philip S. Khoury, *Syria and the French Mandate: The Politics of Arab Nationalism, 1920–1945* (Princeton: Princeton University Press, 1987), p. 14.

5. For background information, see ibid.; Philip S. Khoury, *Urban Notables and Arab Nationalism* (Cambridge: Cambridge University Press, 1983); and Hanna Batatu, *Syria's Peasantry, the Descendants of Its Lesser Rural Notables, and Their Politics* (Princeton: Princeton University Press, 1999).

6. Text reproduced in Nissim Bar-Yaacov, *The Israel-Syrian Armistice: Problems of Implementation, 1949–1966* (Jerusalem: Magnes Press, Hebrew University, 1967), pp. 339–346.

7. See Khouri, "Friction and Conflict," p. 16; and Susser, "Changing the Golan Map," pp. 16–17.

8. Shalev, *Israel and Syria*, p. 31; and Susser, "Changing the Golan Map," pp. 16–17.

9. Patrick Seale, *The Struggle for Syria: A Study of Post-War Arab Politics, 1945–1958* (London: Oxford University Press, 1965), p. 45. This section is slim on Syrian sources partly because the debate took place in Israel and partly because of the nature of the Syrian regime, which allows little or no room for dissenting views.

10. Ibid., pp. 46–57.

11. Miles Copeland, *The Game of Nations* (London: Weidenfeld & Nicholson, 1969), p. 42.

12. Ibid.; and Itamar Rabinovich, *The Road Not Taken: Early Arab-Israeli Negotiations* (New York: Oxford University Press, 1991), p. 84. For Meade's contacts with Zaim, see Douglas Little, "Cold War and Covert Action: The United States and Syria, 1945–1958," *Middle East Journal* 44, no. 1 (Winter 1990); and Andrew Rathmell, *Secret War in the Middle East: The Covert Struggle for Syria, 1949–1961* (London: I. B. Tauris, 1995), pp. 36–44. See also Khaled al-Azm, *Mudhakkirat* (Memoirs), vol. 2 (Beirut: Al-Dar al-Taqaddumiya lil-Nashr, 1973), p. 183.

13. Rabinovich, *Road Not Taken*, p. 69.

14. Ibid.; and Avi Shlaim, "Husni Za'im and the Plan to Resettle Palestinian Refugees in Syria," *Journal of Palestine Studies* 15, no. 4 (Summer 1986).

15. See Simha Flapan, *The Birth of Israel: Myths and Realities* (New York: Pantheon, 1987).

16. See Benny Morris, *The Birth of the Palestinian Refugee Problem, 1947–1949* (Cambridge: Cambridge University Press, 1988); and Benny Morris, *1948 and After: Israel and the Palestinians* (Oxford: Oxford University Press, 1990).

17. Ibid. See also Avi Shlaim, *Collusion Across the Jordan: King Abdullah, the Zionist Movement, and the Partition of Palestine* (Oxford: Clarendon Press, 1988); Avi Shlaim, "The Debate About 1948," *International Journal of Middle East Studies* 27, no. 3 (August 1995); and Ilan Pappe, *Britain and the Arab-Israeli Conflict, 1948–51* (London: Macmillan, 1988).

18. Shlaim, "Husni Za'im," p. 79.

19. Ibid., p. 73.

20. Shlaim, "Debate About 1948," p. 301.

21. Ibid.

22. Ibid.

23. Benny Morris, "A Second Look at the 'Missed Peace,' or Smoothing Out History: A Review Essay," *Journal of Palestine Studies* 24, no. 1 (Autumn 1994), p. 79.

24. Ibid., pp. 79–80.

25. Ibid., p. 81.

26. Ibid.

27. Ibid., pp. 81–82; and Rabinovich, *Road Not Taken*, p. 79.

28. Moshe Ma'oz, *Syria and Israel: From War to Peacemaking* (Oxford: Clarendon Press, 1995), p. 24.

29. Ibid., p. 29.

30. Shalev, *Israel and Syria*, p. 36.

31. Rabinovich, *Road Not Taken*, p. 200.

32. Ma'oz, *Syria and Israel*, p. 30.

33. For details on Shishakli's overthrow, see Seale, *Struggle for Syria*, pp. 131–147.

34. UN S/2157, May 18, 1951; Fred Khouri, "Friction and Conflict," p. 19; and Bar-Yaacov, *Israel-Syrian Armistice*, pp. 93 ff.

35. UN S/1353, special supplement no. 2, July 20, 1949; UN S/2389, November 8, 1951; UN S/2833, November 4, 1952; and Fred Khouri, "Friction and Conflict," p. 17.

36. UN Security Council Official Records, Document S/3343, p. 12.

37. UN S/2049, March 21, 1951; UN S/2157, May 18, 1951; UN S/3343, (UNTSO Chief of Staff) Major-General E. L. M. Burns's report of January 6, 1955; and UN S/5111, April 9, 1962.

38. Israel State Archives (ISA), Foreign Office (FO), 2434/3, February 23, 1953; ISA, FO, 2408/22, April 7, 1953; Fred Khouri, "Friction and Conflict," pp. 23–24; and

Abraham M. Hirsch, "Utilization of the International Rivers in the Middle East," *American Journal of International Law* 50, no. 1 (January 1956), p. 91.

39. UN Security Council Resolution 111, January 19, 1956.

40. UN S/6061, November 24, 1964.

41. Itamar Rabinovich, *Syria Under the Ba'th, 1963–1966: The Army-Party Symbiosis* (Jerusalem: Israel Universities Press, 1972), pp. 84–104.

42. UN S/6248, March 19, 1965; and UN S/7432, July 26, 1966.

43. Yezid Sayigh, "Escalation or Containment? Egypt and the Palestine Liberation Army, 1964–67," *International Journal of Middle East Studies* 30, no. 1 (February 1998), p. 99.

44. Abraham Ben-Tzur (ed.), *The Syrian Baath Party and Israel: Documents from the Internal Party Publications* (Givat Haviva: Center for Arab and Afro-Asian Studies, 1968), p. 4.

45. Ibid., p. 19.

46. See Sayigh, "Escalation or Containment?" pp. 99 ff.

47. For different interpretations of the Khartoum summit, see Nadav Safran, *Israel: The Embattled Ally* (Cambridge: Belknap Press of Harvard University Press, 1981), p. 428; William B. Quandt, *Decade of Decisions: American Policy Toward the Arab-Israeli Conflict, 1967–1976* (Berkeley: University of California Press, 1977), p. 65; Mahmoud Riad, *The Struggle for Peace in the Middle East* (London: Quartet Books, 1981), pp. 54–57; and Kamel S. Abu-Jaber, "United States Policy Toward the June Conflict," in Ibrahim Abu-Lughod (ed.), *The Arab-Israeli Confrontation of June 1967: An Arab Perspective* (Evanston, Ill.: Northwestern University Press, 1970), p. 164.

48. UN Security Council Resolution 242, November 22, 1967. The French version of the resolution states "the territories" and not "territories." This is a major area of dispute.

49. Avigdor Levy, "The Syrian Communists and the Ba'th Power Struggle, 1966–1970," in Michael Confino and Shimoni Shamir (eds.), *The U.S.S.R. and the Middle East* (Jerusalem: Israel Universities Press, 1973), p. 402; Nikolaos Van Dam, *The Struggle for Power in Syria: Politics and Society Under Asad and the Ba'th Party* (London: I. B. Tauris, 1996), p. 63; and Ma'oz, *Syria and Israel*, pp. 117–118.

50. For different interpretations on this episode of Syrian history, see Levy, "Syrian Communists," pp. 408–413; Patrick Seale, *Asad of Syria: The Struggle for the Middle East* (Berkeley: University of California Press, 1988), pp. 158–160; and Ma'oz, *Syria and Israel*, pp. 118–119.

51. Seale, *Asad of Syria*, pp. 190–191.

52. Mohamed Heikal, *The Road to Ramadan* (London: Williams Collins Sons, 1975), p. 12.

53. President Asad announced publicly this policy in a speech in Damascus on March 8, 1972. For more details, see Fred J. Khouri, *The Arab-Israeli Dilemma* (Syracuse: Syracuse University Press, 1985), pp. 367–368.

54. Moshe Dayan, *Moshe Dayan: Story of My Life* (New York: William Morrow, 1976), p. 465.

55. Lieutenant-General Saad el-Shazly, *The Crossing of the Suez* (San Francisco: American Mideast Research, 1980), pp. 164–166; and Heikal, *Road to Ramadan,* pp. 172–173.

56. Dayan, *Story of my Life,* pp. 459–460.

57. Seale, *Asad of Syria,* pp. 197–198. For excellent details and statements on the 1973 war by Egyptian and Israeli officials, see Public Broadcasting Service (PBS), *The Fifty Years War: Israel and the Arabs* (Boston: PBS, 1999), documentary.

58. UN Security Council Resolution 338, October 22, 1973.

59. On condition and treatment of Israel's prisoners of war in Syria, see Hearing Before the Subcommittee on International Organizations and Movements of the Committee on Foreign Affairs, House of Representatives, *Treatment of Israeli POW's in Syria and Their Status Under the Geneva Conventions* (Washington, D.C.: U.S. Government Printing Office, 1974), pp. 13–19.

60. Henry Kissinger, *Years of Upheaval* (Boston: Little, Brown, 1982), p. 561.

61. Ibid., pp. 1253–1254.

62. Ibid.; and Shalev, *Israel and Syria,* map 4.

63. Henry Kissinger, *Diplomacy* (New York: Simon & Schuster, 1994), p. 738.

64. Michel Aflaq, *Fi Sabil al-Ba'th* (For the Sake of the Ba'th) (Beirut: Dar al-Tali'a, 1963), p. 45.

65. Documents of the Arab Ba'th Socialist Party, *Nidal al-Ba'th* (The Struggle of the Ba'th), vol. 1 (Beirut: Dar al-Tali'a, 1963), p. 172.

66. Ibid., p. 175. See also Sylvia G. Haim, *Arab Nationalism: An Anthology* (Berkeley: University of California Press, 1962), p. 236.

67. Aflaq, *Fi Sabil al-Ba'th,* pp. 176–180.

68. Freedom of speech, assembly, and belief was the second principle of the Ba'th Party's constitution. See *Nidal al-Ba'th,* vol. 1, p. 173.

69. For excellent background information on the ANM, see Hani al-Hindi and Abd al-Ilah al-Nasrawi, *Harakat al-Qawmiyyin al-'Arab: Nash'tuha wa Tataworiha 'ibr Wathaiqaha, 1951–1968* (The Arab Nationalist Movement: Its Emergence and Evolution Through Its Documents, 1951–1968), pt. 1 (Beirut: Institution of Arab Research, 2001), pp. 27–187. Both the Ba'th Party and the ANM were heavily influenced by the writings of the pan-Arab nationalist Sati al-Husri. See Bassam Tibi, *Arab Nationalism: A Critical Enquiry,* 2nd ed. (New York: St. Martin's Press, 1990), pp. 123–198.

70. See articles in *Nidal al-Ba'th,* vol. 1, pp. 224–247.

71. Michel Aflaq, *Ma'rakat al-Masir al-Wahid* (The Battle of One Destiny) (Beirut: Dar al-Adab, 1958), p. 97.

72. Ibid., p. 159.

73. Seale, *Asad of Syria,* p. 61.

74. See Avraham Ben-Tzur, "The Neo-Ba'th Party of Syria," *Journal of Contemporary History* (Institute of Contemporary History, London) 3, no. 3 (July 1968), p. 170.

75. Jamal Atasi, "Arab Socialism and the Myth of [Its] Special Qualities," *Fi al-Fikr al-Siyasi* (In the Political Thought), vol. 1 (Damascus: Dar Dimashq, 1963), pp. 170–171.

76. Ibid., pp. 152–155.

77. Ilyas Murqus, "Collapse of the Parliamentary System," *Fi al-Fikr al-Siyasi,* vol. 2, p. 169.

78. Yasin al-Hafiz, "About the Experience of the Ba'th Party," *Fi al-Fikr al-Siyasi,* vol. 1, pp. 194–197. See also Ben-Tzur, "Neo-Ba'th Party of Syria," p. 171.

79. See text in *Nidal al-Ba'th,* vol. 6, pp. 232–291.

80. Ibid., p. 227.

81. Ibid., p. 266.

82. Ibid., pp. 229–230.

83. See Ben-Tzur, "Neo-Ba'th Party of Israel," pp. 174–176.

84. Ben-Tzur, *Syrian Baath Party and Israel,* pp. 4, 6, 8, 21.

85. See Asad's statements in Hafiz al-Asad, *Kadhalika Qala al-Asad* (Thus Asad Said), compiled by General Mustafa Tlas (Damascus: Tlas Press, 1984), pp. 181–183.

86. Kissinger, *Years of Upheaval,* p. 1098.

87. *Al-Nadhir* no. 35, June 17, 1981.

88. *Al-Nadhir* no. 29, February 12, 1981; and no. 35, June 17, 1981.

89. Seale, *Asad of Syria,* p. 141.

90. For background information on the Herut Party, see Yonathan Shapiro, *The Road to Power: Herut Party in Israel* (Albany: State University of New York Press, 1991).

91. For background information on Gush Emunim, see Eliezer Don-Yehiya, "Jewish Messianism, Religious Zionism, and Israeli Politics: The Impact and Origins of Gush Emunim," *Middle Eastern Studies* 23, no. 2 (April 1987).

92. J. C. Hurewitz, *Diplomacy in the Near and Middle East: A Documentary Record, 1914–1956* (Princeton: D. Van Nostrand, 1956), pp. 45–50.

93. Yitzhak Rabin, *The Rabin Memoirs* (Boston: Little, Brown, 1979); Dayan, *Story of My Life;* and Avner Yaniv, "Syria and Israel: The Politics of Escalation," in Moshe Ma'oz and Avner Yaniv (eds.), *Syria Under Assad: Domestic Constraints and Regional Risks* (New York: St. Martin's Press, 1986).

94. Ma'oz, *Syria and Israel,* p. 113. See also Ze'ev Schiff, *Peace with Security: Israel's Minimal Security Requirements in Negotiations with Syria* (Washington, D.C.: Washington Institute for Near East Policy, 1993), p. 40.

95. See, for example, Ariel Sharon's argument in "Why Should Israel Reward Syria?" *New York Times,* December 28, 1999. For further details, see Chapters 5 and 6 in this volume.

96. Sammy Bar-Lev, "Quotes," *Jerusalem Report,* October 20, 1994, p. 8.

2

The Struggle
for Lebanon

Exactly one year after the May 1974 disengagement agreement brought peace and quiet to the Israeli-Syrian front on the Golan Heights, the Lebanese civil war erupted, providing a new arena for the continuation of the struggle between the two embattled neighbors, but by other, indirect means this time. However, it should be made clear from the very outset that the reasons why Syria and Israel vied so fiercely to gain predominance in Lebanon stemmed not only from the nature of the overall Arab-Israeli conflict and its shifting dynamics, but also in equal measure from Lebanon's own highly fragile sociopolitical and religious structures, alignments, and configurations.

As is well known, Lebanon was founded on a delicate balance of religious confessional power in the absence of genuine national integration. This balance came under significant stress when the PLO substituted Lebanon for Jordan as an organizational and operational base for its activities. By and by, the Muslim communities became disgruntled with the old power-sharing arrangements, seeking to enhance their position in the confessional system. The PLO emerged, in their eyes, as an effective instrument for achieving their goal.

As a reaction, the Christians mobilized in defense of the prevailing status quo. More specifically, the Maronites initiated a process of cooperation with Israel that evolved into an alliance. This alliance drew its strength from the rise of the young Christian Maronite leader Bashir Jumayil and from the desire of Israel's Begin government first to reinforce its hold over the West Bank against the backdrop of its withdrawal from the Sinai Peninsula following the peace treaty with Egypt; and second to deny to the PLO and Syria domination over Lebanon. Meanwhile, Syria, feeling isolated and weak, was attempting to prevent Israel from establishing a foothold in Lebanon while seeking to build its regional power especially vis-à-vis Israel.

Naturally, all sides in this deadly contest tried to enlist in their favor the maximum support and involvement of traditional, local, international, and

43

big-power allies such as the United States, the USSR, and the UNO (United Nations Organization). It is this highly complex and intricate situation that I will try to clarify and explain in this chapter.

The Regional Setting

President Nixon planned on making a Middle Eastern trip after Syria had signed the disengagement agreement with Israel in May 1974. His visit to Middle Eastern capitals was the first ever by a U.S. President, except for Cairo. The purposes of the trip were manifold. It symbolized the U.S. commitment to the peace process as well as the indispensable role of the United States in the region. It also served as a great public relations stunt for a domestically wounded president who was exuberantly welcomed by the Middle Eastern public. While celebrating Nixon's visit to Damascus on June 15, President Asad had important things on his mind. He wanted to know the depth of the U.S. commitment to the peace process initiated by Kissinger's step-by-step diplomacy. President Asad put President Nixon through the wringer of penetrating questions, revolving around the future negotiating strategy of the United States and its vision of Israel's future and final borders.[1] He also sought a U.S. pledge to help Syria regain all of the Golan Heights. President Nixon hated this cross-examination and equivocated. But before the meeting was over, Nixon gave Asad the impression that the United States was close to the Syrian position on the final borders with Israel.[2] This Asad interpreted as a U.S. endorsement of Syria's position regarding the Israeli-Syrian frontiers, meaning an Israeli withdrawal from the Golan Heights. Encouraged by the U.S. position, Asad improved his relationship with the United States.

Before the visit, President Asad had set the stage well for a factual encounter with President Nixon. In an interview he had given to Arnaud de Borchgrave of *Newsweek* on June 1, 1974, Asad signaled his desire for peace in the Middle East within the context of Resolutions 242 and 338 and seemed to give the United States a central role in achieving it in the region.[3] A few months later, in February 1975, Asad gave another interview to *Newsweek*'s de Borchgrave in which he said: "If the Israelis return to the 1967 frontier— and the West Bank and Gaza become a Palestinian state—the last obstacle to a final settlement will have been removed."[4] But in the course of the interview Asad revealed that he was really interested in a nonbelligerency agreement. Though falling short of a call for a peace treaty, Asad's statements were conciliatory and promising considering that they coincided with Kissinger's renewed efforts to conclude a second Israeli-Egyptian disengagement agreement. Apparently, President Asad was linking the Israeli-Egyptian agreement with an Israeli-Syrian one, providing for a substantial Israeli withdrawal from the Golan Heights.

By mid-1975, however, President Asad had become disillusioned with U.S. policy in the region. Kissinger had been concentrating all his efforts on an Israeli-Egyptian agreement, leaving Syria out. Asad's fears of a separate accord between Egypt and Israel were confirmed when the two countries signed the second disengagement agreement, known as Sinai II, in September 1975. According to Patrick Seale, President Asad felt "thoroughly betrayed and was angry with himself for having given even a brief credence to Kissinger's assurance that disengagement would proceed in step on both the Egyptian and Syrian fronts and that the United States did not mean to divide the Arabs."[5] The terms of Sinai II were anathema to Asad. Israel and Egypt undertook to resolve their conflict by peaceful means in the interest of a final and just peace settlement. The United States compensated Israel's withdrawal from parts of the Sinai Peninsula with significant economic and military aid, pledging that it would neither negotiate with nor recognize the PLO unless the organization recognized Israel's right to exist and accepted Resolutions 242 and 338. Asad realized that Egypt could no longer exert any military pressure on Israel, and that Syria had lost its strategic military partner. Being the most powerful state in the region, Israel was now in a position to dictate its own peace terms on the Arab states. The Arabs' other option was either to accept or to resign themselves to the continued occupation of their territories. Asad strongly disapproved of such a scenario and sought to reinforce his regional standing vis-à-vis Israel in the region.

On a deeper level, Israel remained for Asad an expansionist state seeking to dominate the region. He was convinced that Zionism's strategic goal was to create a "Greater Israel" extending from the Nile to the Euphrates, a goal to which all plans were subordinated.[6] He perceived the Arab-Zionist struggle as an existential one, and when he took the long view he seemed to think that Israel was just another temporary foreign conquest that would pass like all those conquests that came to and vanished from the region.[7] In sum, the elimination of Israel and the return of all Arab territories figured prominently in Asad's deep-seated ideology. However, he was also a pragmatist. He recognized Syria's weakness. He sought Arab unity and cooperation in the interest of confronting Israel (after all, that had been his plan of action since he seized power), but without enduring success. Egypt had bolted the Arab military camp. Only Lebanon, Jordan, and the Palestinians loomed as potential Syrian allies. Iraq, which helped Syria in the 1973 war, was ruled out at the time due to the deep suspicions and rivalries between the two Ba'thi regimes.

Lebanon, Jordan, and the Palestinians could not be the best of allies, as they were weak on their own and constituted easy political and military targets for Israel. Lebanon was brewing with internal strife exacerbated by the PLO's presence in the country. Jordan rotated within the U.S. political orbit. The Palestinians were striving to break free from Arab tutelage, and to build their autonomous political and military organizations in Lebanon. To many, it seemed that Asad's efforts to build such an alliance were an attempt at reviving the concept of "Greater Syria"—that is, the union of Jordan, Lebanon, Palestine, and present-day Syria. But Asad's main concern was the balance of power in the region, which he wanted to adjust, if not tip, in Syria's favor. What mattered to him was bringing about some Arab unity under Syrian leadership to confront Israel. As he set about to achieve this goal, he faced a grave and immediate challenge from Lebanon.

The Lebanese Morass

Lebanon comprises a patchwork of religious communities. Its hallmark is the absence of national integration. In 1920, the French, with the approval of their political allies, the Christian Maronite community of Mount Lebanon, proclaimed Greater Lebanon. The map of the new country included the Muslim-dominated coastal cities extending from Tripoli in the north to Tyre in the south and the Muslim-dominated Beka Valley. The Maronites assumed political hegemony but had barely a plurality. In 1943 the religious communities, under the leadership of the Maronites and the Muslim Sunnis, worked out a national pact that distributed political power among themselves. The pact assigned a ratio of representation in the parliament favoring the Christians, and stipulated that the president of the republic be a Christian Maronite, the prime minister a Sunni Muslim, and the speaker of the house of representatives a Shia Muslim. Because of its numerical weakness, the Muslim Druze community obtained no privileged office. This is Lebanon's famous confessional system.

The Maronites, who dominated the system, believed in a Lebanon that belonged to neither an Arab nor a Western world, though their ideological commitments were pro-Western. In their view, Lebanon has been and should continue to be a crossroads between East and West. One predominant orientation within the Maronite community came to be represented by the Phalange Party (Kata'ib), founded by Pierre Jumayil in 1936. Its program rested on safeguarding the political autonomy and authority of the Maronites in Lebanon against Arab Muslim pretensions. The Phalange Party defined Lebanon as a historical political community with Maronitism, which Jumayil equated with patriotism, as its basis.[8] This Maronite nationalist outlook ran counter to that of Lebanon's Muslims, whose pan-Arab sentiment had been rising since Lebanon's independence in 1946. Though at various times interests overlapped among the confessional groups, communal solidarity and feudal leadership further weakened the fabric of Lebanese society. Loyalty, in the absence of a national sentiment, went to sect and leader.

A weak state enjoying a quasidemocratic system, Lebanon became a playground for competing movements in the Arab world, revolving around grievances against imperialism and Zionism. The first challenge to confront the state occurred in 1958, when civil war broke out. Muslim (Sunni and Druze) pro-Nasser Arab forces confronted Christian pro-Western forces. At the time, President Camille Chamoun, who supported the Eisenhower Doctrine, called on the United States for help. The response took the form of landing U.S. Marines in Beirut and slowly putting a negotiated end to the fighting. Stability was restored but rested again on a delicate balance of power among the confessional groups. This balance was disrupted when the Palestinians residing in Lebanon became an additional actor in the country, grafting their "Palestine problem" onto Lebanon's domestic politics.

Some 100,000 Palestinian refugees came to Lebanon during the 1948 war. Their numbers increased dramatically to approximately 300,000 following their defeat at the hands of the Hashimite regime in Jordan's civil war in 1970. The bulk of the PLO moved out of Jordan to Lebanon via Syria. The geographic contiguity of Lebanon with Israel, the appeal of pan-Arabism and Palestine to Lebanon's Muslim population, and the weakness of the Lebanese state made Lebanon a highly congenial place for PLO activities. The Palestinians immediately reinforced their presence in southern Lebanon, particularly in the Arqub and Kharoub region, which had been largely neglected by the government. From there they staged guerrilla attacks against Israel. In 1969 the armed presence of the PLO in Lebanon was enhanced following the Cairo Agreement, which provided extraterritorial rights for the PLO, particularly in the refugee camps. Southern Lebanon was becoming a Palestinian stronghold, deserving of the name "Fatahland."

Already before 1970, Palestinian attacks were leading to severe Israeli retaliations. In December 1968, Israel raided Beirut's international airport and blew up thirteen Lebanese airplanes, precipitating the fall of the government. Following the influx of the PLO into Lebanon and its increased border infiltration into Israel, Israeli counterattacks made parts of southern Lebanon uninhabitable. This had two immediate bearings on Lebanon's politics. First, the accelerated flight of the indigent Shia inhabitants of southern Lebanon to the slums around a predominantly Sunni West Beirut led to the destabilizing of the homogeneous religious societal composition of that part of the capital, and set in motion an irreversible radicalization of the Muslim community. Second, the Muslim and Christian communities became polarized, because the leadership of the first supported the PLO and criticized the weakness and neutrality of the army in the face of Israeli aggression, while the leadership of the second opposed the very presence of the PLO on Lebanese soil.

Compounded by serious internal issues about power sharing (and economic disadvantage), this started the creation of two diametrically opposed camps in Lebanon's politics. The Muslim camp sought to alter the status quo and to gain political advantage, moving Lebanon unequivocally in the direction of pan-Arabism. The Christian camp sought to maintain the status quo and keep Lebanon out of the Arab-Israeli conflict, thereby preserving their political predominance. The PLO naturally sided with the Muslims, who not only

Lebanese-Israeli Frontier

Former Israeli Security Zone

UNIFIL Area of Operation

• Population Center
▲ Refugee Camp
∴ "Seven Villages"

·········· Armistice Demarcation Line, 1949

Purple Line Incursions

Line of June 4, 1967

LEBANON

Litani River

Awwali River

SIDON • EIN AL-HILWEH ▲

MIEH MIEH ▲

JEZZIN •

Hasbani River

Mediterranean Sea

Litani (Qasimiyah) River

SHEBAA •

AL /MAJIDIYA

⁺ Mt. Dov

AL WAZZANI

METULLA

TYRE • AL-BUSS ▲

BURJ AL-SHEMALI ▲

RASHIDIEH ▲

ADAISSEH

MISGAV AM

HOULA

AL-QAMH

∴ HUNIN

• QIRYAT

MANARA SHEMONA

ABIL

AL GHAJAR

BANIAS •

UNDOF

Ra's an Naqurah

YARIN •

NABI

QADAS YUSHA

∴ MALIKIYA

RMEISH •

TARBIKHA ∴

SALIHA

Jordan River

QUNEITRA •

GOLAN HEIGHTS

ISRAEL

ACRE •

N

0 —————————— 15 mi
0 —————————— 15 km

Lake Tiberias (Kinneret)

TIBERIAS •

Christine Epperson/Equator Graphics, Inc.
©2000 *Middle East Insight*

Reprinted from *Middle East Insight,* May–June 2000, © 2000 *Middle East Insight.* Used with permission of the publisher.

gave it support but also allowed it to gain a political say in the affairs of the country due to its military strength. Thus, although the Palestinians were not at the root of Lebanon's weak system, they were the catalyst of the system's downfall. Civil war broke out in April 1975 when, avenging the killing of Pierre Jumayil's bodyguard, Phalangists opened fire on an armed Palestinian bus passing through the Maronite suburb of Beirut, Ayn al-Rumane.

The civil war initiated the process of dividing Lebanon along heavily armed sectarian lines, with many Christian and Muslim villages and towns sacked and cleansed along confessional lines. The Christian camp comprised a coalition of three main groups, the Phalangist Party and its armed militia; the National Liberal Party (founded by Camille Chamoun) and its armed militia, known as the Tigers; and the followers of Suleiman Franjieh (then president of Lebanon) and their armed militia, known interchangeably as the Zugharta Liberation Army and the Mara'da. The Muslim camp consisted of a coalition of groups. Its mainstay was the National Movement, founded in 1973, which rallied most Arabist, leftist, and radical groupings and parties in Lebanon (including communists, pro-Iraq Ba'thists, Nasserists, and a faction of the Syrian Social Nationalist Party) and then fronted for the PLO. Its outspoken leader was Kamal Jumblat, an enigmatic, cynical, quasifeudal, and controversial figure.

The founder of the Progressive Socialist Party, Jumblat was a genuine man of the left, who had won the Lenin Peace Prize. He was also a sectarian Druze leader who sought to overthrow Maronite hegemony over the Lebanese system. He abhorred Maronite privileges in Lebanon; he was most probably the person who coined the term "isolationists" to describe the Maronites. He perceived them as central players in a U.S. and Zionist conspiracy against Lebanon and the Arabs in general. According to him, the Maronites strove to cut Lebanon off from its Arab surroundings in the hope of creating a "Christian Zion" called Lebanon, serving to undermine Arab unity. Thus, according to Jumblat, the "battle of the National Movement was to save Lebanon and its Arabism and to reaffirm Lebanon's commitment to the Palestinian cause, foiling the Phalangist conspiracy."[9] In fact, Jumblat, in the name of Arabism, was recruiting the PLO to fight his war against the Christians. This posture was grist for the mill of the PLO, which eventually became a decisive player in Lebanon's civil war. The Popular Front for the Liberation of Palestine (PFLP) and the Popular Democratic Front for the Liberation of Palestine (PDFLP) (both radical factions of the PLO) played a major role in the fight against the Christians as well.

As the civil war intensified and the partition of the country along sectarian lines was becoming a daily reality, Lebanon posed a security problem for Syria as partition of Lebanon could well become de jure. Driven by Muslim and Palestinian pressure, the Maronites could well be provoked to declare their own independent state, opting for close cooperation with Israel. Growing Palestinian activity and power in Lebanon could well draw the Israelis in to destroy Palestinian military bases. Syria faced a dilemma. On the one hand, it wanted to control Lebanon and the Palestinians, but on the other hand, it could not do so without provoking an Israeli intervention. The memory of Syria's involvement in Jordan's civil war was still too fresh. Lebanon bristled with dangers for Syria. President Asad felt that unless the fighting was stopped, his chances for building Syria's regional power were doomed.[10]

The Red Line Agreement

Early on in his rule, President Asad was interested in building good relations with Lebanon, a country, unlike Syria, with an open political and economic system. In December 1970 a Syrian delegation, under Foreign Minister Abd al-Halim Khaddam, traveled to Lebanon and signed an agreement to establish a joint commission, known as the Permanent Authority, "whose main job [would] be to strengthen and improve relations between the two countries and solve problems that may arise."[11] Holding its first meeting in January 1971, the Permanent Authority agreed on a wide variety of issues ranging from economic affairs to security matters. A provision of the Permanent Authority called for the establishment of offices in each capital to carry out coordination and administrative work. But Syria continued to oppose diplomatic relations of any kind. Syria had never opened an embassy in Lebanon. Equally significant, Damascus had always tried to play a significant role in Lebanese politics through the office of the president, which Syria eagerly sought to fill with a loyal candidate. In addition, President Asad forged relations outside the traditional Lebanese establishment. He developed an interest in the Shia community, which had become the single largest confession in Lebanon. He cultivated his relationship with the powerful Shia leader Imam Musa al-Sadr, who issued a *fatwa* (a juridical-religious opinion) declaring the Alawis a part of (Twelver) Shia Islam. This helped Asad's Alawi regime to put on the defensive those Sunni critics who questioned the authenticity of the Alawi confession as a part of Islam, as well as to draw on Shia support in Lebanon.[12]

By early 1976 the last vestiges of communal coexistence in Lebanon had disappeared. The Christians overran and cleared out the Palestinian Dba'ye camp, which lay astride the main road linking Christian East Beirut to the north with Mount Lebanon, and then destroyed the Shia slum of Karantina, situated between East Beirut and the port area. The Muslims and Palestinians razed the Christian towns of Damour, Ji'ya, and Sa'adiyat, lying astride the roads linking Muslim West Beirut to southern Lebanon. As the fighting intensified and the antagonists clearly prepared themselves for the possibility of partition, President Asad decided to intervene to prevent the total collapse of the Lebanese system and state. He dispatched units of Al-Saiqa and the Syrian Palestine Liberation Army (consisting of Palestinians under the control of the Syrian army) into Lebanon in January. At first these units fought alongside the

Muslims and Palestinians, but shortly thereafter they began to separate the combatants as President Asad pressed for a cease-fire.

In February, Asad managed to work out a compromise with President Franjieh, known as the Constitutional Document, in which the Maronites gave up some of their constitutional privileges. This did not prevent the further deterioration of the Lebanese situation. In March, the Lebanese army faced a religious mutiny, with Christian officers breaking ranks to join the Phalangists and Tigers while Muslim officers joined the National Movement. Propped by a phalanx of mutineers, the Muslims and Palestinians went on the offensive and closed down on the Christians, whose military situation turned shaky. The forces of Jumblat's National Movement and the PLO's radicals scented victory.

President Asad was alarmed at the shift in the military balance. He feared that a victory of the left and the PLO would bring in Israel's intervention on behalf of the Maronites. Asad called on Jumblat and Arafat to stop the offensive. In March, he had a long stormy meeting with Jumblat during which the latter refused to obey a Syrian request for an immediate cease-fire. Jumblat recalled the meeting in his posthumously published memoirs:

> The Syrian president misunderstood our intentions. He would not accept the refusal regarding the cease fire. . . . The struggle which had turned from defensive to offensive was very important to [the National Movement], we could not let the opportunity of turning the confessional organizations into secular and democratic ones pass away. We say this because we could not let this historic opportunity evade us. And the revolution does not forgive you: You have to seize it the moment destiny appears propitious and victory within hand's reach.[13]

According to Jumblat, President Asad frankly told him the following:

> Listen to me. It is an historic opportunity for me to orient the Maronites in the direction of Syria, to gain their confidence, and to convince them that their protector is neither France nor the West. We ought to assist them not to request aid from the Westerner. Hence, I can not accept your victory over the Christian military camp in Lebanon.[14]

President Asad realized that he had to immediately intervene in order to prevent the military downfall of the Christian side. Israel would not stand idly by and witness the creation of a radical country, swarming with Palestinian militants, along its border. It would undoubtedly help the Maronites create their own state, thus establishing a permanent foothold in Lebanon. Israel could easily then use Lebanon to militarily outflank Syria's defenses. At this point, it becomes clear that the idea of Syrian intervention in Lebanon was born out of Asad's strategic security needs rather than his ideological convictions about Greater Syria.

At the same time, Syria's military intervention in Lebanon would provoke an Israeli counterintervention. Through the United States, Israel made it

clear to the Syrians that it considered the intervention of foreign armed forces
in Lebanon a grave threat to its security, something that Israel would not allow
to happen.[15] Meanwhile, however, the situation in Lebanon had alarmed the
United States, which at first had paid little attention to Lebanon, concentrating its diplomatic efforts on Egypt and Israel. Now the United States could no
longer ignore Lebanon, particularly when victory of the left and the
Palestinians seemed likely. The Soviet Union had been supporting the winning side, and it would inevitably gain valuable ground in case its clients won.
Moreover, as both Syria and Israel perceived Lebanon as crucial to their security, they might clash and lead the region to another war. Therefore the idea of
Syrian intervention in Lebanon to rein in the radicals and adjust the military
balance appealed to the United States. The irony of the situation was that
Syria, the advocate of Arab nationalism and the Palestinian cause, was
embarking on a course so contradictory to its traditions. Patrick Seale commented that "the benefits for the United States and Israel could be great
indeed: the Palestinians would be humbled, the left reined in, Moscow thwart-
ed, and Asad himself tarnished by a deed heinous in Arab eyes."[16]

The U.S. task was, on the one hand, to convince Israel to consent to the
Syrian military intervention in Lebanon, and on the other hand, to persuade
the Christians (through the Lebanese Christian president) to invite the Syrians
so that Syrian military intervention would appear legitimate. After a difficult
internal debate, Israel consented to the Syrian intervention. Chief of Staff
Mordechai Gur and Chief of Military Intelligence Shlomo Gazit argued that
"it was better for Israel to have the Syrian army deployed on two fronts—the
Golan Heights and Lebanon—and thus stretched thin."[17] Not only would the
Syrian army weaken, but also the Golan Heights would become a lower priority. Prime Minister Yitzhak Rabin supported this logic.

However, Israel made its consent conditional on certain demands, which it
conveyed to Secretary of State Henry Kissinger. The United States, functioning
as an emissary between Jerusalem and Damascus, endorsed Israel's demands
and passed them on to the Syrians. Apparently, the Syrians agreed to Israel's
conditions, and Washington gave its "green light" for the Syrian army to enter
Lebanon. This unsigned, oral U.S.-Israeli-Syrian understanding regarding
Lebanon came to be known as the "Red Line" Agreement. According to Ze'ev
Schiff, the agreement contained three key elements: "(1) The Syrian army
would not enter southern Lebanon and would not cross a line starting south of
Sidon, on the coast, and running east to Aysiya and from there towards the
Syrian border; (2) the Syrian army in Lebanon would not be equipped with sur-
face-to-air missile batteries; (3) and the Syrian army would not use its air force
against the Christians in Lebanon."[18] On the night of May 31, 1976, Syrian
armored columns crossed the border into Lebanon.

Acting on the advice of Secretary of State Kissinger, President Gerald
Ford chose the veteran official, Dean Brown, as the presidential envoy to handle the Lebanese end of the Red Line Agreement. While the Syrians were

entering Lebanon, Brown met with Jumblat in his Druze stronghold of Mukhtara. He conveyed to Jumblat the U.S. concern with Lebanon's independence and the unity of its lands. Jumblat expressed to Brown his fears about the surprising Syrian infiltration into Lebanon at a time when the isolationists (Phalangists) were being defeated on most fronts. Brown replied that the Syrians "would not cross Deir Zanoun," meaning the Syrians would not get involved in the fighting.[19] But as it soon became evident, the Syrians speedily pressed forward in strength and broke the Muslim, leftist, and Palestinian siege on the Christian areas. Jumblat accused the United States of deception. He wrote in his memoirs: "The green light had been given to the Syrians to infiltrate Lebanon, and Kissinger, the German Semite, has applied his sorcery."[20]

The Christian decision to invite the Syrians into Lebanon was one of stoic resignation. The Christians had always been wary of Syrian ambitions in Lebanon, particularly of the notion of Greater Syria. However, their decision was a consequence of two factors. The Christian military camp was threatened by defeat. Jumblat's and Arafat's forces were gaining the upper hand on several fronts in Beirut, Mount Lebanon, including the gates of Kisrwan, and Zahle in the Beka Valley.[21] Dean Brown had continuously refused Christian persistent requests for U.S. intervention, such as in 1958. As a result, the Christians resigned themselves to calling in Syrian help and found consolation in their immediate rescue. It was at this juncture that some Maronites began to entertain close cooperation with Israel as a hedge against the Syrian intervention.[22]

New Developments, New Realities

By late June 1976, and after sharp engagements, Syrian forces put the forces of the National Movement on the defensive and turned the tide of the civil war. Rescued from near defeat, the Christian forces moved to strengthen their military situation by removing hostile enclaves in their territory, notably the Palestinian camps of Jisr al-Basha and Tal Za'tar. Located in Beirut's eastern suburbs, these fortified camps hampered Christian military movements and threatened the unity of East Beirut. Palestinian guerrillas in the camps could engage and occupy Christian forces, while at the same time, leftist, Palestinian, and Muslim militias could attack East Beirut from Al-Shiah in West Beirut. Consequently, important Christian suburbs such as Hazmieh, lying astride the Damascus-Beirut highway and bordering the camps, could fall. With the support and planning of Lebanese Christian army officers, the Tigers led the attack on the camps. After fierce fighting and hand-to-hand combat that lasted for almost two months, the adjacent camps fell in August. These two camps, especially Tal Za'tar, were built not only to withstand Israeli air attacks, but also as a rampart with many subterranean tunnels and

caches for ammunition.[23] No wonder Arafat wanted to continue the fighting—
he had enough men, ammunition, and military bases to wear down his enemies. The death toll on both sides was high. But after the defeat of the camps,
members of the Christian forces, avenging their fallen brethren and
Palestinian ingratitude as guests in Lebanon, committed atrocities against
Palestinians, including civilians.

A few days before the fall of Tal Za'tar, the military chief of the
Phalangists, William Hawi, died mysteriously far from the actual fighting, and
was replaced by Bashir Jumayil, the younger son of Pierre Jumayil. While the
battle for Tal Za'tar was raging, Syrian troops engaged leftist and Palestinian
forces on several fronts to keep them from relieving Christian pressure on the
camps. Obviously, Syria indirectly helped the Christians in removing the
Palestinians from the Christians' heartland. But when in late September and
early October the Phalangists and Tigers tried to take advantage of the Syrian
offensive to expand their territory, Syria checked their moves.[24] Syria's objective was to stop the fighting and to make sure that no party in Lebanon gained
the upper hand. This approach was at the heart of Syria's divide and conquer
strategy in Lebanon. No party was allowed to become strong enough to rally
sufficient resistance against the Syrians, and most parties needed Syria when
their fortunes were at a low ebb. During the long course of the civil war, Syria
deftly played one party against the others.

The intervention of Syria in Lebanon to protect the Christians heaped
opprobrium on President Asad coming from the Arab leaders, as well as from
the Soviet Union, whose position in Lebanon was undermined as a result of
the near rout of its protégés, the National Movement forces. However, in mid-
October Saudi Arabia, with the tacit approval of the National Movement,
invited Syria to a peacemaking summit in Riyadh. A plan was worked out to
send an all-Arab "deterrent force" to Lebanon to keep the peace. Syrian troops
constituted the major contingent of this force, which in effect legitimized and
endorsed Syria's preeminence in Lebanon. In mid-November 1976, Syrian
forces entered West Beirut and the civil war was declared over. In fact, it was
the beginning of a new phase in the war for Lebanon. All parties were unsat-
isfied with the status quo in Lebanon. Major disputes among the antagonists
remained unresolved, and now another actor, Syria, had imposed itself on the
country. In addition, Syria's objective of denying Israel a pretext to intervene
in Lebanon was being undermined as a new era of cooperation between Israel
and the Maronites had dawned with the rise of militia leader Bashir Jumayil.

Already Israel had been cooperating with the Christian forces, mainly
with Camille Chamoun's militia, the Tigers. But this cooperation rested largely on the friendship between the Israelis and Chamoun and his son Dany,
which went back to 1958, and on Israel's military aid to the Christian forces.[25]
Thanks to Dany Chamoun's efforts, Bashir Jumayil hit it off well with the
Israelis after he became the military chief of the Phalangists. The Israelis and

Phalangists easily forged a rapport based on mutual respect and close ideological affinity. Many Maronite Phalangists envisioned the creation of a
Maronite "Zion" state that would serve as a refuge for all Christians in the
Arab world. They were encouraged by the presence of a Jewish state along
their border, serving as a testimony to religious diversity and the ability of
minority states to exist in the largely Muslim Middle East. This strategy dovetailed well with that embraced by some Zionists who entertained territorial
maximalism based on security and economic (water) dimensions.[26] In fact,
predating the creation of Israel, important Maronite figures had contacts with
the Zionists and called for the creation of Palestine and Lebanon as homelands
for the Christian and Jewish minorities.[27]

Bashir Jumayil was a baby-faced, charismatic, vigorous, paradoxically
cruel and kind man. His vision of Lebanon rested on strengthening Christian
power, doing away with external meddling in Lebanese affairs, and uniting
the whole of Lebanon under a strong government. He compared Lebanon to a
farm that he wanted to change into a modern, strong, and totally independent
state, reflecting Lebanon's 6,000-year civilization.[28] Bashir's immediate goal
was to unify the various Christian political and military forces. In September
1976 the Maronite leaders formalized their unification efforts by establishing
the Lebanese Front and its armed militia, the Lebanese Forces. Although
Camille Chamoun was chosen president of the front, Bashir Jumayil controlled the Lebanese Forces and wielded real power. Israel figured predominantly in Bashir's thinking, for it served as an exemplar and as the means for
achieving his vision of a new Lebanon. Aside from ideological affinities,
Israel had also the military power and the international clout that Bashir needed. So, he cultivated his relationship with Israel with gusto. By early 1977,
Israel had established a solid relationship with the Christian forces to the chagrin and infuriation of Syria.

It did not take the Lebanese Front long to discover that the end of the civil
war was remote and that the Syrian forces were planning to stay. Their rescue
at the hands of the Syrians was made neither out of altruistic motives nor for
noble purposes. Greater Syria and Ba'th unity ambitions notwithstanding,
Syria was solely concerned with its security vis-à-vis Israel, and Lebanon was
crucial to this security. Bashir's strategy to mobilize the Christians and
strengthen their power did not go unnoticed by the Syrians. Nor did the expectation of the Lebanese Front that a future showdown with the Syrians was
inevitable. Chafing over the Maronites' close cooperation with Israel, Syria
decided to whittle away at Maronite power and began a process of rapprochement with the Palestinians and Muslims. The assassination of Kamal
Jumblat, the leader of the National Movement and outspoken critic of Syria,
whose death was allegedly orchestrated by the Syrians, made the rapprochement less troublesome. Against this background, internal, regional, and international developments brought Israel and Syria face to face in Lebanon.

The Shia Awakening and the Creation of
the South Lebanon Security Zone

The Shia community in Lebanon, unlike the Maronite and Sunni communities, had been the least privileged politically and economically. This became all the more problematic considering their growing numbers and their respective underrepresentation in the Lebanese confessional system of government. During the mid-1960s, an Iranian-born Shia cleric of Lebanese descent by the name of Musa al-Sadr left Iran for Lebanon and settled in the southern city of Tyre. Imam Sadr immediately took note of the Shia predicament and undertook the task of improving their political and economic standing. Imam Sadr was charismatic and tall, with striking looks and an imperious manner. His physical features complemented his strong personality, which was underpinned by a dogmatic, persuasive character and a boundless energy.[29]

Imam Sadr had great ambitions for his people. He set out to empower the Shia community, to strip it of its quiescence, and to whip up the urgency of its political awakening. Cognizant of Shia deprivation and the government's negligence and lack of support for public investment in Shia neighborhoods, particularly in the south of Lebanon, Imam Sadr railed against Lebanese inequalities. He approached his constituency through religion and emphasized for them the importance of Shia tradition and history. He reconciled the community's dispossession in Lebanon with Shia rituals that glorified sacrifice and daring deeds. He read into the Shia reality of today the inequity and injustice committed against the Shiites throughout the years, emphasizing that the Shia community was at a crossroads and the time had come to set right their condition. The outcome was a strong commitment to bringing about a new era of politics in Lebanon based on Shia centrality.[30]

Imam Sadr established separate religious institutions such as the Supreme Shiite Council and the Movement of the Deprived (Mahrumin), and in 1975 founded the first armed Shia militia, known as Amal, meaning "hope." When the civil war in Lebanon broke out, Imam Sadr had already set the stage for the Shia community's political transformation into a principal and powerful actor. The civil war hastened this transformation. As mentioned earlier, the influx of Palestinian guerrillas into the south of Lebanon, home of the majority of Shiites, turned it into a virtually Palestinian military base and thus into an area of high volatility. Palestinian guerrilla infiltration into Israel and Israeli reprisal raids made living conditions so hard for the Shia population that many migrated to the slums of Beirut. Although initially the Shiites did not play a major role in the civil war, their concentration in West Beirut was soon felt by the Sunnis as well as the Christians. Not only did they undermine Sunni as well as traditional Shia leadership in the capital, but they also managed to build a strong military base around the Da'hia and el-Shi'ah, two Beiruti quarters from which they controlled the military operations against the Christians of East Beirut. Before long, Amal became a powerful militia to be reckoned with, extending its influence from West Beirut to significant parts of southern Lebanon.

Imam Sadr's personal ties with Iran and his political awakening of the Shia community brought to the fore the close ties between the Shiites of Lebanon and those of Iran. Sadr's niece had become Ayatollah Khomeini's daughter-in-law by marrying his son, Ahmad.[31] Southern Lebanon welcomed opponents of the shah, while Amal and Fatah, the PLO's main faction, trained Iranian dissidents. Fouad Ajami remarked that "among those who returned to Iran in 1978 were guerrillas trained by Fatah in Lebanon, including Mohammad Ghazani, the future Islamic Oil Minister; Ayatollah Ali Janati, who had taken part in several Fatah operations against Israel. In addition, Khomeini's sons, Mustafa and Ahmad, frequently visited Lebanon and received military training in the south at the hands of Amal and Fatah."[32] In sum, southern Lebanon became the liaison between Iran and Lebanon, and a hotbed for Islamic activism.

Although the PLO and Amal dominated most of southern Lebanon, some Christian and Druze villages remained beyond their control. Southern Lebanon resembled a patchwork of Muslim, Druze, and Christian villages. Facing a strong and hostile Palestinian garrison and being cut off from their brethren in East Beirut, the Christians turned south toward Israel for protection and work. A significant swath of the Lebanese-Israeli border became known as the "good fence," a name symbolizing the easy access into Israel and its readiness to help stranded Lebanese families. The development of ties between East Beirut and Israel reinforced those between Christian southern Lebanon and Israel. This was reinforced by the arrival of a Lebanese army unit to the south of Lebanon after the disintegration of the Lebanese army. A Christian army officer by the name of Sa'd Haddad moved to the south of Lebanon with fellow officers and their troops. Hailing from the South, Major Haddad was welcomed by many villagers who preferred order under the Lebanese army to anarchy under all other militias, especially the PLO. Major Haddad controlled some villages and eventually structured the relationship between Israel and southern Lebanon.

Paralleling these developments in Lebanon, significant changes were taking place on the international and regional levels. In January 1977, Jimmy Carter and his team replaced the Ford administration. The new president disapproved of Kissinger's realpolitik and step-by-step diplomacy in the Middle East. He inaugurated a foreign policy that gave serious consideration to humanitarian issues and preferred a general approach to the Middle East whereby Israel's security was weighed against a consideration of Arab interests.[33] The Carter administration was the first to publicly admit to Palestinian rights and to work for the convening of a peace conference in Geneva, under the cochairship of Washington and Moscow, where all parties to the Arab-Israeli conflict, including the Palestinians, would be represented. But this U.S. Middle East policy ran counter to the platform of the newly elected Begin government in Israel. An advocate of Vladimir Jabotinsky's revisionist Zionist ideology, Begin took the world by surprise when he defeated, for the first time in Israel's history, the Labor Party at the Israeli elections of May 1977. Begin rejected Palestinian participation in the Geneva conference, and significantly disagreed with the Carter administration over the interpretation of Security Council Resolution 242, especially concerning the West Bank. Alternatively, Syria pressed for a unified Arab delegation to Geneva and for an active Palestinian role.

The impasse resulting from Carter's Middle East policy was broken when Egypt and Israel, fearing Soviet participation in the Geneva conference, began a process of rapprochement that culminated in the historic visit of President Sadat to Jerusalem in November 1977. President Sadat initiated a peace process that sat well with Israel and fundamentally altered the comprehensive approach of the U.S. administration, which now concentrated all its efforts on concluding an Israeli-Egyptian peace treaty. Israel worked, on the one hand, to remove Egypt, once and for all, from the Arab military camp, and on the other hand, to reinforce its hold over the West Bank by accelerating the building of Jewish settlements there. This left Syria in the lurch, scrambling to put teeth in its sought-out goal to build regional power vis-à-vis Israel. During the ongoing Egyptian-Israeli peace negotiations, on March 11, 1978, Fatah guerrillas set out from the southern city of Damour on the Lebanese coast and landed on the Israeli coast south of Haifa. They hijacked an Israeli bus and fired randomly at passersby. When the incident was over, thirty-four Israelis—men, women, and children—had been killed and many more wounded. Prime Minister Begin affirmed that "those who killed Jews in our time cannot enjoy impunity."[34]

On March 14, Israel retaliated and invaded southern Lebanon with the objective of destroying the military bases of the PLO and weeding them out from there. The invasion was large in scope and destructiveness. Israel seized the whole of southern Lebanon up to the Litani River, after which the operation took its code name, "Operation Litani." In the process, hundreds were killed and thousands of civilians were displaced. President Carter considered the Israeli reprisal to have far exceeded the provocation that incited it. He stated: "I consider this major invasion to be an overreaction to the PLO attack, a serious threat to the peace in the region."[35] President Carter told Prime Minister Begin to pull his troops out and on March 19 he instructed the U.S. ambassador to the UN to propose that Israeli forces in southern Lebanon be replaced by a UN force. This proposal resulted in the adoption of Security Council Resolution 425, which called for strict respect of Lebanon's territorial integrity and sovereignty, and called upon Israel to cease all military actions and to "withdraw forthwith its forces from all Lebanese territory." The resolution also established the UN Interim Force in Lebanon (UNIFIL) "for southern Lebanon for the purpose of confirming the withdrawal of the Israeli forces, restoring international peace and security and assisting the government of Lebanon in ensuring the return of its effective authority in the area."[36]

Approximately three months from the date of invasion, Israel withdrew from the south of Lebanon, but not before establishing a buffer zone to protect its border from guerrilla attacks. The objective was to extend the territory under the control of Major Haddad to a ten-kilometer security belt along Lebanon's southern border. Israel reinforced its support of Major Haddad with closer relations with Bashir Jumayil, whose forces were at the time fighting the Syrian army around the capital. Israeli military advisers and arms flowed into East Beirut. Syria was taken aback by Israel's forceful invasion. Given Israel's military superiority and Syria's military clash with the Lebanese Forces, Syria refrained from engaging the Israelis. President Asad found himself in a situation where his plan to build his country's regional power and control Lebanon had turned on its head. Not only did Israel establish a security zone in southern Lebanon, but it also became deeply involved with the daring Lebanese Forces in East Beirut and Mount Lebanon. President Asad felt besieged and concentrated his efforts on building a defensive position in the strategic Beka Valley in eastern Lebanon, the western gate to Damascus and a potential front from which Israel could outflank Syria's main defense line. While Syria was not ready to give up its influence in Lebanon, Israel was reinforcing its position with the rising power of the Lebanese Forces. The struggle for Lebanon simply intensified.

Israel's Invasion of Lebanon

Israel's military support of the Lebanese Forces and the rising leadership of Bashir Jumayil increased Maronite confidence and sharpened Maronite reservations about Syria. Whereas a few years earlier, the Maronites grudgingly accepted Syrian intervention because of their near defeat, now because of their newly gained confidence they found it hard to swallow Syria's military presence and influence in Lebanon. With his charisma and appeal, coupled with his principal position within the Lebanese Front, Bashir was able to mobilize the Christian community and draw support from a large segment of the population who not too long before disapproved of and even despised the Phalangists. Bashir's vision of a unified Lebanon free from foreign influence strongly appealed to the Christian community at large. But behind this vision lay Bashir's serious ambitions for himself and his Maronite flock.

Bashir had a clear-cut plan. First, he perceived power as emanating from the barrel of a gun. He believed that political predominance in Lebanon had to be based on military power in order to be effective. For this reason, he strove to unify Christian military power under his command. Inveterate Maronite squabbling was a luxury he could not afford. Second, he was adamantly opposed to any foreign armed presence on Lebanese soil, including Syrians and Palestinians. He wanted these forces out of Lebanon. Finally, he pursued the creation and institutionalization of a Christian-Maronite "mini-Prussia" inside Lebanon that in due time could rally the whole of Lebanon around its centrality. Bashir never gave up the idea of a unified Lebanon; he envisioned himself as the uncontested future leader of Lebanon, the Lebanon with territorial integrity and sovereignty over its 10,452 square kilometers.[37]

Bashir set out to implement his three-tiered plan. From their "fiefdom" in northern Lebanon, the Franjieh family maintained a cordial relationship with President Asad, which Bashir frowned upon. This relationship went back to the 1950s, when Suleiman Franjieh, escaping a death sentence from a rival clan, found refuge with the Alawis in Syria. Friction between Bashir and the Franjieh family sharpened when Suleiman's son Toni struck a business partnership with President Asad's brother Rif'at, while Bashir tried to extend his political and military organizations into Franjieh's stronghold. Reacting to Bashir's maneuvers to undermine their political and economic base, the Franjieh clan killed Judd Bayeh, the Phalangist political organizer in northern Lebanon. In a dramatic and cruel manner, the Phalangists sent a squad, headed by Samir Ja'ja, to Toni Franjieh's home in the town of Ehden, killing him and his family. Only his son Suleiman Jr. survived. While the attack caused the Franjieh family to sever all relations with the Phalangists, its savageness sent a harrowing message about Phalangist brutality.

Next, Bashir focused on the Tigers, who enjoyed significant independence in the "free" territories of Lebanon.[38] Led by Dany Chamoun and with significant fire power at their disposal, the Tigers were not easily intimidated by the Phalangists, although they admitted Phalangist supremacy. Under the slogan of "uniting the Lebanese Forces' gun," Bashir ordered a surprise attack on the Tigers' headquarters in summer 1980, forcing their leadership to surrender to the Phalangists and to give up all their arms and ammunition. He then dismantled the Tigers' organization and merged its members with the Lebanese Forces.

But if the first objective of Bashir's strategy was within reach, the other two proved difficult and inherently contradictory. Bashir understood clearly that his forces on their own, even with Israeli military aid, could not dislodge the Syrians and the PLO, the first a well-equipped army and the second a well-trained paramilitary organization. Making this doubly difficult was the support the Muslim population and its armed militias lent to the Syrians and the PLO. This support was largely motivated by the Muslim opposition to the growing cooperation between the Maronites and Israel, which served as a rallying cry for all non-Christian parties to oppose the Lebanese Forces. Thus, Bashir needed Israel's army to push the Syrians and the PLO out of Lebanon. He needed to create a situation whereby Israel could be enticed to intervene militarily in Lebanon and thus help him to get rid of the Syrian and PLO forces. There was no other solution if his vision of a unified Lebanon under his leadership was to be fulfilled. Herein lay the roots of the ambivalent Phalangist relationship with Israel.

Bashir wanted to reconcile his objective of ridding Lebanon of all foreign forces, which meant an Israeli military intervention, with his other objective of ruling over Lebanon, which meant ruling over a Muslim majority that opposed Israel and supported the pan-Arab mainstream. This led to Bashir's dilemma: how to cooperate with Israel without totally alienating the Muslim communities in Lebanon. Bashir seemed to think that he would be able to win over the Muslims once he drove all foreign forces out of Lebanon and built his mini-Prussian state. This dilemma was further aggravated by the split in opinion within the Phalangist leadership regarding Israel and Syria. A considerable segment of the Phalangist leadership, represented mainly by Pierre Jumayil, Amin Jumayil, Elie Karame, and Karim Pakradouni, took the middle ground, if not the noncommittal ground, on all issues. They wanted to cooperate with Israel but keep that cooperation opaque and under the rug, so as not to sever their relations with the Arab world. They wanted to get Syria out of Lebanon but maintain good neighborly relations with Syria. Unlike Bashir during that phase, they aspired for Christian hegemony, under the pretense of protecting Christian minority status, without ever relinquishing the idea of concluding a compact with the Muslims that guaranteed this hegemony. Their strategy smacked of confusion at the time.

On the other hand, a younger generation, catapulted to leadership positions by their militant participation in the civil war, represented by Samir Ja'ja, Fadi Frame, Fouad Abou Nader, and Elie Hobeika, unquestionably and enthusiastically endorsed the policy of their leader, Bashir Jumayil. As Bashir held the military sway in the party, his policy line predominated. But again there loomed on the horizon the disparity between his ambitions and his inability to fulfill them without Israeli help. However, Bashir's ambivalent relationship with Israel did not have any effect on either side as long as he was the leader of his Maronite flock and tried to build his own mini-Prussia within Christian Lebanon. Dedicated to his vision, overly confident, and driven by an uncritical ambition, Bashir pressed on with his plan.

The writing on the wall had been clear. Isolated incidents between the Lebanese Forces, including allied Lebanese army officers, and Syrian forces had become a pattern by early 1978. On February 2, 1978, a fight broke out in Fayadiyya, next to the Lebanese army barracks, between members of the Lebanese army, allied with the Lebanese Forces, and Syrian troops. The skirmish escalated into a fierce battle and marked the beginning of the Lebanese Front's open confrontation with Syria. Armed engagements became the order of the day, interrupted by intermittent cease-fires only to prepare for the next round. When Israel invaded Lebanon in March 1978, Syria thought that the attack was a prelude to an Israeli invasion of Syria because it coincided with an ongoing armed engagement with the Lebanese Forces. However, there was no decisive outcome favoring either the Syrian or the Christian side and the whole confrontation degenerated to Christian provocations of Syria and Syrian attempts to check the Christians.

Bashir's provocation of Syria turned its conventional political wisdom on its head. In contrast with the recent past, Syria had to rein itself in and refrain from dealing a severe blow to the Christians, which would provoke an Israeli intervention on their behalf. After all, that was what Shaikh Bashir wanted; his provocation not only was a manifestation of his growing self-confidence and his military support by Israel, but also served as a bait for Syria. This constant provocation could not have come at a more unfortunate time in the history of Asad's regime. After the Israeli invasion of Lebanon, President Sadat of Egypt signed the Camp David Accords with Israel in September 1978, following which Egypt and Israel signed their peace treaty in March 1979. This left Syria isolated, weakened, and at the mercy of Israel's uncontested power in the region. In addition, Syria was facing domestic opposition that almost toppled Asad's regime. The Muslim Brotherhood stirred up dissent against the Alawi regime and launched a wave of attacks against it that almost claimed the life of President Asad himself in June 1980.

Neither Bashir nor the Israelis failed to notice Syria's weakness and preoccupation with domestic matters, which limited its ability to influence events in Lebanon. Bashir decided to take a bold step and extend his power to Zahle, linking it to the Maronite heartland. Zahle is the principal Christian town in the Beka Valley, which was crucial to Syria's security. Bashir had already been reinforcing the Phalangists of Zahle since 1978. He infiltrated special units of the Lebanese Forces into the town, using the mountainous and valley roads of Ouyoun Siman, Qanat Baqish, and Mount Sanin (the series of mountains composing Mount Lebanon). Skirmishes took place between the Lebanese Forces and Syrian forces in the city in the latter part of December. But they were contained by the intercession of Zahle's notables with both Syria and the Maronites of East Beirut. However, on March 30, 1981, the Lebanese Forces ambushed a Syrian transport vehicle crossing a bridge in the outskirts of Zahle. The Syrian government responded by besieging Zahle and sending into its midst a special commando contingent to attack the Lebanese Forces' positions. By early April, cat-and-mouse skirmishes, which had been taking place on Mount Sanin, escalated into a ferocious battle as the Syrian army and the Lebanese Forces fought to capture the mount's French Room.[39] At its eastern edge, Mount Sanin looked down on Zahle from a strategic mountaintop on one side and afforded access to the Maronite heartland on the other.

The Syrians were concerned that, at a maximum, Bashir's move was part of a Christian-Israeli scheme to invite Israel into Lebanon and then to jointly push Syria out of the country, and that, at a minimum, he was precipitating an Israeli-Syrian confrontation that he could use to his own advantage.[40] Whether or not these were Bashir's intentions, Asad was not ready to risk his defensive position in the Beka Valley, nor let Bashir enhance his power in

Lebanon by taking Zahle two years before the upcoming Lebanese presiden-tial elections. President Asad called in special commando units, landing them by helicopters on Mount Sanin. On April 11, the Syrian forces took over Mount Sanin, cutting off the supply road to Zahle and prompting Bashir to appeal to Israel's Prime Minister Begin for help. Israel faced a dilemma: Should it intervene in a crisis initiated by Bashir and risk a general war with Syria, or turn down Bashir's requests for help and let Syria maintain its strong position in the Beka Valley, knowing full well that Syria had contravened the terms of the 1976 Red Line Agreement by using helicopters? Israel's second choice seemed intolerable, for it had pledged to the Lebanese Front in 1978 that it would not allow the Syrian air force to operate against Christian forces.[41]

On April 28, Israel shot down two Syrian transport helicopters flying to Mount Sanin. According to Itamar Rabinovich, Israel signaled to Syria that "neither the use of the air force nor the advance toward Mount Lebanon would be tolerated." But he added that "implicit in the signal was the message that Israel was willing to accept Syrian hegemony in Zahle."[42] In response, Syria introduced surface-to-air missile (SAM) batteries into the Beka Valley, and precipitated what came to be known as the "missile crisis." Although he most likely preferred a military strike to destroy the SAMs, Prime Minister Begin decided to try Washington's hand at solving the crisis. He was preoccupied campaigning for the upcoming general elections in June, an unpropitious time to open a front. In addition, he may have been concerned about the U.S. reac-tion. There was Israel's ongoing tussle with the Reagan administration over its decision to sell AWACS (airborne warning and command systems) to Saudi Arabia, as well as Israel's planning to launch an air strike against Iraq's Osirak nuclear reactor in June. These were two important developments that could have grave implications for the U.S. attitude toward Israel were Israel to pre-cipitate a military confrontation with Syria.

President Reagan sent his envoy, Philip Habib, to the region to defuse the crisis. On the way, his mission was expanded to deal with a major flare-up between Israel and the Palestinians along the Lebanese border. Concerned with the buildup of the PLO's military infrastructure in Lebanon, Israel launched air strikes to cripple that infrastructure. The PLO retaliated by shelling northern Israel. With the assistance of the Saudis, Habib was able to temporarily defuse the crisis. He managed to conclude an "understanding" (i.e., a cease-fire) between Begin, Asad, and Arafat (the contacts with Arafat went through the Syrians and the Saudis) in late July. According to Patrick Seale the unsigned understanding provided that Syria would keep its missiles in the Beka Valley, but on the condition that they would not be fired; Israel would continue reconnaissance flights over Lebanon, but would not attack the missiles; and Israel and the Palestinians would stop firing upon each other across the Lebanese border.[43] What Seale failed to mention was that the spe-cial units of the Lebanese Forces had to leave Zahle, the decisive factor in defusing the crisis.[44] Knowing full well his limits without Israel's intervention on his behalf, Bashir, disappointed with Israel's consent to the cease-fire, agreed to withdraw his men from Zahle. Though Bashir's gambit there returned him no immediate advantage, it highlighted Lebanon's centrality to Israel's and Syria's security policy, the role that Bashir could play to enhance or weaken the security of those countries, and the growing untenability of that status quo in Lebanon.

Between July 1981 and June 1982, a combination of trends and developments, originating both in the wider context of the Arab-Israeli conflict and in the dynamics of the struggle for power in Lebanon, converged to create a situation in which Israel found it expedient to invade Lebanon. Before the missile crisis, Syria decided to revamp its security doctrine with regard to Israel. After President Sadat signed the Camp David Accords and took Egypt irretrievably out of the Arab military camp, Asad tried to compensate for the loss by trying to draw Iraq into an alliance. He had attended the Baghdad summit in November 1978, convened to condemn Egypt, and conducted a dialogue of rapprochement with Iraqi strongman Saddam Hussein. But the rapprochement foundered on the rock of suspicion and rivalry between the two countries, and all expectations of Iraqi commitments to help Syria in the event of a war with Israel collapsed when Iraq invaded Iran in September 1980. Faced with an aggressive Israel, which invaded Lebanon in 1978, and with frustrated plans to build Syria's regional security, especially in Lebanon, President Asad strove to achieve a kind of military parity with Israel. This is what President Asad used to call a "comprehensive strategic balance."[45] Asad was determined not only to build up his regional security, but also to stand up to Israel alone if necessary.

Losing Egypt for the United States, the Soviet Union was eager to support Syria in its quest for military parity. Faced with few choices, in a departure from his past position of refusing to enter into treaties with the Soviet Union, President Asad signed a twenty-year Treaty of Friendship and Cooperation with Moscow in October 1980. As soon as he had regained his confidence with Soviet support and weathered his domestic crisis, he acted on his determination to protect his regional position and stand up to Israel. For example, when King Hussein of Jordan convened an Arab summit in November 1980 to deal with the Iran-Iraq War and to seek Arab approval for his plans for a future Jordanian-Palestinian West Bank federation negotiated with Israel, Asad not only boycotted the summit but also sent troops to the Jordanian frontier. It was within this context that when the Lebanese Forces challenged his authority in Zahle and Israel shot down two Syrian transport helicopters, Asad moved Syrian missiles into the Beka Valley, contravening the terms of the Red Line Agreement. In sum, President Asad's actions were no longer defensive but rather offensive, indicating his determination to confront Israel.

Asad's new posture in Lebanon, coupled with an unchecked and escalating Palestinian activity there, aggravated Israeli concerns. The cease-fire brokered by Habib did not arrest the PLO's drive to continue building its military infrastructure in Lebanon. Rather, it invigorated the PLO and emboldened it to play an overzealous, militant role in Lebanon's internal politics, making a mockery out of what remained of the country's sovereignty. However, the PLO observed the cease-fire and refrained from carrying out cross-border raids into Israel. Meanwhile, Israel was in the process of returning the Sinai Peninsula to Egypt and strengthening its hold over the West Bank (Judea and Samaria), territories considered ideologically part and parcel of Israel by the current Likud government. But although these territories might not be outrightly annexed to Israel, they definitely were not to enjoy any prospective Palestinian sovereignty. The second electoral victory of the Likud Party in June 1981 only reinforced its determination to live up to its ideology. Despite the expansion and creation of Jewish settlements there, Begin's government felt that its plan to implement a limited autonomous form of rule in the West Bank and Gaza was impossible unless the PLO's influence with the Palestinian population was curtailed. In a departure from past policies, Begin's government began to intervene in all aspects of Palestinian daily life, trying to cultivate new leaderships disassociated from the PLO and to undermine the PLO's influence with the population. However, the government's efforts did not bear any fruit, and the PLO kept its hold over the Palestinians, to the chagrin of Prime Minister Begin and his hawkish defense minister Ariel Sharon.[46]

Faced with a failed policy aimed at suppressing Palestinian nationalism in the West Bank and Gaza, Begin's government began to deliberate the necessity to clip the PLO's wings (the embodiment of Palestinian nationalism) in Lebanon, while at the same time holding the belief that a limited operation in Lebanon was insufficient. Another Litani operation could temporarily dent the PLO's power but could not crush it. Given its widespread military and political infrastructure, the PLO could recover quickly enough. At this juncture, other regional and international considerations encouraged Israel to further ponder how to deal with the PLO. The Reagan administration was dedicated to combating communism and regarded Israel as a bulwark against Soviet expansion in the Middle East. The Begin government unfailingly probed for how the Reagan administration would react to an operation against the PLO in Lebanon, and it frequently received the same ambiguous replies, which it interpreted as an endorsement.[47] The Arab-Israeli military balance was in Israel's favor. Not only was Egypt out of the Arab military camp, but it was also ostracized by the rest of the Arab states.

An additional significant consideration was Bashir's quest for the presidency of Lebanon. The Israeli government was aware of Bashir's efforts to involve the Israeli Defense Forces (IDF) in his struggle for power in his country. His latest gambit in Zahle was a clear indication. But whereas in the past Israel had refrained from direct intervention on behalf of his Lebanese Forces, now the idea seemed appealing to the Israeli government. Begin's government was quick to combine Bashir's quest for the presidency with a deep military campaign into Lebanon to deal primarily with the PLO and then with Syria. A grand plan ensued. Israel would invade Lebanon, destroy the military infrastructure and political position of the PLO in the south of Lebanon and in Beirut, and thus end the PLO's hold not only over the Lebanese Muslim population but also over the Palestinian population in the West Bank. Syrian forces and missile batteries would be attacked with the objective of undermining Syria's power in Lebanon, leading to its withdrawal. Bashir Jumayil would be elected president and the Lebanese state would be reconstructed under his legitimate leadership. Israel would then conclude a peace treaty with Lebanon, strengthen its hold over the West Bank, secure its northern border, and put Syria on the defensive for quite some time.[48]

On June 3, 1982, Palestinian extremists (from Abu Nidal's organization and not part of the PLO) shot and gravely wounded Israel's ambassador to Britain, Shlomo Argov, in London. The incident served as the needed provocation for the Begin government to launch its attack on Lebanon. On June 6, Israel launched "Operation Peace for Galilee." The code name falsely implied that its objective was to push back the PLO forty kilometers from the Israeli frontier in order to protect the settlements in the Galilee. From the Knesset's podium Prime Minister Begin called on President Asad to stay out of the fight, as the operation was not directed against Syria. As it turned out, in a few days, the IDF swept through Lebanon, going beyond its stated limited goal. Surprised by the scope and depth of the Israeli invasion, the Reagan administration immediately dispatched presidential envoy Philip Habib to the region, and also voted for Security Council Resolutions 508 and 509, which called for an unconditional Israeli withdrawal. On June 9, while Habib was in Damascus, Israel's air force raided and destroyed the whole Syrian SAM network in the Beka Valley. President Asad ordered his air force to intercept the Israeli planes, thus sustaining severe losses.

Knowing full well the strategic importance of the Beka Valley, Asad was determined to protect his defensive position there and thwart the Israeli offensive. Deprived of air cover, Syrian forces engaged the IDF in fierce battles along the approaches of the Beka Valley. According to Syrian defense minister Mustafa Tlas, the Syrian troops were able to halt the Israeli advance and even push it back six to ten kilometers.[49] Though Israel indeed did not advance into the Beka Valley, in reality the Syrian forces were saved by a cease-fire brokered by Habib on June 11. President Asad explained that Syria had agreed to the cease-fire on the condition that Israel would totally withdraw from Lebanon.[50] Israel had a different interpretation of the cease-fire, as it scurriedly moved its troops toward the Shouf, Baabda, and the outskirts of

Beirut. After all, the cease-fire went against the grain of Begin's and Sharon's main objective in Lebanon, the destruction of the political and military infrastructure of the PLO. PLO guerrillas had withdrawn from southern Lebanon to the capital, dramatically increasing their numbers there. West Beirut swarmed with Syrian and PLO fighters, let alone other militias.

By June 13, the IDF had linked up with the Lebanese Forces and laid siege to West Beirut, beginning a ground and aerial campaign of shelling the city and demanding the surrender of the PLO. PLO chairman Yasser Arafat vowed steadfastness and a fight until victory, while Syria declared its commitment to stand by the PLO and the Lebanese "Nationalist" Forces.[51] On June 22, the IDF attacked Syrian units on the Beirut-Damascus highway east of Beirut, pushing them far enough from the approaches of the city. Not only did the IDF cut the Syrian army off from its troops in West Beirut, but it also deprived the Syrian army from playing any significant role in the defense of the city. Sharon was ready to "cleanse" the capital of the PLO.

At this point the ambivalent relationship between Bashir and Israel came to the forefront. The Begin government wanted Bashir's forces to enter West Beirut and fight out the PLO and Syrian forces. The prospect of the IDF entering West Beirut, fighting close battles on the enemy's turf and sustaining high casualties, inhibited Begin's government from undertaking such a daunting task. But at this crucial time, Bashir wavered in his commitment to the Begin government. He was fully aware of the political and human cost he would have to pay if he entered West Beirut. If the human cost was inhibitive, the political cost was prohibitive. Bashir was preparing himself for the presidential election in August, and did not want to completely alienate the Muslim population. Admittedly, the younger Jumayil wanted to be a constitutionally elected president, meaning he needed a majority of deputies in parliament to vote him in. Bashir's main concern was how to muster enough votes for his election, including the many Muslim votes hanging in the balance. Moderate Muslim deputies, such as Kamil al-As'ad, Kazim al-Khalil, and Talal Mer'ebi, were leaning toward supporting Bashir's presidential bid, but had balked at the slightest intimation of a Lebanese Forces attack on West Beirut. Bashir had been especially courting Kamil al-As'ad, the traditional Shia leader of Lebanon and the then speaker of parliament, who subsequently played a pivotal role in making Bashir president.[52] At this critical time Bashir decided to substitute partial cooperation with the Begin government for the earlier policy of full and complete coordination with this ally.

In addition, Bashir, thrown into the spotlight of international diplomacy at the age of thirty-four, began to slough off his impulsive, combative character and to mature into a prudent presidential hopeful. He found in Habib, who was of Lebanese descent, a paternal diplomatic figure whose advice he sought and appreciated. Habib was against any military action in West Beirut. He strove to effectuate a deal whereby the PLO and Syria would withdraw from the capital. Habib advised the younger Jumayil against entering West Beirut, remonstrating him to behave as a presidential candidate for all Lebanese and not only the Christians.

Bashir's change of tactics was reinforced by the "backdoor" politicking conducted by the Phalangist leadership against Israel's request that the Lebanese Forces enter the capital. Israel's invasion of Lebanon made most of the civil wing of the Phalangist Party, including Pierre Jumayil, draw a sharp distinction between accepting help for the Maronites from Israel and carrying out orders from Israel the ally. Jumayil, the patriarch of the party, accepted everything so long as the alliance with Israel did not sever the Maronite relationship with the Muslims, even if the Maronites had the opportunity to rule by force over the whole of Lebanon. Still, the elder Jumayil mobilized the energies of the party to take advantage of the Israeli invasion, which moved Lebanon to center stage of world diplomacy.

In a Phalangist meeting at the Lebanese Forces headquarters in East Beirut (Karantina), urgently convened following the Israeli invasion, Jumayil spoke of Israel's invasion as the single most important event in Lebanon's civil war. He emphasized that for years the Christians had been struggling to mobilize world opinion in favor of their predicament, but to no significant result. Now, thanks to Israel's invasion, the Western world, particularly the United States, had shown an interest in resolving the conflict in Lebanon, an interest that the Christians should harness to their own benefit. It was clear to me, at the time, that the underlying expectation was that, on one end of the spectrum, U.S. involvement in Lebanon would enable the Christians to wean themselves from total dependence on Israel, making it possible for them to cooperate again with the Muslims and at the same time limit Israel's expectations from the Christians. On the other end, the Christians would impose on the Muslims a situation where it would be more advantageous for them to cooperate with the Christians. By playing on their own ability to restrict their relations with Israel in favor of putting Maronite-Muslim interests ahead of Maronite-Israeli ties, the Maronites could score doubly with the Muslims. Not only could they extract concessions from the Muslims, but they could also prevail on them to start wooing the Christians away from Israel for the right political price—preserving Christian privileges. And in the middle space of this spectrum, the Christians would cooperate with Israel and the United States to remove the PLO from Lebanon within the framework of a wider plan that envisaged the future withdrawal of all foreign forces from Lebanon. Jumayil exclaimed that if the Christians played their cards right, they would emerge as the real victorious party in the war for Lebanon. In the meeting, Jumayil brushed away questions about creating a Maronite state in Lebanon, stressing the urgency of seizing the opportunity that Israel's invasion made available.[53]

Bashir did not send his forces to West Beirut, infuriating both Begin and Sharon. However, he remained their man in Lebanon, the hinge upon which the Maronite-Israeli alliance and Begin's postwar hopes for Lebanon rested. For the next two months and while Habib was mediating the withdrawal of the PLO and Syrian forces from West Beirut, Sharon saturated the city with heavy bombardment. Finally, in mid-August 1982, Habib's mediation efforts bore fruit as he hammered out an agreement among the Israelis, the Syrians, the PLO, and the Lebanese government providing for an immediate cease-fire and an evacuation of Syrian and PLO forces from Beirut. A multinational peacekeeping force (MNF), composed of troops from Italy, France, and the United States, would monitor the evacuation and help the Lebanese government to reassert its authority over the city.[54]

While the Palestinian withdrawal was taking place, the speaker of the parliament, al-As'ad, approved a parliamentary meeting to elect a president at the military school in Fayadiya on August 23. By both wooing and intimidating the Lebanese deputies, the Lebanese Forces were able to muster enough votes to declare Shaikh Bashir president of Lebanon. Sharon and Bashir appeared to have won the day.

Consolidation of Syrian Power in Lebanon

Immediately after his election, Bashir set about mending fences with most non-Christian communities. He called for Lebanon's territorial integrity and proclaimed that all holders of Lebanese citizenship regardless of origin, race, or religion would live in peace and be equally treated by the government of the new Lebanon. Bashir was aiming first at gaining Muslim confidence and support, and then reconciling this with Syria's and Israel's withdrawal from Lebanon, thereby proving his ability to establish Lebanon's total sovereignty. At the same time, he would be building his state power. He believed he could untangle the Lebanese mess, entertaining a wishful if not a naive thought on that matter.

According to the best information available to the party cadres at the time, Bashir thought, first, that by delaying a peace treaty with Israel, he would prove to the Muslims that he was no Israeli stooge. Second, he would continue his policy of strengthening certain sectarian leaders who supported him while undermining those who opposed him, a policy seemingly at odds with the most recent developments in confessional Lebanon (Christian and Phalangist leaders, including the Jumayils, are trying to pacify their relations with most confessional leaders, particularly the Druze leadership). Bashir had been courting and supporting Emir Talal Arslan, the son of Emir Majid Arslan, whose family had a long history of rivalry with the Jumblats for Druze leadership. He also had been propping up the traditional Shia leadership of Kamil al-As'ad. Despite Bashir's support, and in fact partly in reaction to it, the Druze and Shia communities had appreciably rallied respectively around Walid Jumblat's Progressive Socialist Party and the emerging leadership of Nabih Berri's Amal movement. Third, he would depend on U.S. mediation for the withdrawal of Israel and Syria from Lebanon. Knowing full well that Israel would not withdraw without concluding a peace treaty with Lebanon and ensuring Syria's withdrawal, Bashir's objective was to pass the peace treaty over the heads of the Muslims as part of a wider U.S. effort to resolve the Arab-Israeli conflict. Faced with a Lebanese government requesting its withdrawal, Syria would have no legitimate reason to remain in Lebanon. Finally, Bashir would make a great effort to building a strategic cooperation with the United States, based on checking Soviet expansion in the region. This cooperation would also lead to the creation of a strong army and serve as a hedge against Syrian and Israeli ambitions in Lebanon.

Apparently, Bashir conspicuously underestimated the centrality of Lebanon to Israel's and Syria's security, as well as the extent of Israel's strategic cooperation with the United States. In addition, he failed to realize the immensity of the centrifugal forces inherent in Lebanon's position as a weak state sandwiched between two powerful adversaries and to give due credit to Lebanon's harsh domestic incongruities.

Bashir's wishful thinking soon clashed with the hard realities of the Lebanese conflict, which by now became an extension of the Israeli-Syrian conflict. On September 14, 1982, Bashir was assassinated by a bomb explosion while attending a meeting at the Phalangist local headquarters in Ashrafieh. The explosive device was planted by Habib Tanyus el-Shartouni, a clandestine member of the Syrian Social Nationalist Party (SSNP). The SSNP was ideologically committed to Greater Syria and was a staunch ally of Syria against Israel. The death of Bashir shook not only the Lebanese Front and its armed militia, the Lebanese Forces, but also the Maronite-Israeli alliance. A great feeling of gloom, coupled with a clamor for revenge, prevailed over the leadership of the Lebanese Forces, which was disoriented by the loss of decisive authority and direction.

The next day Sharon ordered the IDF into West Beirut and allowed the Lebanese Forces to enter the Palestinian refugee camps of Sabra and Shatila to ferret out PLO guerrillas who had not withdrawn from the capital.[55] On the evening of September 16, the security forces of Elie Hobeika, the head of intelligence in the Lebanese Forces, entered the camps. During the next forty-eight hours Hobeika's forces would go on a rampage of random killing that claimed the lives of hundreds of innocent Palestinians, including children and women. Hobeika's forces committed a massacre that far exceeded the norm of revenge killings in Lebanon, indelibly and bloodily staining Maronite history. Throughout the carnage the IDF cordoned off the camps and provided at night the flares needed by Hobeika's forces to continue their massacre.

The Phalangist leadership denied all involvement in the face of the international outcry this massacre elicited, although Hobeika's fingerprints were everywhere. One immediate reason for this behavior was that the Phalangists were preparing Amin Jumayil, the brother of Bashir, for the presidency, and were terrified that any Phalangist complicity in the massacre would ruin Amin's electoral chances.[56] The irony of the Maronite-Israeli alliance lay in the fact that while the Maronites pursued a policy that enhanced the inclusion of the Muslims, Israel pursued a policy that ensured the exclusion of the Muslim communities. The opportunistic nature of the alliance far outweighed the affinity between the two sides, leading to the alliance's gradual dissolution. The impact of the Sabra and Shatila massacre on the Maronite-Israeli alliance marked the beginning of its end.

Begin's government had to face an outraged Israeli public who, unlike any other Arab public, took to the streets in the largest demonstration in Israel's history protesting the horrendous killing. Pressured by an unyielding and angry public, Begin appointed the Kahan Commission to look into the IDF involvement in the massacre. Sharon was pressured to remove his troops from Beirut. Meanwhile Amin Jumayil presented himself as the presidential candidate of unity. Unlike his brother, Amin had had reservations about close cooperation with Israel and maintained polite relations with the Syrians as well as with the Muslim leadership of Beirut even while the city was under siege. Amin believed in political compromise, rather than the application of force as an effective policy. The Muslim leadership supported Amin's bid for the presidency and he was elected with wide national unanimity on September 21, 1982. Although Begin and Sharon did not regard Amin as their ideal choice for president, they saw in him, as a Jumayil, continuation to their policy in Lebanon.

Upon his election, Amin proceeded with his plan for Greater Beirut, that is, uniting the whole of Beirut under his authority. With the help of the MNF, Amin began gradually to take control of Beirut. In the meantime, by early October, Sharon completed his withdrawal from the capital. But Amin's initial successful thrust at extending his authority was parried by the dilemma he faced as to how to secure Israel's and Syria's withdrawal from Lebanon. Much like the rest of the Phalangist leadership, Amin believed that the United States held the key to resolving his dilemma. By relying on the United States, Amin could pressure Syria into withdrawing and sign a treaty with Israel without an exorbitant political price. However, Syria's attitude was that the Syrian army, unlike the invading Israeli army, was legitimately invited into Lebanon to end the war and establish peace. Alternatively, Israel saw no sense in concluding an agreement with Lebanon entailing its complete withdrawal so long as the Syrian army remained entrenched in the country. In a speech on November 20, 1982, delivered before the Syrian federation of labor unions, President Asad, remarking on the presence of Syrian forces in Lebanon, stated: "We affirm today that when the invading Israeli forces withdraw from Lebanon, there will be no problem with respect to [the withdrawal of] our forces. But it should be understood that the Israeli withdrawal should impose no conditions on Lebanon limiting its sovereignty and freedom. We have been always with Lebanon and we shall always remain, for Syria and Lebanon are two brotherly countries."[57] In a nutshell, Asad wanted Israel out of Lebanon unconditionally.

Amin took the middle road by calling on all foreign forces to leave Lebanon, a position all the more repugnant to Syria because it dealt with Syria on an equal footing with Israel. Facing public revulsion on account of the Sabra and Shatila massacres, a growing number of casualties, and growing opposition to its policy in Lebanon, Begin's government felt pressed to justify its war in Lebanon. So it sought to negotiate a treaty directly with the Lebanese government. Relying on U.S. mediation, headed by Secretary of State George Shultz, Amin went along and commenced negotiations with Begin's government. The negotiations culminated in the May 17 Agreement (1983), which was the closest to a peace treaty that these parties could achieve. The two countries terminated the state of war between them, agreed that their territories would not be used as a base for hostile activity against the other party, and prohibited the deployment in their territories and airspaces of any forces hostile to the other partner. Israel was to withdraw from the whole of Lebanon. And short of the normalization of diplomatic relations, the two countries agreed on creating a liaison office in each other's territory.[58] But in a separate addendum to the agreement, Israel incorporated a pledge from the U.S. government to the effect that its withdrawal would be conditional on Syria's and the PLO's withdrawal. In short, Israel imposed on Lebanon conditions that spelled disaster for Syria, not only calling for its withdrawal but also reducing to naught its position in Lebanon. Israel appeared to have won the war for Lebanon and to have spoiled Asad's plan for building his regional power.

Asad was quick to reject the agreement and to denounce the "isolationists" who had signed it.[59] Encouraged by Soviet support, he was adamant about abrogating it. He encouraged the creation of the National Salvation Front, bringing together Lebanese factions that opposed the agreement. The core of the opposition comprised the Sunni leader from Tripoli in northern Lebanon, Rashid Karame; Druze leader Walid Jumblat; SSNP leader In'am Ra'd; and former president Suleiman Franjieh. The opposition accused Amin of resisting change to perpetuate Maronite privileges and advancing Israel's ambitions in Lebanon. But behind this oppositional facade there existed particular grievances. Karame resented Amin's maneuvers to marginalize his leadership in favor of the Sunni leaders of Beirut. Jumblat was concerned about his lordship over the Shouf Mountains, for the Lebanese Forces had managed, with Israel's help, to take up positions there and pose a threat to his fiefdom. In addition, Jumblat was incensed by humiliating acts perpetrated by members of the Lebanese Forces against his community. Although those acts were of an isolated nature, they ignited anew the perennial recriminations between the Maronite and the Druze communities. Franjieh on his part had not given up on his vendetta against the Jumayils for killing his son and the son's family.

While opposition was rapidly building up against him, Amin's position became precarious. He was caught in the maelstrom of contradictions involving his relations with the Lebanese Forces, the Reagan administration, and Israel, the three backers of the May 17 Agreement. Amin needed the support of the Lebanese Forces, being the strong military arm of his community. But this support hampered his political maneuvering. He was in a double bind: as president of the state there were limits on his cooperation with a partisan militia, yet as Phalangist and senior leader of his community he could not but depend on the full support of the Lebanese Forces, which had evolved into a strong, institutionalized, and independent organization with its own political outlook that resisted the Phalangist leadership's attempt to depoliticize it and reduce its power.[60] This attempt had grown out of the Phalangist desire of securing Maronite predominance by channeling it through the legitimate apparatus of the state. As a result, an ambivalent relationship developed between Amin and the Lebanese Forces that inevitably enfeebled him.

Another dimension of the relationship between the Lebanese Forces and Amin involved Israel. Following the May 17 Agreement, Israel planned to withdraw from Lebanon, vacating the parts to which Amin could extend his authority, thus keeping his opponents from reclaiming their earlier control. To achieve this result, he needed Israel's cooperation concerning the timing and method of its withdrawal. But Amin had a reserved, if not awkward, relationship with Israel, while the Lebanese Forces were Israel's ally. So Amin felt insecure with both Israel and the Lebanese Forces. Would Israel undertake a unilateral withdrawal that would put him on the defensive facing his numerous opponents? Would the Lebanese Forces cooperate with Israel behind his back and bypass his attempts to extend his authority?

Amin all along had relied on the Reagan administration to extend his authority and build his army. But in the face of growing opposition from the National Salvation Front to Amin's government and continued violence, the Reagan administration began to have doubts about his ability to govern without making concessions to some of his opponents. The Reagan administration did not permit its troops in the MNF to help fight Amin's war. With tenuous and uneasy relations with the Lebanese Forces, Israel, and the United States, and with Syria successfully fomenting opposition against him, Amin's political fortunes speedily deteriorated. In less than a year, Amin, the candidate of national consensus to save Lebanon, had become the symbol of disunity and the target of attack.

Yet the first major challenge to Amin's rule came from the Shia militia, Amal. After the withdrawal of PLO and Syrian forces from Beirut, Amal emerged as the largest and strongest militia in Muslim West Beirut. Waves of Shia emigration from southern Lebanon to the city had significantly enlarged the community there. Amal's quest for political and military power had not subsided with the disappearance of their leader, Imam al-Sadr, while on a visit to Libya in 1978. Sadr's legacy had been inherited by the savvy and militant lawyer Nabih Berri. Berri sought to control parts of West Beirut in order to break the political alliance Amin's government had struck with the Sunni leadership of the city, as well as to claim the political role commensurate with his community's numerical strength. Wary of Amal's relationship with Syria and the potential of its power, Bashir and later Amin had tried to undercut Amal's leadership by throwing their weight behind both the traditional Shia leadership and the Sunni leadership of Beirut. Buoyed by Syrian encouragement, Amal's fighters in late August and early September 1983 attacked the Lebanese army to wrest control of West Beirut. The fight immediately took on an additional political dimension in which Amal opposed Amin's government and sided with Syria against Israel.

Although the Lebanese army was able to hold its grounds, its position in West Beirut was badly shaken. Immediately after the conflagration there, the IDF decided to withdraw from the Shouf Mountains without coordinating with either the Lebanese Forces or the Lebanese army. The IDF's decision was the product of several factors reflecting the Israeli government's determination to revise its policy in Lebanon. The authors of this policy were simply gone. In February 1983, Sharon had to resign after the publication of the Kahan Commission's report; in early September, Begin, depressed over the death of his wife, submitted his resignation. Their departure reinforced the voices within the government questioning Israel's involvement in Lebanon, particularly after the Sabra and Shatila massacres. In fact, the massacres damaged U.S.-Israeli relations, thus hastening Israel's withdrawal from Lebanon. Already after the massacres and while Begin was still in office, his government began to ponder the viability of Israel's policy of relying only on the Maronites in Lebanon. This inclination gathered momentum when the Druze community in Israel began to voice its displeasure at the Begin government's disregard for the Druze community's security in the Shouf Mountains, which had come under the threat of the Lebanese Forces when Israel brought them there following the invasion.

Several Israeli Druze army officers journeyed to Mukhtara and Ba'aqlin, the centers of Druze leadership in Lebanon, held meetings with fellow religionists, and showed their sense of communal solidarity. With the tacit approval of Begin's government, channels of communication were opened with the Druze leadership, including Walid Jumblat. The IDF did not hesitate to offer some military and economic aid to the Druze in Lebanon. The Lebanese Forces caught wind of the emerging Druze-Israeli relationship and frowned upon it. They had plans to extend their influence to significant parts of the Shouf, hoping to connect Bhamdoun, a Christian town straddling the

Beirut-Damascus highway, with Deir al-Qamar, another Christian town in the Shouf Mountains southeast of the capital. Israel's overtures of friendship to the Druze community meant grave consequences not only to the plans of the Lebanese Forces but also to their newly acquired positions in the Shouf Mountains.

The trend that highlighted Israel's undue reliance on the Maronites became the norm for Israel's policy toward Lebanon with the government of Prime Minister Yitzhak Shamir and Defense Minister Moshe Arens. The new Israeli government tried to reconcile a number of incompatible policies simultaneously: developing relations with the Druzes and the Shiites, withdrawing from parts of Lebanon, and minimizing its exposure to Lebanon's violence. Rebuffing requests from the Lebanese Forces to postpone its withdrawal, the IDF, on September 3, 1983 withdrew all the way to the Awali River. The Lebanese Forces and the Druzes jumped at the opportunity to fill the vacuum created by Israel's withdrawal. They fought each other fiercely. Jumblat instantly denied any Israeli connection and professed again his undivided loyalty to Syria. With significant Syrian and Palestinian help, Jumblat's fighters were able to rout the Maronite forces in the Shouf. In the process, the Druzes slaughtered hundreds of Maronites, many of whom had surrendered.[61] The Lebanese army intervened in the battle for the Shouf but failed to turn the tide. However, it was able to defend the eastern approach of the city by holding a line at Suq al-Gharb. With Jumblat's fighters controlling the Shouf Mountains overlooking the capital, Amin's government not only had failed to extend its authority but also was now surrounded by powerful militias backed by an unrelenting Syria. Another political consequence of the Shouf battle was that it marked the end of the Maronite-Israeli alliance, as the Lebanese Forces considered Israel's withdrawal in this fashion a betrayal.

The final blow to Amin's government came when Shia extremists, with the help of Iran and the probable connivance of Syria, attacked the headquarters of the MNF, including U.S. troops. On October 23, a Shia extremist drove a truck filled with explosives into the U.S. Marine headquarters in West Beirut, killing 240 troops. This act of terror greatly weakened the U.S. will to stay in Lebanon and soon turned the cautious U.S. support of Amin into abandonment. Before long, in February 1984, the Reagan administration redeployed its troops to U.S. ships offshore, leaving Amin under the mercy of President Asad, whose will to abrogate the May 17 Agreement and push the Israelis out of Lebanon had only stiffened. At the same time that the Reagan administration decided to abandon Lebanon, Amal took on the Lebanese army in West Beirut and precipitated its collapse there. Deserted by the United States and humbled by a powerful opposition, Amin finally succumbed to Asad's will in Lebanon and in late February visited Damascus, where he paid homage to its master. In March, Amin's government abrogated the May 17 Agreement. Asad and his allies had turned Israel's objectives in Lebanon on their head.

Still, the war for Lebanon had not been decisively won. The Lebanese Forces remained outside the purview of Syrian influence, although the Phalangist president had become an instrument of Syrian policy in Lebanon. Israel had kept significant territories under its control. But with Asad and his Lebanese allies having wrested the initiative from Israel in Lebanon, it was only a matter of time before Israel and the Lebanese Forces would cave in to Asad's political will in the country. Significantly, Lebanon had been rapidly mutating into hostile territory for Israel's army. The Maronite-Israeli alliance had foundered. The Druzes had shunned all Israeli connections as they followed their leader Jumblat, who through his military conduct in the Shouf battle had established his political dominance in the Druze heartland. And most important, the Shia community had begun its war on the raiding Israelis.

Initially, many in the Shia community welcomed Israel's invasion as a way of ending PLO activities in southern Lebanon. But that initial feeling quickly faded in response to the anti-Israel political climate that the Shia community found itself living under due to later developments. Amal had emerged as the military strong arm of the community and had taken the initiative in staking its claim to power in Lebanon. Notwithstanding the Shiites' close relationship with Syria, Amal's objective of undermining Maronite political hegemony converged with that of Syria, although the two objectives were pursued for different reasons. This automatically tied Amal's struggle to that of Syria against the Maronite-Israeli alliance and thus against Israel.

In addition, Iran's contacts with the Shiites of southern Lebanon provided the seeds for the emergence of an Islamic movement opposed to the Israeli occupation of southern Lebanon. Iran's theocratic leaders strove to expand their revolution by exporting it to Lebanon, building a political base among the Shiites that supported their radical and anti-Israel ideology. The new movement considered Israel a usurper of Muslim land and a tool in Satan's imperialist hands (i.e., the United States). This was reinforced, on the one hand, by Syria letting into the Beka Valley some 2,000 Iranian revolutionary guards, who disseminated Iran's radical ideology to the Shia community, and on the other hand, by Iran backing the spread of its ideology with military and financial rewards. This not only had served to turn many Shiites into radical Iranian disciples, but also had put pressure on the Shia mainstream to consider any relationship with Israel as taboo.

Many Shiites made a connection between Israel's invasion of Lebanon and their own understanding of the Iranian revolution. The revolution convinced those Shiites that armed struggle could win and Islamic fundamentalism could serve as an instrument for achieving political predominance: What could be more behooving to advance an Islamic political movement seeking predominance in a confessional country like Lebanon than embracing the struggle against Israel's invasion? Thus, fighting Israel became the central tenet of an extremist Islamic political movement. It was within this climate that extremist organizations like Hizbollah, or the Party of God, were created.

The current secretary-general of Hizbollah, Hasan Nasrallah, claimed that his party was founded by those embracing an Islamist jihadist (crusaderist) ideology in response to Israel's invasion of Lebanon in 1982. He also implied that those Islamists, who had belonged to Amal, came to be guided in their decision to establish Hizbollah by their disagreement with Amal over the methods to confront Israel.[62]

While Hizbollah embodied Iran's ideological fervor and received its full support to spread the message of the "Islamic Revolution," Syria found in the Party of God a fortuitous instrument for both preserving its interests in Lebanon and putting military pressure on Israel. Syria, through Hizbollah, could strike indirectly at Israel as well as at anti-Syrian groups in Lebanon. Hizbollah readily accepted Iran's and Syria's support to shrewdly transform its fight against Israel into a nationalist struggle. Deftly and courageously conducted and led by Hizbollah, this struggle not only enhanced the image of the party but also laid the ground for Hizbollah's entrance into the realm of Lebanese politics, a move spurned on ideological grounds not long ago.

Hizbollah is an indigenous organization whose fighters are totally integrated into Lebanese society. Hizbollah listens to its patron, Iran, and defers to Syrian influence in Lebanon. However, secular Syria, theocratic Iran, and Islamist Hizbollah have no neat overlap of their interests. A focal point of their interests is the struggle against Israel, albeit a struggle pursued for different objectives. Whereas Syria seeks to retrieve the Golan Heights, Hizbollah is concerned with its political base of support while at the same time remaining loyal to its patron in general and to its ideology in particular. According to Augustus Richard Norton, Hizbollah's leaders understand that the party's role in Damascus's eyes is utilitarian and transient, and they are ever aware that alliances of convenience may eventually become inconvenient.[63] The implication of all of this translates into limits on Syria's influence over Hizbollah.

The cumulative effect of these developments created an anti-Israel politically "correct" environment within the Shia community. When on October 16, 1983, an Israeli convoy inadvertently clashed with a Shia crowd in the southern city of Nabatiya celebrating the day of Ashura, Shia's holiest day, the spiritual leaders of all colors and hues were quick to denounce Israel. Shaikh Muhammad Hussein Fadlallah, the spiritual leader of the new movement, called it a religious duty to destroy Israel. Shaikh Muhammad Mahdi Shamseddine, then deputy president of the Supreme Shiite Council, associated with Amal, and known for his centrist views, urged resistance against Israel.

Consequently, Amal avoided any contact with Israel, opting instead to embrace a militant posture against it in order to enhance its prestige and fend off any radical threat to its political predominance within the Shia community. Before long, Shia attacks not only increased on the IDF in Lebanon but also became a symbol of the perpetrator's preeminence in the Shia community. With its Maronite alliance gone and Lebanon having become a hostile territory overseen by Syria, Israel continued its withdrawal from Lebanon throughout 1984 and 1985. The vacuum created by Israel's withdrawal was speedily filled by Amal and Hizbollah. No longer did Israel entertain ambitious ideas for Lebanon. It reduced its efforts to support its proxy militia, the South Lebanese Army (SLA), which came under the leadership of Colonel Antoine Lahd after the death of Major Sa'd Haddad, in its ten-kilometer-wide security zone in southern Lebanon. Still, Shia attacks on the IDF and the SLA in the security zone had not subsided, with Hizbollah leading the campaign against Israel.

As pointed out earlier, throughout most of his presidential term, Amin had a tenuous and uneasy relationship with the Lebanese Forces. The Lebanese Forces accused Amin of threatening the fate of the Maronite community by being a puppet in Syrian hands. Amin, on the other hand, accused the Lebanese Forces of undermining his authority by undercutting his diplomatic maneuvering with Syria. This relationship was further aggravated by Amin's attempts to co-opt the Lebanese Forces. He tried to oust oppositional figures, involving himself in a power struggle with the leadership of the Lebanese Forces over the proper way of protecting the Maronite community. He also wanted to fight off their charge that he had become a weak president beholden to Syria. However, the two sides refrained from severing their relationship or engaging in armed conflict, understanding fully well that their survival depended on each other.

The fortunes of the Christian camp suffered a serious blow in 1988 when President Jumayil prepared himself to leave office. The president, torn between domestic, regional, and international pressures, was unable to present to the Lebanese parliament an agreed-upon list of presidential hopefuls, as mandated by the constitution. Thus he appointed General Michel Aoun to head an executive cabinet until a president was agreed upon and elected.[64] Immediately after his appointment, Aoun opposed Syrian presence in Lebanon. However, many pro-Syrian deputies disapproved of Aoun's appointment, regarding it constitutionally illegitimate, and lent their support to the government of Prime Minister Salim al-Hoss. At the time, Lebanon witnessed two authorities: one formal, led by Aoun and exercising its authority over the Christian area, the other de facto and pro-Damascus, led by Hoss and extending its authority over the areas under Syrian control.

In March 1989, General Aoun proclaimed a "liberation war" against Syria and requested help from the Muslims of West Beirut. His liberation war was to take the form of an "intifada" against Syria similar to that of the Palestinians in the West Bank.[65] Aoun also invited Iraqi meddling in Lebanon, which infuriated Syria, by accepting Iraqi military aid. Syria responded by shelling the Christian area and imposed on it a sea-and-land blockade, especially on East Beirut. In view of the constitutional impasse and the escalation of hostilities, Lebanese deputies left for the city of Taif in Saudi Arabia. At the meeting there, the Lebanese deputies, with the intercession of Arab delegates from Saudi Arabia, Algeria, and Morocco, managed to introduce significant amendments to the Lebanese constitution. The new version of the constitution became known interchangeably as the Document of National Understanding, and the Taif Accord. In addition, over Aoun's objections the deputies elected Elias Hrawi president, whom Aoun refused to recognize.

General Aoun opposed the Taif Accord as a Syrian scheme to whittle away at Maronite power and called on the Lebanese Forces to stand by him in order to meet the Syrian challenge. Contemplating the surge of Maronite support for Aoun, the Lebanese Forces, in addition to considering Aoun's liberation war against Syria as political suicide, reckoned that under the pretext of meeting the Syrian challenge, Aoun was paving the way for dismantling them. Deadly hostilities broke out between the Lebanese Forces, commanded by Samir Ja'ja, and Aoun's forces in Christian East Beirut. The fighting shattered whatever was left of Christian unity. While both Aoun and Ja'ja bore responsibility for the inexcusable crime of destroying the Christian camp, Aoun's political shortsightedness was the main culprit. Karim Pakradouni remarked on Aoun's losing battles with Syria and the Lebanese Forces: "The General lost the 'liberation war' against Syria because it was bigger than him, and he lost 'the eastern battle' [East Beirut] against the Lebanese Forces because he considered it smaller than him."[66] It was against this backdrop that Iraq rocked the region by invading Kuwait in early August 1990. The United States needed Syria's help in forming the international and Arab anti-Iraq coalition to extract Iraq from Kuwait.

Significantly enough, following the visit by John Kelly, the deputy secretary of state for Middle Eastern affairs, to Syria on August 20, the U.S. ambassador in Damascus, Edward Djerejian, announced that Washington wanted to immediately implement the Taif Accord.[67] Equally important, on September 13, Secretary of State James Baker visited Damascus for the first time and discussed with President Asad the means of managing both the Gulf and the Lebanese crises.[68] On October 13, the Syrian army, along with a unit of the Lebanese army under the command of Colonel Emile Lahoud, launched an all-out attack on Aoun's forces. The Syrian air force intervened for the first time in the history of the Lebanese conflict and raided Aoun's headquarters. Within hours, East Beirut, the last bastion of Lebanese opposition to Syria, fell. Obviously, the United States had yielded to Asad's demand for total hegemony over Lebanon as a price for bringing Syria into the anti-Iraq coalition.

The collapse of East Beirut and the emergence of a "new Lebanon" under Syrian hegemony expedited the implementation of the Taif Accord. The accord reduced the prerogatives of the Maronite president of the republic and enhanced the positions of both the Sunni prime minister and the Shiite speaker of the parliament. It called for (1) building the armed forces to shoulder

their national responsibilities in confronting Israeli aggression, (2) dismantling all militias, (3) implementing UN Resolution 425, and (4) taking the necessary measures to liberate all Lebanese territory from Israeli occupation. The
accord also provided that the Syrian forces shall assist the legitimate Lebanese
Forces in establishing the state's authority within a period not exceeding two
years and that the two governments shall decide on the future redeployment
of Syrian forces. With regard to Lebanese-Syrian relations, the accord underscored that "Lebanon, which is Arab in affiliation and identity, is bound by
fraternal, sincere relations to all Arab states and has special relations with
Syria that draw their strength from the roots of kinship, history and common
internal interests."[69]

In line with the Taif Accord, on May 22, 1991, the Syrian and Lebanese
presidents signed a Treaty of Brotherhood, Cooperation, and Coordination
calling for the closest coordination in all political, security, cultural, scientific, and other matters between the two countries. On the internal level, the
treaty stipulated that neither Lebanon nor Syria shall pose a threat to each
other's security under any circumstances. On the external level, the treaty
stipulated that each country's foreign policy shall support the other's in matters relating to its security and national interests, and that the two governments shall strive to coordinate their Arab and international policies.[70] In a
nutshell, since the Syrian-Lebanese relationship was asymmetrical, the agreement would permit Syria to have its own way in Lebanese affairs.

Whether President Asad wanted to achieve his Greater Syria plan or build
his regional power, his aim of controlling Lebanon had been largely achieved
militarily, politically, and legally. Moshe Arens, Israeli defense minister at the
time, compared Syria's swallowing up of Lebanon with Iraq's annexation of
Kuwait, with the only difference being that the Syrians had taken a more ele-
gant and clever approach.[71] As it turns out, with Syria controlling Lebanon,
Hizbollah has become the most significant instrument at Damascus's disposal to put military pressure on Israel.

Notes

1. Henry Kissinger, *Years of Upheaval* (Boston: Little, Brown, 1982), p. 1135.

2. Ibid.; and Moshe Ma'oz, *Asad: The Sphinx of Damascus, a Political Biography*
(New York: Weidenfeld & Nicolson, 1988), p. 100.

3. See Asad's interview with Arnaud de Borchgrave, *Newsweek*, June 10, 1974;
and Kissinger, *Years of Upheaval*, p. 1133.

4. See Asad's interview with Arnaud de Borchgrave, *Newsweek*, March 3, 1975.

5. Patrick Seale, *Asad of Syria: The Struggle for the Middle East* (Berkeley:
University of California Press, 1988), p. 261.

6. Hafiz al-Asad, *Kadhalika Qala al-Asad* (Thus Asad Said), compiled by
General Mustafa Tlas (Damascus: Tlas Press, 1984), p. 183.

7. Ibid., pp. 181–183.

8. See Pierre Jumayil, "Lebanese Nationalism and Its Foundations: The Phalangist Viewpoint," in Kemal H. Karpat (ed.), *Political and Social Thought in the Contemporary Middle East* (New York: Praeger, 1970).

9. Kamal Jumblat, *Lubnan wa Harb al-Taswiya* (Lebanon and the War for a Settlement) (N.p.: Center of Socialist Studies, Progressive Socialist Party, 1977), pp. 19–21. See also Kamal Jumblat, *Hadhihi Wasiyati* (This Is My Will) (Paris: Stok, 1978), pp. 12–16; and Kamal Jumblat, *Fi Majra al-Siyasah al-Lubnaniya* (In the Course of Lebanese Politics) (Beirut: Dar al-Tali'a, 1962), pp. 42–60.

10. For more details on Syria's policy regarding Lebanon, see Itamar Rabinovich, *The War for Lebanon: 1970–1985* (Ithaca: Cornell University Press, 1985), pp. 36–37.

11. *An-Nahar Arab Report,* February 8, 1971.

12. See *Al-Nahar,* July 6, 1973, and March 27, 1974.

13. Jumblat, *Hadhihi Wasiyati,* p. 24.

14. Ibid., p. 110.

15. Ibid., pp. 232, 235.

16. Seale, *Asad of Syria,* p. 279.

17. Ze'ev Schiff, *Peace with Security: Israel's Minimal Security Requirements in Negotiations with Syria* (Washington, D.C.: Washington Institute for Near East Policy, 1993), p. 26.

18. Ibid. See also Seale, *Asad of Syria,* pp. 279–280.

19. Jumblat, *Hadhihi Wasiyati,* p. 23.

20. Ibid.

21. As a member of the Lebanese Red Cross, I served on the Beirut and Mount Lebanon fronts.

22. Based on my frequent discussions with Phalangist leaders, including Abdu Sa'ab, former Lebanese deputy and head of the Phalangists in Baabda district, July 1980. See also Jumblat, *Hadhihi Wasiyati,* p. 25.

23. I served with the Lebanese Red Cross at Tal Za'tar's front and entered it after its fall.

24. Syria tipped Jumblat's forces about a Christian surprise attack from Kahale on Aleyh with the result that the Christians were ambushed and many of them perished. I transported a significant number of casualties to the Sacre Coeur hospital in Hazmieh.

25. Based on my discussions with many Phalangist leaders and Lebanese deputies, including deputy Kazim al-Khalil, who was a Chamoun supporter, June, July, and August 1982.

26. The Zionist Organization's memorandum presented to the Supreme Council at the Peace Conference following World War I included in its proposed boundaries of Palestine a significant Lebanese swath of territory extending up to the vicinity of Sidon. Importantly, the Zionist Organization aimed at including the Litani and Hasbani rivers in its proposed state. See J. C. Hurewitz, *Diplomacy in the Near and Middle East: A Documentary Record, 1914–1956* (Princeton: D. Van Nostrand, 1956), p. 46. For a critical perspective on Israel's strategy, see Livia Rockah, *Israel's Sacred Terrorism: A Study Based on Moshe Sharett's Personal Diary and Other Documents* (Belmont, Mass.: Association of Arab-American University Graduates, 1980).

27. See the statements of Maronite archbishop Ignace Mubarak in Bat Ye'or, *The Dhimmi: Jews and Christians Under Islam* (London: Associated University Presses, 1985), pp. 401–403. See also Eyal Zisser, "The Maronites, Lebanon, and the State of Israel: Early Contacts," *Middle Eastern Studies* 31, no. 4 (October 1995), pp. 889–918.

28. Shaikh Bashir frequently repeated these statements in Phalangist meetings on the local, regional, and central levels. With the exception of explicit statements about Christian power, his other pronouncements were broadcast and given special emphasis on *Voice of Lebanon.*

29. I resided next to Imam Sadr's headquarters, the Supreme Shiite Council, in Hazmieh, a suburb in East Beirut. I met Imam Sadr on coincidental occasions between 1974 and 1977.

30. For details on Imam Sadr's role in the Shia community, see Fouad Ajami, *The Vanished Imam: Musa al Sadr and the Shi'a of Lebanon* (Ithaca: Cornell University Press, 1986).

31. Ibid., p. 48.

32. Ibid., p. 224.

33. The Carter administration's strategy for the Middle East peace process was largely based on a study conducted at the Brookings Institution by sixteen experts, among them Morroe Berger, Zbigniew Brzezinski, John C. Campell, Malcolm Kerr, William Quandt, Nadav Safran, and Charles W. Yost, some of whom subsequently joined the administration. See Brookings Middle East Study Group, *Toward Peace in the Middle East* (Washington, D.C.: Brookings Institution, 1975).

34. Beate Hamizrachi, *The Emergence of the South Lebanon Security Belt* (New York: Praeger, 1988), p. 112.

35. Jimmy Carter, *The Blood of Abraham* (Boston: Houghton Mifflin, 1985), p. 96.

36. See text of Resolution 425 in Fida Nasrallah, *Prospects for Lebanon: The Questions of South Lebanon* (Oxford: Centre for Lebanese Studies, 1992), p. 33.

37. I attended several Phalangist party meetings at the regional and central level, including a meeting with Shaikh Bashir at his Lebanese Forces office in Ashrafieh in July 1981. "The Lebanon of 10,452 square kilometers" had become the slogan in the Phalangist Party propaganda.

38. The territories under the control of the Lebanese Forces.

39. The French Room is the highest peak on Mount Sanin, and was used by the French during the mandate to monitor the Lebanese-Syrian border.

40. General Mustafa Tlas et al., *Al-Ghazu al-Israili li-Lubnan* (The Israeli Invasion of Lebanon) (Damascus: Tlas Press, 1985), pp. 106–108.

41. Rabinovich, *War for Lebanon,* p. 117; and Seale, *Asad of Syria,* p. 369.

42. Rabinovich, *War for Lebanon,* p. 118.

43. Seale, *Asad of Syria,* p. 371.

44. I observed the arrival of the Lebanese Forces unit that left Zahle to Hazmieh.

45. See articles on the subject in *Tishrin,* November 28, May 30, and August 9, 1981.

46. See Rabinovich, *War for Lebanon,* pp. 127–131.

47. After Begin and Sharon probed Secretary of State Alexander Haig about the U.S. reaction in the event Israel invaded Lebanon, Haig maintained an attitude that "unless there is a major, internationally recognized provocation, the United States will not support such an action." In addition, Haig remarked in public that "the time has come to take concerted action in support of both Lebanon's territorial integrity . . . and a strong central government." These attitudes were construed by Begin as an endorsement of Israel's invasion under the right circumstances. See respectively, Alexander M. Haig Jr., *Caveat: Realism, Reagan, and Foreign Policy* (New York: Macmillan, 1984), pp. 326–328; and Alexander Haig's statements before the Chicago Council on Foreign Relations on May 26, 1982, in *U.S. Department of State Bulletin,* July 1982, pp. 44–47.

48. This was the widespread Phalangist understanding regarding Israel's invasion. See also Rabinovich, *War for Lebanon,* pp. 122–125, especially the statement by the Israeli cabinet issued on the day of the invasion, June 6, 1982.

49. Tlas, *Al-Ghazu al-Israili li-Lubnan,* p. 368.

50. See the Syrian official statement regarding the cease-fire in *Al-Nahar,* June 12, 1982.

51. See *Al-Nahar,* June 22, 1982.

52. At the time I was privy to Shaikh Bashir's attempts to persuade the Lebanese deputies to support his presidential election.

53. A meeting of high-ranking civil and military Phalangist leaders and officials on June 8, 1982, which I attended.

54. See *Al-Nahar,* August 19, 1982.

55. Some Phalangists claim they were called upon by Sharon to enter the refugee camps. See following endnote.

56. After a silence of many years and in light of the case brought against all those involved in the Sabra and Shatila massacres before the Belgium court, Hobeika and some members of the Phalangist Political Bureau, such as Karim Pakradouni, are stressing Sharon's culpability, explaining that he set a trap for the Lebanese Forces while its leadership and that of the Phalangists were in a state of mourning over the death of Bashir Jumayil. Pakradouni has emphasized that the Christian leadership had no idea what Israel was planning, given their preoccupation at the time with Bashir's funeral services and accepting condolences. See Hobeika's public statements on major Lebanese television stations, including the Lebanese Broadcasting Company (LBC) in July 2001. See also Pakradouni's interview with the LBC on July 29, 2001.

57. *Tishrin,* November 21, 1982.

58. See text of the agreement in Nasrallah, *Prospects for Lebanon,* p. 63; and in Tlas, *Al-Ghazu al-Israili li-Lubnan,* pp. 749–750.

59. Ibid., pp. 751–752. See also *Al-Ba'th,* May 15 and May 18, 1983.

60. The Phalangist leadership, including Pierre Jumayil and Elie Karame, called for many meetings on the local and regional levels in order to mobilize support for Shaikh Amin. Their line was that Shaikh Amin was their own and that they should entrust him with strengthening the power of the state in the interest of the Maronites. I attended several meetings at the Phalangist local headquarters in Hazmieh, and at the regional Phalangist military police headquarters (Baabda district), also in Hazmieh, in July and August 1983.

61. In Bhamdoun alone, over eighty Maronite fighters were either shot in the head or knifed. Firsthand accounts from Maronite fighters who managed to escape.

62. See interview with Hizbollah's secretary-general, Hasan Nasrallah, in *Al-Wasat,* March 18, 1996, p. 30.

63. Augustus Richard Norton, "Hizballah and the Israeli Withdrawal from Southern Lebanon," *Journal of Palestine Studies* 30, no. 1 (Autumn 2000), p. 33. For more details on Hizbollah, see also Augustus Richard Norton, *Hizballah of Lebanon: Extremist Ideals vs Mundane Politics* (New York: Council on Foreign Relations, 1999).

64. The United States, Israel, Syria, and the Lebanese Christians and Muslims all preferred different candidates, who were rejected either by lack of consensus or by Shaikh Amin. Frustrated, Amin appointed General Aoun. I sat in on a meeting with Shaikh Amin, Archbishop Elia Elia of the Catholic Orthodox Church, and Maronite Chairbishop Joseph Lahoud at the Sheraton Commander in Cambridge in September 1991, during which the question over Aoun's appointment was discussed.

65. Karim Pakradouni, *La'nat Watan: Min Harb Lubnan Ila Harb al-Khalij* (Curse of a Fatherland: From the Lebanese War to the Gulf War) (Beirut: Trans-Orient Press, 1992), p. 205.

66. Ibid., p. 219.

67. Ibid., p. 223.

68. Ibid.

69. See text of Taif Accord in Nasrallah, *Prospects for Lebanon,* pp. 71–74.

70. See text of the treaty in *Al-Nahar,* May 23, 1991.

71. *Economist Intelligence Unit,* "Country Report: Lebanon, Cyprus," 3rd quarter 1991, p. 93.

3

The Role of the
United States in the
Israeli-Syrian Relationship

No account of the relations between Israel and Syria is anywhere near adequate without taking into full consideration the history of the relationship of the United States to the two countries and to their fierce enmity. Taking as its starting point the Gulf War (1990–1991), this chapter examines the U.S.-Israeli-Syrian triangular relationship to identify patterns and the changes they have produced in U.S. foreign policy toward the Middle East.

U.S. foreign policy toward Israel and Syria, though it went through many developments (leading to significant changes in the nature of Israel's and Syria's relations with the United States), has kept a strong degree of continuity. The United States has maintained a belief in Syria's key regional role and in its capacity to influence events in the area. At the same time, although the United States has unequivocally supported Israel's security and most of its policy objectives in the region, questions about Israel's regional role and the future prospects and nature of the U.S.-Israeli cooperation began to preoccupy the two countries. Upon analysis it becomes clear that while U.S. administrations have been closer to the Syrian position regarding resolving the Arab-Israeli conflict (and have thereby been judged tacitly biased toward Syria), Congress has always greatly supported Israel. This dual attitude in the U.S. government has affected the country's role in dealing with the two embattled neighbors, particularly its attempt at making peace between them.

Background

Chief among the reasons keeping relations between the United States and Syria from improving are the sanctions imposed upon Syria. The U.S. Congress passed two acts, the International Security Assistance and Arms

Export Control Act of 1976 and the Export Administration Act of 1979, which respectively terminated foreign assistance to countries that aid or abet international terrorism and required the secretaries of commerce and state to notify Congress before licensing exports of goods and technology to countries that support acts of international terrorism.[1] A by-product of these laws was the creation in 1979 of a "terrorism list" by the State Department to identify such countries. Syria has been on this list since its creation, and thus has been barred from receiving any type of assistance from the United States.

Ironically, the terrorism issue, which precluded the United States from improving its relationship with Syria, became the issue responsible for bringing the two countries together. In the late 1980s and early 1990s, Syria played a significant role in securing the release of U.S. hostages in Lebanon. John H. Kelly, assistant secretary for the Bureau of Near Eastern and South Asian Affairs, testified in 1989 before the Committee on Foreign Affairs that "Syria has told us that they will be as helpful as possible on the question of hostages in Lebanon," adding, "I think that Syria was indeed helpful in the case of Charlie Glass who was kidnapped and held for a couple of months."[2] The first George (H. W.) Bush administration made it publicly known that Syria was assisting the United States in its efforts to release the hostages.[3] The avenue to freedom for the hostages was through Damascus, where the Syrians basked in the flashbulbs of the international press.[4]

Syria's cooperation with the United States stood well with the Bush administration but had little effect on Congress, whose majority remained adamant about keeping sanctions on Syria so long as it harbored and abetted terrorist organizations on its soil. There were also limits on the extent to which the administration could cooperate with Syria. In addition to being on the State Department's terrorism list, Syria had been denied certification for U.S. international aid as a result of its inadequate effort to stop drug production and drug trafficking.[5] Further, when Syrian intelligence was implicated in an aborted attempt to place a bomb on an El Al airliner at Heathrow Airport in 1986, the U.S. government added further controls to detailed trade restrictions on exports to Syria.[6] Consequently, Syria's relationship with the United States had become both contradictory and perplexing. Inasmuch as the United States wanted to punish Syria for its involvement in terrorism, it needed Syria's help in dealing with terrorism and was trying to maintain, if not improve, its relations with Damascus at a time when Washington had to limit its cooperation in consideration of a Congress that was adamant in its negative attitude toward Syria.

True, U.S.-Israeli relations had developed largely on their mutual interests to ward off Soviet threats to the security of the region, but Israel had more than the Soviet threat on its mind. The political right in Israel, headed by the Likud Party, had at the center of its platform the annexation of the West Bank and Gaza and the creation of settlements there. This policy ran counter to that of the U.S. administrations and threatened to deteriorate relations between the United States and Israel. Likud governments feared that the values Israel shared with the United States, such as commitment to freedom, human rights, and democratic principles, which elevated Israel in the minds of Americans in contrast to other Middle Eastern countries, would not hold with respect to its policy in the West Bank and Gaza. And those values, even if not flouted, would not be adequate to check a deterioration in relations with the United States. Consequently, barring the Soviet threat or a U.S. foreign policy inimical to Israel, Israel's rationale for developing and expanding its relations with the United States had been partly designed to counteract an expected erosion of the "common values" foundation of U.S. support for Israel and partly to keep U.S. support—political, diplomatic, economic, and military—constant.[7]

Priorities Reordered

In a departure from the Reagan administration's policies, which kept U.S. objections to Israeli settlement in the West Bank and Gaza on a low rung on the ladder of U.S.-Israeli relations, the Bush administration considered the settlements to be obstacles to peace and went on to publicly criticize Israel for human rights abuses.[8] At a time when Israel was absorbing Soviet Jewish immigrants, Secretary of State James Baker summed up the position of the administration in the following words:

> Under both Democratic and Republican administrations . . . American policy has always made a clear distinction between the absorption of Jews into Israel itself, and the settling of them in the occupied territories. Early in the administration, we'd concluded that such settlements constituted a serious obstacle to peace in the Middle East, and as a matter of principle, we believed that we should not in good conscience allow U.S. tax dollars to fund activities contrary to American policy and peace.[9]

America's relationship with Syria remained difficult and contradictory at best, straddling the grounds from sanctions to cooperation. In February 1990, President Bush decided that Syria did not meet the necessary certification standards to control narcotics production or trafficking.[10] In April 1990, State Department spokesperson Margaret Tutwiler briefed the press on the U.S. position toward Syria:

> Most of the sanctions imposed in November 1986 remain in place, including strict export controls, the cancellation of Syrian eligibility for Export-Import Bank credits and concessionary wheat purchases, the termination of our bilateral air transport agreement, the prohibition of the sale of Syrian airline tickets, a travel advisory alerting Americans to the potential for terrorist activity originating in Syria, among others. . . . Our relations with Syria have

been difficult for a number of years. Notwithstanding Syrian assistance with the release of Robert Hill [U.S. hostage], there remain important impediments to improved U.S.-Syrian relations, particularly the continued presence of terrorist groups in Syria and Syrian-controlled areas of Lebanon.[11]

When Iraq invaded Kuwait in August 1990, it violated the sovereignty of an independent state and threatened the security of the Arab Gulf, an oil-producing region deemed vital to U.S. interests. President Bush committed himself to reversing Iraq's aggression by leading an international coalition of forces to extract Iraq from Kuwait. The inclusion of Arab forces in the anti-Iraq coalition became paramount as Saddam Hussein, president of Iraq, tried to portray the coalition's war effort in anti-Islamic, anti-Arab terms. Later he tried to precondition the resolution of the crisis by linking it to a comprehensive regional settlement of outstanding conflicts of occupation, mainly Israel's withdrawal from the occupied territories and Lebanon, and Syria's withdrawal from Lebanon.

Iraq's maneuvers convinced the Bush administration to lure Egypt and Syria into the anti-Iraq coalition, and subsequently to isolate the resolution of the crisis from other regional issues. The corollary of this policy entailed the reordering of U.S. priorities in the region, including a rapprochement with Syria, keeping Israel out of the efforts to end the crisis, and supporting an international conference to settle the Arab-Israeli conflict once the liberation of Kuwait was achieved. Syria's regional role had come to the forefront again. Secretary of State James Baker attested to Syria's prominent role in the coalition. In a press conference on September 10, 1990, he stated: "I don't think anything highlights more the isolation of Saddam Hussein in the Arab world than Syria's opposition to Iraq's invasion and occupation of Kuwait. It has contributed forces to the multinational effort—significant forces. I think its presence is significant."[12] Baker emphasized the importance of face-to-face dialogue with Syrian officials as he prepared himself to travel there, the first visit by a high-level official in years. When members of the press raised the question of Syria's involvement in terrorism and America's "patting them on the back" because they supported the United States in the Gulf crisis, Baker responded that "it's very important . . . in a situation such as we have in the Gulf that we cooperate with a major Arab country who happens to share the same goals we do."[13]

The United States, with Syria's manifest eagerness, pressed ahead with improving its relations with Syria. Suddenly, as the documents examined show, the thorny issue of terrorism, which had marred the U.S.-Syrian relationship, now appeared in a different light. When Baker met President Hafiz al-Asad of Syria on September 14, 1990, in Damascus and raised the subject of terrorism with him, he recalled in his memoirs that Asad "made no apologies for supporting terrorism against Israel, which to him was simply part of an armed struggle for liberation from unjust occupation, but insisted that he had agreed to condemn acts of violence elsewhere."[14] Asad maintained that "any person in the land of Syria who is carrying out or planning a terrorist operation outside of the occupied territories will be tried."[15] He also denied any Syrian involvement in the 1988 bombing of Pan American flight 103 over Lockerbie, Scotland. After the meeting with Asad and Syrian officials, Baker and Syria's foreign minister, Farouk al-Shara, held a press conference at which Baker talked about the subject of terrorism and the problems the United States had with Syria on this matter. In a new formulation of the definition of terrorism, Baker was close to Asad's interpretation:

> We consider any violent act outside the occupied territory is a terrorist act. But, at the same time, we cannot consider the legitimate struggle against the occupation forces as a terrorist act. Now we are talking about Kuwait, for instance. The Kuwaiti resistance to the Iraqi occupation is legitimate in every sense of the word. We believe that, so far, Syria was put on the terrorist list without any justification. We believe that the Pan Am 103, the disaster of that flight, did not, until this moment, bring hard evidence to who is responsible and for who is behind that terrorist act. But in our estimation, the accusation addressed to Syria in this respect is meant for political objectives rather than analyzing an objective situation.[16]

Baker's position on Syria's involvement in terrorism was a far cry from the positions of previous administrations. By professing that Syria had been put on the terrorism list without any justification, Baker was not only mending fences with Syria, but also drawing the administration closer to the Syrian argument on terrorism. Because the terrorism issue figured so prominently in U.S.-Syrian relations, Baker's position could be interpreted as a harbinger of change. The United States seemed to be moving closer to the Syrian position on resolving the Arab-Israeli conflict. Nevertheless, despite Baker's words, the U.S. government made no attempt to remove Syria from the terrorism list, opting instead to support Syria's hegemony over Lebanon as a reward for its pro-U.S. involvement in the Gulf crisis.[17] On November 23, 1990, President Bush and President Asad met in Geneva, where they discussed the restoration of Kuwait's territory and legitimate government; the necessity of implementing the Taif Accord in Lebanon; the importance of moving ahead with the Middle East peace process in accordance with UN Resolutions 242 and 338; Syria's help in bringing about the release of all hostages held in Lebanon; and continuing the dialogue on the question of terrorism with the goal of achieving positive results.[18]

Syria went along with U.S. plans to successfully extract Iraq from Kuwait, and by the end of the Gulf War the last of the hostages held in Lebanon, Terry Anderson, saw the first glimpse of freedom when Syrian liaison officers removed the blindfold from his eyes and led him to Damascus.[19]

Standoff and Changing Perspectives

Israel, unlike Syria, now presented a vexing problem to the U.S. government. The Bush administration wanted Israel to stay completely out of the Gulf crisis, so that Iraq could neither link it to the Arab-Israeli conflict nor cause a split in the anti-Iraq coalition, which included Arab forces. Israel became more of a liability to U.S. efforts in the region. Nevertheless, when Iraq launched Scud missile attacks against Israel during the U.S.-led campaign against Iraq, Desert Storm, the U.S. government immediately enhanced its strategic cooperation with Israel. The United States sought to improve Israel's security and at the same time to prevent it from striking back at Iraq. According to Shai Feldman, an entirely new phase of U.S.-Israeli strategic cooperation occurred in late 1990 and early 1991, which included dramatic developments. Most important, the United States sent Patriot surface-to-air missile units to Israel to intercept and destroy the Scuds in the air, and for the first time members of the U.S. armed forces were sent to operate the Patriot units in Israel.[20]

However, this new phase of cooperation gave way to a situation that not only put a damper on U.S.-Israeli relations, but also placed these relations out on a limb. This new condition developed when the Bush administration tried to make good on its promise to the Arab allies in the anti-Iraq coalition to convene a peace conference after the war as part of a U.S. effort to bring about a comprehensive settlement of the Arab-Israeli conflict. This situation unfolded in the form of a standoff between the Bush administration and Israel and its American Jewish supporters over the $10 billion in loan guarantees, requested by Israel at a time when the United States was shoring up support for the peace process. The standoff underscored (1) Israel's diminished status as a strategic ally for the United States in the aftermath of the Cold War, (2) the divergence of U.S. and Israeli policies on resolving the Arab-Israeli conflict, (3) a renewed desire on the part of the U.S. administration to end the Middle East conflict as satisfactorily as possible for both sides, and (4) a subtle U.S. tilt in the direction of the Arab side of the conflict, including Syria.

This problem had its provenance in the reservations the U.S. government had about Israel's settlement activity in the occupied territories. In 1989, Israel requested $400 million in U.S. housing-loan guarantees to enable it to absorb Soviet Jewish immigrants. On May 25, 1990, Congress approved the aforementioned amount for "the purpose of providing housing and infrastructure in Israel for Soviet refugees."[21] Already in March, Baker had informed the House Appropriations Subcommittee on Foreign Affairs that "support for the $400 million in loan guarantees was contingent upon 'satisfactory assurances' from Israel that none of the money would be used in the territories."[22] As settlements sprang up in the occupied territories, the Bush administration refused to release the loan guarantees.

As the coalition forces launched the air campaign against Iraq's forces in Kuwait in January 1991, Iraqi Scud missiles hurled down on Israel, which for the first time in its history refrained from swift retaliation. Though the Bush administration appreciated Israel's restraint, it was taken aback when Israeli finance minister Yitzhak Modai announced that his government would ask for $13 billion in additional aid from the United States—"$10 billion in loan guarantees for settling Soviet Jews, and $3 billion in compensation for the damage inflicted on Israeli cities by Scud attacks."[23] The timing and the size of the request were considered inappropriate and audaciously presumptuous by the Bush administration. Nevertheless, a compromise was worked out whereby Israel would defer its request ($10 billion) until September, and the United States would release the $400 million and pay $650 million as compensation for Israel's damage.

Shortly afterward, Israel's ambassador to the United States, Zalman Shoval, was quoted by the *Washington Post* on February 14 as saying that "we sometimes feel we are being given the run-around" by the United States. This and other remarks so enraged Secretary of State Baker that he asked his staff "to research the legal requirements for declaring Shoval persona non grata and expelling him from the United States."[24] Baker later summoned Shoval to his office, where the secretary of state subjected the Israeli ambassador to a barrage of poignant questions. As the United States concentrated its efforts on winning the Gulf War and restarting the Middle East peace process, tensions between the United States and Israel over Jewish settlements in the West Bank and Gaza heightened. Ariel Sharon, the Israeli housing minister, aggressively expanded the settlements, and Prime Minister Yitzhak Shamir turned down Baker's suggestion that Israel "curtail the expansion of settlements as a goodwill gesture for peace."[25]

In midsummer 1991 the Bush administration received information that the American Israel Public Affairs Committee (AIPAC), headed by Thomas Dine, and its allies in Washington were preparing a campaign to win congressional approval for the loan guarantees regardless of the administration's position. Furthermore, Dine and his colleagues transmitted a message to Shamir that the president "did not have the political will to take on AIPAC and, in any event, would quickly succumb to the legislative juggernaut."[26] Among the many supporters AIPAC had on Capitol Hill, Senators Bob Kasten (R–Wis.) and Daniel K. Inouye (D–Hawaii) stood at the vanguard. However, in order for AIPAC to deliver the administration a blow, it needed the endorsement of the guarantees by Senate Majority Leader George Mitchell (D–Maine) and House Speaker Thomas Foley (D–Wash.), both reliable supporters of Israel.

The Bush administration launched a campaign of its own to undercut AIPAC's efforts. It targeted not only Senators Mitchell and Foley but also congressional leaders Senator Patrick Leahy (D–Vt.) and Representative David Obey (D–Wis.), both of whom respectively chaired the Senate and

House committees for foreign aid appropriations, and both of whom supported Israel. It was mainly Baker who approached the congressmen and called
upon them to give peace a chance. With the peace conference looming close
in the air, around late October, Baker argued that proceeding on the subject of
guarantees and settlements would doom the peace process. The administration
also perceived that the issue of loan guarantees had become a litmus test of its
evenhandedness.

On September 6, 1991, Shoval made a formal request for the guarantees.
AIPAC and its friends from the political action committees (PACs) and the
Council of Presidents of Major American Jewish Organizations rallied influential personalities to descend on Capitol Hill on September 12 to press their
case. The president countered by going public, remarking that he was "'one
lonely guy' fighting 'powerful political forces' amounting to 'something like
a thousand lobbyists.'"[27] On October 2, the president won the day as the
Senate agreed to defer the loan guarantees for 120 days.

Although Israel had agreed to participate in the Madrid peace conference
(see below), the tug-of-war between the two sides over the loan guarantees
and settlements continued unabated, particularly after the 120-day deferral
period had passed. Shamir, in an angry message to the administration, publicly defied "the gentiles of the world" and said that "the settlements expansion will continue, and no power in the world will prevent this construction."[28] Shamir's attitude only further exacerbated the relations between the
United States and Israel. The U.S. government rejected any idea of compromise short of a settlement freeze, conspicuously linking the loan guarantees
with the administration's policies. In late February 1992, Baker appeared
before the Senate Operations Subcommittee and pointedly emphasized:

> We simply believe that if we are going to talk about providing assistance of
> this magnitude over and above the generous assistance that is already pro-
> vided on an annual basis with no conditions whatsoever—that is, the $3 bil-
> lion to $4 billion—then we have a right to know, and frankly, we have an
> obligation to the American taxpayer to know, that we're not going to be
> financing something directly or indirectly that American policy has opposed
> for 25 years.[29]

This firm U.S. posture coincided with the recent victory of Yitzhak Rabin
in Israel's Labor primaries, sending a message to the Israeli public that U.S.
ties with Israel were at a crossroads, hence indirectly boosting the chances of
a Labor victory in the upcoming summer elections. In March, stories began to
surface in the press that Israel had been transferring U.S. technology to China
and South Africa, among other countries, without permission.[30] This came in
the wake of the 1985 arrest of Jonathan Pollard, a U.S. mole recruited by
Israel. All this had strained relations between U.S. officials who advocated
strategic cooperation with Israel and others who shunned such a policy.
Adamant about his position, the president rejected a compromise deal sub-

mitted by Senator Robert Kasten, and under the veto threat to any legislation that did not include a freeze on all new settlements, the president stifled all congressional opposition.

The Bush administration's position was reinforced by other factors on the loan guarantees contest. Since the intifada, U.S. public opinion had been shifting toward a more sympathetic view of the Arabs, partly at the expense of Israel's popularity. When the president went public to counter the pro-Israeli lobbyists, he received wide support. In a Wall Street Journal/NBC News poll on August 2, 1991, that asked who "was the biggest obstacle to peace, 37 percent of the respondents said Israel, to 35 percent who said the Arab countries."[31] A Wall Street Journal/NBC News national telephone survey conducted from February 28 to March 2, 1992, on the question of linking the loan guarantees to the resettlement of Soviet Jewish immigrants revealed that 49 percent opposed the guarantees under any circumstances, 32 percent linked them to a freeze on new settlements, and only 13 percent supported unconditional guarantees.[32] This mood over foreign aid had been partly caused by its general unpopularity, and partly by a recession at home. Already in 1990, Senator Bob Dole (R–Kans.) had proposed a 5 percent cut of foreign aid to major recipients, including Israel, and Representative John Bryant (D–Tex.) had proposed for the 1992–1993 foreign aid budget a reduction of economic aid to Israel by $82.5 million. Though both proposals were defeated, they reflected the unpopularity of foreign aid.

The standoff over the loan guarantees laid bare the newly changed position of Israel after the Cold War. Senator Robert Byrd (D–W.Va.), chairman of the Senate Appropriations Committee, addressed the Senate in early April 1992 on loan guarantees and U.S.-Israeli relations. He critically scrutinized U.S.-Israeli relations, stressing the overriding interests of the United States. On the issue of settlements, Byrd emphasized that "the stated and demonstrated policy of the state of Israel is in direct contradiction to that of the United States regarding such settlements."[33] On the issue of U.S. aid to Israel, Byrd elaborated:

> We have provided Israel with multibillion-dollar aid packages since 1974, and both the United States and Israel have very little progress to show for it. Israel has become dependent on both our economic and military assistance. Our aid has enabled Israel to maintain its enormous military capability, put off much needed economic reform, and avoid making serious progress in solving its problems with its neighbors. Israel must, for its own good, start to stand on its own and cut itself free of a dependence that is really a roadblock to progress, both economically and from the standpoint of achieving security, and it is a dependence that will have no end otherwise.[34]

Senator Byrd went further and exposed Israel's transformed image from a bulwark against Soviet expansionism in the Middle East into a liability to stability:

We should wake up to the reality which has been slow to dawn on many, including our own Pentagon, that the Cold War is over and the real threat to stability in the Middle East lies in the tension between Israel and its Arab neighbors. And that tension only increases as a result of the continued expansion by Israel of settlements in the occupied territories.[35]

Breaking the Ice:
The Madrid Peace Conference

Among the important developments to occur in the aftermath of the Gulf War and the end of the Cold War was the U.S. ability to conduct its policy in the Middle East unhindered by the traditional Soviet considerations. In addition, the countries of the region could no longer play on the old superpowers' rivalries there. Capitalizing on this development, President Bush on March 6, 1991, addressed a joint session of Congress outlining his Middle East objectives:

First, we must work together to create shared security arrangements in the region. . . . Let it be clear: Our vital national interests depend on a stable and secure Gulf. Second, we must act to control the proliferation of weapons of mass destruction and the missiles used to deliver them. . . . And third, we must work to create new opportunities for peace and stability in the Middle East. . . . A comprehensive peace must be grounded in the UN Security Council Resolutions 242 and 338 and the principle of territory for peace. This principle must be elaborated to provide for Israel's security and recognition and at the same time for legitimate Palestinian political rights. . . . The time has come to put an end to the Arab-Israeli conflict.[36]

Late in March, Egypt and Syria issued a call for an international peace conference on the Arab-Israeli conflict. Israel, as always, was not enthusiastic about an international conference. In any event, during May the issue of the loan guarantees surfaced and the Bush administration made clear its position on settlements as obstacles to peace.[37] Responding to the president's speech and his administration's stand on settlements, Prime Minister Shamir stated on July 24: "I don't believe in territorial compromise. Our country is very tiny. . . . I believe with my entire soul that we are forever connected to this homeland."[38] What Shamir was really hinting at was a concurrence to negotiations but without prior commitment to the principle of territory for peace.

During this period (as we have seen), the battle over the loan guarantees prompted the president to speak forcefully against the Israeli settlements and the Israeli lobby. At the same time, the president called for a repeal of the UN Resolution 3379, which labeled Zionism as racism. Eventually, the Israeli government caved in to U.S. pressure and voted to attend the Madrid peace conference on October 20, 1991, after Washington acceded to Shamir's demands concerning the Palestinians: no PLO members, no one from East Jerusalem, and no one from outside the territories was to be present in the peace negotiations. On closer examination, however, two other momentous developments contributed significantly to bringing Israel to Madrid: the strategic geopolitical implications of the Gulf War and the impact of the intifada on Israel.

The Gulf crisis, in the words of Aharon Yariv, a former intelligence chief, appears to have substantiated many lessons and truths for Israel, including: the United States was the superpower, both politically and militarily, hence the inconceivability of any world order without its involvement and leadership; Israel depended on the United States and was vulnerable to missile attacks; the despotic regime in Iraq was durable; and Syria had had a change of heart concerning the peace process.[39] Bearing this in mind, Yariv expounded why Israel should participate in the peace process:

> Continued confrontation will inevitably increase tension and sharpen the feelings of mutual enmity and hatred. Estrangement between Israel and most countries in the world will become progressively stronger. A situation of "no peace, no war," accompanied by an escalating arms race, will sooner or later bring about the crystallization of an Arab military coalition that will go to war against Israel. . . . Then, under new circumstances, we shall again face peace negotiations. Shall we then be able to get a better deal than now, when we are in a strong position and enjoy the support of the U.S. as well as many other countries of the world?[40]

The implications of the intifada for Israel were ponderous as well. As the Palestinian uprising spread in the territories, Israeli defense minister Yitzhak Rabin adopted strong measures to quell it in January 1988. He sanctioned what came to be termed as a policy of "breaking bones" to subdue the intifada.[41] His policy proved futile and counterproductive, as the intifada continued with a vengeance. It brought the Palestinian problem before the eyes of the world and most importantly inside the Israeli home. Suddenly, Israel appeared as an oppressor nation, an image that tormented the conscience of a nation whose history had been replete with oppression. In addition, the intifada had many damaging effects on the country, including an adverse effect on the esprit du corps in the armed forces. Soldiers faced the psychologically excruciating experience that they were fighting children, an experience that had far-reaching dehumanizing effects on the one hand, and lowered the morale of the Israel Defense Forces on the other. This was exacerbated by the Palestinian belief that the IDF was incapable of stopping the intifada. The peace process loomed as a sound alternative for Israel to fight back the intifada's effects.[42] As Itamar Rabinovich admitted:

> The Palestinians' uprising in the West Bank and in Gaza in late 1987, the *intifada,* had a long and profound effect on the Israeli public. Ever since the 1967 war twenty years before, Palestinians had failed to devise an effective

strategy for their struggle against Israel, and whenever Israeli society
weighed the costs of keeping the status quo or working out a new compromise, the balance had tilted toward maintaining the status quo. But in 1988,
a significant body of opinion in Israel was no longer willing to pay the costs
of a perpetuated status quo. It is impossible to understand Yitzhak Shamir's
acceptance of the "Madrid framework" or the Labor Party's victory in the
1992 elections without understanding the effect of this change.[43]

For Syria, the march to Madrid was greatly influenced by international,
regional, and domestic factors. On the international level, the world's stage
was being set for a unipolar power, led by the United States. Syria's old
patron, the Soviet Union, was beginning to disintegrate. Its inability to either
protect the Iraqi regime or mediate the Gulf conflict had weeded out any influence the Soviets may have had with their client's state in the region. Syria saw
the Gulf War as an opportunity to mend its relations with the United States
and to reposition itself under the novel circumstances of a unipolar world. The
United States, on the other hand, sent positive signals to Syria about a new
world order from which Damascus could benefit. Both countries quickly
reached an understanding on how to handle the Gulf and the Lebanese crises
(see above and Chapter 2). In addition, the Syrians, like most Arabs, saw a
credible U.S. president unhindered by Jewish pressure. His stand on the loan
guarantees was a tangible proof of his administration's evenhandedness.

On the regional level, the alignment of forces in the Gulf War translated
itself to a great extent into an alignment of policies after the war. Syria, Egypt,
and Saudi Arabia, the states that joined the U.S.-led coalition against Iraq,
became more attuned to U.S. policies in the region. This was bolstered by the
dawning reality that the actors in the region could no longer play on the historical rivalry of the two superpowers. Equally significant, the Gulf War terminated the once idealized concept of pan-Arabism, under which pretext Arab
countries, especially Syria, had meddled in the internal affairs of each other.
For the first time in recent history Arab forces joined Western ones to attack
an Arab state. The national interests of each Arab state preceded those of pan-
Arabism. On the level of inter-Arab relations, the fragmentation of the Arab
world in the aftermath of the Gulf War suddenly seemed more dangerous than
a negotiated settlement.[44]

In addition, Syria's regional influence with the Arab states and the
Palestinians appeared to be beating a retreat. After the Gulf War, the Gulf
states signed an agreement with Egypt and Syria, called the Damascus
Declaration, that would provide Egypt and Syria with a security role in return
for financial remuneration. However, the integration of the United States in
the Gulf through bilateral security pacts with the Gulf states reduced, if not
scrapped outright, Syria's role there.[45] Significantly enough, Jordan and the
PLO had lost ground in the Gulf War by siding with Iraq. They were resented by the Arab states and the West. At this critical juncture, the United States

might capitalize on their weakness and pressure them into signing separate peace agreements with Israel that would leave Syria behind.

On the domestic level, Syria realized that its quest for strategic parity with Israel, while it could deter an Israeli attack, could not give Syria a war option.[46] In time, Syria might even lose its deterrent capability due to the collapse of the Soviet Union and Israel's advanced weapon supply from the United States. With Egypt locked into a peace treaty and Iraq incapacitated, Israel might preemptively attack Syria, the only looming danger for the Jewish state. If Syria could not retrieve its occupied territory by force, the only other option available would be the peace process. Indeed in this instance, Syria could well prevent Israel from capitalizing on the region's weakness and launch an attack against it.

On October 30, 1991, under the joint chairmanship of Bush and Gorbachev, the Middle East Peace Conference opened in Madrid with Israel, Syria, Lebanon, and a joint Palestinian-Jordanian delegation in attendance. Meanwhile, the U.S. administration initiated changes in export laws in favor of Syria and other Arab states that had helped the United States win the Gulf War. The documents I examined show that in September 1991, the U.S. Commerce Department made "significant changes in U.S. export regulations applying to Syria and Iran."[47] This had the effect of releasing dual-use technology (militarily applicable) to Syria, giving it a way to circumvent the Export Administration Act (EAA). Representatives Mel Levine (D–Calif.) and Howard Berman (D–Calif.) took heed of the changes and petitioned the chairman of the House Committee on Foreign Affairs, Dante B. Fascell (D–Fla.), to reconsider the release of export licenses that would permit the sale of dual-use items to Syria and Iran.

Although the terms of the EAA protect information regarding the control of exports from disclosure, in order to safeguard the "property" rights of U.S. companies and their competitiveness, Section 12(c) of the EAA requires that its full committee meet and determine whether the withholding of that information is contrary to the national interests.[48] In letters to Fascell dated May 1 and July 1, 1992, Berman and Levine compared the U.S. export policy toward Syria and Iran with that of Iraq, a policy that provided sophisticated technology to terrorist countries and led to war. The representatives were concerned with the possible diversion of some of the technology to military use, and with the contribution that such technologies would make to the economic advancement of Syria and Iran.

True, the changes in export laws were made in the aftermath of the Soviet Union's demise; still, they could be viewed as preliminary steps to the removal of sanctions on Syria. Since mid-1990, relations between the Bush administration and Syria had improved substantially and peaked when Syria joined the anti-Iraq coalition. Seemingly, members of Congress were concerned with any promises the administration might have made to Syria in return for its participation in the coalition and its subsequent agreement to attend the Madrid peace conference along with holding bilateral talks with Israel, a position Syria had consistently rejected in the past. Not surprisingly, the supporters of Israel in Congress stood in the vanguard to observe closely the administration's dealings with Syria, in an effort to prevent the administration from laying the groundwork to remove Syria from the terrorism and narcotics list, thus making it eligible for U.S. financial and military support.

Various measures and reports were introduced in Congress to highlight Syria's record and urge the administration to make its cooperation with, and consequently its assistance to, Syria contingent upon its satisfying a number of conditions. In the same month, March 1992, that sixty-eight senators released a letter to Syria expressing their gratitude for Syrian participation in the Gulf War, a House resolution was introduced in Congress that placed several restrictions on Syria. Section 609 of the 1992 H.R. 4546 ruled that U.S. assistance might not be provided to Syria until the president determined, and so reported to the appropriate congressional committees, that (1) Syria had demonstrated its willingness to enter into direct bilateral negotiations with Israel; (2) it was not denying its citizens the right or opportunity to emigrate; (3) it was no longer supporting groups responsible for acts of international terrorism and was no longer providing safe haven for terrorists; (4) it was withdrawing its armed forces from Lebanon; (5) it was no longer acquiring chemical, biological, or nuclear weapons; (6) it was fully cooperating with U.S. antinarcotics efforts and was taking steps to remove Syrian officials who were involved in the drug trade; and (7) it had made progress in improving its record of respect for internationally recognized human rights. In addition Section 608 of the same resolution affirmed that it was U.S. policy to oppose Syrian control of Lebanon and ensure that no assistance provided to Lebanon would benefit Syria.[49] Although Syria had satisfied the first condition, the others had gone to the heart of Syria's domestic politics and were regarded as meddling in Syrian national interests.

Obviously, the administration and Congress had been conducting a tug-of-war over Syria during the delicate time of the ongoing peace process. The administration wanted to improve its relations with Syria by paving the way to removing sanctions on Syria, thereby ridding itself of the legislative shackles either to reward Syria for its participation in the anti-Iraq coalition or to provide it with incentives to enter into a peace agreement with Israel. Farouk al-Shara, Syria's foreign minister, made it clear to Senators James M. Jeffords and Hank Brown during their visit to Syria that if the United States wanted good relations with Syria, it must remove Syria from the terrorism list.[50] Congress, spearheaded by Israel's supporters, had been circumspect with Syria's type of government and the administration's rapprochement. It toughened the restrictions on Syria in order to constrict the administration's maneuverability and to make sure that Syria would comply with certain conditions before receiving any U.S. assistance. The conditions laid down by Congress

heavily intruded upon the domestic politics of Syria, making improved relations between the two countries extremely difficult, if not impossible.

As a result of all these developments, the American Jewish community
along with Israel perceived the Bush administration as harsh on Israel.
Spokespersons for the former expressed much criticism in the U.S. press and
media of the Bush-Baker policies, to which Baker is reputed to have reacted
by making his famous comment in reference to the American Jews: "They did
not vote for us anyway."[51]

But contrary to the belief that Bush and Baker were the sole authors of a
more critical and tougher U.S. policy toward Israel, a group of foreign policy
experts, mostly Jews, known as the "Israelists," were behind it. Leon H.
Hadar summarized their logic:

> Israel's long-term existence could only be assured through the maintenance of
> American hegemony in the Middle East. However, without a solution to the
> Arab-Israeli conflict, the U.S. role could be challenged in the long run by the
> rise of radical forces, especially Muslim fundamentalists, as well as by grow-
> ing isolationist voices in America who might question the need to pay the costs
> of intervention in that far-away region. In that case, Israel would be left alone
> and isolated in the region facing growing threats from militant Islamic gov-
> ernments who perhaps even have nuclear weapons at their disposal.
>
> Hence, since the first days of the Bush administration, the "Israelists"
> have recommended that Washington work to reach as quickly as possible
> some kind of an accommodation between Israel and the Palestinians and the
> Syrians, even if that would mean painful concessions on the part of the
> Jewish state.[52]

Oddly enough, a strange coalition between neoconservative Republicans
and Democrats developed to counter the policy of the Bush administration on
Israel. The Committee on U.S. Interests in the Middle East, headed by Frank
Gaffney, a neoconservative and former Pentagon official who highlighted
Israel's role as a strategic asset during the Reagan years, typified such a coalition. Despite a hopeful Labor election campaign in Israel, which held promise of warming the relations between the Bush administration and the government of Israel if successful, AIPAC and its affiliated PACs had other plans
on their mind. Most AIPAC strategists believed now that their political lot was
more secure with the Democratic Party than with the Republicans, and that
they should revert to reactivating their political base of support in Congress
rather than largely concentrate on lobbying the executive branch, a tactic
adopted during the Reagan years.[53] Consequently, the Democratic presidential
hopeful, William Clinton, received most of the Jewish vote, contributing not
insignificantly to his election.[54]

The tensions between the United States and Israel appreciably dissipated
when the Labor government, headed by Prime Minister Yitzhak Rabin,
assumed office in Israel. Unlike Shamir's tactics, which mocked the substance
of a "land for peace" formula at the Madrid peace conference, Rabin's platform

fit well with the peace process, as he became a central figure pressing for peace with all his Arab neighbors, including the Palestinians. Rabin's policies complemented by his leadership traits and his excellent credentials smoothed out the rough edges of U.S.-Israeli relations. He was well aware of the need to retailor Israel's policies and tactics in pursuing its national interests within the context of U.S. interests, thereby effectively reversing the negative trend set in motion by the end of the Cold War and Shamir's militant policies.

The Clinton Years: Cooperation Versus Limits

President William Clinton inherited the framework of the peace process from the Bush administration, giving it his full support. In 1994 he met twice with Asad, once in January in Geneva, and again in October in Damascus. In his first meeting, the president described Syria as the "key to the achievement of enduring and comprehensive peace."[55] He also expressed his hope that Israel would "respond positively" to Asad's call. It should be remembered that Asad had called for "the peace of the brave," a peace that secures the interests of each side and emphasizes that if the "leaders of Israel have sufficient courage to respond to this kind of peace, a new era of security and stability in which normal peaceful relations among all shall dawn."[56]

Itamar Rabinovich, Israel's ambassador to the United States and chief negotiator with Syria, underscored that President Clinton had put the onus on Israel by expressing "hope" that Asad's call "would provoke a positive response in Israel."[57] He also noted that the president "went along with emphasizing the importance of comprehensiveness in the Arab-Israeli peace process and practically endorsed Syria's policy in Lebanon."[58] In his second meeting, a week after a terrorist bus bombing occurred in Tel Aviv, the president affirmed the resolution of the Arab-Israeli conflict on the basis of UN Resolutions 242 and 338 and the principle of land for peace, and added that peace must guarantee security against surprise attack by any side.[59] The meeting underscored the philosophical differences between the two heads of state on terrorism. While the issue of terrorism was not openly discussed, Clinton regretted that Asad did not publicly denounce the recent terrorist (bus) attack in Israel.[60]

Still, the Clinton administration, virtually like its predecessor, put much emphasis on Syria's key role in regional stability to the point of downplaying the issue of terrorism in the interest of the peace process. In a lecture delivered at the Washington Institute for Near East Policy in May 1994, Anthony Lake, the U.S. national security adviser, emphasized:

> A decisive Syrian-Israeli agreement would allow Jordan and Lebanon to resolve their differences with Israel in a short order. Full normalization of relations between Israel and the Arab states of the Maghreb and the Gulf would follow. An Israel-Syria peace would thus shore up the agreement

between Israel and the PLO and greatly advance U.S. efforts to widen the circle of peacemakers, bolster the network of Middle East moderation, and construct a bastion against backlash states. Syria plays a critical role in the wider sweep of regional peace.[61]

When the Clinton administration's policy is juxtaposed against Clinton's expressed hope that Israel respond positively to Asad's call, the administration's strategic desire to settle the Israeli-Syrian conflict on terms adequate to Syria becomes clear. This is reinforced by Clinton's continuing emphasis on UN Resolutions 242 and 338 as the basis for such a settlement. The endless number of shuttle trips that Secretary of State Warren Christopher made to Damascus, let alone the diplomatic slight he received on one occasion when Asad kept him waiting but never met with Christopher, were testimonials to the administration's willingness to travel the extra mile rather than see Syria become a source of regional instability.

But it was the administration's ambiguous language about Syria's involvement in terrorism that demonstrated its complex position on Syria. The State Department's 1994 annual report on terrorism stated:

> There is no evidence that Syrian officials have been directly involved in planning or executing terrorist attacks since 1986. Damascus is publicly committed to the Middle East peace process and has taken some steps to restrain the international activities of these groups. . . . However, Syria continues to provide safehaven and support for several groups that engage in international terrorism. . . . In addition, Damascus grants a wide variety of groups engaged in terrorism basing privileges or refuge in areas of Lebanon's Bekaa Valley under Syrian control.[62]

In its 1995 report, the State Department emphasized that "Syria continues to use its influence to moderate Hizbollah and Palestinian rejectionist groups. . . . It has, however, allowed Iran to resupply Hizbollah via Damascus."[63] The 1996 and 1997 reports, with slight variations, had the same intent and message.[64] The administration found Syria innocent of the charge of terrorism, but found it to be an accomplice. This paradoxical, noncommittal position could best serve the administration when it decided to remove Syria from the terrorism list. So this position had been none other than a lubricating process to smooth out the give and take with Syria, whereby, in exchange for Syrian concessions on the peace process, the administration would remove it from the terrorism list. In such an event, the United States could benefit from Syria's key role in order to bolster regional stability, widen the circle of peacemakers, restrict fundamentalism, and rein in terrorism.

The administration had not been alone in devising plans regarding Syria and the peace process. When the idea circulated in Washington of stationing U.S. troops on the Golan Heights to monitor an Israeli-Syrian peace accord in the event it occurred, a campaign that included right-wing organizations and individual activists in the Jewish community, supported and goaded by Israel's Likud Party, was organized to bring the idea to naught.[65] Beginning in May 1994, the organized campaign focused on Congress, the media, and the Jewish community, conveying the message that sending U.S. soldiers to the Golan Heights would be a catalyst to severing the U.S.-Israeli relationship. Though in different tones or styles, the message read the same:

> I as an American citizen believe that relinquishing the Golan Heights will necessitate the stationing of U.S. troops who will be exposed to murderous attacks from Arab irregulars. The American people will not accept casualties among the U.S. peacekeeping forces and rightly so. Any such deployment of U.S. troops will begin with good intentions and end with American body bags and vehement American protest demonstrations. This will no doubt lead to a rise in anti-Semitism.[66]

Making such a circumlocution to link anti-Semitism with peacemaking was far from diplomatic stonewalling. The writers of the message obviously refused to acknowledge, or make known, that such a U.S. role had indeed been undertaken. U.S. troops compose half of the Multinational Force and Observers (MFO) in Sinai who monitor Israeli and Egyptian adherence to the security provisions of their 1979 peace treaty. Furthermore, Syria has scrupulously observed the 1973 disengagement agreement with Israel on the Golan Heights, and there has been no incident of terrorism by Arab irregulars. Nevertheless, as Republicans took over both houses of Congress in November 1994, the campaign to kill the idea of stationing U.S. troops on the Golan Heights gained momentum. The designated chairman of the Committee of Foreign Affairs, Senator Jesse Helms, lambasted the idea of sending U.S. troops to the Heights to monitor a future peace accord between Israel and Syria.[67]

The Labor government was taken aback by the negativity of the organized campaign. Ambassador Rabinovich wrote: "We saw the campaign as a shrewd effort to controversialize the Israeli-Arab peace process and to provide an American peg for opposing the notion of an Israeli-Syrian settlement. After all, why should an American senator or columnist take exception to the fact that Israel and Syria decided to end their conflict?"[68] However, soon enough, a critical attitude toward Syria prevailed in Congress as Senator Jesse Helms became the chairman of the Senate's Committee on Foreign Relations, and Representative Benjamin Gilman became the chairman of the House Committee on International Relations. Gilman at first spoke in favor of placing U.S. troops on the Golan Heights, but then, probably due to pressure from his New York constituency, became critical of Asad's regime.[69]

To the harsh criticism of Syria by Helms and his staff, *Al-Ba'th,* the mouthpiece newspaper of Syrian government, featured several articles responding to Helms and others. In one article, Muhammad Kheir al-Wadi questioned Helms's motives in maligning Syria's reputation, especially when he did not have any relations with the Syrian people, did not know its geographic location and its political weight, and did not know its civilizational role in human history.[70] The article added that Syria did not depend for its livelihood on the United States the way Israel does; Syria respects the American people.[71] When Syria did not attend the March Thirteenth (1996) Terrorism Summit in Egypt, following suicide bombings in Israel, opposition to Syria increased in Congress to the chagrin of the administration. Gilman chaired a hearing before the House Committee on International Relations that questioned whether Syria was a peace partner or rogue regime. Gilman stated that "the Administrations' efforts to convince Syria to cease and desist from these activities [narcotics trafficking and terrorism] have been paltry, subsumed by the greater desire to achieve a comprehensive peace in the Middle East."[72] He emphasized that as Syria had been acquiring unconventional weapons, had refused to crack down on terrorist groups based in Syria, and had kept its close relationship with Iran, it had renewed the suspicion that it does not desire peace, but rather a "peace process."[73] In the hearing, Patrick Clawson, of the Washington Institute, and Daniel Pipes, editor of *Middle East Quarterly,* among others, spoke of Syria as being a "rogue regime," deserving of U.S. toughness rather than "cajoling." This campaign against Syria put a damper on Syria's expectations of improving its relationship with the United States, diminishing Syrian hopes of any U.S. financial or military rewards in the event of an Israeli-Syrian peace agreement. Therefore, while this campaign had not brought Israeli-Syrian negotiations to a halt, it had put serious obstacles in its path.

Even though the Labor government in Israel lost to the Likud Party in May 1996, when Benjamin Netanyahu was elected prime minister, and the chances of an Israeli-Syrian peace agreement foundered, the campaign against Syria lost no steam. The focus was mostly from Congress, reinforcing legislation that punished Syria. Though the Foreign Operations, Export Financing, and Related Programs Appropriations Act of 1991 had banned any direct U.S. assistance to eight countries, including Syria, other resolutions were introduced to strengthen this act, namely H.R. 4569 of the 105th Congress. Section 507 of this 1998 House resolution prohibited direct funding for certain countries, including Syria. The prohibition on obligations or expenditures included direct loans, credits, insurance, and guarantees of the Export-Import Bank or its agents. Furthermore, Section 523 prohibited indirect funding to certain countries, including Syria.[74] The cumulative effects of the tall list of sanctions against Syria indeed punished Syria and shackled the hands of the president.

The Clinton Years: Cooperation Versus Interests

The Clinton administration's relationship with Israel had been warm and supportive, but not to the extent of distancing Arab states and the Palestinians.

The participation of Israel in the peace process further improved the U.S.-Israeli relationship.[75] Prime Ministers Yitzhak Rabin and Shimon Peres enjoyed a good working relationship with the Clinton administration, despite the fact that Israel had perceived the administration as supportive of Syria in the sense that the onus of the peace negotiations had been placed on Israel's shoulders. But as is apparent from Rabinovich's account, the Israeli government obviously was at one with the administration on the importance of concluding an Israeli-Syrian peace agreement, given the fact that Israel criticized the organized campaign to thwart such an agreement. However, the Israeli government believed that the administration had not done enough to achieve a breakthrough. Rabinovich claimed that had the United States not been "soft" on Syria, the latter would have signed a peace deal.[76] This argument supports the notion that the United States had obviously been sensitive to Syria's concerns, and that it had been trying to dovetail Syria's strategic key role in the region with U.S. interests. Though this position could be interpreted as even-handed, surely it could not be regarded as blind support for Israel as Arabs often claim.

In fact, it was the peace process that highlighted again, but in a different form, the determining factors of U.S. strategic cooperation with Israel. In April 1996, President Clinton together with Israeli prime minister Shimon Peres issued a joint statement that "anchored their 'strategic partnership' in two main principles: the U.S. commitment to Israel and a mutual determination to achieve a 'comprehensive peace settlement.'"[77] Joseph Alpher, former director of the Jaffee Center for Strategic Studies at Tel Aviv University, asserted that a commendable condition for future American strategic support for Israel may be one which requires that "Israel remain pledged to a workable peace process."[78] When Benjamin Netanyahu replaced Peres as prime minister and challenged the conditions of peace with Syria and the Palestinians, relations between the Clinton administration and the Israeli government became strained.

Netanyahu's policies ran counter to the "land for peace" formula of the peace process, and included the expansion of Israeli settlements in the occupied territories. However, whereas the Bush administration regarded the settlements not only as obstacles to peace but also as contradictory to U.S. policy and illegal, the Clinton administration regarded them only as the former. The Clinton administration had unfailingly supported Israel in the United Nations. It had vetoed Security Council resolutions that criticized Israeli settlement policies in the occupied territories, and had voted against General Assembly resolutions with the same intent. Moreover, the United States had reduced the amounts supposed to be deducted from the annual $2 billion housing-loan guarantees for settlement activities. Walid Khalidi noted that at a time when Netanyahu was expanding Israeli settlements in the West Bank, the deduction decreased from $437 million in 1994 to $60 million in 1996 and

1997. So what was the signal the Clinton administration was sending to Netanyahu?[79]

But despite his favorable attitude toward Israel, President Clinton snubbed Netanyahu and disapproved of his blustering. On one occasion Netanyahu threatened that if Clinton publicly blamed him for the breakdown of the peace process, he would "set fire to Washington."[80] What Netanyahu meant was a mobilization of forces to fight back Clinton's political preferences, forces such as "the Congress, the Jewish lobby, highly influential members of the press— A. M. Rosenthal, Charles Krauthammer, William Safire, Martin Peretz, to name a few—the Christian fundamentalists, politically powerful members of the Jewish community and a strong embassy with excellent connections in the right places."[81] Hirsh Goodman of the *Jerusalem Report* remarked: "Netanyahu has done everything he can to infuriate Clinton. Worse, he has forgotten that while Congress and Bill Safire are important, so is the President."[82]

Clinton's warm relationship with the Jews cushioned the effects of Netanyahu's policies. The *Jerusalem Report,* on May 25, 1998, featured a cover-story article titled "Clinton's Intriguing Kinship with the Jews." The author wrote: "Bill Clinton feels an affection for the Jewish people wholly unprecedented among even the most supportivé of U.S. Presidents. From personal friends to professional appointments, he is an insider and admirer—a fact that underlies his stance on Israel as well. His inspiration for this warmth: the Bible."[83] Clinton's good friend Menachem Genack, an Orthodox rabbi and Democratic Party activist, remarked that Clinton has a "special sensibility for Jews unprecedented in a U.S. president. In this light, even perceived White House hostility to the Israeli government and Benjamin Netanyahu's lack of enthusiasm for the peace process falls into perspective."[84]

Before he became Israel's prime minister, Netanyahu was well aware of Israel's diminished role as a strategic asset for the United States. During the episode of the loan guarantees, Netanyahu, among other Israeli spokesmen, dropped the language describing Israel as a strategic asset for the United States against Soviet expansion and substituted it with one describing it as "democratic," while the loan guarantees were characterized as "humanitarian."[85] In his book *Fighting Terrorism,* Netanyahu wrote about the rise of militant Islam in the United States and the world and on other terrorism-related issues, with the objective first of alerting the Western democracies to the new terrorist threat, and second, once the nature of the threat was understood, of explaining the need for the Western democracies to understand that the threat could be fought effectively.[86] The book came out at a time when fighting terrorism and fundamentalism had been high on the U.S. foreign policy agenda. Netanyahu's position on and approach toward terrorism could well be interpreted as a further means to converge Israel's national interests with those of the United States. Thus Israel would remain a focal point in U.S. foreign policy and consequently would have more chances of upgrading its strategic cooperation with the United States, apparently to the level of a strategic alliance.

This line of reasoning was not new to Israeli officials. To some, strategic alliance has meant a reliable way to maintain Israel's qualitative military edge while safeguarding the U.S.-Israeli relationship against an expected erosion of the "common values" foundation shared by the two countries. Menachem Begin was one of those who favored a formal alliance that included a defense treaty. Netanyahu had favored a strategic alliance, given his position on the peace process, which had the effect of rapidly eroding the "common values" foundation. When signing the Wye River Agreement in October 1998 with the United States and the Palestinians, the Israeli government obtained a provision that had nothing to do with security or other issues on the West Bank. The nature of the provision underscored decisively Israel's concern with upgrading U.S.-Israeli cooperation to the level of strategic alliance.

The provision created the Joint Strategic Planning Committee (JSPC), which would coordinate U.S.-Israeli cooperation on Israeli security against weapons of mass destruction. This marked the first time such a cooperation on Israel's security had taken place between the two countries. Noting the threats of biological and nuclear weapons, Uzi Arad, Netanyahu's foreign policy adviser, in a meeting with foreign policy specialists at Harvard's Kennedy School of Government, explained that the agreement would commit the United States and Israel to "achieving two specific goals: enhancing Israel's defense and deterrent power; and upgrading military, strategic, and technical cooperation between the US National Security Council and the Departments of Defense and State, and their counterparts in Israel."[87] Arad added, "It is about to cross the threshold from a partnership to a virtual strategic alliance. . . . Clearly there is a desire to move to an elevated stage in our cooperation."[88] He had been concerned with the threat from Iran, which had recently launched a long-distance missile, the Shihab.

The director of the Belfer Center for Science and International Affairs at the Kennedy School, Graham Allison, commented that the language of the agreement was very far reaching.[89] Some specialists "questioned the benefits of the cooperation, suggesting it could entangle the United States in Middle East conflicts without providing any significant benefit."[90] Allison echoed some of his colleagues when he asked: "What's in it for the US?"[91] Some specialists were concerned that this agreement would set a precedent in that other countries could claim to be equally threatened and ask for similar agreements with the United States. To that Arad replied: "I don't think there is any country in the world that has the same kind of animosity and real threat, as opposed to imagined threat, than Israel."[92]

When Ehud Barak, who ran for the office of prime minister on a platform of peace, replaced Netanyahu in May 1999, U.S.-Israeli relations speedily improved. Barak's desire for peacemaking was matched by Clinton's enthusiasm. At a joint news conference in the White House in July 1999, the two leaders appeared eager to "show that the nations' relationship had been rein-vigorated."[93] This was openly conveyed by their agreement to a series of pro-posals and plans to enhance the two countries' relationship. Chief among them were plans to increase U.S. military assistance to Israel; to provide financing for Israel's acquisition of additional Arrow antimissile systems (this measure was not new but rather had been delayed during Netanyahu's tenure); and to sign an accord "allowing for 'broad cooperation' between various agencies of both governments on responding to the threat of weapons of mass destruction."[94]

Clinton was able to help bring the Israelis and Syrians to resume their peace talks after a hiatus of almost four years. Not surprisingly, Likud leader Ariel Sharon assaulted liberal U.S. lobbying groups, especially the Israel Policy Forum, a peace group that advocates an active U.S. role in the peace effort, for trying to persuade members of Congress to "overcome 'their natu-ral resistance' to provide Syria money as part of a peace package."[95] Thomas Smerling, director of the Israel Policy Forum's Washington center, said that his group "did not lobby for aid to Syria, but encouraged Congress to see the strategic value of peace with Syria and 'not to foreclose any options before a deal is struck.'" Added Smerling, "Opponents of peace have long viewed Congress as the soft underbelly of Israel's initiative."[96]

It seemed hardly possible that Congress would change its attitude toward Syria, let alone consider financial assistance. Although Syria had asked mili-tant groups based in Damascus to end their armed struggle against Israel even before Israeli-Syrian peace negotiations resumed, no serious effort was under-taken in Congress to try to remove Syria from the terrorism list. In any event, the peace talks failed and Clinton made a last-ditch effort to meet with Asad in Geneva, the final meeting between the two presidents before Asad died. The summit in Geneva collapsed as Asad rejected Clinton's peace offer, which promised the return of almost all of the Golan Heights to Syria, a posi-tion the U.S. administration apparently felt fair enough to produce a peace deal. According to former secretary of state James Baker, Clinton "may sim-ply have presented the Israeli position to President Asad and recommended that he accept it, because it offered to return practically all of the Golan."[97]

Patterns and Expectations

An interplay of factors have determined the nature and extent of Syria's and Israel's relationships with the United States. Whereas the Arab-Israeli conflict has set limits on the scope of both relationships, domestic and international considerations have affected their nature. Syria's key role in the region and its capacity to influence the outcome of events beyond its borders have kept U.S. foreign policy toward Syria generally constant. Syria's direct or indirect involvement in terrorism by no means pushed U.S.-Syrian relations to the point of open hostilities. U.S. foreign policy toward Syria has been ambivalent, for better or for worse. But this ambivalence often translated itself into a tacit bias toward the Syrian position on how to resolve the Arab-Israeli conflict. And whereas the executive branch of the U.S. government defended this bias and tried to improve U.S.-Syrian relations, the legislative branch passed legislation punishing Syria, thereby countermanding the executive branch and undermining the effect of the bias.

Israel, on the other hand, has strengthened its U.S. relationship, partly because of its own volition to stand by the United States, partly because of a "common values" foundation shared by both Israel and the United States, and partly because of a robust American Jewish community that has nurtured this relationship. However, inasmuch as the U.S.-Israeli relationship has expanded, a limiting effect was exercised on the U.S. position by the Arab-Israeli conflict, Syria's key role in the region, and U.S. interests in the Arab Gulf. This made U.S.-Israeli strategic cooperation feasible but a U.S.-Israeli strategic alliance questionable, especially after the disappearance of the Soviet threat to the region.

As a result of this ambivalence, U.S. foreign policy toward Syria and Israel, while maintaining its continuity, suffered some loss in its political coercive power on account of the difference noted above in the approaches of the executive and legislative arms of the government on Israeli-Syrian peacemaking. The inevitable conclusion is that unless the United States reaffirms its coercive power, Israel and Syria will not be able to thresh out an initial agreement on their own.

The election of George W. Bush as president may have complicated matters. While it would be expected that Bush continue Clinton's peace efforts, which began under George Bush Senior, it appears doubtful that the new president will give priority to peacemaking between Israel and Syria. The composition of the Senate—initially split fifty-fifty between Democrats and Republicans and later Democrat-controlled by a single vote—together with a weak presidential mandate (losing the popular vote in a hotly contested election) could diminish the will of President Bush to undertake a task fraught with political perils. In fact, early on in office, the Bush administration made it clear that its main foreign policy concern in the Middle East was to reinvigorate the sanctions against Iraq.[98]

The Bush administration had set the tone of a policy best described by the State Department's parlance as a "minimalist" approach to peace talks in contrast to the hands-on approach of the Clinton administration. Following the election of Likud leader Ariel Sharon as prime minister of Israel in early February 2001, largely in response to escalating violence in the Palestinian occupied territories (Al-Aqsa intifada), the Bush administration formally abandoned former President Clinton's peace proposals concerning the Palestinian-Israeli conflict. Condoleezza Rice, President Bush's national security adviser, emphasized in an interview: "We shouldn't think of American involvement for the sake of American involvement."[99] In a speech considered as the first major description of the Bush administration's Middle East policy, Secretary of State Colin L. Powell signaled a break with the Clinton administration's hands-on approach to the Palestinian-Israeli conflict by saying, "The United States stands to assist, not insist."[100]

This minimalist approach harks back to the days of President Bush's father, when Secretary of State James Baker was so frustrated with the rightist government of Yitzhak Shamir that he famously told the Israelis, "When you are serious about peace, call us."[101] Then Secretary Baker announced the White House phone number. A clear distinction, however, must be drawn between these two approaches. While frustration with Israel's policy of expanding the settlements in the occupied territories set the mood of Bush Senior's administration, cautiousness seemingly characterizes the mood of the current administration. Apparently, it is wary about any new U.S. role after the heavy involvement of the Clinton administration wound up in violence. In addition, it is trying to look at the Arab-Israeli conflict within the context of the overall U.S. policy in the Middle East, which still has not yet crystallized. Disagreements over U.S. foreign policy between the State and Defense Departments have yet to be sorted out. For example, Secretary of State Powell prefers to modify the sanctions on Iraq, while Secretary of Defense Donald H. Rumsfeld proposes a tougher stance against Iraq and support for Iraqi opposition.[102]

In the meantime, Sharon's government has been quick in advancing policies consistent with the pattern established by other Likud governments. Immediately following his election, a high-level Israeli foreign policy team consisting of Zalman Shoval and Moshe Arens, both former ambassadors to the United States, and Dore Gold, a former ambassador to the UN, was dispatched to Washington to try to change the foundation upon which the United States and Israel based their policy in the Middle East. All three opposed the 1993 Oslo Accords and criticized the Barak and Clinton administrations for making the peace process a cornerstone of the U.S.-Israeli relationship. In much the same vein as their Likud predecessors, the essence of their mission was to argue for a closer U.S.-Israeli relationship, paying greater emphasis on regional security concerns apparently with the objective of shifting the focus of the relationship from the peace process.[103] Thus Israel could remain a focal point in U.S. foreign policy while at the same time preventing a potential deterioration of U.S.-Israeli relations.

After meeting with Secretary Powell, Dore Gold said: "We see many things eye to eye, and we believe that with the forthcoming visit of Secretary Powell to Jerusalem we will see a continuation and actually an upgrading of the relationship between our two countries."[104] Secretary Powell did indeed travel to Jerusalem as part of his larger tour of Middle Eastern capitals. But his trip centered more than anything else on reinforcing the sanctions against Iraq and rebuilding Arab support for them. With the Al-Aqsa intifada continuing unabated in the Palestinian occupied territories, many Arab countries have come under pressure from their populations to assist the Palestinians and to support the removal of sanctions against Iraq. Many Arabs have lost faith in U.S. evenhandedness in the region, citing favoritism toward Israel. Correspondingly, several Arab countries, including Syria, have begun to sign trade agreements with Iraq and fly their planes to Baghdad's international airport in defiance of the sanctions.[105] All this had made Powell's efforts to solicit strong support for his policy crucial as well as onerous.

Inadvertently, Syria reemerged as a country that could make or break what had been considered as the Bush administration's highest foreign policy priority. Bearing in mind the geostrategic position Syria commands, bordering Iraq, the Bush administration has been specifically interested in preventing Saddam Hussein from using revenues of Iraqi oil flowing through Syrian pipelines (which opened recently after many years of closure) to acquire weapons, whether sophisticated or unconventional. As part of his strategy, Secretary Powell sought to convince President Asad to place into a UN escrow account those oil revenues flowing into Saddam's pockets. After meeting with President Asad on February 26, 2001, Secretary Powell was able to obtain a commitment in this respect from the Syrian president. According to the New York Times the "commitment from the Syrian was so firm—Mr. Asad stated it three times during the meeting, General Powell said—that the secretary said he had telephoned President Bush to tell him."[106] In the meantime, Washington adopted a neutral position (considered a sign of approval) regarding Syria's prospects of an appointment (as a nonpermanent member) to the UN Security Council, despite pressure to oppose the appointment from supporters of Israel in Congress, led by Eliot Engel (D–N.Y.).[107] This undoubtedly illustrates the premium the Bush administration places on Syria's key regional role and cooperation, without which the chances of reinforcing sanctions on Iraq appear dim. However, in the absence of an efficient and clear U.S. policy on Iraq, and hurt financially by sanctions on Iraq, Syria, Turkey, and Jordan have increased their trade with Baghdad. In contradiction to what Asad promised Powell, approximately 150,000 barrels of Iraqi oil pass daily through Syrian pipelines, with revenues split between Baghdad and Damascus.[108]

A few weeks later, Prime Minister Sharon visited Washington and met President Bush. Most of the discussion revolved around defense and broader regional issues. According to a senior administration official, the two leaders found a "convergence of interest" in missile defense.[109] On the eve of Sharon's visit, however, President Bush called President Asad to discuss with him the situation in the Middle East. According to Syrian sources, the two leaders "discussed bilateral ties and the need to improve them 'for the benefit of regional security and stability.'"[110] At the same time, the State Department expressed its concern over, and discouraged the Israeli government from approving, a plan to expand the Har Homa housing project in East Jerusalem.[111] This came in the wake of another message to Israel that, according to then–prime minister Ehud Barak, unjustifiably equated Israeli response to violence with Palestinian terror.[112] Apparently, this administration does not shy from taking a critical position toward Israel. However, one should not interpret this to mean that the Bush administration would deal with Israel and the Palestinians on an equal footing. Still, President Bush has not invited PLO chairman Yasser Arafat to the White House and so far has put most of the blame for escalating the violence in the Palestinian occupied territories squarely on Arafat's shoulders.[113]

Following a sharp twist of events, the Bush administration's desire for a minimalist approach to the Arab-Israeli conflict quickly dissipated in the wake of the most tragic, horrific, and unprecedented acts of terror ever to have taken place on U.S. soil. Targeting U.S. symbols of economic and military power, Islamic extremists, followers of Osama bin Laden, using hijacked planes as high-explosive bombs, struck the World Trade Center and the Pentagon on September 11, 2001, killing thousands of innocent victims. The sheer magnitude and enormity of this seminal event altered irreversibly not only the American way of life but also U.S. foreign policy priorities. Splitting the world between those "with the United States" and those "with the terrorists," President Bush declared a war on terrorism and built an international coalition to fight terrorists and those countries that harbor them. The initial objectives of the war, mainly to destroy Bin Laden's Al-Qaeda organization and remove from power the Afghani Taliban rulers who harbored it, have been largely accomplished.

Given the ultimate determination and motive of the United States to lead this campaign, Washington's coalition-building efforts and fight against terrorism reshaped the world's balance of power and alignment of forces in a way much more profound than that during the Gulf War (1990–1991). Consequently, the Bush administration could no longer pursue its initial minimalist approach to the Arab-Israeli conflict while it needed Arab participation in the U.S.-led coalition. Violence in the Palestinian occupied territories added urgency to a new approach. On October 2, 2001, President Bush endorsed the creation of a Palestinian state. "The idea of a Palestinian state has always been a part of a vision, so long as the right of Israel to exist is respected," President Bush told reporters after a meeting with congressional leaders.[114] His comments followed reports from Washington that, prior to the terror attacks on September 11, the Bush administration had been planning a new Middle East initiative. This announcement was followed by a speech by Secretary Powell in which he called on Palestinians to stop terrorism and incitement and on Israelis to stop settlement activity and occupation.[115]

However, this did not amount to an enunciation of a Powell plan. Apparently, by taking up the issue of the Arab-Israeli conflict and not offering any policy innovation (sticking to the Mitchell and Tenet recommendations), Powell realized the importance of adopting to a certain extent a hands-on approach (appointing retired Marine Corps General Anthony Zinni as a special envoy to help the parties achieve a durable cease-fire), while at the same time perceiving that the success of any major initiative was highly unlikely. This balancing act is no more than a U.S. unwillingness to articulate a well-defined concept for settling the Arab-Israeli conflict. This is set in sharp relief with respect to Syria. Syria condemned the September 11 terror attacks and pledged to combat terror as part of the international coalition. Damascus has cooperated with and helped top U.S. intelligence officials who traveled to Syria.[116] In fact, U.S. officials have praised the Syrians for contributing to the antiterrorism effort. Even Secretary Powell admitted that the Syrians "have said and done some things, and have cooperated with us."[117] In addition, U.S. officials expect Syria to play a more important role in the next phases of the war against terrorism. Damascus has been recently the hub of diplomatic activities for many U.S. congressional delegations.[118]

Yet Damascus remains on the State Department terrorism list and has been mentioned peripherally in the U.S. media and some diplomatic quarters as a possible future target because of its support for and harboring of groups such as Hizbollah, Hamas, and the Palestinian Islamic Jihad (PIJ), which Washington has labeled as terrorists. Damascus, for its part, has called for a specific definition of terrorism, especially with regard to making a distinction between fighting occupation and acts of terror.[119] All this is a reflection of the persistent ambivalent attitude of the United States toward Syria: the United States knows it has a conflict with Syria, yet Washington recognizes that it needs Syria inasmuch as it hates to admit it.

Since the Bush administration's Middle East foreign policy has not yet taken a final shape, especially with regard to what to do with Iraq, one could expect a stronger U.S. support to Israel than to Palestinians or Syrians. But as history has witnessed, the Arab-Israeli conflict has a way of imposing itself on all U.S. administrations. Compelled to reach a decision over what to do with Iraq's alleged pursuit of weapons of mass destruction (whether to enforce smart sanctions or topple the regime) and faced with a situation fast deteriorating in the occupied territories, threatening regional violence, and complicating Arab and Muslim participation in the coalition, the Bush administration might unwillingly be forced not only to adopt a somewhat hands-on approach to the Arab-Israeli conflict but also to dovetail it with its overall Middle Eastern foreign policy. This could well spell a future crisis in U.S.-Israeli relations given the Sharon government's overall ideology and attitude toward the peace process and the Palestinian occupied territories. In sharp contrast, the Bush administration would need Syria's cooperation in order to put teeth in its foreign policy in the Middle East.

When all is said and done, the Bush administration, like its predecessors, appears beset by domestic, regional, and international considerations potentially rendering its policy ineffective in the region in general and in the triangular relationship in particular.

Notes

An adaptation of this chapter appeared in *Middle East Journal* 55, no. 3 (Summer 2001).

1. See Alfred B. Prados, "Syrian-U.S. Relations," *Congressional Research Service,* May 12, 1992, p. 11.

2. Hearing Before the Subcommittee on Europe and the Middle East of the Committee on Foreign Affairs, House of Representatives, *The Situation in Lebanon, July 1989* (Washington, D.C.: U.S. Government Printing Office [GPO], 1989), pp. 118–119.

3. See Hearing Before the Subcommittee on International Operations of the Committee on Foreign Affairs, House of Representatives, *American Hostages in Lebanon* (Washington, D.C.: U.S. GPO, 1990); and U.S. Department of State, *American Foreign Policy: Current Documents 1990* (Washington, D.C.: U.S. GPO, 1991), p. 622. See also Margaret Tutwiler's statement later in this chapter.

4. For vivid accounts on U.S. hostages in Lebanon, see their memoirs, one of which is Terry A. Anderson, *Den of Lions: Memoirs of Seven Years* (New York: Crown Publishers, 1993).

5. U.S. Department of State, *American Foreign Policy: Current Documents 1988* (Washington, D.C.: U.S. GPO, 1989), p. 216.

6. Padros, "Syrian-U.S. Relations," p. 13.

7. For details, see Shai Feldman, *The Future of U.S.-Israel Strategic Cooperation* (Washington, D.C.: Washington Institute for Near East Policy, 1996); and Thomas L. Friedman, "U.S. and Israel at Sea," *New York Times,* March 22, 1992.

8. Middle East Watch, "Human Rights Watch World Report 1992: 'The Israeli-Occupied West Bank and Gaza Strip,'" *Journal of Palestine Studies* 21, no. 4 (Summer 1992), p. 123 (reproduced from *Human Rights Watch,* December 1991).

9. James A. Baker III, *The Politics of Diplomacy: Revolution, War, and Peace, 1989–1992* (New York: G. P. Putnam's Sons, 1995), p. 542.

10. U.S. Department of State, *American Foreign Policy: Current Documents 1990* (Washington, D.C.: GPO, 1991), p. 111.

11. Ibid., pp. 621–622.

12. Ibid., p. 622.

13. Ibid., p. 623.

14. Baker, *Politics of Diplomacy,* p. 426.

15. Ibid., p. 426.

16. U.S. Department of State, *American Foreign Policy: Current Documents 1990,* p. 626.

17. See Karim Pakradouni, *La'nat Watan: Min Harb Lubnan ila Harb al-Khalij* (Curse of a Fatherland: From the Lebanese War to the Gulf War) (Beirut: Trans-Orient Press, 1992), pp. 205–224. See also Chapter 2 in this volume.

18. U.S. Department of State, *American Foreign Policy: Current Documents 1990,* p. 627.

19. Anderson, *Den of Lions,* pp. 343–345.

20. Feldman, *Future of U.S.-Israel Strategic Cooperation,* p. 15.

21. Baker, *Politics of Diplomacy,* p. 542.

22. Ibid., pp. 542–543.

23. Ibid., p. 544.

24. Ibid., p. 545.

25. Ibid., p. 547.

26. Ibid., p. 549.

27. Ibid., p. 552; and William B. Quandt, *Peace Process: American Diplomacy and the Arab-Israeli Conflict Since 1967* (Berkeley: University of California Press, 1993), p. 403.

28. Leon T. Hadar, "The Last Days of Likud: The American-Israeli Big Chill," *Journal of Palestine Studies* 21, no. 4 (Summer 1992), p. 81; and Mark Shields, "The Gulf War Fades," *Washington Post,* March 6, 1992.

29. Hadar, "Last Days of Likud," p. 82; and Thomas L. Friedman, "Senators Press Baker on Help to Israel," *New York Times,* February 26, 1992.

30. Bill Gertz and Rowan Scarborough, "China May Have Patriot from Israel," *Washington Times,* March 12, 1992; and Edward T. Pound, "U.S. Sees New Signs Israel Resells Its Arms to China, South Africa," *Wall Street Journal,* March 13, 1992.

31. Nathan Jones, "Skepticism About Israel Accompanies Opposition to Loan Guarantees," *Washington Report on the Middle East Affairs,* April–May 1992, p. 18.

32. Ibid., p. 18.

33. Senator Robert Byrd, "Senator Byrd on Loan Guarantees and U.S.-Israeli Relations," *Journal of Palestine Studies* 21, no. 4 (Summer 1992), p. 131.

34. Ibid., p. 137.

35. Ibid., p. 138.

36. For text of the speech, see *Washington Post,* March 7, 1991.

37. See Thomas L. Friedman, "Baker Cites Israel for Settlements," *New York Times,* May 23, 1991; and Thomas L. Friedman, "Bush Backs Baker View of Mid-East Barriers," *New York Times,* May 24, 1991.

38. Linda Gradstein, "Shamir Bars Losing Territory," *Washington Post,* July 25, 1991.

39. See Aharon Yariv, *War in the Gulf: Implications for Israel* (Boulder: Westview Press, 1992), pp. 382–397.

40. Ibid., p. 395.

41. Quandt, *Peace Process,* p. 364.

42. See Aryeh Shalev, *The Intifada: Causes and Effects* (Boulder: Westview Press, 1991), pp. 163–175.

43. Itamar Rabinovich, *Waging Peace: Israel and the Arabs at the End of the Century* (New York: Farrar, Straus, and Giroux, 1999), p. 36.

44. For a detailed account on the impact of the Gulf War on the Arab world, see Muhammad Faour, *The Arab World After Desert Storm* (Washington, D.C.: U.S. Institute of Peace Press, 1993).

45. For details on security, see Chapter 6.

46. Nadav Safran, "Dimension of the Middle East Problem," in Roy Macridis (ed.), *Foreign Policy in World Politics,* 8th ed. (Englewood Cliffs, N.J.: Prentice Hall, 1992), p. 393.

47. Hearing Before the Committee on Foreign Affairs, House of Representatives, July 22, 1992, *To Consider Release of Dual-Use Export Licenses to Iran and Syria Pursuant to Section 12(c) of the Export Administration Act* (Washington, D.C.: U.S. GPO, 1992), p. 19.

48. Ibid., pp. 2, 19.

49. See *Congressional Information Service,* H.R. 4546, 102nd Congress, 1992.

50. Report to the Committee on Foreign Relations, U.S. Senate, by Senator James M. Jeffords and Senator Hank Brown, *Trip to Croatia, Syria, Jordan, Israel, and Egypt* (Washington, D.C.: U.S. GPO, 1993), p. 10.

51. William Safire, "Blaming the Victim," *New York Times,* March 19, 1992.

52. Leon T. Hadar, "High Noon in Washington: The Shootout over the Loan Guarantees," *Journal of Palestine Studies* 21, no. 2 (Winter 1992), pp. 77–78. The for-

eign policy experts included Richard Haass, Dennis Ross, Aaron Miller, and Daniel C. Kurtzer.

53. Hadar, "Last Days of Likud," p. 92. Some Jewish leaders had already predicted that President Bush would not receive Jewish votes. "There is anger and dismay in Jewish communities over Bush administration policy that is increasingly perceived as one-sided and unfair against Israel," said Jess Hordes, Washington director of the Anti-Defamation League. "I imagine it will be translated into an unwillingness to vote for this administration or contribute funds." Thomas L. Friedman, "Damage to Bush Seen,'" *New York Times,* March 19, 1992.

54. In 1992, Bush Senior received 11 percent of the Jewish vote, to Bill Clinton's 80 percent. See Thomas B. Edsall, "GOP Eyes Jewish Vote with Bush Tack on Israel," *Washington Post,* April 30, 2002.

55. Excerpts from President Clinton's news conference with President Asad of Syria, "Asad and Clinton Speak: New Commitment to Peace," *New York Times,* January 17, 1994.

56. Mary Curtius, "Asad Calls for 'Normal' Relations with Israel," *Boston Globe,* January 17, 1994.

57. Itamar Rabinovich, *The Brink of Peace: The Israeli-Syrian Negotiations* (Princeton: Princeton University Press, 1998), p. 129.

58. Ibid.

59. Excerpts from remarks by President Clinton and President Hafiz al-Asad of Syria, "Asad and Clinton Speak: Shared Quest for Peace," *New York Times,* October 28, 1994, p. A21.

60. Ibid., p. A20.

61. Quoted from Rabinovich, *Brink of Peace,* p. 145.

62. U.S. Department of State, *Patterns of Global Terrorism 1994* (Washington, D.C.: U.S. Government Printing Office, April 1995), pp. 23–24.

63. U.S. Department of State, *Patterns of Global Terrorism 1995* (April 1996), p. 28.

64. See U.S. Department of State, *Patterns of Global Terrorism 1996* and *1997* (April 1997 and April 1998). The 1997 report claimed that Syria continues to provide safe haven and support for radical terrorist groups, including the Popular Front for the Liberation of Palestine–General Command (PFLP-GC), the Palestinian Islamic Jihad (PIJ), the Palestinian-Islamic Resistance Movement (Hamas), and the Kurdistan Workers Party (PKK).

65. Among those involved were Frank Gaffney, who ran a conservative think tank in Washington—the Center for Security Policy—and Yossi Ben-Aharon, the predecessor of Rabinovich as chief negotiator with Syria. Key Republicans such as Dan Quayle, William Bennet, and Jack Kemp have supported Gaffney.

66. Quoted from Rabinovich, *Brink of Peace,* p. 166.

67. Steven Greenhouse, "Dole May Moderate Helms Conservatism," *New York Times,* December 9, 1994, p. 3.

68. Rabinovich, *Brink of Peace,* p. 165.

69. On Gilman in favor of deploying U.S. troops, see Greenhouse, "Dole May Moderate Helms Conservatism," p. 3.

70. Muhammad Kheir al-Wadi, "Helms . . . wa al-Nazzara al-Israiliya" (Helms . . . and the Israeli Binoculars), *Al-Ba'th,* March 28, 1995.

71. Ibid.

72. Hearing Before the Committee on International Relations, House of Representatives, *Syria: Peace Partner or Rogue Regime?* (Washington, D.C.: U.S. GPO, 1996), p. 31.

73. Ibid., p. 32.

74. *Congressional Information Service,* H.R. 4569, 105th Congress, 1998.

75. Human rights considerations have been of second importance in formulating U.S. foreign policy in the region. Rarely has the United States criticized Israel for human rights abuses. When it had done so, during the Bush administration, Human Rights Watch claimed that the criticism "has been less effective than it could have been for two principal reasons. Foremost is the Administration's unwillingness to link, at least publicly, Israel's human rights record with the amount of aid it receives or the favorable trade relations it enjoys. . . . Second, the United States has long made clear that its concern for human rights abuses committed by Israel is subservient to the goal of bringing Israel and her neighbors into a peace process." See Middle East Watch, "Human Rights Watch World Report 1992," p. 123. The Human Rights Committee's 1998 report on Israel confirmed Israel's "serious shortcomings in meeting its obligations under the [International] Covenant [on Civil and Political Rights]." The committee also deplored the controversial guidelines in Israel's Landau Commission (which has been recently revised) as constituting violations. See Human Rights Watch, *Israel's Record of Occupation: Violations of Civil and Political Rights* (New York: Human Rights Watch, 1998), p. 3. The 1995 State Department report on Israel's human rights practices stated that the main problems in Israel have arisen from its policies and practices in the occupied territories. "The redeployment of the IDF from most major Palestinian population areas [is] significantly reducing these problems." The 1995 State Department report on Syria indicated that despite some improvements, the government continues to restrict or deny fundamental rights. Serious abuses include the widespread use of torture in detention, arbitrary arrest, and fundamentally unfair trials in the security courts. See U.S. Department of State, "Israel Human Rights Practices 1995," March 1996, p. 2, and "Syria Human Rights Practices 1995," March 1996, p. 1.

76. Author interview with Itamar Rabinovich, November 12, 1998.

77. Thomas W. Lippman, "Anti-Terrorism Accord Signed," *Washington Post,* May 1, 1996, p. A23; and Duncan L. Clarke, "U.S. Security Assistance to Egypt and Israel: Politically Untouchable?" *Middle East Journal* 51, no. 2 (Spring 1997).

78. Joseph Alpher, "Israel: The Challenge of Peace," *Foreign Policy* 101 (Winter 1995–1996), pp. 142–143.

79. Walid Khalidi, "The American Factor in the Arab-Israeli Conflict," *Middle East International,* January 30, 1998, p. 17.

80. Hirsh Goodman, "The Wrong Enemy," *Jerusalem Report,* June 8, 1998, p. 56.

81. Ibid.

82. Ibid.

83. Netty C. Gross, "Clinton's Intriguing Kinship with the Jews," *Jerusalem Report,* May 25, 1998, p. 28.

84. Ibid.

85. See Hadar, "High Noon in Washington," p. 81.

86. Benjamin Netanyahu, *Fighting Terrorism: How Democracies Can Defeat Domestic and International Terrorists* (New York: Farrar, Straus, and Giroux, 1995), pp. 130–131.

87. Kate Zernike, "U.S., Israel to Hold Talks on Upgrading Strategic Relations," *Boston Globe,* January 12, 1999, p. 2.

88. Ibid. On Israel's nuclear capability and its implications for U.S.-Israeli relations, see Feldman, *Future of U.S.-Israel Strategic Cooperation,* pp. 17–18; and Shai Feldman, *Nuclear Weapons and Arms Control in the Middle East* (Cambridge: MIT Press, 1997).

89. Zernike, "U.S., Israel to Hold Talks," p. 2.

90. Ibid.

91. Ibid.

92. Ibid.

93. Jane Perlez, "Clinton to Press Syria to Reopen Talks with Israel," *New York Times*, July 20, 1999.

94. Ibid. Under a new formula to restructure U.S. aid to Israel, the administration outlined a plan whereby the United States would phase out economic assistance, now $1.2 billion a year, while increasing military aid. Israel now receives $1.8 billion a year in military assistance. Over the next ten years, this would be increased to $2.4 billion a year.

95. Deborah Sontag, "Sharon Cautions West Against Aid to Syria in Any Peace Deal," *New York Times*, March 1, 2000.

96. Ibid.

97. James A. Baker III, "Peace, One Step at a Time," *New York Times*, July 27, 2000.

98. See statements by the newly appointed secretary of state, General Colin Powell, and the national security adviser, Condoleezza Rice, respectively in Steven Erlanger, "A Higher Threshold for U.S. Intervention Means Adjustments Abroad," *New York Times*, December 18, 2000, and "Promoting the National Interest," *Foreign Affairs*, January–February 2000.

99. Jane Perlez, "Bush Officials Pronounce Clinton Mideast Plan Dead," *New York Times*, February 9, 2001.

100. Jane Perlez, "Powell Stresses Responsibility of Mideast Policy," *New York Times*, March 20, 2001.

101. Perlez, "Clinton Mideast Plan Dead."

102. Jane Perlez, "Bush Team's Counsel Is Divided on Foreign Policy," *New York Times*, March 27, 2001. This has become more pronounced within the Bush administration following the September 11, 2001, terror attacks on the United States.

103. William A. Orme Jr., "Sharon Starts Out by Trying to Assemble a Coalition," *New York Times*, February 8, 2001.

104. Marc Lacey, "Bush Condemns Attack and Calls for End to Mideast Violence," *New York Times*, February 15, 2001.

105. See *Al-Hayat*, March 11, 2001.

106. Jane Perlez, "Powell Proposes Easing Sanctions on Iraqi Civilians," *New York Times*, February 27, 2001.

107. See *Al-Hayat*, March 31, 2001.

108. Alan Sipress and Colum Lynch, "U.S. Avoids Confronting Syrians on Iraqi Oil," *Washington Post*, February 14, 2002.

109. Jane Perlez, "Bush and Sharon Find Much in Common," *New York Times*, March 21, 2001.

110. Nitzan Horowitz and Daniel Sobelman, "Bush Calls Asad," *Ha'aretz* (Internet edition), March 18, 2001.

111. Ibid.

112. Deborah Sontag, "Seventeen Hurt in Hit-and-Run Rush Hour Attack," *New York Times*, February 15, 2001.

113. Jane Perlez, "Bush Hammers Arafat; Takes a Softer Tone with Israel," *New York Times*, March 30, 2001. President Bush became more critical of Arafat following suicide bombings in Israel carried out by Palestinian extremists.

114. CBS News, "Bush Backs Palestinian State," www.cbsnews.com/stories/2001/09/03/world/main313042.shtml.

115. See Secretary Powell's Louisville speech on the State Department website, www.state.gov/secretary/rm/2001.

116. James Risen, "New Allies Help C.I.A. in Its Fight Against Terror," *New York Times,* October 30, 2001.

117. Neil MacFarQuhar, "Syria Repackages Its Repression of Muslim Militants as Antiterror Lesson," *New York Times,* January 14, 2002.

118. For the names of congressional leaders who visited or are planning to visit Damascus, see *Al-Hayat,* January 7 and January 17, 2002.

119. For a complete view of Syria's stand on the issue of terrorism, see its official position with respect to UN Security Resolution 1373, which created a UN committee to combat terror, in *Al-Hayat,* January 3, 2002.

4

Syria: Peacemaking and Domestic Politics

It should be evident that the large efforts invested by the United States to bring about a substantive and lasting resolution of the conflict between Syria and Israel have not born fruit as yet. The historical factors contributing to this unfortunate situation are many and complex. Most important among them are complicated domestic situations producing conflicting impulses, pressures, and constraints that affect the movement toward peace in contradictory ways.

Chapters 4 and 5 will be devoted, therefore, to an account of the domestic conditions that the governments of Syria and Israel have to contend with respectively as they act, choose, and make policies concerning peace with each other.

Politico-Economic Considerations

As noted in Chapter 1, during the French mandate over Syria, French policy favored the recruitment of minorities in the Troupes Speciales du Levant, which evolved, after Syrian independence, into the Syrian army. The Alawis in the army were gradually able to consolidate their position partly due to the numerous army purges that decreased at first Sunni and later on Druze and Ismaili representation in the upper echelons of the officer corps.[1] This process unfolded more systematically after the military-Ba'th seizure of power on March 8, 1963. The new leadership, deprived of mainstream urban support, expanded its political base of support to the rural classes, which cut across religious sectarian lines, and pursued two broad but complementary policies to secure its hold on power. The first sought to augment the numbers of military and civilian personnel of rural extraction in the Ba'thi state—mostly favoring Alawi recruitment—while the second worked on setting up "popular organizations" (general peasant unions, a general federation of trade unions, teacher unions, etc.) as a means of mobilizing popular support across the whole country.[2] This attempt to penetrate the whole of Syrian civil society was coupled with a policy of economic nationalization and land reform, which destroyed the economic basis of the bourgeoisie and curbed the power of the landed aristocracy.

What showed these policies to be more or less successful was the resulting political fragmentation of Syrian society, conspicuously revealed when the Ba'thi regime lost the 1967 war but faced no serious threat to its rule. As explained in Chapters 1 and 2, in November 1970, then–defense minister Hafiz al-Asad, who supported a nationalist policy that advocated Arab cooperation and gave priority to the armed struggle against Israel, ousted, in a bloodless coup, Salah Jadid, who supported a leftist radical transformation of Syrian society. Asad's immediate concerns were to break Syria out of its regional isolation and win the support of the urban bourgeoisie. On the one hand, Asad embraced the Ba'th Party's ideological commitment to pan-Arabism, which not only transcended tribal, regional, and sectarian differences in Syria but also gave him the ideological legitimacy to win over the different segments of the population, especially the Sunnis. This was translated into building a consensus on a political program that revolved around confronting Israel. Arab nationalism and military confrontation with Israel became the twin pillars of the regime's policies.

On the other hand, Asad set about to restructure the political system by introducing economic and political reforms. First he relaxed the previous control of the state over economic activity and partially liberalized trade in order to strike a modus vivendi with the bourgeoisie, especially that of Damascus, who were happy with the overthrow of the radical Jadid regime. Then he appointed a parliament in 1971, established the Progressive National Front (PNF) in 1972, and promulgated a "permanent" constitution in 1973. The explicit function of the PNF was to rally the progressive forces in Syria around the Ba'th Party in the interest of confronting Israel.[3] The preamble of the Syrian constitution emphasized the revolutionary direction of the Ba'th, establishing a nexus between the national and socialist struggle, the unity of Arab republics, and the struggle against colonialism and Zionism.[4] The obvious reason of these laws was to strengthen the link between Arab nationalism and military confrontation with Israel, underpinning it with Ba'thi ideology and socialist economy. This is what constituted the external raison d'être of the regime.

These reforms came to be known as the "corrective movement." They created the formal structure of the regime by which Syrian politics have been conducted. The formal structure comprised several institutions and organizations: (1) the presidency, to which the constitution gave vast powers, (2) the cabinet, whose ministers represented the Ba'th Party and the PNF, (3) the Ba'th Party, which the constitution decreed as "the vanguard party in the society and state," (4) the leadership of the PNF, (5) the Majlis al-Sha'b, or the

parliament, and (6) the popular organizations, which according to the constitution comprised the popular forces striving for the progress of society.[5]

However, power resided in an informal structure based on a nexus
between the mostly Alawi officers, the Ba'th Party, and regime loyalists,
which constituted the inner circle of the president and the network attached to
it. This group has controlled the functioning of the formal structure. But the
essence of these reforms was to legitimize the regime and institutionalize it.
While the army, the Ba'th Party, and bureaucracy constituted the primary base
of support for the regime, the formal structure served to expand that base to
reach all segments of Syrian society. In a way the formal structure, especially
the parliament, the PNF, and the popular organizations, along with the public
sector, played a multidimensional role, that of mobilization, control, and representation, leading to the co-opting of potential opposition. The greater its
expansion, the more the regime widened its base of support.

For example, the Arab Socialist Party, the Arab Socialist Unionist Party,
the Arab Communist Party, the Syrian Arab Socialist Union Party, the Unionist Socialist Democratic Party, and the Union Socialist Party have all joined the
vanguard party—the Ba'th—to form the PNF. But by opting for political participation and legality, the PNF parties have given up much of their independence and of course their potential for opposition. The parliament represented
the Ba'th Party apparatus and leadership along with the PNF parties, the popular organizations, the religious establishment, and the commerce and industry
chambers. In 1990 the parliament was enlarged from 195 to 250 members.
One-third of the seats have been reserved for independent deputies. While the
PNF has kept its majority and control of the parliament, the independent elements represented social forces that hitherto had not been represented.

As a rentier state with a "socialist" system, Syria controlled and divided
its economy along functional lines. The regime developed the popular organizations into hierarchical, quasigovernmental bodies to uphold the national
priorities of the state. The peasant union has represented the peasants; the
trade unions have represented all workers in the public sector; and the teachers, artisans, writers and all other unions and associations have represented the
segment of society corresponding to their respective functional purpose.
These organizations, however, have been the perfect fronts for mobilization
and control of Syrian society at large.[6]

The expansion of state institutions and popular organizations went hand
in hand with the growth of both the public sector and of course the military
institutions. The expansion of the political base of support of the regime did
not depend only on co-optation and representation. The regime has had no
qualms about using whatever means at its disposal to squelch any opposition,
from arbitrary arrests, to long-term imprisonment, to assassination. Battling
the Muslim Brotherhood (1976–1982, more on this below), the regime waged
an indiscriminate, brutal war in the city of Hama that left thousands dead.[7]

In addition, the regime filled the formal structure with Sunni appointees and sustained a balance, on the one hand, among the various organs of the formal and informal structures, and on the other hand, among the elites to keep Asad's absolute power overarching. The vice presidents, Abd al-Halim Khaddam and Muhammad Zuhair Mashariqa; the former and present prime ministers, Mahmoud Zubi and Muhammad Mustafa Miro; the deputy prime minister and defense minister, Mustafa Tlas; and the foreign minister, Farouk al-Shara, are all Sunni Muslims. This reflected the genuine need of the regime to conspicuously depict the state as nonsectarian, while at the same time gaining the compliance of the predominant Sunni majority. Through their control of the army, party, and security apparatus, and their closeness to Asad's decisionmaking process, the Alawi officials in the informal structure have guaranteed the survival of the regime and have controlled the functioning of the formal structure. But their wings can be clipped if they overstep their boundaries. At one time, an influential personality, the brother of Asad, Rifa't, who commanded the then–praetorian guard, the defense companies (brigades), was exiled along with high-ranking Alawi officers in 1984 for questioning the policies laid down by Asad when he had suffered a heart attack.[8]

What made possible the expansion of the regime's political base of support was in large part Syria's strategic position in the regional balance of power, which revolved around confronting Israel. As a confrontational state, Syria had been able to benefit from its strategic and regional position and military credibility by receiving significant military and nonmilitary aid from the Arab countries and the former Soviet Union since the 1973 war. This allowed Syria to invest in the military institutions to enhance its strategic position. The nonmilitary aid went to finance public investments. In fact, immediately after the 1973 war, a vast inflow of capital from Arab countries, supplemented with a strong rise in oil rent, inflated Syrian budgets. Ambitious development projects proliferated and Asad had at his disposal the wherewithal to begin expanding the state's army, party, public sector, and popular organizations.

After the 1973 war and especially after 1979, when Egypt signed the peace treaty with Israel, Syria became the confrontational state of note in the region. Its arms imports were paid mainly by the Arab Gulf states (and Libya) and financed by the former Soviet Union on a concessionary loan basis. Between 1973 and 1978, nonmilitary Arab financial aid averaged $600 million yearly. After the Baghdad summit in 1978, Arab aid drastically increased to Syria, which received an annual average of almost $1.6 billion during the 1979–1981 period. This aid declined to an annual average of $670 million until 1987, and dwindled to almost nothing in the years 1988 and 1989.[9] The decrease in aid was due to Syria's support of Iran in the Iran-Iraq War. However, Iran partially offset the decrease by granting Syria oil deliveries, which were reduced significantly by 1990. When Syria joined the anti-Iraq coalition in the second Gulf War, Arab aid resumed to Syria. It obtained since the beginning of 1990 nearly $3 billion in development aid.[10] Most of the funds went into infrastructural developments. In addition, Syria received from 1992 to 1996 a total of $668.4 million in net official development assistance from the Arab countries.[11]

As the evidence shows, Syria gained both economic and political advantages from its regional position. It has been able to support a hegemonic and militarily credible policy, as well as a foreign policy based primarily on confronting Israel, which produced a stable domestic policy. Simply put, domestic and foreign policies with regard to Israel have enhanced the regime's security. Therefore, one could safely conceptually argue that Syria's confrontational "dividend" from its regional position makes the regime reluctant, if not unwilling, to forego it in return for peace with Israel, which would largely pacify the region. But on closer examination, the domestic situation in Syria is more complicated and precarious, which could make the prospects of peace with Israel a direct threat to the regime's survival. A perforce economic liberalization in Syria combined with a commitment to making peace with Israel could undermine all the political structures that the regime built to support itself.

Asad's corrective movement, which had encouraged a limited private-sector role in the economy to appease the urban bourgeoisie, fared well with the expansion of the economy after 1973. Many old bourgeois families of Damascus took advantage of the new opportunities and cooperated with the regime's elite. Various elements of the private sector prospered as either contractors for the state or middlemen between the state and foreign firms. Political, business, and marriage alliances were formed between the two classes and a new bourgeoisie emerged. At its core was a military-merchant complex of Alawi officers and Damascene merchants.[12] So the regime supported a huge bureaucracy to bring about its socialist contract—provision of work—and obtain a wide societal support, while at the same time it created a new class depending on a market economy for its prosperity.

By the mid-late 1970s, oil rent had decreased and the regime found it necessary to introduce cautious economic reforms as part of its corrective movement. Laws were passed setting up mixed-sector companies in tourism and transportation to encourage private-sector activities. "Mixed" companies refers to state-private joint ventures run independently of government interference in the conduct of business. By the mid-1980s, the regime faced increased black-market imports, rising inflation, and a decrease in the value of the Syrian pound, all of which brought Syria to the verge of foreign-exchange bankruptcy. The regime again introduced reforms to encourage further private-sector activities in the economy. It passed a law in 1986 that gave considerable privileges to Syrian expatriates, and it set up mixed-sector companies in agrobusiness.[13]

Despite a certain improvement in the economy in the early 1990s, particularly after an infusion of Arab capital into Syria, the country remained cash-strapped. In addition, the Soviet Union no longer existed, depriving Syria of much material support. The regime responded by further liberalizing the economy. It passed Law no. 10 of 1991, which opened up the public sector to private investment and granted qualifying investors tax holidays and duty-free privileges for the import of capital goods.[14] The law was designed to repatriate the Syrian capital saved abroad, estimated at about U.S.$60 billion. Syria, however, remained in need of financial aid to balance its budgets. This chronic want is best illustrated by the spiraling increase of Syria's debt. The country has seen its total external debt—long-term debt and short-term debt—rise exponentially throughout the years from U.S.$3.522 billion in 1980, to U.S.$15.668 billion in 1987, to U.S.$20.577 billion in 1994, to U.S.$21.420 billion in 1996.[15] In balancing its annual general budget, the Syrian government took respectively from 1994 to 1997 foreign loans in the amounts of 24.530 billion Syrian pounds, 24.282 billion pounds, 22.396 billion pounds, and 22.184 billion pounds.[16]

One might ask what kind of reforms Syria has been undertaking that its economy continues ailing? And what is the relationship of these reforms to peace with Israel? On the surface, the regime could claim that these reforms offer representation, since they opened up the public sector to private investment and the state to political inclusion. In official Syrian parlance, this is called *ta'adudia* (economic and political pluralism). However, as we have seen, representation has been none other than a means for co-optation and containment. On a deeper level, the regime has controlled the reform process largely to prevent any bourgeois pretensions to political power. The reforms have been of an ad hoc nature, selective, and in service of the state.[17] Until spring 2000, Law no. 24, which punished private-sector foreign exchange, though rarely invoked, had not been annulled and thus far had been in conflict with Law no. 10. A multilayered foreign-exchange rate makes accounting difficult, corruption easy, and currying favor from the regime's elite the norm of business and investment procedures.[18] This situation has been aggravated by the absence of stock exchange and privately run commercial institutions.

The regime has been aware of the gradual transformation of its social basis, which has placed it in a difficult position. From the 1960s until late 1970s, rural peasants and urban workers all benefited from the Ba'thi state's land reforms and nationalization of industries. Social classes, cutting across sectarian lines, represented in government institutions and organizations and in the public sector, formed the social basis of the regime. But as the regime has been compelled to introduce reforms, the military-merchant complex has gained advantages at the expense of the public sector, gradually becoming the dominant alliance of the regime's composition. What is of great significance is that the entrepreneurial class has been gaining economic influence, which could well be translated into political influence under certain conditions. The regime has been aware of this development and has been trying to co-opt this class. The enlargement of the parliament in 1990 to include the independents, particularly the Damascene entrepreneurs, illustrates the regime's awareness.

Under these circumstances, peace with Israel will not only rob the regime of its raison d'être, but also make the justification of the maintenance of Syria's authoritarian rule and the privileges granted to the mostly Alawi military officials difficult to justify. This would weaken the leverage the Alawi officials have in their alliance with the merchants, whose own leverage consequently would strengthen. Eventually, the merchants would press for more substantial reforms to advance their economic interests and transform Syria's rustic socialist economic system. Any modicum of economic liberalization will have the effect of further enhancing the economic power of the merchant class. Equally significant, economic liberalization will create pressures for some political restructuring that will only continue to weaken the Alawi officials' leverage over their merchant allies. The regime will find it harder and harder to uphold its authoritarian structure.

As a result, on the one hand, the military-merchant complex could split, as the relationship between the two allies would become inversely proportional, leading to divergent interests. On the other hand, the regime would lose the support of the public sector, which would inescapably bear the brunt of any reforms. All this could threaten political instability.

Some scholars point out that the regime is solely concerned with its Alawi nature, which a peace with Israel will put at risk.[19] Others argue that a regional peace will partly aggravate the divergent interests of the military-merchant complex, resulting in political instability. At the heart of this hypothesis lies the concept that undertaking reforms would "greatly enhance the power of Syria's business community, split the dominant military-merchant coalition, and thus threaten political stability."[20] While both analyses have a degree of truth, particularly the second, they dismiss the role of the public sector and the popular organizations in ensuring regime stability. This is well illustrated by the regime's reluctance to trim the numbers and sizes of public-sector and popular organizations, even when it has been encouraging private activities going against their interest. Out of a labor force of less than 3.5 million, the number of members in the agricultural union in 1992 stood at 697,820; in the consumer union, 598,850; in the professional union, 3,288; in the building union, 218,410; in the social services union, 1,780; and in the transport and communications union, 45,499.[21]

I would like to point out that democratization need not follow economic liberalization in Syria. The bourgeoisie is mainly interested in stability and advancing its economic interests. And the one important thing that has to be borne in mind is that Asad's regime has provided stability and to a significant extent national integration in Syria. However, the bourgeoisie, which has been included in the political process through parliament, has been vocal in expressing Syria's need for economic reform. Witnessing the erratic pace of reforms in Syria, Riad Seif, a prominent Damascus businessman and parliament member, wrote an open letter in 1996 painting a bleak picture of Syria's economic conditions and recommending a bold agenda for change.[22] This daring act, unimaginable only few years ago, is a testimony to the enhanced status of the bourgeoisie and its platform.

It is of great value to examine further the economic and demographic conditions in Syria in the 1990s and their effect on the political decisions of the regime. The inflow of Arab aid in the early 1990s, combined with rising levels of fixed investment and oil exports, fueled Syria's economic growth from 1990 to 1995. However, after reaching a high of 10.6 percent in 1992, Syria's economic growth declined to 6.7 percent in 1994 and 1995, dropping significantly to 2.2 percent in 1996.[23] This drop was affected by lower production of oil. In addition, Syria's general budget, also an indicator of economic growth, has been steadily increasing. This increase, however, has been partly due to pegging the Syrian pound to a higher U.S. dollar conversion. For example, while the 1997 budget showed an increase of 23.075 billion Syrian pounds over the preceding year and the 1998 budget showed an increase of 26.175 billion pounds over 1997, the real change has come from a conversion of 1 U.S. dollar to 35 Syrian pounds in 1997 rather than 23 pounds (conversion rate of 1996), and to 45.5 pounds in 1998.[24]

Although the government explained this method of calculating the budget as a means to unify foreign-exchange rates, it artificially inflated the budget. Meanwhile, while Syria's level of fixed investment has been falling and Arab aid dwindling, Syria has become more dependent on its oil exports, which accounted for 63.3 percent of the value of exports in 1996 and 20 percent of gross domestic product (GDP). Agriculture has remained the largest contributor to Syrian economic activity, accounting for approximately 26 percent of GDP.[25] Consequently, the Syrian economy in large measure has become vulnerable to erratic or harsh natural conditions, which could affect harvests, and to falling oil prices and/or production. Equally significant, the economy has been suffering from a high inflation, estimated at 20 percent.[26] Inflation has eroded any gains in Syrian budgets, as well as the buying power of the salaried middle class, who have constituted the bulk of Syria's work force. Syria's trade balance, which could increase foreign exchange, had shown negative bottom lines. While Syria's trade balance (exports versus imports) showed a surplus of 7.438 billion Syrian pounds in 1991, from 1992 to 1996 its trade balance showed a continuous deficit, reaching 27.123 billion pounds in 1994 and 15.498 billion pounds in 1996.[27]

At the same time, Syria's population has been exploding, with a growth of slightly over 3 percent per year. Its population was over 6 million in 1970, increasing to over 9 million in 1981, 13 million in 1994, and 15 million in 1997. Most of Syria's population is under 30 years of age. In 1994 the age groups ranging from 5 to 9, from 10 to 14, and from 15 to 19, constituted the bulk of the population, numbering respectively 2.1 million, 2.0 million, and approximately 1.6 million. The level of urbanization has been high, reflecting the growth of urban centers especially in Damascus, Aleppo, Homs, and

Hama. In 1994, Damascus had 22.7 percent of the total population, followed by Aleppo at 21.4 percent, Homs at 8.8 percent, and Hama at 7.9 percent.[28]

Population growth, a high level of urbanization, and the cash-strapped economy have put great pressure on the government to create jobs and sustain stability. However, the regime has not followed up on Law no. 10; no significant reforms to improve the country's economic conditions have been introduced. In fact, because of bureaucratic red tape, only 775 projects out of 1,177 granted permits under Law no. 10 have been implemented.[29]

The reasons lay squarely in the fact that reforms have benefited the merchant bourgeoisie more than any other group in Syria. This became highly disturbing for the regime at a time when it committed itself to peace negotiations with Israel, and thus might have robbed itself of its own raison d'être. The conflict with Israel had been the main pretext under which the regime controlled the slowly but surely increasing economic strength of the Syrian bourgeoisie, preventing it from translating that strength into political clout and power-sharing arrangements. The regime thus found itself in the quandary of wanting to maintain the military's highly privileged position at a time when the justification for such a position seemed to be eroding. This is aggravated by the fact that the dominant faction in the military, the Alawis, never succeeded in creating a business class of their own.[30] It is interesting to note the coincidence that no economic reforms were introduced in Syria during negotiations with Israel. The regime confined itself to the same contradictory policies, represented by its efforts to co-opt the bourgeoisie on the one hand, and to ensure the loyalty of the public sector and the popular organizations on the other. In this respect, as the evidence shows, perforce piecemeal reforms were introduced only to maintain regime stability and to deny any bourgeois pretension to power. It is this intricate and complex situation in Syria that acted as an obstacle to peace with Israel, because peace not only would weaken the Alawi military class vis-à-vis the merchant bourgeoisie, but also would prevent the regime from cashing in on its regional strategic position—that is, the regime would lose its confrontational dividend, at a time when its needs are significant in the face of the country's chronic economic condition. In any case, peace or no peace with Israel, Syria will have to enact major economic reforms if it is not to be marginalized in a rapidly changing Middle East.

Lebanon as a *Qutr?*

As we have seen in Chapter 2, Syria achieved a crowning success in Lebanon. The Asad regime viewed Lebanon as both a foreign and a domestic policy matter, since it combines geostrategic concerns with internal power considerations for Syria. Lebanon served the Asad regime tremendously in many different ways, as a medium of political and military leverage against Israel, as a patronage system to reward the regime's loyalists, and as an outlet to relieve internal politico-economic pressures. The regime has been eagerly trying to entrench its presence in Lebanon and to bring the country irreversibly within its sphere of influence, if not as an integral part of Syria, then as a quasi-colony. As I shall show, regional peace has the potential of changing the dynamics of the Lebanese-Syrian relationship, undermining Syria's elite cohesion.

The Taif Accord spelled out the future nature of Lebanon's relations with Syria, special as they were, basing them on roots of kinship, history, and common fraternal interests. But it was the Treaty of Brotherhood, Cooperation, and Coordination, signed in May 1991 between the two countries, that governed their relations since then by defining a framework that made possible the "colonization" of Lebanon by Syria.[31] The language of the treaty's preamble smacks of Ba'thi ideological expressions that emphasize the "distinctive brotherly ties" between the two sides. In its first article, the treaty calls for the highest levels of cooperation and coordination between the two states in political, economic, security, cultural, scientific, and other areas. Article 3 emphasizes the interconnectedness of the security of the two countries, which "requires that Lebanon never constitute a source of threat to Syria's security and vice versa under any circumstances whatsoever." The article adds that "Lebanon shall not become a passageway or a base for any power, state, or organization aiming to violate its security or that of Syria," and that "Syria, which desires the security, independence and unity of Lebanon and harmony among its people, shall not allow any action that threatens Lebanon's security, independence and sovereignty."[32]

Article 3 is formulated in a way that guarantees Syria the right of intervention in Lebanon. It gives the former the right to defend the sovereignty of Lebanon according to Syria's evaluation of the impending threat, as if Lebanon had delegated to its neighbor the power to do so. This is bolstered by the lack of any reciprocity: Lebanon undertakes not to become a source of threat to Syria's security while the latter undertakes no similar obligation toward Lebanon. Article 5 defines the basis upon which the two countries will pursue their foreign policies: "Each shall support the other in matters relating to its security and its national interests. . . . The governments of the two countries shall therefore strive to coordinate their Arab and international policies."[33] Finally, Article 6 creates a Higher Council composed of the leaders of the two countries that defines this general policy of coordination and cooperation and oversees its implementation. It also designates a number of committees to deal with all aspects of this cooperation (foreign affairs, economic and social affairs, defense and security affairs, etc.), with specific tasks spelled out. Clearly, the conspicuous aim of the Higher Council and its committees is to institutionalize these lopsided relations between the two countries. Since Syria is the senior partner, this institutionalization allows Syria to dominate the Lebanese decisionmaking process.

This treaty served as a baseline for a slew of agreements that have put Lebanon in the shadow of the Syrian state. In August 1991 the two countries signed a defense and security agreement that allows Syria to intervene in an unprecedented way in Lebanese internal affairs, infringing on the country's sovereignty. The agreement "prohibits all organized activities in the military, security, political and media realms the purpose of which is to harm and damage the other country."[34] The agreement also "binds the two sides to offer no refuge, passageway or protection to persons or organizations working against the security of the other country," and states that such persons shall "be arrested and handed over upon request."[35] With Syria as the hegemonic state, this agreement goes to the heart of Lebanon's civil society, for it not only allows Syria to extradite Lebanese or other oppositional figures deemed subversive by Syria, but also allows Syria to muzzle any criticism directed at the regime, particularly in the Lebanese media, curtailing free speech.[36]

Coinciding with the signing of the Oslo Accords (September 1993), the Syrians unveiled four agreements with Lebanon: a social and economic cooperation agreement, an agricultural cooperation agreement, a health agreement, and an agreement on the movement of individuals and goods.[37] In line with the others, these agreements have worked well for Syria's benefit. Interestingly enough, Lebanon was referred to as a *qutr* (province or region). Simone Ghazi Tinaoui notes that in the minutes of the meeting held on September 1993 for the signature of the social and economic cooperation agreement, Lebanon is officially described, for the first time, as a *qutr*.[38] The word has a symbolic meaning in Ba'thi ideology, as it denotes that all Arab states are no more than provinces in a potentially united Arab nation, with the added implication in this context that Lebanon is merely a province of Syria.

The barrage of agreements did not stop. Several were unveiled in 1994: an Orontes River agreement, a cultural agreement, a labor agreement, and a tourism agreement. These agreements reveal again the scope and extent of Syrian-Lebanese relations in the direction of deepening and reinforcing Syrian control of Lebanon, while enhancing the economic and political stability of Asad's regime. For example, in the past Lebanon and Syria had not been able to agree on sharing the waters of the Orontes, which springs from Lebanon and runs through Syria. In the 1950s, Lebanon proposed exploiting 250 million cubic meters, or almost 40 percent, of the river's waters, a proposal rejected then by the Syrians. Under the new agreement, Lebanon will be allowed to use only 80 million cubic meters to irrigate the arid Hermel region.[39]

The cultural agreement encourages all aspects of cultural cooperation and coordination between the two countries, including establishing joint cultural organizations, facilitating the entrance of printed matter to each other's countries, and producing joint cultural and artistic ventures, such as films and plays, with a view to serving "the common cultural, civilizational and national aspirations of the two neighbors."[40] This agreement seeks to blend the two cultures, blurring Lebanon's cultural distinctiveness. The labor agreement is the culmination of several attempts to remove travel barriers between the two countries, facilitating the entrance of Syrian labor into Lebanon. The agreement also seeks to legalize the status of the large number of Syrian workers in Lebanon, many of whom are working illegally there.[41]

Lebanon has become an oasis of opportunity for the unemployed in Syria, whose number, due to Syria's high population growth, is increasing at a fast rate. Estimates differ on the number of Syrian workers in Lebanon, ranging from 300,000 to 900,000.[42] The controversy over this number has been further complicated by the fact that the Lebanese government had already naturalized a significant number of long-term residents, many of whom are Syrians.[43] This step will have important repercussions on the demographic structure of Lebanon in terms of disrupting the delicate confessional balance, considering that the Lebanese Christians have a century-old legacy of emigration. The labor agreement facilitates and legalizes the status of Syrian illegal laborers in Lebanon and entitles them to the same treatment and rights as Lebanese workers.[44] This migrant work force has siphoned hard currency out of Lebanon, negatively affecting the country's balance of payments, while positively affecting that of Syria.

The tourism agreement simplifies and rationalizes administrative procedures for traveling between and to the countries, apparently aiming at the creation of a single tourism zone for both. It also refers to Syria and Lebanon as the *al-qutrayn al-taw'amayn,* meaning the twin provinces or regions.[45]

Other agreements emerged coinciding with the delicate Israeli-Syrian negotiations at the Wye Plantation in Maryland in January 1996. While shrouded in secrecy, these agreements focused on strengthening economic ties and on sharing water resources. However, their character evoked a daring response from the Lebanese editor in chief of *Al-Nahar,* Ghassan Tueini, who criticized the whole span of Syrian moves aiming at "unifying" the two countries.[46] Other agreements followed regarding the free exchange of products and unification of tariffs between the two countries.[47] And in October 1999, in a show of respect to Asad, most of Lebanon's ministers traveled to Damascus to sign yet more accords on farm produce and tourism. This time it was the turn of Jibran Tueini, son of Ghassan and managing director of *Al-Nahar,* to speak out against Syrian efforts to swallow up Lebanon. In an open letter addressed to Bashar al-Asad (at the time heir apparent and in charge of Lebanese affairs), Jibran openly declared that many Lebanese were neither comfortable with Syrian policy nor comfortable with the Syrian presence in Lebanon, and that Lebanon was not a Syrian province.[48]

As my research concerning these agreements shows, Syria is indeed "colonizing" Lebanon in a subtle way. This has been done with the objective of drawing economic and political dividends in the interest of the stability of Asad's regime. From the start, Syria had used Lebanon as a system of patronage to reward its loyalists. Legally and administratively privileged in Lebanon,

Syria offers its almost 40,000 troops (and an unknown number of Mukhabarat) an unmatched opportunity to supplement their meager incomes, whether from legal or illegal activities, such as drug smuggling and rackets. Syrian interventions and intercessions *(wasta)* are needed to secure and expedite such transactions. For example, high-ranking military officials have allegedly amassed illicit fortunes from the drug trade in Lebanon. According to a report of the U.S. Congressional Committee on the Judiciary, these Syrian beneficiaries include Defense Minister Mustafa Tlas; General Ali Dubah, the commander of Syrian military intelligence; General Ghazi Kenaan, the commander of Syrian military intelligence in Lebanon; and Rifa't al-Asad, the famous brother of the Syrian president.[49]

Politically controlled, but with an open capitalist market, Lebanon has taken the pressure off the Ba'thi regime to liberalize the Syrian economy, preventing the enhancement of the power of the merchant bourgeoisie there. Responding to the bourgeoisie's calls for introducing more reforms (particularly in the banking industry), the Ba'thi regime has one thing to say to them: "You have Lebanon, go transact your business and invest there."[50] And indeed, this is what the Syrian merchants have been doing. This has allowed the Alawi officials to maintain leverage in the merchant-military complex, while at the same time satisfying the capitalist needs of their merchant allies to prosper. Meanwhile, the Ba'thi regime has safeguarded itself against any of the bourgeoisie's pretensions to power, while keeping the public sector under the control of the state and thus maintaining its support.

Peace with Israel will undoubtedly put Syrian interests in Lebanon at risk and thus may very well disrupt the stability of the Ba'thi regime. In the event of a peace treaty, Syria will have no reason to keep its military in Lebanon. It will come under Lebanese, regional, and international pressure to withdraw its troops in accordance with the Taif Accord. Once the troops are out, the Syrian officials, particularly the Alawis, will lose much of their military clout with the Lebanese merchants (in part under the guise of protection) and much of their ability to transact legal as well as illegal activities, and thus forfeit all *wasta*-related income. Equally significant is the fact that the regime will lose Lebanon both as a system of patronage to reward loyalists, and as an economic sop for the merchant bourgeoisie. Herein lies the dilemma for the Syrian regime.

On the one hand, peace will make Syria face the formidable challenge of creating alternative means for rewarding its loyal military officers, especially at a time when the state will lose its primary, confrontational position. On the other hand, the regime will no longer be able to point to Lebanon as a "backdoor" for the economic liberalization of Syria, prompting the merchant bourgeoisie to make Syria the focus of its demands for economic liberalization. In addition, Lebanon will certainly become more restrictive toward the Syrian migrant work force, especially in locations where it has enjoyed significant privileges thanks largely to the ubiquitous presence of the Syrian army there.

Therefore, if the Ba'thi regime contemplates withdrawing its troops from Lebanon following a peace treaty with Israel, it will run the risk of (1) facing resistance from many Alawi officials who stand to lose economic and political resources from Lebanon, (2) becoming the focus of pressure from the merchant class to introduce substantial reforms, and (3) losing hands-on control over an economy employing a significant number of Syrian laborers. All this will have the potential of straining elite cohesion and undermining political stability in Syria itself.

One could argue that all those bilateral agreements between the two countries would protect Syrian interests in Lebanon and turn the country into a sort of economic and political compensation for the negative effects of a regional peace. This is highly speculative, as the Ba'thi regime knows very well that it lacks significant numbers of admirers on the whole Lebanese popular spectrum and that it faces a vibrant civil society that rarely condones the authoritarian nature of Syrian rule.[51] Oppositional voices to Syria's hegemony in Lebanon have been subdued and fragmented but not silenced, particularly that of the Maronites. During the 1990s, for example, notwithstanding the opposition outside Lebanon (Amin Jumayil, Michel Aoun, and Raymond Edde), the Maronite patriarch Nasrallah Boutros Sfeir has been vocal in expressing his reservations about Syria's upper hand in Lebanon. In an interview with *Al-Wasat,* Sfeir stated: "We want brotherly relations with Syria but between two independent states."[52] In fact, this Maronite attitude has sharpened after the unilateral Israeli withdrawal from Lebanon in May 2000, pulling the legitimization rug from underneath Syrian feet in Beirut. Many Christians, supported by the Druze leadership, have called on Syria to redeploy in preparation for its withdrawal.[53]

Based on my research and experience in Lebanon, a withdrawal of the Syrian troops from the country will diminish to a significant extent Syrian power there. This diminution will be balanced by the cumulative effect of the bilateral agreements between the two countries. A consensus will probably emerge about letting Lebanon run its own domestic affairs, with special consideration given to Lebanese-Syrian "brotherly" relations, while Syria will have the final say in Lebanon's foreign policy, especially when it comes to Syria's vital national interests. In this scenario, the challenges to the Ba'thi regime noted above will still apply. As such, the Lebanese issue could form an obstacle to regional peace, as it will deprive the Ba'thi regime of economic and political resources needed for its stability.

The Islamist Opposition

The Syrian Islamists have been the radical opponents of the Ba'thi state since its inception. This opposition goes back to the early mid-1960s and was led by the Muslim Brotherhood, who resented Ba'thi secularism, minority dominance, and attempts to nationalize key sectors of the Syrian economy. The Muslim Brotherhood forged an alliance with the urban bourgeoisie, whose power the regime was trying to curb. A local incident in Hama was transformed by the city's imams into an insurrection against the regime. The Ba'thi rulers quelled the insurrection by force. Although the regime weathered the crisis, its tenuous hold on power was exposed.[54] It was at this time that the regime began to consolidate its rule through the expansion and organization of the bureaucracy and the popular organizations.

The respective establishment and reorganization of new and existing state institutions touched all spheres of Syrian societal life except the suq (market or bazaar). Despite the regime's efforts to recast the organs of society along functional lines, and despite the expansion of both the bureaucracy and the popular organizations, the suq maintained its relative autonomy from the state. It is the place where the traditional urban quarters and markets have fused with the religious institutions and trading economy. The ulema, the learned men of Islam, and the heads of religious institutions commanded a pious following in the suq. Since they were not "organized in a state controlled hierarchy comparable to al-Azhar, the Ulema retained considerable autonomy of and capacity to resist the regime."[55]

By 1976–1977, discontent with and reservations about the Asad regime were almost endemic in the urban areas. A crippled trading economy exacerbated by high inflation and an interventionist policy in Lebanon on behalf of the Maronite Christians and against the Muslims, pushed the Muslim Brotherhood to again lead the opposition against the regime. Violence broke out in the form of assassinations of Alawi officials and regime supporters, and the use of car bombs to attack Ba'th Party and government offices. The Islamist activists operated in different parts of Syria, especially the cities. By the late 1970s, the opposition seemed to hold the initiative and the regime appeared unable to stem the tide of violence and was in danger of collapsing.

A tougher stance was adopted toward the Muslim Brotherhood, at the Ba'th Party's Seventh Regional Congress during December 1979–January 1980. Behind this new stance was Asad's brother, Rif'at, who called for an all-out war against the terrorists. According to Patrick Seale, Rif'at declared that "what was demanded was absolute loyalty: Those who were not with the regime must now be considered against it. The Ba'thist state had to be defended, in blood if necessary."[56] After the congress, the regime wasted no time and began to purge all skeptical elements within its ranks and to secure its base of support by substantially raising military and civil service salaries, and setting up militias of the party and the popular organizations.

Meantime, the Muslim Brothers expanded their offensive by instigating and staging large-scale urban uprisings. Aleppo's business quarter shut down in March 1980, and open defiance spread to Homs, Hama, and many other cities. Damascus, at this critical juncture, due to the efforts of Badr al-Din al-Shallah, the head of the chamber of commerce there, kept its business quarter open. According to Seale, this turned the tide in favor of the regime.[57] Apparently, the modus vivendi struck between the regime and the Damascus urban bourgeoisie paid off.

The wrath of the regime climaxed when Asad narrowly escaped an assassination attempt in June 1980. The reaction was a gory, merciless campaign against the Brotherhood. The regime was able to quell and expunge the opposition in most parts of Syria. However, with its strong religious roots and historical defiance of the center, Hama remained a bastion of opposition. Meanwhile, the Brotherhood released a document titled *Declaration and Program of the Islamic Revolution in Syria* on September 11, 1980.[58] They accused the regime of sectarianism and contended that one of the mocking acts of this sectarianism was the promotion of Asad, defense minister at the time, who was directly responsible for the defeat in the 1967 war, to the highest office in the land. They also contended that the true battle of the "Islamic Revolution" was with the Zionists, and that the struggle against the sectarian regime was but a prelude to that decisive fight. According to the declaration, the Syrian regime was brought about anyway to act as a front that distracts the people of Syria and diverts them from their real battle with the Zionists.[59]

After five years of battling the opposition, the regime had failed to stamp out the underground movement of the Brotherhood, now centered in Hama, a testimony to their entrenched power. When Hama rebelled in February 1982, the regime knew that its survival depended on totally crushing the insurrection. Special units led by loyalist Alawi commanders (such as Ali Dib, Ali Haydar, Nadim Abbas, Shafiq Fayyad, Fu'ad Ismail, and Yahya Zaydan) were dispatched to Hama and backed by the Ba'thi militias. The battle for Hama raged for over a month. The regime used scorched-earth tactics, employing indiscriminate, brute force that left thousands dead and bulldozed almost a quarter of the city to rubble.[60] The regime won the day.

After Hama, opposition to the Syrian regime was reduced to insignificance, without completely vanishing. Despite its defeat, the Syrian Muslim Brotherhood continued to be active in the Arab world, particularly in Jordan, lingering as a potential threat to the regime. Unable to confront the regime directly, the Brotherhood tried mobilizing segments of the population through continuous and unabated propaganda campaigns. The basis of such campaigns was the charge that Asad's regime was not only sectarian but also a Zionist collaborator. *Al-Nadhir*, the mouthpiece of the Brotherhood, emphasized at one time that a U.S.-Zionist plan made the reinforcement of Asad's sectarian (barbarian) regime a priority, for it perpetrated what no one else except Genghis Khan, Timorlene, and Hulaku had perpetrated against the Syrian people.[61] In addition, the Brotherhood continued to be vocal in expressing its objective of dislodging the regime. In the same publication, a declaration by the Brotherhood's consultative council affirmed the movement's continuing armed struggle against the regime until its overthrow.[62] In 1990, Ali Sadr al-Din al-Bianouni, then deputy controller-general of the Brotherhood, confirmed the movement's position on overthrowing the regime, using all means available.[63]

This unrelenting position made the regime ever more careful and anxious to monitor all oppositional efforts conducted by the Brotherhood. This borderline paranoia on the part of many regime officials was due to the fact that the regime had barely escaped the Brotherhood's onslaught and survived only by waging a vicious and murderous campaign. Despite the stability and the large measure of national integration that the Asad regime brought to Syria, the political and social repercussions of its monstrous Hama campaign are still too fresh in the collective memory of the Syrians to be overlooked, particularly by the regime itself. This is exacerbated by the fact that the majority of the population is Sunni and the Alawi officials wield the real power in the country. The regime, understandably, fears that under certain circumstances the Brotherhood might strike again a chord with the urban population and foment dissent.

The one scenario that could play into the hands of the Brotherhood is the regime's readiness to conclude a peace treaty with Israel. Once a treaty is signed, the Brotherhood could claim that all its charges against the regime were true. It could then assume the high moral and political ground and try to mobilize oppositional elements against the regime. This scenario was not overlooked by Asad. In fact, during the 1990s he pursued a policy based on preemptively foiling the Brotherhood's expected attempts to foment dissent.

When the Oslo Accords between the Israelis and the PLO were signed in 1993, most Islamist groups in the Arab world were united in condemning them. This position had not changed, despite certain breakthroughs in the peace process. Fathi al-Shiqaqi, secretary-general of the Palestinian Islamic Jihad (PIJ; Al-Jihad al-Islami fi Filastin), not only opposed the Oslo Accords but also questioned the legitimacy of the peace negotiations.[64] Islamic Jihad had been behind terrorist bombings in Israel to torpedo the peace process. Shiqaqi claimed responsibility for the Beit Lid junction bombing in Israel on January 22, 1995, while peace negotiations were under way. He boasted: "It gives satisfaction to our people."[65] Ramadan Abdallah Shalah, who replaced Shiqaqi after his assassination in 1995, adopted his predecessor's policy, declaring that the Israelis should expect new strikes.[66] The Muslim Brotherhood in Jordan joined Hamas (Harakat al-Mujtama' al-Islami, or the Palestinian-Islamic Resistance Movement) in questioning the legitimacy of the Oslo negotiations as well. They even declared that every agreement with the "enemy" should be regarded as a betrayal of God, the prophet Muhammad, the Arab nation, and the Muslim people.[67] They criticized harshly the Israeli-Jordanian agreement, signed in 1994, and rejected any dialogue with Israel.[68] A few years after that agreement, the superintendent-general of Jordan's Brotherhood, Shaikh Abd al-Majid Zuneibat, not only opposed normalization with Israel but also stated that the agreement itself—with God's permission—would vanish.[69]

In much the same vein as Islamic Jihad, Hamas has sponsored terrorist bombings in Israel. During the 1990s, Hizbollah fought Israel in the south of Lebanon and promoted itself as the vanguard of Islamic resistance. Hizbollah's spiritual leader, Muhammad Husayn Fadlallah, delegitimized Israel's existence, whether in the south of Lebanon or in Palestine.[70] At the height of the Israeli-Syrian negotiations in 1996, Fadlallah stressed that "Islamists reject Israel's legitimacy and believe that a peace based on justice can only be achieved when the Jews, who came from faraway regions of the world, leave and the Palestinians return to Palestine."[71] Fadlallah's position mirrors that of Iran.

Many of these Islamist groups have found a safe haven of support from an unusual quarter: Syria. Ironically, the authoritarian, secular Ba'thi state, which fiercely battled the Muslim Brotherhood, has been giving political support to Islamic Jihad, Hamas, and Hizbollah, along with hosting the headquarters of Islamic Jihad, as well as an office for Hamas.[72] Meanwhile, the regime has been making an effort to enhance its image in the Muslim world by participating in Islamic conferences organized by the Islamic Conference Organization (ICO), sponsored by Muslim and Arab states. The platform of the ICO addresses issues of concern to the Muslim world ranging from the ideological to the economic, including the projection of an improved and more palatable image of Islam to the West. For example, Damascus hosted the conference of the ICO ministers of information in May 1994. The main theme of the meeting centered on correcting the image of Islam in the Western media. High-ranking Syrian officials have always attended ICO conferences.[73]

In addition to supporting non-Syrian radical groups and putting on a pious face, the Ba'thi regime has been trying, with a significant measure of success, to co-opt the moderate Islamists inside the country. The mufti of Syria, Shaikh Ahmad Kaftaro, and the religious scholar Muhammad Said Ramadan al-Bouti have maintained good relations with the regime and have not hesitated to support its policies. During the Israeli-Syrian negotiations, Kaftaro professed that Islam accepts the politics of the possible and the reconciliation with the Jews, however fraught with danger the normalization of relations with Israel may be. He also added that Islam rejects extremism.[74] One may wonder what kind of contradictory policy the regime had been following: negotiating with Israel and at the same time supporting the radical opponents of peace, while repressing its own Islamist opposition groups,[75] and dealing with moderate Syrian Islam and Islamists who accept peace but not normalization with Israel, all under the umbrella of a secular nationalist Ba'thi ideology?

This contradictory policy serves the regime (1) to put the Syrian Muslim Brotherhood on the defensive, (2) to take precautionary measures by conditioning the Syrian people to the possibility of peace with Israel and keeping the Brotherhood from galvanizing the population, especially at the suq, where the regime has minimum influence, and (3) to have leverage against Israel. Supporting some radical Islamist groups and advancing Muslim issues help take the wind out of the Brotherhood's sails. Furthermore, the Brotherhood cannot attack a regime supported by many Islamists who perceived it as the "last ditch of resistance" against Israel. After Oslo and the Israeli-Jordanian peace treaty, Syria, according to many Islamists, remained the only Arab state unbent by U.S. and Zionist pressure. Shaikh Ahmad Yassin, a founder of Hamas, remarked that Oslo breached the wall of Arab resistance while Syria stood high before pressure.[76]

The opinion voiced by the Syrian mufti regarding the peace process gave the regime the religious cover needed to negotiate with Israel. At the same time, it served not only to condition the Syrian people for the possibility of peace, but also to head off other religious views. Finally, by supporting the Islamists, the regime sends a clear message to Israel that Syria not only has at its disposal tools of political pressure, but also holds the cards for either enhancing or curbing future radical Islamic activism.

The regime's concern with further neutralizing the radical elements of the Syrian Brotherhood became obvious in the mid-1990s. Concerned about stability in Syria, Asad attempted in 1995 to reconcile with parts of the Islamist movement, a process that had gradually begun a few years earlier. He released 1,200 Muslim Brotherhood prisoners (arrested between 1976 and 1982) as part of a general amnesty declared in honor of the twenty-fifth anniversary of the corrective movement.[77] In addition, he allowed the return from exile of the former superintendent-general of Syria's Muslim Brothers, Abd al-Fatah Abou Ghudda (Al-Bouti played a significant role in mediating the release of the prisoners and the return of Abou Ghudda). Asad went as far as expressing his willingness to permit the return of all exiled Brotherhood members to Syria. After Abou Ghudda left Syria again for Saudi Arabia and died there, Asad in a symbolic gesture offered to repatriate his body for burial.[78]

However, the regime's overture to the Muslim Brotherhood was tactical and did not reflect any change in its basic position. It fell largely in the context of Syria's policy of co-opting the moderate Islamic opposition and marginalizing and liquidating the radical elements with the objective of further fragmenting the Brotherhood. Abou Ghudda was allowed to return because he was considered moderate. However, despite his cooperation with the authorities, he left Syria allegedly on account of the regime's tight security, which hindered his free movement. Of more significance was the regime's conditions for the Brotherhood's return. In this instance, it demanded that the organization issue a declaration condemning its past mistaken behavior and commending the right policy of the state. In addition, the regime insisted that the members of the Brotherhood return as individual citizens and not as party members, meaning that they were prohibited from engaging in political activity.[79] As expected, these conditions were rebuffed by the radical wing of the Brotherhood.

So, on the surface, the contradictory policy that the regime pursued not only put the Syrian Muslim Brotherhood out on a limb, but at the same time served Syria to negotiate from a position of strength with Israel. But on a deeper level, this policy, which emanated from purely domestic considerations, became an obstacle to peacemaking as well. First, by supporting the Islamists, Syria sent conflicting messages to Israel, as if it were more interested in the peace process than in making peace. To all intents and purposes, Syria remained hostile to the Jewish state. Second, the emphatic efforts of the regime to counteract the Syrian Muslim Brotherhood, whose efforts had become confined to a maligning propagandist campaign, inadvertently undercut the regime's flexibility in negotiating with Israel. How could the regime negotiate a peace treaty with the enemy without perpetuating the old treason charge? This partly reinforces and explains the regime's adamant insistence on Israel's full withdrawal from the Golan Heights to the June 4, 1967, lines. This inflexibility was compounded by the Syrian tacit acceptance that normalization of relations with Israel need not accompany a peace treaty, a position endorsed by the mufti. Thus, Syria's contradictory policy degenerated into one that safeguarded the regime on the one hand, while laying out obstacles to peace on the other.

The Succession Struggle

During his reign, Asad had been the locus of power in the structure that he built for Syria and the Syrian state. But along with him a small group of men, mainly Alawi officials, controlled the levers of power in the country through the army and the security apparatus. This group of men formed the hard core that guaranteed the security of the regime and the stability of the country. It was no idle speculation that without a smooth transition of power, the whole structure may have broken down, leaving Syria at the mercy of grim uncertainties. At the same time, as Asad grew frail and old, the question of succession most likely absorbed all his attention and efforts, making his involvement in the peace process and other affairs of foreign policy precarious.

The first succession crisis erupted in November 1983, when Asad suffered a heart attack. He appointed a council of six members, all Sunnis and most of them bureaucrats, to run the day-to-day affairs of the state until he recuperated. He included neither his brother Rifa't nor any other powerful Alawi general.[80] Rifa't had been a pillar of the regime and had commanded the strong and well-equipped defense companies. As Asad's health situation became more uncertain, some generals and members the Ba'thi regional command rallied behind Rif'at's bid to assume leadership of the country. However, Asad gradually convalesced and was extremely upset by what had happened. Tensions grew between the two brothers, splitting the organs of the state, especially in the armed forces, as everyone had to take sides. A deadly confrontation between the two brothers and their supporters loomed over Damascus, as Rifa't moved his strike forces to the city.

Damascus narrowly escaped a disaster when Asad managed to outwit Rifa't (who in the end deferred to his older brother's wishes) by sending him, his supporters, and his opponents on a trip to the Soviet Union to cool off. In reality, Rifa't was exiled and subsequently his power base rooted out. He retained, however, his official but symbolic position as vice president, to which he had been appointed in March 1983.[81] Damascus averted a bloodbath, the regime survived intact, and the question of succession was put on the back burner.

In the early 1990s, the question of succession began to gain momentum as Asad was seen grooming his eldest son, Basil, to succeed him. Basil adopted a military career throughout which he rapidly advanced through the ranks and joined the presidential guard, a military elite unit charged with protecting the president and the capital. He also got involved in Lebanese affairs and led a campaign against corruption and drug smuggling and trafficking. He was given wide press coverage for his activities, including his supposedly superb equestrian ability. His picture appeared alongside his father's all over the country. Basil supposedly enjoyed wide popularity as a tough but decent and down-to-earth man. To many in Syria, he appeared not only as the heir apparent, but also as the guarantor of political stability who had what it takes to rule.

Obviously, Asad promoted his son by delegating to him wide powers to build his base of support. But at the same time, Asad did not declare Basil as his heir. In any event, he died in a car accident while speeding to Damascus's international airport in January 1994. The Syrian public sincerely grieved Basil's death, as hundreds of thousands participated in the funeral procession first in the capital and then in Qardaha, where the Asads hail from. Basil's unexpected death rekindled the undeclared but momentous issue of succession. Asad's other son, Bashar, studying ophthalmology in London at the time of his brother's death, returned home and received broad media coverage while attending the mourning ceremonies. Apparently, Bashar emerged as the convenient replacement of his brother for the succession.

Gradually, Bashar began to follow in the footsteps of his late brother. He joined the presidential guard, got involved in Lebanese affairs, and took interest in equestrian sports. He also paid significant attention to the importance of technology for Syria's future, particularly the Internet. Meanwhile, Asad began a politico-administrative process by which he removed too well entrenched officials who could become future opponents of his son while promoting loyal supporters ready to transfer allegiance to him. At the same time, Bashar had been steadily promoted, along with his circle of loyal young officers, in the army. And following the same method as with Basil, Asad did not declare Bashar his heir, although Bashar's promotion and grooming showed otherwise.

Major-General Ali Haydar, commander of the special forces, was arrested in summer 1994 and stripped of his post, which was assigned to Major-

General Ali Habib. His closest supporters were also ousted from their posts.[82] Haydar hails from the powerful Alawi Haddadin clan, a traditional supporter of the regime, and he was instrumental in subduing the Muslim Brotherhood. His fall from grace was reportedly the consequence of his criticism of Asad for deviating from Ba'thi principles and joining the peace process.[83] Also in 1994, Major-General Muhammad Khuli was appointed commander of the air force. His appointment came as a surprise to many, since Khuli had been implicated in the attempt to blow up an El Al airplane at London's Heathrow Airport in 1986. Because of that attempt and under international pressure, mainly from the United States and Britain, Khuli was dismissed from his post as chief of the air force security directorate. By bringing him back into his inner circle, Asad indicated that his need to reinforce his regime with a loyal associate overrode his concern with the possible anger of the United States and Britain. This was so in spite of the fact that Syria was trying to enhance its image and improve its relations with both powers.[84] Asad undertook that step because he knew he could rely on a grateful Khuli to support his policies, particularly with regard to the succession issue.

This process of establishing Bashar as the successor gathered steam from the mid-1990s to the late 1990s. Reportedly, Major-General Adnan Makhluf, commander of the presidential guard and a relative to Asad by marriage, was dismissed from his post in 1995 following disagreements with Bashar. He was replaced by a young officer with no political power, Major-General Ali Hussein, making Bashar the strongman of the guard.[85] In the same year, two long-time loyalists of Asad, Generals Ibrahim Safi and Shafiq Fayyad, were promoted respectively to commanders of the Second Corps (Syrian forces in Lebanon) and Third Corps. Their former posts as commanders of the First Division and Third Division were filled by young Alawi officers whose loyalty went to Bashar. Other appointments of Bashar loyalists had taken place in 1995 and 1996 as well.[86]

In 1997 Bashar received a retroactive promotion from major in 1995 to lieutenant colonel. His speedy promotion, which started with the rank of captain in 1994, was attributed to his excellent achievement in the army.[87] Asad's son-in-law, Asef Shawkat, was appointed to the Department of Military Intelligence, headed by General Ali Duba, making him the second strongman in that all-important department and presumably placing Shawqat in line to replace Duba upon his retirement. Major military changes took place in 1998 as well. General Hikmat Shihabi, army chief of staff and a Sunni, was retired and was replaced by an Alawi, General Ali Aslan. Some analysts claim that Shihabi did not get along well with Bashar. Meanwhile, four major-generals were promoted to generals: Abd al-Rahman al-Sayadi, Ali Habib, Toufic Jaloul, and Farouq Issa Ibrahim, all considered longtime loyalists to Asad. In addition, Major-General Mahmoud al-Shaqa, an Alawi and commander of the Syrian forces in the Gulf War, was appointed head of civilian intelligence.[88]

At the same time, Bashar's activities were given wide press coverage, reflecting his elevated status in the higher echelons of the regime. For example, he was projected as a modern man bent on reforming the socioeconomic condition of the country, as well as an advocate of combating corruption. He actively promoted computer awareness in Syria and emphasized the need of the country to acquire new technologies.[89] He appeared alongside Defense Minister Mustafa Tlas at the military graduation ceremonies in Homs and attended the war games of certain commando units of the Syrian army along with General Tlas.[90] He also deepened his involvement in Lebanese state affairs, the former province of Vice President Khaddam.[91]

All of these appointments, promotions, and removals reveal the fact that Asad was delegating power to Bashar while he was still alive with the ultimate objective of preparing a smooth transfer of power to his son. However, what was happening was extremely hazardous in light of the fact that throughout Asad's presidency few changes in the makeup of the elites in the military had taken place before 1994–1995. This indicates that Asad was really concerned about a power struggle for succession that could split the organs of the state, a situation that had occurred before. Certain rumblings within the civil and military wings of the state and party that Bashar "does not have it in him to rule" exacerbated this state of uncertainty in the higher echelons of the regime.[92]

A possible contender for power remained Rifa't, who returned to Syria in 1992. During his exile, he did not disappear into obscurity. He built a wide network of connections with the leadership of the Arab world, partly woven through his array of businesses. He still commands a loyal following in Syria, particularly among his former associates and supporters, and is regarded by many as a veteran politician and able commander, an image starkly in contrast to that of nephew Bashar. Rifa't retained the post of vice president until recently and kept a low profile. Still, while Asad was alive, Rifa't never stopped promoting his political image and his status as a potential successor to the throne. Through several communications and media companies that he and his sons owned in Paris and London, Rifa't kept nurturing his image as a statesman and an advocate of freedom, modernity, and democracy.

During the early 1990s, Rif'at's son Dorid published a monthly magazine in Paris called *Al-Fursan* (The Knights), a title with a hint of Arab traditional chivalry that Rifa't had frequently used.[93] Dorid's themes revolved around the usefulness of democracy and free dialogue.[94] In 1997, another son, Sumar, edited a weekly magazine called *Al-Sha'b al-Arabi,* which featured articles about the establishment of democracy in the Arab world, as well as critiques of the Arab regimes. The magazine also served as a mouthpiece for the Arab Democratic People's Party (Hizb al-Sha'ab al-Arabi al-Dimuqrati), established in the same year in London with the apparent objective of promoting Rifa't. The party calls for the establishment of democracy and a free dialogue to solve current problems in the Arab world. When a member of the party and reportedly a close associate of Rifa't, Zubayda Muqabil, was arrested by Syrian security, Sumar featured an article calling the arrest arbitrary and implicitly criticized the regime with much irony.[95] Also in 1997, an Arabic-language satellite television station was set up in London, called Arab News Network (ANN). The chairman of its board of directors was none other than Sumar, who asserted that the station would be independent and dedicated to promoting democracy.[96]

Apparently Asad frowned upon his brother's activities. Reportedly, Rifa't was put under house arrest in 1996. In late 1997, skirmishes and exchanges of fire were reported even in the Alawi-inhabited areas, including Qurdaha, between Rif'at's supporters and those of Bashar. Asad's concern about Rifa't mounting a challenge against the candidacy of his son was conspicuously revealed when he stripped Rifa't of his title as vice president in February 1998. Equally significant, in October 1999, Syrian troops raided the port facility in the Latakia area, a hub for Rif'at's supporters, killing many of them in the process. The facility was subsequently closed down.[97]

Throughout the late 1990s, the battle of succession in Syria had become a critical political issue. According to a prominent Damascene personality, the regime had been so absorbed by the succession question that it had not given due attention to other critical affairs of state.[98]

Considering all of this, Asad undoubtedly paid increasing attention to domestic affairs, affecting his posture on the peace process with Israel. On one end of the spectrum, Asad may have chosen to postpone indefinitely making peace with the old enemy while still alive. This option would have left no room for any expected dissent resulting from an Israeli-Syrian peace treaty. By committing Syria to peace, Asad ran the risk of alienating some of the regime's veterans who had not yet come to terms with the idea. This may have further exacerbated the state of fluidity in the regime's cadres by provoking an unpredictable shift of alliances or coalition building, ruining in the process Asad's plans for Bashar. In this instance, Asad would have worked to widen Bashar's political base of support in the army and the security apparatuses. On the other hand, Asad may have preferred to conclude a peace treaty with Israel to pass the reins of government to Bashar free of the burdens of having to make peace with the enemy. This would have taken place at the expense of those veterans in the regime who either opposed Bashar's candidacy or opposed peace with Israel, or both. Between these two extremes, Asad would have been unlikely to agree to any peace treaty regarded at home as too flawed (or dishonorable, in the regime's parlance), as this could become a source of instability for the regime especially when Bashar assumed power. This was literally spelled out by Shara: "Lieutenant Colonel Bashar Asad informed me more than once that President Asad does not accept to leave behind for him a dishonorable peace."[99] Consequently, Asad adopted a principled position on the peace process.

As this analysis has shown, the struggle for succession in Syria constituted an internal constraint to making peace with Israel by being a double-edged sword in Syria's hands.

The Psychological Factor

Another Syrian domestic constraint to making peace with Israel involves the intangible psychological factor. Since the founding of the state of Israel, Syrian propaganda against the Jewish state, whether out of conviction or out of need for public consumption, had undoubtedly created an odious image of the mortal enemy in the Syrian collective mind. This was perfected by the Ba'th Party when it came to power, especially by the Asad regime, which embraced the concept of confrontation with Israel as one essential pillar of its raison d'être. Early on in his rule, Asad was aware of the impact this had on the psychological state of his country. When he was negotiating the May 1974 disengagement agreement with Kissinger, Asad tried hard to get concessions from the secretary of state to vindicate his claimed victory in the 1973 war. One reason why he feared accepting less than he was asking for was his concern with what the Syrian people would think of him. Referring to the country's state of mind, Asad said:

> The Syrian difficulty is that people here who have been nurtured over 26 years on hatred, can't be swayed overnight by our changing our courses. We would never take one step except in the interests of our people. We are all human—we all have our impulsive reaction to things. But in leadership, we have to restrain ourselves and analyze and take steps in our own interest.[100]

The intensity of the Syrian propaganda against the Jewish state did not diminish after the 1974 agreement. Rather, it became more pronounced and better articulated in the official discourse of the regime, which began to enhance the personality cult of the leader. Lisa Wedeen identified three widely shared beliefs of political life in Syria that the regime capitalizes on in its contemporary official discourses: first, the regime defends Syrians against Israeli threats; second, the Golan Heights must be returned to Syria; third, Asad's rule has produced unprecedented stability in Syria, which is desirable.[101] Parallel to this discourse, Asad was regularly depicted by the state-controlled media as the "father," the "first teacher," the "leader forever," the "gallant knight" (compared favorably to Salah al-Din al-Ayyubi, who wrested Jerusalem from the crusaders in 1187), as well as "a man of the people," among other attributes. He personified qualities such as steadfastness (sumud), willingness to struggle (nidal), and sacrifice (tadhiya). Portraits, pictures, and banners glorifying his qualities adorn almost all significant public places. One could not but feel his omnipresence and absorb the subliminal message that he was not only to be followed but also to be emulated.

One could logically infer that the official discourse that really highlights the achievements of the regime serves as proof of the personal qualities of Asad. Therefore, the significance of Israel in the official discourse is no less important than in the symbolic world, magnifying Asad's cultist qualities. In other words, Israel serves not only as a basis for the regime's legitimacy, but also as a reflection of the leader's qualities. This centrality of Israel in Syria's political and social life obviously posed a double problem for Asad's regime when it negotiated peace with its old enemy. Asad, therefore, was to a great extent no less attentive to the state of mind of his nation than to his conscious concern with his own image.

Before Syria joined the peace process, the favorite and ubiquitous adage embossed on the banners and placards filling Damascus streets was, "what was taken by force could be retrieved only by force," in reference to the Israeli-captured Golan Heights. After Syria joined the peace process, this adage was deleted in favor of another, "we fought with honor *(Sharaf),* we negotiate with honor, and we make peace with honor."[102] Another widespread terse adage was "peace of the brave." These sayings work not only to condition the Syrian people for the idea of peace, but also to highlight even the regime's achievements in waging peace. The qualitative words of "brave" and "pride" hint directly at the personal qualities of the leader as he sits atop the pyramid of the regime's achievements. This only reveals that despite his tight grip on power, Asad paid significant attention to public opinion. What he confessed to Kissinger in his early years of power, continued to hold true twenty years later when his power was firmly consolidated.

In addition, Asad in his decisionmaking process involved the organs of the Syrian state most likely as a way of covering his steps and of spreading accountability. He regarded the state's institutions and organizations as representative of the Syrian people. As such, they constituted the consensus upon which the regime depended to formulate its policies. In this respect, Asad blamed the West for looking at him as the sole source of decisionmaking in Syria, emphasizing instead the contribution of all the state's institutions.[103] Arlen Specter, a Republican senator, in a meeting with Asad, told him that if he were to arrange peace he would get the Nobel Peace Prize in Oslo. Asad replied that if he got that, he would not be able to come back to Damascus.[104]

All this indicates that the Syrian regime's psychological barrier to negotiating peace with Israel has not yet crumbled. Based on my research and discussions with the Syrians I know, I assume that it is the regime and not so much the Syrian people that is a prisoner of its own dogma, symbolism, and rhetoric. While this does not preclude negotiating peace, it surely does not help with achieving it.

Notes

1. See Nikolaos Van Dam, *The Struggle for Power in Syria: Politics and Society Under Asad and the Ba'th Party* (London: I. B. Tauris, 1996), pp. 34–62. See also Hanna Batatu, "Some Observations on the Social Roots of Syria's Ruling Military Group and the Causes of Its Dominance," *Middle East Journal* 35, no. 3 (Summer 1981).

2. Itamar Rabinovich, *Syria Under the Ba'th, 1963–1966: The Army-Party Symbiosis* (Jerusalem: Israel Universities Press, 1972), pp. 76, 131, 174.

3. Volker Perthes, *The Political Economy of Syria Under Asad* (London: I. B. Tauris, 1995), p. 162.

4. *Al-Thawra,* February 1, 1973; and Peter B. Heller, "Document: The Permanent Syrian Constitution of March 13, 1973," *Middle East Journal* 28, no. 1 (Winter 1974).

5. Ibid. (both sources).

6. Perthes, *Political Economy of Syria,* pp. 170–171. On the political economy of Syria, see also Raymond Hinnebusch, *Authoritarian Power and State Formation in Baathist Syria: Army, Party, and Peasant* (Boulder: Westview Press, 1990).

7. See Middle East Watch, *Syria Unmasked: The Suppression of Human Rights by the Asad Regime* (New York: Vail-Ballou Press, 1991), pp. 18–21.

8. Patrick Seale, *Asad of Syria: The Struggle for the Middle East* (Berkeley: University of California Press, 1988), pp. 421–440.

9. For an excellent account on Arab aid, see Pierre Van Den Boogaerde, *Financial Assistance from Arab Countries and Arab Regional Institutions* (Washington, D.C.: International Monetary Fund, 1991). See also Volker Perthes, "From Front-Line State to Backyard? Syria and the Economic Risks of Regional Peace," *Beirut Review* no. 8 (Fall 1994), pp. 81–95.

10. *Economist Intelligence Unit,* "Country Profile: Syria 1998–1999," p. 29.

11. Ibid., tab. 22.

12. Based on discussions with Sadek al-Azm, who coined the term "military-merchant complex" on September 19, 1999. See Seale, *Asad of Syria,* p. 456.

13. Sylvia Polling, "Syria's Private Sector: Economic Liberalization and the Challenges of the 1990s," in Gerd Nonneman (ed.), *Political and Economic Liberalization: Dynamics and Linkages in Comparative Perspective* (Boulder: Lynne Rienner, 1996), p. 169; and Volker Perthes, "The Private Sector, Economic Liberalization, and the Prospects of Democratization: The Case of Syria and Some Other Arab Countries," in Ghassan Salame (ed.), *Democracy Without Democrats? The Renewal of Politics in the Muslim World* (London: I. B. Tauris, 1994), p. 248.

14. *Economist Intelligence Unit,* "Country Profile: Syria," p. 11.

15. World Debt Tables, "External Finance for Developing Countries," *World Bank* vol. 2 (1996), p. 454.

16. Central Bank of Syria, *Quarterly Bulletin* 35, nos. 1–2 (1997), tab. 38.

17. See Steven Heydmann, "The Political Logic of Economic Rationality: Selective Stabilization in Syria," in Henri Barkey (ed.), *The Politics of Economic Reform in the Middle East* (New York: St. Martin's Press, 1992), pp. 11–39.

18. For example, the exchange rate for U.S.$1 in 1995 was 11.22 Syrian pounds according to the official exchange rate, 23.00 Syrian pounds according to the customs rate, 42.00 Syrian pounds according to the neighboring countries' rate, and 49.50 Syrian pounds according to the Beirut market rate. See *Economist Intelligence Unit,* "Country Profile: Syria," tab. 25, p. 42.

19. See Daniel Pipes, *Greater Syria: The History of an Ambition* (Oxford: Oxford University Press, 1990); and Daniel Pipes, *Syria Beyond the Peace Process* (Washington, D.C.: Washington Institute for Near East Policy, 1996).

20. See Glenn E. Robinson, "Elite Cohesion, Regime Succession, and Political Instability in Syria," *Middle East Policy* 5, no. 4 (January 1998), p. 163.

21. Syrian Arab Republic, *Statistical Abstracts* (Office of the Prime Minister, General Bureau of Statistics, 1993), p. 412.

22. See *MEED (Middle East Economic Digest)* 41, no. 36 (September 5, 1997), p. 4.

23. *Economist Intelligence Unit,* "Country Profile: Syria," pp. 13, 33.

24. See respectively, *Al-Ba'th,* May 19, 1997, and June 3, 1998.

25. *Economist Intelligence Unit,* "Country Profile: Syria," pp. 22–23.

26. See Aref Dalila, "Al-Siyasat al-Iqtisadiya wa al-Ijtimai'ya wa al-Maliya fi Suriya" (Economic, Social, and Fiscal Policies in Syria), *Dirasat Ishtirakia* (Social Studies) vol. 169 (Damascus, 1997).

27. Central Bank of Syria, *Quarterly Bulletin* 35, nos. 1–2 (1997), p. 69.

28. Syrian Arab Republic, *Statistical Abstracts* (1995), p. 53.

29. *Economist Intelligence Unit,* "Country Report: Syria," 3rd quarter 1998, p. 13.

30. Author interview with a prominent Arab public intellectual, October 19, 1999.

31. See full text of the treaty in *Al-Nahar,* May 23, 1991.

32. Ibid.

33. Ibid.

34. See text of the agreement in *Al-Nahar,* September 7, 1991.

35. Ibid.

36. See Habib C. Malik, *Between Damascus and Jerusalem: Lebanon and Middle East Peace* (Washington, D.C.: Washington Institute for Near East Policy, 1997), pp. 64–65.

37. For texts of the agreements, see *Al-Nahar,* September 17, 1993. Also in 1993, agreements on telecommunications (March) and tourism (May) were signed.

38. Simone Ghazi Tinaoui, "An Analysis of the Syrian-Lebanese Economic Agreements," *Beirut Review* no. 8 (Fall 1994), p. 102.

39. See *Al-Nahar,* September 19 and September 22, 1994.

40. See full text of the agreement in *Al-Nahar,* September 22, 1994.

41. See full text of the agreement in *Al-Nahar,* October 19, 1994.

42. See *Economist Intelligence Unit,* "Country Profile: Syria," p. 15; and Malik, *Between Damascus and Jerusalem,* pp. 40–42. See also Michel Murkos's articles in *Al-Nahar,* October 14 and October 24, 1994, and July 24, 1995.

43. See Malik, *Between Damascus and Jerusalem,* pp. 42–43. See also *Al-Nahar,* June 22, 1994.

44. *Al-Nahar,* October 19, 1994.

45. See Tinaoui, "Analysis," p. 109.

46. See *Al-Nahar,* January 29, 1996.

47. See *Tishrin,* August 20, 1997.

48. See *Al-Nahar,* March 23, 2000.

49. See Staff Report Issued on November 23, 1992, by the Subcommittee on Crime and Criminal Justice of the Committee on the Judiciary, *Syria, President Bush, and Drugs: The Administration's Next Iraqgate* (Washington, D.C.: U.S. Government Printing Office, 1993).

50. Author interview with Sadek al-Azm, October 18, 1999; and with a prominent Syrian businessman, October 5, 1999.

51. A significant precautionary measure that Syria has been undertaking in Lebanon to secure the implementation of all those bilateral agreements is strengthening Lebanese state institutions and filling them with individuals thought favorable to

its schemes. The election of Emile Lahoud, commander of the Lebanese army, as president of the republic in 1998 confirms this trend.

52. See Patriarch Sfeir's interview with *Al-Wasat,* November 18, 1996, pp. 20–21.

53. For complete details on Lebanese opposition to Syrian presence in Lebanon, see Robert G. Rabil, "The Maronites and Syrian Withdrawal from Lebanon: From 'Isolationists' to 'Traitors'?" *Middle East Policy* 8, no. 3 (September 2001).

54. See Seale, *Asad of Syria,* p. 94.

55. Raymond A. Hinnebusch, "State, Civil Society, and Political Change in Syria," in Augustus Richard Norton (ed.), *Civil Society in the Middle East* (Leiden: E. J. Brill, 1995), p. 225.

56. Seale, *Asad of Syria,* p. 327.

57. Ibid., p. 326.

58. Higher Command of the Islamic Revolution in Syria, *Declaration and Program of the Islamic Revolution in Syria* (Damascus: N.p., 1980).

59. Ibid.

60. For details, see Middle East Watch, *Syria Unmasked,* pp. 8–21.

61. *Al-Nadhir* no. 117 (September 1989), pp. 3–4.

62. Ibid., p. 8.

63. *Al-Nadhir* no. 122 (April 1990), p. 7.

64. See *Al-Mujahid,* January 1, 1994.

65. Lara Marlow, "Interview with a Fanatic," *Time,* February 6, 1995, p. 34.

66. See Ramadan Abdallah Shalah's interview with *Al-Wasat,* April 1, 1996, p. 14.

67. See *Al-Sabil,* May 10, 1994. Quoted from Eyal Zisser, "Syria," in Ami Ayalon and Bruce Maddy-Weitzman (eds.), *Middle East Contemporary Survey* (Boulder: Westview Press, 1994), p. 115.

68. See *Al-Sharq al-Awsat,* June 18, 1994; and *Al-Sabil,* July 19, 1994. Quoted from *Middle East Contemporary Survey* (1994), p. 115.

69. See Shaikh Abd al-Majid Zuneibat's interview with *Al-Wasat,* May 12, 1997, p. 23.

70. See *Al-Ahd,* March 3, 1994.

71. Al-Hayat, "Fadlallah Sees 'Positive Conclusion' to Talks," in *Foreign Broadcast Information Service: Near East and South Asia,* January 17, 1996, p. 67.

72. Throughout the 1990s, Damascus has been a pilgrimage stop to many Islamists, such as Rashid al-Ghannushi, exiled leader of the "Awakening" movement in Tunisia; Mahfuz Nahnah of the Algerian Hamas movement; and Hasan al-Turabi of the Islamic National Movement in Sudan. For the first time in over twenty-five years, the leadership of Jordan's Islamic Action Front (Muslim Brotherhood), headed by the party's secretary-general, Ishak al-Farahan, paid a formal visit to Damascus in 1997. According to *Al-Wasat,* the visit not only brought reconciliation between the Ba'th and the Brotherhood in Jordan, but also resulted in the signing of a "Memorandum of Understanding" containing a program of action for the future. See *Al-Wasat,* January 13, 1997.

73. For example, Asad attended the ICO conference in Tehran in 1997 while Mubarak of Egypt and King Hussein of Jordan absented themselves.

74. See Shaikh Ahmad Kaftaro's interview with *Al-Wasat,* March 6, 1996, p. 18.

75. The regime maintains Law no. 49, enacted in 1980, and punishes membership in the Syrian Muslim Brotherhood by death, as a threat against future religious political activities.

76. See Shaikh Ahmad Yassin's interview with *Tishrin,* May 5, 1998, p. 10.

77. *Tishrin,* December 12, 1995; and *Al-Hayat,* November 28, 1995.

78. See Ibrahim Hamidi in "Al-Awda Tashuk al-Ekhwan" (The Return Divides the Brethren), *Al-Wasat,* February 24, 1997, pp. 24–25; and Riad Alam al-Din in "Dimashq: Khutat al-Ekhwan al-Muslimin Letasi'id didd Nizam" (Damascus: The Plan of the Muslim Brethren to Escalate Against the Regime), *Al-Watan al-Arabi,* February 13, 1998, pp. 18–19.

79. Ibid. (both sources).

80. For excellent details, see Seale, *Asad of Syria* (revised chapter "The Brothers' War"), pp. 421–440.

81. The presidential decree of March 11, 1983, appointed three vice presidents.

82. *Al-Hayat,* September 3, 1994.

83. For more details and different interpretations on the cause of Haydar's sacking, see Eyal Zisser, "The Succession Struggle in Damascus," *Middle East Quarterly* 2, no. 3 (September 1995), pp. 56–57. See also *Middle East Contemporary Survey* (1994), pp. 613–614.

84. Zisser, "Succession Struggle in Damascus," p. 58; and *Middle East Contemporary Survey* (1994), p. 615.

85. *Middle East Contemporary Survey* (1995), p. 595.

86. *Middle East Contemporary Survey* (1996), p. 634.

87. See *Al-Wasat,* July 14, 1997, p. 5.

88. See *Al-Wasat,* July, 13, 1998, p. 5; *Middle East International (MEI),* July 17, 1998, p. 3; and *Economist Intelligence Unit,* "Country Profile: Syria," p. 7.

89. See *Al-Hayat,* October 12, 1997; and *Tishrin,* May 28 and July 13, 1997.

90. *Al-Ba'th,* June 8, 1998.

91. *Al-Watan al-Arabi,* September 11, 1998, pp. 16–18.

92. Author interview with a prominent Damascene personality, October 27, 1999. In addition, certain reservations about Bashar were based on his young age. Born on September 11, 1965, Bashar had been too young to become president in the near future, as the Syrian constitution provided that the president of the republic should be at least forty years of age at the time of his election.

93. While in power in Syria, Rifa't published a magazine of the same name, *Al-Fursan,* and used this appellation for his estate in Mezze as well.

94. See, for example, *Al-Fursan,* January 20, 1992.

95. See *Al-Sha'b al-Arabi,* July 21, 1997.

96. See *Al-Watan al-Arabi,* October 28, 1997.

97. See *Al-Hayat,* October 21, 1999.

98. Author interview with a prominent Damascene personality, October 27, 1999.

99. This quote was reproduced from an interview with Foreign Minister Shara granted to *Al-Mustaqbal* (Lebanese newspaper) by *Al-Hayat,* April 1, 2000, p. 4.

100. Henry Kissinger, *Years of Upheaval* (Boston: Little, Brown, 1982), p. 1067.

101. Lisa Wedeen, *Ambiguities of Domination: Politics, Rhetoric, and Symbols in Contemporary Syria* (Chicago: University of Chicago Press, 1999), p. 7.

102. See Jeffrey Aronson, "Lafitat fi Shaware' Dimashq: Harabna Bisharaf wa Nufawed Bisharaf" (Banners in the Streets of Damascus: We Fought with Honor and We Negotiate with Honor), *Al-Wasat,* September 5, 1994, p. 18.

103. See Asad's interview with Patrick Seale in *Al-Wasat,* May 5, 1993, pp. 12–15.

104. See Arlen Specter's interview with Daniel Pipes, "Arlen Specter: Invite Asad to the White House," *Middle East Quarterly* 4, no. 1 (March 1997), p. 57.

5

Israel: Making Peace at Home and Abroad

Kissinger's famous saying to the effect that Israel has no foreign policy but a domestic one rings true especially when it comes to peacemaking with the Arab states and the Palestinians. This is so because the democratic political system in the country has transformed it into a party state, constantly embroiled in party politics that cut across the whole political spectrum. As a result, the political system does not functionally separate highly sensitive issues, such as peacemaking, from the typicalities of domestic politics. While this political system does not preclude peacemaking, it imposes extra complications, obstacles, and restraints on the process.

Political parties played an important role in the political development of the Yishuv (prestatal Israel). Ideological, economic, political, and even security issues not only were identified with the parties but also were determined by them. At the time, the parties created a framework for a party system where every member of the Yishuv was represented. This translated, after the establishment of the state of Israel, into an electoral system based purely on proportional representation, with the whole country regarded as one constituency. This way, the political parties safeguarded their predominance in the state through parliament, known as the Knesset, and supposedly made sure that every vote counted.[1] In addition, the ideological rivalries among the parties subsided significantly as the state became the focus of their loyalty and politics.

This political system failed to generate a single party with a parliamentary majority, thereby making coalition building the inescapable means of forming a government (minimum 61 out of 120 seats). During the early years of the state, the labor socialist party, Mapai, had a predominant position in the system that allowed it to choose its coalition partners from a wide array of small parties with little effort and bargaining.[2] However, from the mid-1960s on, the situation changed when one-party dominance began to give way to two large parties in the system. This change enhanced the bargaining power of the small parties, as they eventually became not only indispensable to coalition building but also the key to determining which of the two largest parties would form a government. Consequently, the small parties, mainly oriented toward single issues, used their leverage to impose their platforms on the big parties, which represented the bulk of the population.

After the 1967 war, ideas started circulating in Israeli political society about the possibility of achieving peace with the Arabs in exchange for the occupied territories. This spurred an internal debate between and among the parties and their leaders, sharpening the political divide between the left and right.[3] The territories not only were perceived by some as ideologically, religiously, and historically indispensable for Israel, but also were perceived by many as vital for its security. However, the debate long remained hypothetical, because no peace efforts had materialized. At the same time, settlements began to expand in the occupied territories, further hindering the return of some Arab occupied territories in exchange for peace. Significantly enough, all of this turned the issue of peacemaking into more of a domestic matter than it should have been, since it involved territorial concessions.

The 1973 war, in which the Arab armies made initial advances, affected the psychology of Israel as it realized its narrow margin of error. The war hastened the decline of Labor, which many blamed for the debacle, and the ascendance of the right wing. It also began to transform the historical relationship between Labor and the National Religious Party (NRP), as the latter shared the right-wing ideology of Greater Israel. At the same time, Israel depended more than ever on the support of the United States. Following the war, the internal debate sharpened as Israel prepared itself to negotiate a disengagement agreement with Egypt entailing an Israeli withdrawal from the Suez Canal zone.[4] The entire right wing combined into a new bloc, Likud, which led the opposition against the government.[5] In the elections of December of the same year, the Labor Party (Big Alignment) lost 5 seats (from 56 to 51) while the right wing gained 13 seats (from 26 to 39). While the right wing, headed by Menachem Begin, was in no position to form a government, the Labor Party, despite its numerical dominance in the Knesset, could not escape the dawning reality that small parties had begun to hold the big parties to ransom for joining a coalition. According to Moshe Dayan, Labor's ability to form a government depended on having to "make far-reaching concessions to a few small parties for joining a coalition."[6]

Given the surprise of the war and the growth of domestic opposition, the government came under increasing pressure to demonstrate that it was not making any territorial concessions endangering the security of the state. The government felt that it had to legitimize the disengagement agreement with Egypt by submitting it to the Knesset for approval. Indeed, the agreement was submitted in January 1974, drawing 76 votes in favor and 35 against.[7] This set a precedent for future agreements with Arab states that involved territorial concessions.

Israel went on to negotiate two other disengagement agreements, one with Syria signed in May 1974 and the other with Egypt signed in September 1975. As expected, the negotiations sparked domestic opposition. In the first case, the fact that the negotiations were led by an interim government, shielded therefore from domestic opposition, greatly helped to finalize the agreement, although other factors contributed to its successful conclusion. In the second, a mix of internal and external factors helped to bring about cabinet approval of the agreement. Externally, the United States pressured Israel to make territorial concessions in the Sinai Peninsula, even going as far as initiating a policy of reassessment of the relationship between the two countries.[8] Internally, the new prime minister, Yitzhak Rabin, preferred a second agreement with Egypt that would terminate the state of belligerency between the two countries, thereby reducing the prospects of another war.[9]

Following in the new tradition set by the first disengagement agreement with Egypt, the government submitted the two agreements to the Knesset for approval in order to legitimize them. While both were ratified, the one with Syria received more support than the one with Egypt. The predominance of Labor in the political system, although with no parliamentary majority, helped the government in getting the agreements ratified. Likud again attacked both agreements on the ground that they endangered the security of Israel for mere cease-fires. It claimed that the second agreement in particular constituted a pure surrender to the United States, increasing Israel's dependence on the Americans. Interestingly enough, the second agreement triggered opposition from within the government and from extraparliamentary groups. As Yaacov Bar-Simon-Tov noted, for the first time ever, three members of Labor, among them Moshe Dayan, joined the opposition in voting against the agreement in the Knesset. At the same time, two members of the coalition government from the NRP voted against.[10] At this juncture, the alliance between Labor and the NRP, maintained since the founding of the state, began to crack. Many members of the NRP, especially the youth (Young Guard), identified with Likud regarding expanding the settlements in the occupied territories and retaining them. Consequently, they schemed to take over the party and to move it decisively to the right.[11]

In addition to the wide opposition within the Knesset, the government was attacked by the settler movement Gush Emunim. The right wing organized demonstrations against the government and U.S. Secretary of State Henry Kissinger, who was mediating the second disengagement agreement with Egypt. Rabin was greatly disturbed by Gush Emunim's behavior.[12] Interestingly enough, the opposition that those agreements provoked encompassed the ruling party itself, the coalition, the Knesset, and extraparliamentary groups. Meanwhile, Likud was making inroads in the political system. Through its hawkish positions and promises of economic reform, Likud appealed to the poorest segment of the population, many of whom were of sephardic origin, who felt discriminated against by the Labor establishment.[13]

The electoral trend toward having two large parties with roughly equal strength crystallized in the 1977 elections. The ruling party since the founding of the state, Labor suffered a disastrous loss in the elections—19 seats in the Knesset (from 51 to 32)—while Likud gained 4 seats (from 39 to 43).[14] This ended one-party dominance in the system, enhancing the leverage of the small parties over the big ones to form a coalition government. From 1948 to 1977, no government could be formed without the dominant leftist socialist party (Mapai and then Labor). Therefore, Mapai/Labor had the leverage to control key ministries in a government and to limit payoffs demanded by potential coalition partners. The small parties had little option for developing political alternatives. Now the situation was reversed.

Immediately after the elections, Begin entered into laborious negotiations with the small parties to form his coalition government, especially the religious parties, Agudat Yisrael (4 seats) and the NRP (12 seats). He needed them in his coalition because they supported his nationalistic policies. Capitalizing on their essential participation in a Likud coalition, the religious parties bargained for far-reaching concessions with Begin. In turn, Begin gave them sweeping policy privileges regarding some socioreligious issues, including a pledge to try to amend the Law of Return under which only conversions in accordance with Halakah (Jewish religious law) would be recognized. He then gave them patronage concessions, rewarding the NRP with the coveted Ministry of Education and Culture, as well as the important Ministry of Interior and Ministry of Religious Affairs.[15]

In June 1977, Begin was able to form his coalition government, approved by the Knesset in a 63–53 vote, two votes above the minimum requirement (45 Likud votes, 12 NRP, 4 Agudat Yisrael, and 2 Independents). In October, he enlarged his parliamentary base of support by bringing the recently established Democratic Movement for Change (DMC) (15 seats) into his coalition. Begin lured the DMC by patronage concessions (cabinet posts), pledging no policy concessions. The DMC called for reforming the electoral system and maintained a flexible position on territorial concessions, favoring restricted Jewish settlements on the West Bank. With regard to the latter position, the DMC was closer to Labor than Likud.[16]

However, the fact that Likud was not a dominant party in the political system opened for the coalition government a Pandora's box of domestic politics. The coalition government could be held hostage by small parties whose political appetite had been whetted by payoffs, as well as by members of Likud threatening defection. Significantly enough, the small parties had acquired not only the ability to decide which party would form a coalition government, but also the ability to bring down a coalition. All this had an immediate bearing on the government's capacity to pursue peacemaking with the Arabs in exchange for territorial concessions, since the issues cutting across party lines moved to center stage.

Given the diverse ideological, economic, historico-religious, and security importance of the occupied territories to the parties, on the one hand, no party had a predominant position in the political system enabling it to overcome domestic opposition without running the risk of collapsing. On the other hand, a large party would have to go through a balancing act to see how to keep those members and coalition partners who opposed territorial concessions from bolting the coalition, while protecting its platform from being hijacked by the single-issue small parties.

Although Begin advocated the concept of Greater Israel, he agreed to peace with Egypt after Sadat came to Jerusalem. He realized that removing Egypt from the Arab-Israeli conflict once and for all, expanding control over the West Bank and Gaza, and enhancing the U.S.-Israeli relationship were benefits worth the costs of giving up the strategic Sinai. In addition, peace could well give Begin's Israel wide domestic and international legitimacy, as well as prove his statesmanship in the annals of history.[17] The historic visit by President Anwar Sadat to Jerusalem in November 1977 helped Begin domestically in his peace policies. Through the mediation of the United States, Begin negotiated the Camp David Accords with Egypt, which contained two parts, one dealing with withdrawal from the Sinai and the other with Palestinian autonomy in the West Bank and Gaza.[18] Besides a few officials, mainly Foreign Minister Moshe Dayan, Begin did not let his government or the Knesset in on his decisions during the negotiations. Initial domestic opposition to Begin's peace policy was almost benign, partly because of the support it elicited from the public, partly because of his status as a charismatic right-wing leader making peace, and partly because he assured his party and the Sinai settlers that he would not dismantle any settlements there. Ironically, the threatening opposition came from within Likud's main faction, Begin's Herut. Herut members were particularly wary of Begin's autonomy plan for the West Bank and Gaza. However, their opposition remained inconsequential, since they could not be perceived as acting against their own leader (although some members voted against the plan).[19]

But soon after he signed the accords, Begin faced increased domestic opposition, mainly from within his government and some extraparliamentary groups such as Gush Emunim, the Movement of Greater Israel (a secular right-wing nationalist movement), and the Sinai settlers. Dismantling the Sinai settlements and professing Palestinian autonomy over the West Bank and Gaza raised the specter of party defections. Two Likud members, indeed, later left the party and established a new ultranationalist party called Tehiya (Renewal), which vehemently attacked Begin.[20] In fact, Tehiya, a single-issue party (to retain the territories), sponsored two bills in the Knesset regarding East Jerusalem and the Golan Heights to make them nonnegotiable in the future, while at the same time pressuring Begin to affirm his Greater Israel position.[21] This opposition, however, was sufficiently counteracted by a combination of a significant segment of Likud and the other coalition partners (the NRP, Agudat Yisrael, and the DMC), on the one hand, and Labor, some other small parties, and the grassroots movement Peace Now, on the other.[22] In the Knesset vote on the Camp David Accords, 84 members (MKs) voted in favor, 19 opposed, and 17 abstained. Interestingly enough, only 46 MKs from Likud and its partners voted for the accords, meaning that had it not been for the opposition parties, Begin's government would not have won the Knesset's approval.[23]

The Camp David Accords laid the ground for an Israeli-Egyptian peace treaty, which Begin concluded. The government widely approved the treaty in March 1978. In the Knesset vote, 95 MKs voted in favor, 18 against, 2 abstained, and 5 did not participate. Obviously, Begin's peace policy had significant support. But the fact remained that the opposition parties largely helped Begin in his policy. Although some Likud and coalition members changed their mind and voted for the treaty (53), the opposition parties again gave Begin a majority vote (42), legitimizing his policy.[24] Gush Emunim (and its offshoot, Movement to Stop the Withdrawal) and the Sinai settlers immediately led the domestic opposition after the Knesset vote. They even crossed swords with the Israeli army, charged with implementing the peace treaty. But their oppositional efforts fizzled in light of the massive Knesset support for the treaty.

In 1981 the Israelis went to the election booth and cast the bulk of their votes almost evenly between Labor and Likud, together winning approximately 80 percent of the Knesset seats (Labor 47, Likud 48). The small parties lost a considerable number of seats in comparison with the 1977 elections.[25] The election proved that Likud's popular base of support was not as ephemeral as many had thought. It also highlighted the importance of the sephardic vote, which largely favored Likud. Begin was able to form his coalition government depending on the religious parties, whose eventual disproportional representation in the government belied their weakening electoral position. Begin gave them again significant economic and patronage support, including a renewed pledge to deal with the highly sensitive question, "Who is a Jew?"[26] With a highly nationalist right-wing government, which got involved militarily in Lebanon, no substantial peace policy could be pursued. Indeed, Begin was eager to reassert his right-wing position and pacify his opposition in light of his country's withdrawal from and dismantling of the settlements in the Sinai in compliance with the implementation of the Israeli-Egyptian peace treaty. In winter 1981, he single-handedly considered the introduction of the Golan bill to the Knesset, where it was swiftly passed into law. The bill extended Israel's law, jurisdiction, and administration to the Golan Heights. Besides Likud's ideology of territorial maximalism, security and economic considerations were at the center of Begin's decision. The Reagan administration criticized the Israeli action and endorsed UN Security

Council Resolution 497 of December 17, 1981, which declared the Israeli action "null and void and without international legal effect."[27]

The elections of 1984 sustained the trend of having two large parties with almost equal strength in the system. At the same time, the two large parties' share of Knesset seats had shrunk, with Labor obtaining 44 seats and Likud 41. This reduction meant that the other small parties had received an increase in their share of Knesset seats, which could translate to a rise of their coalition bargaining power. However, the small parties were so fragmented that the large parties did not perceive them as plausible partners in building a stable coalition. Even the religious parties were so rife with dissent among themselves that some groups split and founded their own separate parties. Although the religious parties received the same number of electoral Knesset seats as in the 1981 elections (13), this number was divided among five instead of previously three parties. The major happening was the establishment of a party to cater for the religious, economic, and political needs of the growing sephardic community. This new party, the Sephardic Torah Guardians, known as Shas, received four Knesset seats.[28]

Meanwhile, Begin, the charismatic and undisputed leader of Likud, resigned from office and party. He was replaced by the uncharismatic Yitzhak Shamir, who was eager to assert his authority. The two large parties' shrinkage in electoral size, the fragmentation of the small parties, and Shamir's lack of assertive leadership led the two large parties to join their forces and form a national unity government.[29]

Forming a unity government cluttered the national agenda with many issues of real concerns to both coalition partners, such as how to deal with a staggering inflation, a difficult involvement in Lebanon, and peacemaking. But on the same grounds, being a unity government allowed each party to thwart the efforts of the other. That was especially true with regard to the issue of peacemaking, on which the two parties disagreed the most. The parties had only two options: break the coalition or do nothing. Opting for sustaining the government, there was little hope for peacemaking.[30]

Another national unity government was created following the 1988 elections, reflecting the distribution of electoral strength in the Knesset. As in the preceding elections, Likud (40 seats) and Labor (39 seats) emerged in equal strength in the elections, suffering a shrinkage in their electoral vote. Surprisingly, the religious parties emerged from the elections with 18 seats, with Shas (6 seats) leading the others. Although most of the religious parties later joined the coalition, their position was that of a junior partner. With neither of the two large parties able to muster a majority (minimum 61 seats), the religious parties held sway. But their rivalries and their persistent demand to amend the Law of Return helped to pull the two large parties together.[31]

Again with a national unity government adopting different perspectives on the question of what to do with the occupied territories, it was hardly possible to get the peace process off the ground. In addition, the idea of peace-making did not generally appeal at the time to the Israeli public because of the outbreak of the intifada. This, however, did not prevent the labor leadership from trying its hand at peace efforts undertaken by the U.S. and Egyptian governments. With Labor and Likud forestalling each other on the peace initiatives, the national unity government collapsed in spring 1990.[32]

Labor leader Shimon Peres failed to form a government, while Likud's Shamir was able to do so. But this came at the expense of his own power in the cabinet and the disappearance of the center in Israeli politics. Shamir gave key cabinet posts to his radical intraparty rivals and had to rely on far-right parties as well as the religious parties to form his government.[33] Meanwhile, his government witnessed two cataclysmic world events having immediate impact on Israel: the second Gulf War and the collapse of the Soviet Union. On the one hand, one consequence of the Gulf War was the revival of the peace process under the leadership of the United States, which Shamir reluctantly agreed to participate in (see Chapter 3). On the other hand, Shamir had to deal with immigration of the Russian Aliya, which dramatically increased following the collapse of the Soviet Union.

Shamir's failure to deal adequately with the absorption of the new immigrants, his clash with the United States, and his inability to improve the economic conditions of the country were all detrimental to Likud's election prospects in 1992, while being grist for the mill of Labor.[34] While Likud was suffering a defection of its supporters to parties of the right, Labor, under the leadership of Yitzhak Rabin, strove to attract segments of the sephardic and former Soviet communities.[35] As a result, Labor defeated Likud in the 1992 elections, with the former winning 44 Knesset seats and the latter 32.

Despite its victory, Labor remained a large, although a nondominant party in the political system. Labor could depend on Meretz (a far-left spin-off of Labor, 12 seats) to form a coalition government, but still needed 5 seats to achieve the minimum required (61). The Arab-Israeli parties won 5 seats (Hadash 3, United Arab List 2), a number that could solve Rabin's problem.[36] However, he could count on the Arab parties to block Likud from forming a government and to support a Labor government in votes in the Knesset, but could not include them in a Labor coalition or give them cabinet positions.[37] Rabin simply could not depend on Arab parties to legitimize his government, especially when he was girding himself for peacemaking. The implicit assumption of Israeli politics requires the procurement of a "Jewish majority" for such major decisions. Alternatively, Likud and its affiliated parties, which included Tsomet (8), the NRP (6), Shas (6), the United Torah Jewry (UTJ, a religious party, 4), and Moledet (3), received a total of 59 Knesset seats. Barring the Arab parties, Likud had an advantage of Knesset seats over Labor. This meant that what Rabin needed was to attract a party out of the Likud bloc to form a coalition. Rabin's choice fell on Shas.[38]

While the NRP opposed Labor mainly because of its position on the occupied territories, Shas never made this issue a determining factor in its political affiliation. Shas perceived itself as a religious movement dedicated to Torah education and to the bettering of conditions for its sephardic community. Political maneuvering and power were means for religious ends, especially to support its religious schools and socioreligious programs. Shas abhorred sitting in the opposition, as this would undermine its political standing, and thus its effectiveness in spreading its message. Rabin gave Shas the choice to pick its portfolios in the coalition, of which the Ministry of Interior was the most covetous. By controlling the Ministry of Interior, coupled with taking up important posts in the Ministries of Education and Religion, Shas could well channel funds to support its programs.[39] With Shas joining a Labor-led coalition, Rabin formed his government.

Rabin, Israel's hero and foremost advocate of security, and Peres, the party strongman, embarked on the path of the peace process. But unlike in the past, peacemaking with Syria and the Palestinians involved deeply embedded competing values that touched Israel's existential roots. The Golan Heights, the West Bank, and Gaza, unlike the Sinai, represented the core of Israel's ideological, security, territorial, and settlements values. Alternatively, Syria and the Palestinians presented the most threatening militarily, political, and ideological challenges to the state of Israel. More specifically, the peace process sparked again the divisive debate on the future of the occupied territories, but this time reaching a level of polarization of Israeli politics unseen throughout the country's history. The conflict not only involved the two main rival camps, but became extremely personalized, leading to an ominous process of political demonization by the opposition. It seemed as if Labor's leadership did not foresee the extent and intensity of domestic opposition.

Rabin and Peres negotiated the Declaration of Principles (Oslo I Agreement) with the PLO, signed in September 1993. Although the agreement drew significant public support, this support was fragile. The almost homogeneous nature (Labor-Meretz) of the Labor coalition helped Rabin's government in approving the agreement. But his government had a hard time legitimizing Oslo I, and thus its peace policy, in the Knesset. Only 61 MKs voted in favor of Oslo I, while 50 opposed it; the others either abstained or did not participate. Significantly enough, had it not been for the Arab parties, which were not part of the coalition, the government could not have ratified Oslo I in the Knesset.[40] On such a vital issue to the Jewish people, the fact that non-Jewish votes enabled the passage of the agreement intensified domestic opposition. How could Labor's peace policy reflect the will of the Jewish people when it depended on Arab support?

When the Likud-led opposition failed to frustrate the government's peace policy in the Knesset, it turned to right-wing extraparliamentary groups for mounting a public campaign to delegitimize the government and its policy.

The opposition parties cooperated with groups such as the Yesha Council, representing the settlers in the West Bank and Gaza, as well as with ultra-right groups such as Kach.[41] When a spate of suicide bombings in Tel Aviv, Jerusalem, and Beit Lid illustrated the fragility of the peace process, the opposition quickly exploited the situation as proof of Oslo's failure. In July 1994 the opposition organized an antigovernment demonstration in Jerusalem, which was addressed by prominent Likud leaders Benjamin Netanyahu, Ariel Sharon, and Yitzhak Shamir. Characterized by a demonization of the government and its leaders, the demonstration ended in violence. Rabin was referred to as a traitor. Subsequent demonstrations followed in which the chants and slogans that Rabin and Peres were "murderers and traitors," and that the government's policy was an "act of national treachery," became the rallying cry of the opposition. Many in Israel believed that this demonization campaign created the volatile climate leading to Rabin's assassination.[42]

Meanwhile, the idea that the Golan Heights might be relinquished in exchange for a peace treaty with Syria added more fuel to the polarization of Israeli politics. Rabin was so taken aback by the intensity of domestic opposition that he declared that any withdrawal from the Golan Heights would be conditional on a referendum. In early August 1993 he conveyed this pledge to U.S. Secretary of State Warren Christopher, and he reiterated this pledge to the Israeli public whenever necessary.[43]

In addition, the question of the return of the Golan Heights was potentially explosive for the Labor Party itself. After all, it was Labor that encouraged the creation and expansion of settlements on the Golan. More specifically, although the settlements there were encouraged largely for security rather than political reasons, the paramountcy of the Golan's relevance to Israel's security in light of the historical mistrust between the two countries has become deeply embedded in the psyche of the Israeli public. Many military leaders across the political spectrum think that the Heights are indispensable to Israel's security, constituting a buffer zone against a Syrian surprise attack, although an increasing number of top military brass have been counteracting this argument (see Chapter 6 for details). Before long, in June 1994, an extraparliamentary group was founded under the name "Third Way," comprising mostly Labor members and sympathizers, many of whom had a military background. According to Itamar Rabinovich, the members argued that "in the negotiations with the Palestinians and with the Syrians Rabin and his government had drifted to the left, and vowed to return Labor to its centrist tradition by exerting pressure from outside."[44]

Simultaneously, the Golan settlers organized themselves into an effective pressure group with close connections to the Third Way. Indeed, the settlers cultivated ties with some hawkish Labor MKs opposing the relinquishing of the Golan, notably Avigdor Kahalani and Immanuel Zissman. This Golan lobby formulated a law, the "Golan entrenchment law," to be passed in the Knesset. The law would require a majority (70 or 80 members) in the Knesset in order to repeal the 1981 Golan annexation law, as well as a majority (65 percent) in the national referendum on the question of Israeli withdrawal from the Heights that Rabin had promised. The lobby unsuccessfully tried twice to pass the law in the Knesset, once in September 1994 and again in July 1995. However, while in the first case the law was voted down, in the second case the vote came to a draw of 59–59, meaning that the law had an equal number of supporters and opponents.[45] In fact, spearheading the Golan campaign, Kahalani and Zissman eventually bolted the Labor Party and transformed the Third Way into a party.[46]

In the meantime, Rabin negotiated a peace treaty with Jordan, signed in October 1994. Unlike other agreements, the treaty was widely supported by the public and the Knesset. This was so because the treaty did not involve any territorial concessions and the king had an empathetic relationship with Israel. But as Rabin began negotiating the Oslo II Agreement with the Palestinians, signed in October 1995, the Likud-led opposition fiercely stepped up its efforts. Although Rabin and Peres joined hands to mobilize support for the agreement despite their longtime rivalry, the Labor leadership had great difficulty legitimizing the agreement. Again, only 61 voted in favor of Oslo II while 59 voted against, including 2 Labor MKs.[47] As previously, the opposition vehemently attacked the agreement, especially the fact that the Arab parties had enabled its passage. Shortly thereafter, in November 1995, Rabin was assassinated.

Peres succeeded Rabin and tried to continue the government's term in following through with the peace process, especially with regard to Syria. However, it soon appeared that a breakthrough was not feasible in the near future (see Chapter 7 for more details). The lack of progress with the Syrians nudged Peres to move up the elections from November to May.[48] Meanwhile, a wave of terrorist attacks during February–April 1996 helped to erode Peres's widespread public support, which was partly the result of the strong feelings of horror caused by the Rabin assassination.[49] At the same time, the attacks were exploited by Likud and its leader, Benjamin Netanyahu, to vilify Labor's peace policy and especially Peres. Likud's famous slogan for the election was "peace with security." Apparently, the slogan was part of a centrist strategy Likud had devised to appeal to many Israeli voters' thirst for peace as well as penchant for security.

At this juncture, a new electoral reform law was adopted in Israel that provided the voter with two ballots, one for the direct election of the prime minister and one for a party in the Knesset. The law was designed to put an end to the type of horse-trading that had characterized previous attempts to form coalition governments, with the small parties holding up the large ones to ransom. The theory behind the law was that by directly selecting a prime minister, much of the bargaining would be taken out of the process. However, the new law produced the very opposite of the intended effect. It ended up increasing the number and strength of small parties, as well as moving much of the horse-trading process from after the election to before it. More specifically, the double choice of the law allowed Israelis to split their vote by permitting them to express two preferences, with the result that Labor and Likud could lose support from their voters, who in the past may have voted for them predominantly on foreign policy issues. For example, an orthodox Jew could vote for a religious party on religious and state issues, and for a moderate or hawkish prime minister on peace process matters.[50] The result of the 1996 elections set in sharp relief the unintended consequences of the new law.

The elections further eroded the strength of the two large parties, with Labor winning only 34 seats and Likud-Tsomet-Gesher 32 seats.[51] Likud's leader, Netanyahu, was elected prime minister. At the same time, the number of small parties increased, with the new Russian immigrant party, Yisrael ba-Aliya, winning 7 seats and the Third Way winning 4 seats.[52] In addition, Shas gained 4 more seats than in the 1992 elections, winning a total of 10 seats. All this meant that Netanyahu faced the specter of putting together a Likud-led coalition government of small parties with significant leverage over their single issues. On the one hand, there would be no escape from forming a coalition running the gamut from the religious and hawkish NRP to the religious and moderate Shas to the secular and hawkish Yisrael ba-Aliya and Third Way. On the other hand, by the end of day, the small parties could threaten the coalition's stability whenever their special demands were not met. As a result, there would be most likely no unity on the government's policy.

Netanyahu was able to form his government depending on the right (Likud with 32 seats, NRP 9, UTJ 4, and Moledet 2) and the center (Shas with 10 seats, Yisrael ba-Aliya 7, and Third Way 4). As expected, this coalition combined the religious and the secular, the moderate and the hawkish. Surely, given the nature of his coalition, Netanyahu would not be under pressure to seek a peace treaty with Syria. Rather, he would find himself bartering over contradictory domestic issues such as marriage laws, Sabbath observance, Jewish education on the one hand, and secularizing social laws and spending on the new immigrants on the other.

However, the implications of such an evolution for the political system would make peacemaking, especially with Syria, a daunting task even in a future Labor-led government. The two large parties' position in the system would only grow worse. Not only would they be weakened, but they also would be faced with a rise of additional small parties. The two large parties would undoubtedly be held hostage by the small ones. The large ones would face the specter of bartering over domestic issues, affecting their own platform. While the parties of the right would naturally oppose concessions to peacemaking with Syria, some parties of the center such as Shas would most likely use peacemaking as a bargaining chip to extract domestic concessions. This is bolstered by Shas's steady rise in electoral votes and thus in Knesset seats. Equally significant is that a future Labor-led government may need the support of the Arab parties for peacemaking, thereby leading many Israeli

Jews to question its legitimacy. As such, peacemaking with Syria would inten-sify an already highly polarized Israeli domestic political system, creating within it centrifugal forces of sorts. The ability of the leaders to mobilize sup-port for peacemaking would be put to the test by a hesitant public torn by peace and security concerns. Only the Knesset and a national referendum will decide if the domestic battle for peace with Syria is to be won. And this is a tough call for prophecy, even in the land of prophets.

The Golan Settlers and the Nation

The future of the Jewish settlements on the Golan Heights and the reaction of the settlers there to peace negotiations with Syria will undoubtedly constitute enormous obstacles to an Israeli-Syrian peace treaty. On the surface, the issue might appear difficult but manageable. The leadership of the country, sup-ported by a majority of the public, would eventually take the political decision to conclude a peace treaty entailing the dismantling of settlements, however painful that may be. After all, is not peace (with security) the pinnacle of Zionism's designs? On a deeper level, the issue is tremendously complicated, as the settlers will harrow next to Israel's ideological and political roots, thereby turning peacemaking into a wrenching psychological process and an explosive domestic political issue. This is further complicated by the decision to hold a referendum over the Golan.

The first settlements on the Heights were built following the 1967 war. At the time, the Labor government was torn between expanding the settlements to enhance the security of the state and entertaining the idea that Syria would eventually press for peace to take back its occupied territory. The Labor party was almost evenly divided between hawkish and moderate wings regarding the occupied territories, such that it did not adopt a formal policy concerning them. Consequently, the government encouraged settling of the Golan, albeit at a slow pace. But as the idea of Syria pressing for peace began to recede, the party began to tilt toward a hawkish position encouraging an accelerated pace of settlement. This attitude was congruent with, if not even part of, the over-all position the party was taking with regard to the occupied territories.

In September 1973, the party released the Galili Document in a major attempt to define its aims for the territories. The document, considered hawk-ish, recommended, among other things, the encouragement of Jewish settle-ment on the Golan Heights.[53] After the surprise of the 1973 war, a new wave of Jewish settlement swept the Golan. Not only the government, but a wide national consensus supported the expansion of settlements there. The surprise war highlighted the Golan's importance for the defense of northern Israel and its water sources. The support of settlements crossed nearly the entire politi-cal spectrum of the country. As it shall be recalled, it was the Likud-led gov-ernment that extended Israel's jurisdiction to the Golan in 1981. Probably the only issue that brought together a significant number on the left and on the right was the importance of the Golan Heights to Israel's security. This issue has been so drummed up by those who insist on retaining the Golan, that it has become a deep-seated, subconscious fact in the collective psychology of the nation.[54]

The settlements spread throughout the region, encouraged on the one hand by the legal belief that the Golan has become an integral part of Israel, and on the other hand by the constant emphasis that the Golan Heights are vital for Israel's security. However, the number of settlements remained low in comparison with those in the West Bank. Scarce natural resources, notably water and land suitable for agriculture, and the remoteness of the Golan from the center of activity in the country, discouraged many from settling there.

By the time the Madrid peace conference convened in October 1991, there were slightly over thirty settlements on the Golan. At the time, the Likud-led government supported a plan to increase them. In 1994, while the Labor-led government was holding peace negotiations with Syria, the settlements numbered thirty-four and had a population of approximately 13,000. The biggest settlement was the town of Katzrin with 1,000 families, followed by the settlement of Bnei Yehuda with 116 families. The others had less than 100 families each.[55] Interestingly enough, although they are spread throughout the Golan, a significant number of settlements had been built next to the border to emphasize their defensive role. The settlers prided themselves on turning the Golan into a prosperous region combining agriculture, wine making, and tourism.

By 1991, many settlers had lived on the Golan for twenty-five years. Many could argue that they had struck roots and that a new generation had been born there. More specifically, the Golan settlers, unlike those of the West Bank, were encouraged to settle there by the Israeli government itself and through a wide national consensus. In addition, the settlers epitomized the pioneering spirit of Zionism. They were contributing not only to the defense of the nation, but also to its economic and social well-being. This gave them the high politico-moral ground to oppose any government's policy entailing a withdrawal from the Golan. Indeed, as we have seen, during the Israeli-Syrian negotiations (1992–1996) the settlers were able to organize themselves into a highly effective pressure group. They cultivated support from the hawks of the Labor Party, who opposed an Israeli withdrawal from the Golan. This support found expression in the Third Way movement.

On close examination, however, what helped the settlers to become an effective pressure group had been the Labor Party's own position on the Golan and the broad consensus in the country that the Heights were crucial for the defense of northern Israel. Since the Galili Document, the party had adopted a hawkish position concerning the Golan. But this decision had not been binding on Labor members, who could adopt their own independent position without being expelled from the party. So long as peace negotiations

with Syria had been perceived as far from imminent, the party had little difficulty containing its hawks and moderates. This, however, became extremely
difficult on the eve of the Madrid peace conference as the party struggled to
adopt a compromise formula reconciling both hawks and moderates. What
emerged was an apparent contradiction with regard to peace with Syria
reflected in the platform adopted by the Fifth Congress of the party in 1991.
Article II states: "The peace agreement with Syria will be based on Security
Council Resolutions 242 and 338, whose meaning is the principle of territorial compromise within the framework of full and viable peace, in which the
security needs of Israel will be provided."[56] Apparently, after pressure from
the Golan settlers, supported by party hawks, the Labor leadership added an
amendment after the congress, stating:

> Israel views the Golan Heights as an area of great importance to its security,
> its welfare and to secure its water resources in peacetime as well. In any
> agreement with Syria and in the security arrangements, Israel's presence and
> control, both settlement and military, in the Golan Heights, to which Israeli
> law, jurisdiction and administration have been applied, will continue. . . .
> The efforts will continue to strengthen the existing Israeli settlements in the
> Golan Heights.[57]

Even after a number of years of peace negotiations with Syria, the 1996
Labor platform returned to an article that was eliminated in earlier delibera-
tions, which stated: "Labor sees in the Golan Heights an area of national
importance for the state of Israel."[58] Although Labor's position could be
understood as a means to garner as many votes as possible, it had nevertheless been an apparent contradiction that made it possible for the Golan settlers
to bring together opponents of Labor and dissidents from within. This is
exactly what happened when some Labor MKs split from Labor and formed
the Third Way, joining thereafter the Likud-led government in 1996. Based on
the aforementioned analysis of the party politics, one could safely argue that
the Third Way would find willing partners (Likud, NRP, UTJ, and Yisrael ba-
Aliya) to form a considerable opposition bloc against a Golan withdrawal.

In addition, although the pace of settlement has been slow on the Golan,
the numbers there have been slowly but steadily increasing. In 1997 the population jumped to over 16,000.[59] The increase included a significant number
of former Soviet immigrants who by and large lean to the right. It is not
unwise to expect that as the number of Golan settlers increases and as their
stay there is prolonged, their collective will to resist a withdrawal will harden.
In fact, the results of the 1996 elections seem to indicate a considerable shift
in Golan votes toward the right, sending a clear message of resistance to
Labor's peace policies. While in the 1992 elections Labor won 60 percent of
the Golan votes, in 1996 Labor drew only 27 percent.[60] Apparently, this was
clearly a protest vote from the many traditionally Labor-affiliated settlers, further constraining Labor's hands at peacemaking.

But all this is actually a product and consequence of the broad consensus in the country that the Golan is vital to Israel's security, a consensus bolstered by the Zionist ideology. This is reflected by the internal debates exposing the fissures and psychological unease in the country. If every Golan settlement has its own hawks, moderates, and all shades in between, not surprisingly the country as a whole could be regarded as a settlement. For example, during the Israeli-Syrian peace negotiations in 1994, a group of Golan settlers went on a hunger strike, drawing more than 200,000 supporters. Prime Minister Rabin at the time blasted the group's action, calling it "undemocratic" and warning that "it could lead to anarchy."[61] The mayor of Katzrin, Sammy Bar-Lev, an activist in the group, proclaimed: "Rabin is just like Chamberlain, who believed he was bringing peace by signing a deal with a ruthless dictator—a deal that led to millions of deaths."[62] This opinion was echoed, though in a different tone, by Yehuda Sinai, a settler of Ein Gev, a kibbutz that was on the front line until Israel conquered the Golan. Like many of his fellow kibbutzniks, the settler entertained doubts about Syrian intentions once they returned to the Heights. Yehuda Sinai said that "Syria is not a democracy. Tomorrow Asad might die. There would be a new leader, who might say, 'to hell with peace.' Then we would have to fight all over again." Sinai then added that "Asad knows we can be in Damascus very quickly if we're on the Golan Heights. But he also knows we want peace very badly. That's our weak point. If Asad really wants peace, he will compromise. If not, so be it. I don't want my children to suffer war again, but I don't want a situation where they face a worse war."[63]

During the 1992–1996 Labor government, the most popular signs and bumper stickers in Israel were "Peace with the Golan" and "The People Are with the Golan."[64] It is difficult to gauge public sentiments, but those opinions and popular signs were a testimony to the country's mixed feeling about peacemaking with Syria, as well as representative of a significant national consensus to retain the Golan. This is further corroborated by the almost successful attempt by the Golan lobby to pass the "Golan entrenchment law" in the Knesset, which came to a draw of 59–59 despite the fact that Prime Minister Rabin led the government. So what makes the Golan issue domestically explosive and psychologically wrenching is not that the Golan settlers had been protesting peacemaking, but rather the settlers' ability to strike a chord with the population at large on account of water and security issues (see Chapter 6). The whole country has yet to be conditioned for peace and to come to grips with the idea of peacemaking with Syria. At this point, much would depend on the ability of the country's leadership to wage a public campaign persuading the population of the merits of peace.

In addition, the Golan settlers were helped to become an effective pressure group not only by the country's mixed feelings about peacemaking with Syria, but also by the fundamental questions that withdrawal raised concerning the country's ideology and values. Are not the Golan Heights an integral part of Israel, same as any other part? Are not the settlements the very proof of Zionism's continuity, and their dismantlement the very proof of Zionism's speedy erosion? How can a Labor government support a withdrawal from the Golan when most of the settlers there have been encouraged by and traditionally affiliated with it? These questions go to the heart of the country's national consciousness, making it wrestle with its present and future values.

It is not the fairly small number of Golan settlers but the encompassing political and psychological process provoked by them that makes it extremely difficult for any Israeli government to decide on the withdrawal and removal of the settlements from the Golan. The battle of the settlers is not only over their homes and the security of the state, but also over the spirit and soul of Zionism: peace versus giving up a part of the land of Israel. Ultimately, this means that peace with Syria will require a much greater effort on the part of the Israeli leaders to convince their public of the advantages of peace over retaining the Heights. The wrenching difficulties of this process reside in the fact that these leaders have to counteract the long-term effects of the indoctrination they had themselves practiced on the Israeli people concerning the paramount security importance of the Golan Heights. In spite of all these considerations, when a peace treaty with Syria is signed, there is no reason to believe that the Israeli government will deal any differently with the Golan settlers than it once dealt with those of the Sinai Peninsula: removal by force if necessary.

Notes

1. For details on the system of government and parties, see Michael Wolffson, *Israel, Polity, Society, and Economy, 1882–1986* (Atlantic Highlands, N.J.: Humanities Press International, 1987), pp. 3–99; Gregory S. Mahler, *The Knesset: Parliament in the Israeli Political System* (Rutherford, N.J.: Fairleigh Dickenson University Press, 1981); and Israel Knesset, *The Knesset: Its Origins, Forms, and Procedures* (Jerusalem: Government Printing Press, 1966).

2. See details on Knesset elections, especially Mapai Knesset seats, in Wolffson, *Israel,* pp. 20–25. See also findings of the Harvard Study Group on Israeli Politics, led by Nadav Safran, *Reforming Israel's Political System: What Needs to Be Done?* (Cambridge: Harvard University Press, 1991), p. 3.

3. Yehoshafat Harkabi, *Arab Strategies and Israel's Responses* (New York: Free Press, 1977), pp. 70–149; and Zvi Yehuda Blum, *Secure Boundaries and Middle East Peace* (Jerusalem: Hebrew University of Jerusalem, Faculty of Law, 1971).

4. For details on the disengagement agreement, see Henry Kissinger, *Years of Upheaval* (Boston: Little, Brown, 1982), pp. 799–854.

5. In 1965, Herut and the Liberals joined to form Gahal. In 1973, Gahal joined three small parties to form Likud.

6. Moshe Dayan, *Moshe Dayan: Story of My life* (New York: William Morrow, 1976), p. 599.

7. Yaacov Bar-Simon-Tov, *Peace Policy as Domestic and as Foreign Policy: The Israeli Case* (Jerusalem: Leonard Davis Institute, Hebrew University of Jerusalem, 1998), p. 9.

8. Yitzhak Rabin, *The Rabin Memoirs* (Berkeley: University of California Press, 1996), pp. 261–263.

9. Ibid., p. 247.

10. Bar-Simon-Tov, *Peace Policy,* p. 14.

11. See Yael Yishai, "Factionalism in the National Religious Party: The Quiet Revolution," in Asher Arian (ed.), *The Elections in Israel, 1977* (Jerusalem: Jerusalem Academic Press, 1980).

12. Rabin, *Rabin Memoirs,* p. 271.

13. On the rise of Likud to power, see Efraim Torgovnik, "Likud 1977–81: The Consolidation of Power," in Robert O. Freedman (ed.), *Israel in the Begin Era* (New York: Praeger, 1982), pp. 9–14.

14. See C. Paul Bradley, *Parliamentary Elections in Israel: Three Case Studies* (Grantham, N.H.: Tompson and Rutter, 1985), p. 60.

15. Ibid., pp. 80–81.

16. Ibid., pp. 52, 82; and Efraim Torgovnik, "A Movement for Change in a Stable System," in Arian, *Elections in Israel, 1977,* p. 91.

17. For details, see Chapters 2 and 3 in this volume; and Ezer Weizman, *The Battle for Peace* (New York: Bantam Books, 1981), pp. 76, 190.

18. For details on the negotiations leading to the Camp David Accords and their contents, see William B. Quandt, *Camp David: Peacemaking and Politics* (Washington, D.C.: Brookings Institution, 1986).

19. Yaacov Bar-Simon-Tov, *Israel and the Peace Process, 1977–1982: In Search of Legitimacy for Peace* (Albany: State University of New York Press, 1994), pp. 67, 73; Bar-Simon-Tov, *Peace Policy,* p. 17; and Moshe Dayan, *Breakthrough: A Personal Account of the Egypt-Israel Peace Negotiations* (London: Weidenfeld & Nicolson, 1981), p. 99.

20. On the defection issue, Begin insisted that the upcoming Knesset vote on the accords be free of coalition discipline. This way, Likud members could vote against the accords without being automatically removed from the party. Torgovnik, "Likud 1977–81," p. 32.

21. At the time (summer 1980), Tehiya succeeded in passing the Jerusalem bill into law, the Jerusalem Law, in the Knesset. However, Begin's government rejected the introduction of the Golan bill to the Knesset.

22. For example, Israel's defense minister, Ezer Weizman, played an important role in nudging Begin toward flexible positions on his peace policy. See Weizman, *Battle for Peace.* Alternatively, Labor refrained from attacking Likud during the negotiations so as not to weaken Begin's negotiating position. See Neill Lochery, *The Israeli Labour Party: In the Shadow of the Likud* (Reading, UK: Ithaca Press, 1997), pp. 79–80.

23. For a breakdown of the Knesset vote, see Bar-Simon-Tov, *Israel and the Peace Process,* p. 148.

24. Ibid., p. 185.

25. For a breakdown of the parties and their respective Knesset seats, see Bradley, *Parliamentary Elections in Israel,* p. 112.

26. For details on the concessions Begin gave to the religious parties, see ibid., pp. 128–129.

27. UN Security Council Resolution 497, December 17, 1981; and U.S. Department of State, *American Foreign Policy: Currents Documents 1981* (Washington, D.C.: U.S. Government Printing Office, 1984), pp. 772–773.

28. On Shas and on the religious parties, see Samuel C. Heilman, "The Orthodox, the Ultra-Orthodox, and the Elections for the Twelfth Knesset," in Asher Arian and Michal Shamir (eds.), *The Elections in Israel, 1988* (Boulder: Westview Press, 1990); and Aaron P. Willis, "Shas: The Sephardic Torah Guardians: Religious 'Movement' and Political Power," in Asher Arian and Michal Shamir (eds.), *The Elections in Israel, 1992* (New York: State University of New York Press, 1995).

29. Asher Arian, "Israel's National Unity Governments and Domestic Politics," Arian and Shamir, *Elections in Israel, 1988*, pp. 209–210.

30. Ibid., pp. 212–213.

31. Ibid., pp. 214–215; and Heilman, "Orthodox," pp. 147–151.

32. For details on this episode of events, see Lochery, *Israeli Labour Party,* pp. 153–155.

33. For example, Shamir gave ultra-right nationalist Ariel Sharon the Ministry of Immigration and Construction. And he relied on Tsomet, Tehiya, and Moledet to form his government. As mentioned before, Tehiya (3 seats) was an extreme single-issue right-wing party. Tsomet (Crossroads) was formed in 1987 by Rafael Eitan, a former chief of staff. What characterized it from other right-wing parties was that it called for the retention of the occupied territories on a security rather than a biblical basis. Tsomet received 2 Knesset seats in the 1988 elections. Moledet (Homeland) was founded in 1988 and ran on the single issue of the voluntary transfer of Arabs from the occupied territories. It received 2 seats in the 1988 elections.

34. See Leon T. Hadar, "The 1992 Electoral Earthquake and the Fall of the 'Second Israeli Republic,'" *Middle East Journal* 46, no. 4 (Autumn 1992), pp. 594–616; and Sammy Smooha and Don Peretz, "Israel's 1992 Knesset Elections: Are They Critical?" *Middle East Journal* 47, no. 3 (Summer 1993), pp. 444–463.

35. The Soviet immigrants shared more the ideology of Likud than that of Labor. Their vote for Labor was regarded by many as a protest vote for Likud. On Soviet immigration and Israel's elections, see Aharon Fein, "Voting Trends of Recent Immigrants from the Former Soviet Union," in Arian and Shamir, *Elections in Israel, 1992;* and Bernard Reich, Noah Dropkin, and Meyrav Wurmser, "Soviet Jewish Immigration and the 1992 Israeli Knesset Elections," *Middle East Journal* 47, no. 3 (Summer 1993). On the shift of the sephardic vote to Labor, see Asher Arian and Michal Shamir, "Two Reversals: Why 1992 Was Not 1977," in Arian and Shamir, *Elections in Israel, 1992,* p. 29 ff.

36. Hadash really represents the Democratic Front for Peace and Equality and the Democratic National Bloc (DFPE-DNB), a coalition of the Israeli Communist Party, independents, and radical groups. The United Arab List included the Democratic Arab Party and a moderate segment of the Islamic Movement. Keeping with the tradition of former communist lists, Hadash maintained its Jewish-Arab character.

37. On the Arab parties, see Majid al-Haj, "The Political Behavior of the Arabs in Israel in the 1992 Elections: Integration Versus Segregation," in Arian and Shamir, *Elections in Israel, 1992.*

38. Lochery, *Israeli Labour Party,* pp. 215, 222.

39. See Willis, "Shas," p. 133.

40. Author interview with Abdel Wahab Darawshe, Knesset member and founder of the Democratic Arab Party, November 23, 1998. See also Bar-Simon-Tov, *Peace Policy,* p. 22.

41. Founded by the radical Meir Kahane, Kach sought the transfer of Arabs from the occupied territories.

42. Lochery, *Israeli Labour Party,* pp. 234, 237; and Bar-Simon-Tov, *Peace Policy,* p. 23.

43. See Itamar Rabinovich, *The Brink of Peace: The Israeli-Syrian Negotiations* (Princeton: Princeton University Press, 1998), pp. 105, 158.

44. Ibid., p. 189.

45. For details, see ibid., pp. 190–191. Shas left the coalition in 1994, making any defection by labor MKs from the party a direct threat to the coalition. Indeed, when Kahalani and Zissman were preparing to leave the Labor Party, their move was balanced by a right-wing defection to the coalition (a right-wing faction of Tsomet, Yi'ud, split from the party and joined the coalition).

46. The Third Way ran in the 1996 Knesset election, winning 4 seats. It subsequently joined a Likud-led government.

47. Author interview with MK Abdel Wahab Darawshe, November 23, 1998; and Bar-Simon-Tov, *Peace Policy,* p. 22.

48. Rabinovich, *Brink of Peace,* p. 211; and Lochery, *Israeli Labour Party,* p. 254.

49. See Michal Yaniv, "Peres the Leader, Peres the Politician," in Asher Arian and Michal Shamir (eds.), *The Elections in Israel, 1996* (Albany: State University of New York Press, 1999), p. 221.

50. See Bernard Susser, "The Direct Election of the Prime Minister: A Balance Sheet," in Daniel J. Elazar and Shmuel Sandler (eds.), *Israel at the Polls, 1996* (London: Frank Cass, 1998).

51. Gesher, a secular right-wing party, was founded by former Likud member David Levy, a sephardic Jew. For a breakdown of party seats in the Knesset elections, see *Jerusalem Report,* June 27, 1996, p. 18.

52. Yisrael ba-Aliya was founded by former Soviet dissident Natan Sharansky. Although the party is considered secular and centrist, it favors a right-wing nationalist policy on the territories, especially with regard to the Golan Heights. For details on the party and the elections, see Tamar Horowitz, "Determining Factors of the Vote Among Immigrants from the Former Soviet Union," in Asher and Shamir, *Elections in Israel, 1996;* and Etta Bick, "Sectarian Party Politics in Israel: The Case of Yisrael Ba'Aliya, the Russian Immigrant Party," in Elazar and Sandler, *Israel at the Polls, 1996.*

53. Lochery, *Israeli Labour Party,* p. 56; and author interview with Moshe Ma'oz, December 15, 1998.

54. Personal impressions from many Israelis of all walks of life gathered in 1998.

55. For excellent details on the settlements, see Aryeh Shalev, *Israel and Syria: Peace and Security on the Golan* (Boulder: Westview Press, 1994), app. 3.

56. Extract from *The Israel Labor Party Platform on Foreign Affairs and Security* (Tel Aviv: Labor Party Headquarters, 1991), quoted from Lochery, *Israeli Labour Party,* p. 198.

57. Ibid.

58. Reuven Y. Hazan, "The Electoral Consequences of Political Reform: In Search of the Center of the Israeli Party System," in Arian and Shamir, *Elections in Israel, 1996,* p. 167.

59. Matti Friedman, "Ignoring the Uncertainty," *Jerusalem Report,* March 20, 1997, p. 21.

60. Ibid.

61. *Jerusalem Report,* October 20, 1994, p. 8.

62. Ibid.

63. Ibid., pp. 18–19.

64. Ibid., p. 18; and Hazan, "Electoral Consequences," p. 174.

6

Regional Security
and Water

The previous two chapters discussed various domestic considerations and constraints that the governments of Syria and Israel had to contend with when seriously contemplating peace with each other. This chapter will continue the earlier discussion by taking up the two most significant and decisive additional factors affecting the peace policies of the two states toward each other, namely security and water. Serving as a potential springboard by either country to launch a surprise attack against the other, the Golan Heights have been the focal point of security concerns for both countries. These concerns have been deepened no less by the two countries' mutual enmity than by their diametrically opposed senses of vulnerability. More specifically, security and water concerns begin with the Golan but branch off to cover hotly debated state security doctrines and regional uncertainties affecting the peace policies of the two states toward each other. This was highlighted by the implications of the Gulf War (1990) for both countries. Although the peace process was launched and new agreements and treaties between Arabs and Israelis were signed, the region still remained in a state of flux and volatility.

The Golan Heights
and Security Perceptions

The Golan Heights are an extension of the Hauran region in Syria. Israel controls an area of 1,158 square kilometers of the Heights, including Mount Hermon, known famously in Arabic as Jabal al-Shaikh (named so because snow covers its peak almost year-round). Israel controls the western and southern extensions of the Hermon, rising 2,224 meters above sea level, while the other parts are divided roughly equally between Lebanon and Syria. The Heights in the hands of Israel are bounded by Mount Hermon in the north, by the Jordan River and the Sea of Galilee (Lake Tiberias) in the west, by the Yarmouk Valley (and River) in the south, and by the disengagement lines drawn by the May 1974 disengagement agreement in the east. Numerous hills exist along these lines, including Mount Fares (Tel Fares) and Mount Avital (Tel Abou Neda). These hills, including the highest peak at Mount Hermon, offer Israel strategic observation posts looking down deep into Syrian and Lebanese territories.[1] Indeed, one can observe Damascus from Mount Hermon.

The Golan is for the most part a rough terrain difficult to cross. Access to it from the north, west, and south is difficult, while access from the east is less problematic. Towering over Israel, the Golan has topographic advantages over most of Israel's approximately 80-kilometer-long border with Syria. This is sharply pronounced along the southern part of the Golan-Israel border, where steep slopes suddenly rise up to 500 meters above the Sea of Galilee. The Golan terrain is narrow in the north and south and wider in the center. In the northern part of the Golan (from the international border of 1923 to the disengagement line), its width is 12 kilometers. In the center, its maximum width is 25 kilometers, and from there southward it becomes increasingly narrow.[2] Because of these narrow distances, the Golan offers no substantial strategic depth to Israel, especially when compared with the Sinai Peninsula and the West Bank. However, given its difficult accessibility, its towering position, and the narrow width of Israel's Galilee panhandle, the Golan constitutes an important buffer zone to Israel despite the Heights' small size. This commanding topographic feature of the Golan gives many Israelis a subconscious attachment to it, imparting to them a certain intangible sense of protection and peace of mind. It gives them a much needed extra-psychological reassurance, knowing that no one, Syrian or otherwise, is looking down on them.

This strategic piece of land plays an important role in Israel's and Syria's security concepts. While many security concerns worry both countries, they place great emphasis on the serious security risk posed by the eventuality of a surprise attack launched by either country against the other using the Golan as a springboard.

Since the founding of the state of Israel, the country has pursued a military doctrine predicated on offensive warfare. The geopolitical position of the Jewish state, lacking strategic depth and situated in a hostile environment, burdened by a psychological insecurity from cruel historical experiences, drove the state to adopt a strategy of deterrence. Out of this strategy grew the doctrine of preemptive offensive, which depended on a preemptive attack, executed by a combination of swift ground and air strikes deep into enemy territory. This meant that the war should be fought inside the enemy's territory, where its forces are to be destroyed, thereby removing the immediate threat to Israel. This doctrine also depended on the successful completion of the mobilization of the Israeli Defense Forces, which relied on a reservist system.[3]

Israel paid significant attention to keep abreast of technological advances and to equip its army with the latest modern weaponry. The astounding success of the 1967 war made many in the military develop a blind faith in

Israel's military doctrine. As it turned out after the war, the Arab territories served as buffer zones, on the one hand, and reduced the risk factor inherent in Israel's lack of strategic depth, on the other hand. The 1973 war shook the foundation of Israel's doctrine, as the Arab armies surprised Israel and won in the early days of the war. A debate erupted in military circles about the viability of Israel's military doctrine and the benefit of the Golan as a buffer zone to the security of the state. Many in the military establishment came to the conclusion that the Golan must be retained in order to preclude another Syrian surprise attack. In addition, the military ought always to maintain a qualitative edge reflected by an ability to repel and overwhelm any combination of Arab forces. The U.S.-Israeli strategic cooperation helped Israel to maintain its military qualitative edge, and to stick to its policy regarding the Golan.

So long as peace with Syria seemed distant, this security debate remained within the confines of the military establishment. But once Syria and Israel joined the peace process, the debate intensified and was even taken up by the public. Many in the military establishment insisted on keeping the Golan as a buffer zone and as an early warning system. Hirsh Goodman, of the *Jerusalem Report,* questioned why former Israeli generals—in some cases members of Prime Minister Yitzhak Rabin's own Labor Party—were heading a campaign to make the Heights nonnegotiable, even if this meant forfeiting a historic chance of peace with Syria:

> I wonder why . . . when these generals speak about the need for continued Israeli civilian settlement on the Golan, they don't remind the public that the first thing the Israeli army did in the 1973 Yom Kippur War was evacuate the Israeli settlements on the Golan.
>
> They also fail to mention that possession of the Golan in 1973 did not prevent war with Syria, did not negate the element of strategic surprise that cost this country dear, did not prevent Syrian missiles from being launched against Israeli population centers and did not cut down on Israeli casualties. We lost 722 men on the Golan in the Yom Kippur War when we had possession of the Heights, more than five times as many as we did in the Six-Day War when we had to conquer them. And what stopped the Syrians from launching more missiles at Tiberias in 1973 was not that we had the Golan, but that we had air superiority. . . . Territory had nothing to do with it.
>
> Furthermore, what ultimately stopped the fast-advancing Syrian armored columns . . . were not only the Israeli tank and artillery units stationed on the Golan but, once again, the Israel Air Force. . . .
>
> Why, if the early-warning stations on Mt. Hermon and two other sites are so crucial to our security now, did they fail to function in 1973? There is no disputing that we were taken by surprise and one of the first positions to fall to the Syrians was the Hermon. Why are these failed warning stations more important than peace, international guarantees and inviolable tripwires that have worked in Sinai and could work on the Golan?
>
> To be sure, if Israel and Syria are to remain in a state of enmity, better Israel be in possession of the Golan Heights than be without it. But if relinquishing that territory can be translated into an iron-clad agreement, better to take the risk than retain the territory.[4]

Before long Goodman's viewpoints and questions were one by one answered and rebuffed by Yoash Tsiddon-Chatto, a colonel in the air force reserves, a former Knesset member, and a member of the Israeli delegation to the Madrid peace conference in 1991:

> First, settlements were seen as defensive positions only through the War of Independence. . . . Settlements in the Golan . . . are a sign of Zionist resolve to develop the land and keep it. The existence of settlements has also resulted in the military doctrine of carrying the war beyond our borders. . . .
> Second, while the Golan did not prevent the Yom Kippur War, it certainly prevented Israel's collapse. Syria's conclusion that it cannot win a war as long as Israel retains the Golan explains why the border has remained quiet since. . . .
> Third, during the Yom Kippur War, the initiative and tactical surprise were Syria's. In the initial stages, Syrian anti-aircraft missiles kept Israel from achieving air superiority over the battle arena and so from providing efficient ground support. . . .
> Fourth, it is true that territory does not prevent the launching of ballistic missiles from far behind the front lines. The air force may. But let's look at the whole picture: Israel's defense doctrine is based upon our regular forces holding the line for 48–72 hours, efficiently covered and supported by the air force, while the reserves mobilize for the counter-offensive. If Syria again goes to war with Israel, the most probable scenario indicates that it would open with a massive missile attack against cities and large military targets. . . . We can assume that the missile attacks will not only inflict damage on Israel but also slow the pace of mobilization.
> The Syrian ground forces' onslaught will therefore have to be blocked by our standing forces for more than 48–72 hours. During that time, our army will be deprived of air support, since the (damaged) air force will be sent to neutralize the ballistic missiles. In such circumstances, the standing ground forces must make maximum use of natural defenses. The only natural defense in Israel's north is a range of hills along the Golan plateau.[5]

This concern over a Syrian surprise attack is compounded by the fact that Syria maintains a strong military presence in Lebanon, especially in the Beka Valley. Syria could launch an offensive through Lebanon and extend its front with Israel.[6] This debate did not stop at this point and took a far-reaching dimension as many in Israel pondered the implications of the Gulf War (1990) for the country. Having no mutual border with Israel, Iraq launched surface-to-surface ballistic missiles against Israel and managed to inflict terror in the country. Despite the mastery of the air and the redoubtable air force attacks by the U.S.-led coalition against Iraq, the coalition did not manage to effectively suppress the launching of Scud missiles against either Israel or Saudi Arabia. The crux of the matter was that Israel's deterrent doctrine did not prevent Iraq from attacking the Jewish state. This further intensified the security debate in Israel, which began to center on the utility of territories in the age of missiles and the methods necessary to adjust the country's military doctrine.

While some maintained that the Gulf War evinced the fact that territories no longer gave Israel strategic depth and that relinquishing them in exchange for peace was the right thing to do, others stressed that, on the contrary, territories are now more important than ever. In fact, for example, the latter emphasized that the Gulf War highlighted the vitality of territory and strategic depth to Israel's security in two contexts: the surface-to-surface missiles (SSMs) threat, and intelligence functioning.[7] In the first context, Aharon Levran argued, among other points, that "conventional wars are decided on the ground, and not by firepower," and added that while SSMs can cause damage and casualties (and disrupt IDF mobilization) they "cannot conquer a single inch of territory."[8]

Levran emphasized that, unlike the proxy harassment of Israel by Syria from southern Lebanon, the Golan has been quiet mainly because Damascus, the capital, is some fifty kilometers away from Israeli lines on the Heights. The presence of Israeli troops and the privileged position of the IDF there deter Syria from initiating a war and from launching SSMs on Israel.[9] Therefore, keeping the Heights is an important lesson from the Gulf War. In the second context, Levran emphasized that in spite of the abundance of U.S. intelligence tools in the Gulf, the United States was taken by surprise when Iraq invaded Kuwait. For small countries such as Israel, the indisputable solution lies in maintaining extensive territory and strategic depth for defense.[10] In this instance, it is the Golan. These Gulf War implications for Israel with regard to the Golan have become more pressing as Syria exerts greater efforts to improve its missile capabilities.[11]

This ongoing debate sharpened when the government of Ehud Barak (1999–2000), top-heavy with former military brass, along with some of Israel's leading strategic thinkers, endorsed the idea of relinquishing the Golan in exchange for peace and security with Syria.[12] Given the wide consensus within the government and among some of Israel's strategists, this marked a considerable shift in the country's strategic, military, and political thinking over the past decade, although by no means unanimous or popular. The strategic thinking behind this position was comprehensively outlined by analysts, including top former army officers, from the Jaffee Center for Strategic Studies at Tel Aviv University in December 1999. Holding a news conference to mark the publication of the *Middle East Military Balance, 1999–2000,* the analysts argued that returning the Golan could be offset by strengthening the IDF and by security guarantees such as early-warning systems and demilitarization of Syrian territory near the Golan. They emphasized that Syria's military has deteriorated since the collapse of the Soviet Union; that Israel's air force has a formidable edge over that of Syria, providing significant battlefield advantage; and that Israel's military is not only technologically advanced but also capable of absorbing dramatic changes in modern warfare.[13]

The leading dissenter of this position was none other than Likud leader Ariel Sharon. Consistent with Likud's philosophy (and some Labor hard-liners), Sharon based his argument against relinquishing the Golan on the assumption that Syria cannot be trusted because of the authoritarian nature of the regime. He stressed that "even in the missile age it is impossible to defend Israel effectively against a ground attack without military control of the Golan Heights. Syria has more than 4,000 tanks and 1,000 missiles, and the last and only line where an assault by them could be stopped runs through the center of the heights."[14]

In addition, this ongoing debate sharply questioned the viability of Israel's military doctrine. As mentioned above, the 1973 war and subsequent events in the region, such as the Gulf War, had raised doubts. Many in Israel believe that the country's strategy of deterrence has been declining and that it should be radically revised. This is compounded by a combination of techno-logical, economic, and social forces that have been pushing the country into undertaking major changes in its security concept.[15]

Apparently, Israel is grappling not only with the question of whether to relinquish the Golan Heights, but also with the related question of what to do with its military doctrine. Undoubtedly, Israel is going through a transition in its security concept, making the country extremely cautious especially with regard to a strategic piece of land. This can only impose heavily on Israel's decisionmakers, as no consensus has yet emerged in the ongoing security debate concerning the Golan Heights. Under these new circumstances and given the history of conflict between the two embattled neighbors, one could expect that even those who call for peace with Syria in exchange for the Heights will be forced to raise the bar of their acceptable minimum security requirements in their peace negotiations (for example, Israel could be adamant about maintaining observation posts on Mount Hermon, demanding the total demilitarizing of the Golan, and asking Syria to move its army away from the border and/or reduce its size). In other words, what supposedly could make a peace agreement with Syria security ironclad, could frustrate peace negotiations with it as well.

Under President Hafiz al-Asad, Syria has maintained a security concept in large measure revolving around the belief that Israel is an expansionist state seeking regional hegemony.[16] This concept is directly linked to the Syrian need to recover the Golan Heights. In the early 1970s, Asad tried unsuccess-fully to establish an eastern front including Iraq and Jordan against Israel. In the end, he opted for a partnership with Egypt, which climaxed in the two countries' surprise 1973 war. However, this partnership quickly dissolved as Cairo pursued peace with its former enemy. Asad believed that the region suf-fered from a strategic imbalance in favor of Israel, largely made possible by U.S. support. Consequently, he wanted to rectify this situation by trying to achieve strategic parity with Israel with the help of the former Soviet Union. Until this day, little has been published on the subject in Syria.[17]

Patrick Seale, Asad's biographer, took up the subject and explained that the Syrian president believed that a balance of power between opponents keeps the peace, while an imbalance causes war. He added that the essence of the Syrian president's "strategic thinking has always been that the Arabs should strive to muster sufficient deterrent power to hold Israel in check."[18] Correspondingly, the rational of Asad's quest for strategic parity lay in the belief in security through an Arab-Israeli balance of power. In his analysis of Asad's concept of strategic parity, Aryeh Shalev deduced three objectives: first, to enable Syria to withstand an Israeli attack; second, to allow Syria to negotiate from a position of strength; and third, to provide Syria with an offensive option to liberate by force the Golan Heights.[19] In much the same vein, Ze'ev Schiff wrote that strategic parity "clearly aims to counter Israel's architecture of defense and deterrence, by acquiring military capabilities to deter Israel and to overcome Israel's defenses on the Golan."[20]

Coincidentally, the civil war in Lebanon (as we have seen in Chapter 2) further convinced Asad to improve and build his country's military capabilities while at the same time projecting its regional power. Israel's invasion of Lebanon in 1982 surely hardened Syria's determination to pursue its plan of strategic parity to deter its enemy. According to my assessment, however, Asad's security concept, though it aspired for strategic parity, was limited. It is hard to envisage that Asad's Syria, a country with far inferior academic, economic, and technologic capabilities and know-how than Israel, could achieve its goal even with the Soviets' help. Asad's concept of strategic parity was most likely aimed at acquiring a deterrent capability along with some sort of offensive option, understandably limited to the Golan Heights and Lebanon.

Israel's swift invasion of Lebanon highlighted to the Syrians not only the notion that the Jewish state is expansionist and aggressive, but also the fact that it could extend its front with Syria from the Golan to the Beka Valley. This is bolstered by Israel's offensive capabilities and military strategy. It could launch a surprise attack from the Golan on Syria and cripple its military and industrial complex, as well as use Lebanese territory, especially the Beka, to outflank the Syrian army. To the Syrians, this is highly exacerbated by two geopolitical and economic concerns, making the country very vulnerable. Most of Syria's industry and population are concentrated in the western part of the country, and this part is in close proximity to the Golan and the Beka Valley in Lebanon. Damascus, the capital, is only fifty to sixty kilometers from the disengagement line on the Golan. In addition to the capital, Syria's main cities, where the country's industrial infrastructure and population centers are located, are all at a close distance from Lebanon. In other words, Syria, like Israel, lacks strategic depth.

Abd al-Halim Khaddam, the Syrian vice president, remarked that "Syria's capital is only 25 km from the Lebanese border. Syria's heartland in Homs is just 30 km from the Lebanese border. Tartus is only 25 km. Should Israel manage to control Lebanon, it will in effect be able to break through Syria from the coast, the middle, and the capital."[21] It shall be recalled that during the Israeli invasion of Lebanon, Syrian troops fiercely engaged the IDF along the approaches of the Beka Valley in order to deny them that strategic area (see Chapter 2). Since then, it seems as if Syria's security concept has treated Lebanon as an extension of the Golan front. Even after its victory in Lebanon and the withdrawal of the IDF to the south and then completely from Lebanon in May 2000, Syria has stationed the bulk of its troops in Lebanon in the strategic Beka.

In the late 1980s, Syria came to the conclusion that its quest for strategic parity with Israel fell short of achieving an offensive option. In addition, whatever ideas Syria entertained about improving its military capabilities vanished with the disintegration of its patron the Soviet Union. The country acutely faced the constant specter of how to neutralize Israel's military superiority. Though Syria joined the peace process, it accelerated its quest for surface-to-air and surface-to-surface ballistic missiles. The lessons of the Gulf War were not lost on the country. Ballistic missiles could deter Israel. In this respect, Asad was furious with U.S. attempts to monitor Syria's weapon imports, especially missiles.[22]

Unlike some analysts who believe that Syria's military situation will improve with time, I find the opposite to be true.[23] Without a patron (the Soviet Union), an economy of scale, and a political system supportive of research and development, Syria will always face a technologically and militarily superior Israel. This is promoted by the U.S.-Israel strategic cooperation, which preserves Israel's qualitative military edge. Since the early 1990s, Syria's military concept has been confined to maintaining a large ground force, acquiring missiles, and fortifying the approaches of the western part of the country from the Golan and the Beka.[24]

While this military preparedness could be looked at as giving Syria an offensive option, it has been undoubtedly designed to deter an Israeli attack on the Golan and Lebanon. Syria is no stranger to Israel's military doctrine. So most of its armed forces have been organized and structured with the aim of preventing Israel from implementing its war doctrine—carrying the war swiftly to enemy territory and destroying the enemy's forces. The size and density of the Syrian forces around the Golan and the Beka, the geographic constraints there (the narrowness of these fronts and the rough terrain of the Golan), and reportedly the depth and complexity of Syria's fortifications there, all limit Israel's maneuverability. Significantly enough, they also raise the specter that an Israeli attack would entail unacceptably high losses. Syria knows full well that the basic cause of the strategic imbalance between the Arabs and Israel lies in the fact that the latter cannot afford a single defeat, while the former surely can.[25] In addition, Israel cannot stomach a high number of casualties, while the Arabs can. As such, according to the Syrians, Israel would be deterred from launching any attack entailing these risks.

Ultimately, the Golan Heights and by extension the Beka Valley are central to Syria's security concept in two contexts: to provide the country with strategic depth and to deter Israel. Apparently, Syria shares the same security concerns as does Israel. But since security is in the eye of the beholder, these concerns are diametrically opposed. Syria's security concept grew not only from the history of the Arab-Israeli conflict, but also from the country's geopolitical and economic conditions. Its lack of strategic depth, its need both to project regional power, especially in Lebanon, and to recover the Golan, and Israel's superior offensive capabilities all heighten Damascus's sense of vulnerability. Accordingly, Damascus would be expected to take an adamant stand against certain security arrangements in the peace negotiations should these arrangements be perceived as increasing the country's vulnerability.

While security concerns involving the Golan are high on the agendas of the two embattled neighbors, they surely do not dominate those agendas. I consider these security worries as part and parcel of the wider regional concerns of the two countries.

Regional Security Perceptions

As we have seen in Chapters 1 and 2, the Middle East has been the stage of constant direct and indirect conflicts between the two embattled neighbors. This condition seemed to be coming to a close as Washington promised the actors in the region a "new regional order" at the end of the 1991 Gulf War. However, this proved somewhat illusory. Although the peace process was launched and new agreements and treaties between the Arabs and Israelis were signed, still the region remained in a state of flux, unpredictability, and volatility, inside an ongoing process of reshuffling alliances. All this fostered a new sense of vulnerability for each of the two embattled neighbors, heightening their fears and intensifying their security concerns over the Golan.

The Gulf War changed the landscape of the region, bringing about new realities in the realm of security with a far-reaching impact on the behavior of Israel and Syria. For Israel, the region as a whole could no longer be divided into heartland and periphery. More specifically, regional developments and conflicts beyond the Arab-Israeli conflict could not be ignored, either as challenges or as threats to the Jewish state. When attacked by Iraqi ballistic missiles, Israel woke up to the reality that such missiles bring distant countries closer, as well as to the fact that it could be attacked even if it had nothing to do with the prevailing crisis. Suddenly, Israel began to face multiple and less tangible challenges and threats in addition to those still emanating from its conflict with the Arabs. These new threats started weighing heavily on the minds of Israeli leaders, because the political reality of the peace process imposed limits on their options, choices, and ability to act.

Under these new circumstances, the Jewish state became deeply concerned not only about a Syrian surprise attack, but also about the possibility of attacks by countries like Iran and Iraq, which have been developing their conventional (and allegedly their unconventional) capabilities. Israel has been trying to meet these new threats by reexamining and revising its military doctrine, on the one hand, and by pursuing two sets of policies to improve its deterrent strategy, on the other hand. The first kind of policy manifested itself in the military alliance with Turkey, while the second took the form of maintaining Israel's long-standing policy of "deliberate ambiguity" about its nuclear weapons.[26]

On the one hand, the Gulf War marked the renewal of Turkey's involvement in the rest of the Middle East. U.S. air bases in Turkey were used to launch bombing attacks against Iraq. More important, the political and military situation in northern Iraq, which the United States designated as a "no-fly zone," deeply worried Turkey. Northern Iraq is the home of the two main Kurdish parties—the Patriotic Union of Kurdistan (PUK) and the Kurdistan Democratic Party (KDP). These two parties have been fighting an insurrectionary war against the Iraqi regime to establish in the north of the country an independent part of historical Kurdistan.[27] With many Kurds living in Turkey and a recent war for independence in the east of the country waged by the Kurdistan Workers Party (PKK), Ankara resisted all Kurdish independence efforts in Iraq for fear that they could spill over into its own territory. This provoked Turkey to intervene militarily in Iraq and pay close attention to what was happening in the region.

On the other hand, although a member of the North Atlantic Treaty Organization (NATO), Turkey feared overall marginalization as a result of the disappearance of the Soviet Union and its threats to the Western alliance. Facing a multitude of regional and internal problems and wanting to stake a claim to a role as a regional power, Syria's northern neighbor sought to improve its relations with the United States and refurbish its armed forces, which are mainly based on U.S. equipment.[28] Ankara met resistance in the U.S. Congress and at the White House, both of which were lobbied by human rights organizations as well as by Greek American and Armenian American pressure groups. Against a background of fledgling Israeli-Turkish military ties, Israel emerged as the solution to Turkey's dilemma. The Jewish lobby could help Turkey counteract the influence of the Greek and Armenian lobbies, and to refurbish its armed forces. Indeed, according to Turkish sources, the United States guided Turkey in the direction of Israel.[29] Non-Arab, largely secular, Western-oriented, and democratic (Israel more so), the two countries shared a wide rationale for close relations.

Israel was more than happy to meet Turkey halfway. Isolated in the region despite its participation in the peace process and concerned with threatening developments all around it, Israel unhesitatingly went headlong into a military alliance with Turkey, negotiated by Prime Minister Yitzhak Rabin in 1994–1995. Two agreements were signed in February and August 1996 and in both some provisions remained secret. They provided for joint air and naval exercises, the opportunity for the Israeli air force to train over the mountainous expanses of Anatolia, intelligence cooperation, and substantial Israeli arms transfers to Turkey.[30] Significantly enough, the military alliance brought Israel closer to the borders of Iran, Iraq, and northern Syria. Using Turkey's strategic location, not only could Israel monitor these countries' development of weapons of mass destruction and their military movements, but it could also undertake deep air raids against them, especially against Iran and Iraq, to destroy the bases of those weapons.[31] With reports circulating that Iran is trying to acquire unconventional (nuclear, chemical, and biological) capabilities with the help of Russia, one could not rule out an Israeli surgical air attack against Tehran to destroy its facilities, an attack similar to that against Iraq's nuclear reactor in 1981.[32]

Israel also held on to its traditional policy on nuclear weapons in spite of its participation in the peace process. For the Israelis, this nuclear potential would always provide the effective deterrence against any Arab state that may think it can destroy Israel. After the Gulf War, within the context of multilateral Arab-Israeli negotiations, Israel and some Arab states convened in Moscow in January 1992 and agreed to create a working group on Arms Control and Regional Security (ACRS). Syria and Lebanon boycotted the negotiations while Iran, Libya, and Iraq were not invited to take part in them. The reported objective of the group was to bring out the fact that meaningful arms control can only be achieved in the context of a wide and stable peace. But after several meetings, two opposing positions crystallized. Egypt emphasized the need to implement nuclear disarmament, while Israel stressed the importance of conflict resolution and confidence building.[33]

Egypt insisted that Israel commit itself to signing the Nuclear Non-Proliferation Treaty (NPT). Syria sided with Egypt. Prior to the 1995 NPT review and extension, Egypt became frustrated with Israel, as the latter gave no indication that it would sign the treaty.[34] Not surprisingly, Egypt lost interest in the ACRS, robbing it of its significance. Israel's refusal to sign the NPT could be explained on the grounds that this nuclear existential deterrence contributes to the country's cumulative deterrence. But as it was recently revealed, other considerations have been on the country's agenda concerning its nuclear policy. The policy of "deliberate ambiguity" has been supported by politicians on the left and the right, who refrained from publicly talking about the nuclear issue. But in a departure from the past that broke the taboo on the nuclear issue, Israel held a debate in parliament on the subject. This quick debate expounded the guiding principles of Israel's nuclear policy. Representing the government, Chaim Ramon, stated:

> Israel will not be the first to use nuclear weapons in the Middle East. Israel, which has not signed the Nuclear Proliferation Treaty, supports, in principle, preventing the spread of nuclear weapons, even though international support of the concept has been ineffective in curtailing Iranian and Iraqi weapons production.

> Israel supports the creation of a region free of nuclear weapons and ballistic missiles once there is a "proven peace over a sustained period of time."[35]

In other words, Israel affirmed its concern over Iran's and Iraq's development of nuclear weapons, and its need to maintain its existential deterrence until it feels secure enough in a peaceful region. This shows that Israel will not compromise on its nuclear existential deterrence, even at the cost of forfeiting arms control cooperation in the region, which creates a regional climate uncongenial to peace.

In addition to these two policies (which cannot be separated from the calculus of Israel's revision of its military doctrine), the political reality of the peace process complicated further the job of the country's decisionmakers with regard to its security. On the Palestinian front, an embryonic Palestinian state is emerging on territories once considered as giving Israel some strategic depth. More specifically, this development created a lightly armed but considerable Palestinian ground force at a hairsbreadth from Israel's main centers. Here, peace is not only taking away Israel's strategic depth but also reducing the country to a space with extremely narrow security margins. In addition, peace has introduced a new element into the equation of Arab-Israeli relations. Israel's decisionmakers can no longer but take into consideration the political impact of the country's use of force on existing Arab-Israeli treaties and agreements.

All this has a direct impact on Israel's security position vis-à-vis Syria, making security arrangements between the two countries all the more difficult. The problem lies in the fact that Israel's decisionmakers have to consider security negotiations with Syria in light of the overall security position of the Jewish state in the region. Regional security concerns begin with the Golan, but surely cannot end with it. It is the political uncertainties of the region that compel those decisionmakers to approach peace while preparing for the unknown. Within this context, Israel's military alliance with Turkey, its position on nuclear weapons, and its military strategy could well be looked at as means to improve and safeguard the overall security of the Jewish state. But the Syrians do not quite see it this way.

The Gulf War was also a watershed for Syria. The country saw its once powerful and rival neighbor, Iraq, soundly defeated. The isolation of Iraq left Syria as the only Arab country of note opposing the Jewish state. In addition, in the event of a Syrian-Israeli war, Damascus could no longer expect Iraqi military support. Damascus took careful note of how efficiently the modern technological war against Iraq was carried out. This highlighted Israel's advanced and superior military capabilities in comparison with Syria's, if only because the Jewish state has been the recipient of advanced U.S. weaponry. Undoubtedly, the Gulf War and the consequent destruction of Iraq's military had tipped the balance of power in the region even more decisively in Israel's favor. Syria joined the peace process partly to neutralize Israel's power and partly to position itself within the context of U.S. plans for a new regional order. But along with that, Syria tried, on the one hand, to strengthen its regional security role, and on the other, to upgrade its military capabilities.

In March 1991 the six Gulf Cooperation Council (GCC) states signed the Damascus Declaration with Egypt and Syria, apparently creating the Arab anti-Iraq coalition.[36] Actually, the declaration provided the poor partners in the coalition, Egypt and Syria, with a security role in protecting the rich Gulf states in return for financial remuneration. However, by the end of the Gulf War, fearing that Egyptian and Syrian troops could become a source of tension in the Gulf, the GCC states were quick to strip the agreement of any significance. In fact, the final text of the agreement did not specify any role for Egypt and Syria.[37] In addition, the GCC states went ahead with signing bilateral security pacts with the United States, further scrapping away any potential Syrian security role in the Gulf.[38]

Another venue for Syria to improve its regional security was its cooperation with Iran. After the Gulf War, Syria continued to promote its relationship with Iran, the state that Syria supported during the Iran-Iraq Gulf War (1980–1988). While many consider this relationship as a strategic alliance, it is really no more than a form of strategic cooperation dominated by realpolitik. The two states are on the extreme ends of the political spectrum in the region: Syria is secular and Iran is theocratic. Fear of potential Iraqi hegemony in the region in the 1980s made Syria support Iran in the first Gulf War, and Syria's weakness vis-à-vis Israel made Damascus more than happy to cooperate with and welcome Iranian support. More specifically, Iran and Syria frequently found themselves on the same side of the political fence facing regional issues, ranging from an unpredictable Iraq to Gulf security to the Arab-Israeli conflict. One aspect of this cooperation had been Syria's benefiting from Hizbollah in Lebanon, Iran's protégé, by waging a guerrilla campaign against the IDF and the South Lebanese Army, while in the south of Lebanon and most recently after the Israeli withdrawal, against Israeli positions in the disputed area of Shebaa Farms (more on this in Chapter 9). Syria has been using this campaign as leverage against the Jewish state.

The realpolitik aspect of this cooperation was revealed when in late 1995 and early 1996 Syria and Israel appeared close to concluding a peace treaty. Suddenly, Iran waged an anti-Syrian propaganda campaign. The propaganda went so far so as to accuse Syria of altering its regional diplomacy and forgetting old friends while at the same time warning Damascene statesmen of the same fate as Anwar Sadat.[39] Iran expressed its concern over a prospective Israeli-Syrian agreement by affirming that the Jewish state was only trying to legitimize its rule in the region. Iran's foreign minister, Ali Akbar Velayati, asserted that "Israel's real objective is not to hold on to the territory [Golan Heights] but to impose hegemony over the entire region."[40]

At the same time, Syria as a member of the Damascus Declaration supported the United Arab Emirates (UAE) in its quarrel with Iran over three

Gulf islands (Abu Musa, Greater Tunb, and Lesser Tunb), claimed by both countries but taken over by Tehran. This made Iran doubly upset with Syria.[41] Apparently, Iran thought that Syria had indeed changed its regional diplomacy and was moving into the political orbit of the United States and Israel. The Persian state feared that the United States and Israel were using the peace process as a means to further contain Tehran (U.S. dual containment of Iran and Iraq) and deny it a regional role by robbing it of its only actual Arab friend, Syria. No doubt, were Syria to join a U.S.-Israeli-Arab alignment, Iran's position in the Gulf would be sufficiently constricted.

Syria understandably knew of Iran's concerns and was quick to allay its fears. Syria conveyed to Iran that Damascus would continue standing on Tehran's side in the international arena and would not relinquish its strategic cooperation with Iran. Damascus asserted that it would not turn its back on its friends in return for whatever was presented to it.[42] In fact, Syria played a mediating role between the Damascus Declaration states and Iran. When the Damascus Declaration states tried to issue a statement supporting the UAE in late 1995, Syria helped alleviate the harshness of the statement against Iran by eliminating a section that described Iran's development of weapons of mass destruction as threatening to the security of the region. Syria's argument was that this section did not distinguish Iran from Israel, the state with the powerful nuclear arsenal.[43] Shortly thereafter, the Syrian foreign minister, Farouk al-Shara, launched some shuttle diplomacy between Iran and Bahrain to help remove their misunderstandings.[44]

As this episode revealed, Iran was concerned with potential regional developments stemming from the peace process that could cause a major disruption in the alignment of forces in the Gulf and affect negatively its regional position. In this respect, one could argue that Iran's opposition to an Israeli-Syrian peace agreement lies in its terms rather than in its very existence. Syria was concerned with strengthening its regional position, especially at a time when it was deeply involved in negotiating a peace treaty with Israel. This, on the one hand, would allow Syria to negotiate from a position of strength; and on the other hand, could be interpreted as a reminder to the United States as well as to Israel that Syria's strategic regional position is irreducible.

By playing a mediating role between the Arabs and Iran, Syria could only enhance its strategic regional role. More specifically, Syria and Iran seemed to share the belief that Israel is bent on achieving hegemony in the region. In addition, the two countries shared another belief that historically they have been the victims of Western conspiratorial plots. Syria looked at Iran both as a means of leverage against Israel and as a counterweight to its power, especially its nuclear capability. This explains why Syria, unlike other Arab countries, did not see Iran's development of weapons of mass destruction as a threat to the region. I would like to emphasize that, absent an Israeli-Syrian peace treaty, Iran-Syria strategic cooperation could transform into a strategic alliance once Iran acquires the nuclear bomb.

This indicates that Syria's quest for strengthening its regional position grew no less out of its military weakness vis-à-vis Israel than out of its sense of vulnerability and insecurity. In fact, Syria took to heart the fact that Israel's security concept rested on the premise that it should maintain its power and superiority over all the Arabs, especially in the technological field. Accordingly, Syria's military strategists held the belief that Israel operates in an environment of peace in the same manner as in an environment of war, meaning through the logic of power and hegemony.[45] It is against this backdrop that Syria bristled with anger against the United States as it monitored Damascus's efforts to upgrade its military capabilities, especially those involving the acquisition of ballistic missiles.

While the issue of how to neutralize Israel's power dominated Syria's security agenda, Damascus had other regional security worries. The country had had difficult relations with Turkey. Historically, in 1939, Turkey with the help of France annexed the formerly Syrian sanjak (district) of Alexandretta, calling it Hatay.[46] Syria never recognized this transfer. Still, tension between the two countries had emanated largely from two additional conflicts, the first over Turkey's Southeast Anatolia Project (GAP) and its building of dams on the Euphrates River (see below), the other over Syria's support for the PKK. Since the 1980s and throughout most of the 1990s, the PKK engaged Turkey in armed struggle and terrorist activities. Ankara accused Damascus of harboring the PKK and its leader, Abdallah Ocalan, and providing them with bases in Lebanon's Beka Valley and in Syria. Ankara believed that the PKK could not continue its terrorist activities without Syria's support.

In 1992 the two countries reached a security agreement, which soon fizzled out as relations between them deteriorated anew. In the mid-1990s, Turkey began to make Syria's suspension of all support to the PKK the focal point of their relationship. Syria denied all Turkish accusations and emphasized that the problem was an internal Turkish one, an emphasis repeatedly voiced by the Ba'thi leaders.[47] Discontented with Syria's responses, Turkey threatened action against its neighbor and suspended all official contacts with it.[48] Tension rapidly rose between the two countries in May–June 1996, leading almost to a military confrontation on the border. The assumption to power of Turkey's Islamic leader, Necmetin Erbakan, temporarily defused the crisis.[49] However, Turkey sent a stern message to Syria in the form of bombing attacks against civilian targets planted by Turkish agents in Damascus and other parts of the country.[50]

Paralleling these developments, the rapprochement between Turkey and Israel during the early 1990s culminated in military agreements, at a time when Turkey was also militarily intervening on a regular basis in northern Iraq. Damascus was quick to interpret Turkey's new assertiveness as a product of the emerging Israeli-Turkish alliance. Syria, which shares an 820-kilometer border with Turkey, saw the alliance as a great geopolitical threat to its regional position and its political cohesion. Not only did Syria become sandwiched by two powerful allies, Turkey and Israel, but it also faced a neighbor, Iraq, threatened by sectarian strife and partition. This, Syria feared, could well spill into its own territory, given the sectarian composition of the country's population. Even before the alliance agreement was signed, some Ba'thi leaders believed that there was a plan to partition Iraq, a plan in sync with a Zionist plot to sow divisions within each individual Arab state.[51] In addition, the timing of the alliance during the Syrian-Israeli negotiations convinced some Ba'thi leaders that the objective of the military agreement was to force Syria to sign a peace treaty with Israel on the latter's terms.[52]

The Turkish-Israeli alliance spawned a flurry of activity in the region. Syria mobilized its efforts to seek regional alliances to offset the impact of the Turkish-Israeli alliance on the regional balance of power. Its previous efforts to strengthen its regional role began to meet positive responses from many Arab countries, which themselves frowned on the Turkish-Israeli alliance. Although Israeli and Turkish leaders affirmed that neither country would assist the other in the event of an attack by a third party, the geopolitical aspect of the agreements and their provisions pointed in another direction.[53] Interestingly enough, Syria's mediation efforts between Iran and the Gulf countries paid off when Saudi Arabia and Iran reached a détente. On the one hand, as a member of the Damascus Declaration, the road was paved for Syria to help bring about a front led by Cairo, Riyadh, and Damascus. On the other hand, Syria deepened its strategic cooperation with Iran.

Contacts between Damascus, Riyadh, and Cairo stepped up. This tripartite entente managed to convene for the first time since the 1991 Gulf War an Arab summit in June 1996 in Cairo. The parties attending the summit expressed their deepest concern over the Turkish-Israeli military alliance and called upon Turkey to reconsider its position with the objective of canceling it. This Arab stance was emphasized in subsequent meetings between the Damascus Declaration states as they called for Arab cooperation. In addition, in a departure from their tough stance on Iraq, they called for protecting the unity of Iraq.[54] Iran was no less quicker than the Arab states to lend its support to Syria. It even proposed the creation of an alliance counteracting that between Turkey and Israel.[55] Syria further improved its strategic cooperation with the Persian state, but short of a military alliance. Following a visit by Asad to Tehran in August 1997, the two countries released a joint declaration in which they emphasized their deepest concern over the Turkish-Israeli alliance, which posed security threats to all neighboring countries and regional stability. They also affirmed the necessity of preserving Iraq's territorial unity.[56]

In retrospect, the Turkish-Israeli alliance apparently evoked Arab suspicions of a Western attempt to establish an alliance, similar to that of the historic Baghdad Pact, to impose its will on the region. Given constant Turkish military interventions in northern Iraq, Syria, like the other Arab states, could not but entertain the idea that Turkey indeed has never given up its ambitions to control the oil-rich provinces of Mosul and Kirkuk.[57] In the vanguard of Arab states, Syria kept affirming that the Turkish-Israeli alliance was directed against the Arabs, with Syria at the center of the alliance's efforts.[58] Heightened Syrian fears of this alliance became all the more telling after these two countries began to flex their muscles against Damascus.

In fall 1996 the Israeli media hyped the possibility of a limited Syrian surprise attack on the Golan Heights. As it turned out, this was fueled in large measure by rumors leaked by a retired Mossad official (Yehuda Gil). But a few months later, the press in Israel began to ask questions about Syria's efforts to quietly acquire ballistic missiles and weapons of mass destruction. Sporadic threats by the government of Israel against Syria accompanied these reports, which centered on Damascus developing Scud assembly lines and chemical and biological weapons. Syria was cautious not to provoke Israel into taking action, but was not reticent. On May 1, 1996, while at a press conference in Egypt, Asad was asked about the Israeli threats and his country's production of the lethal VX gas, which can be carried by missiles. Asad grimly replied that "whoever has nuclear weapons has no right to criticize others for whatever weapons they have. If they [Israelis] want disarmament, let us start with nuclear weapons. We Arabs in general are ready to get rid of the other weapons. We have heard the threats and they did not cause an earthquake, Syria remains unshaken."[59] The conference ended with Syria and Egypt confirming their joint support in facing regional challenges.

Equally significant, Israel, Turkey, and the United States conducted a joint military exercise in the Mediterranean (Operation Mermaid), with Jordan as an observer. Although the exercise was confined to humanitarian purposes, it undoubtedly carried a heavy symbolic message to the region, namely that the United States blessed not only the Turkish-Israeli alliance but also the exercises as a show of force. With the disappearance of the Soviet threat to the region, the Washington-blessed alliance could easily be interpreted by the Arabs as a means to contain and narrow their margin of maneuverability in the area. A few months later in September, tension reached an all-time high between Turkey and Syria as the former massed its troops along the border and appeared ready to invade if Syria did not immediately suspend its support of the PKK. This confirmed Syrian fears not only that Turkey's sudden hardline stand was a product of the Turkish-military burgeoning alliance, but also that Israel was behind this position. The Syrian government's mouthpiece, *Al-Ba'th,* declared on October 2, 1998, that "we in Syria are totally sure that this official Turkish position does not reflect the opinion of the Turkish people. . . . It came as a result of full coordination between Ankara and Tel Aviv in accordance with their alliance."[60]

The gravity of the Turkish-Israeli alliance to regional security and particularly to that of Syria was underscored by Syrian Defense Minister Mustafa Tlas. He stated that "the most serious thing the Arabs are facing is the satanic Israeli-Turkish alliance . . . the Israeli-Turkish alliance is not only aimed at

Syria but at all Arabs."[61] He admitted as well that Israel is also aiming at bringing Jordan into the alliance. However, when Turkish-Syrian relations further intensified in fall 1998 because of alleged Syrian support of PKK activities, Damascus eventually caved in to Turkey's pressure and agreed to suspend all support to the PKK, to bring to court any Kurdish rebel found on its territory, and to no longer allow Ocalan in the country. This was spelled out in an agreement between the two countries signed on October 20, 1998.[62]

As this section has shown, security problems between Israel and Syria start with the Golan and branch off to cover a whole range of issues. This is why security for the two states cannot be separated from overall developments in the area. Conflicts, whether connected or unconnected to the Syrian-Israeli confrontation, eventually affect the two countries' perceptions of all security concerns. What the Gulf War imparted to the region was not cooperation but political competition between the embattled neighbors to adjust to the lessons each side drew from the war. In a climate still charged with old fears, Israeli moves to improve the security of the state were interpreted by Syria as threats of hegemonic expansion by the other side. The two states seemed unable or unwilling to understand each other's security concerns, with each asserting its own concerns without regard to those of the other.

Water Politics and Security

Water is a crucial issue between the two embattled neighbors, affected no less by its scarcity in the Jordan River basin than by the politics of the Arab-Israeli conflict. Eventually, it became the focal point of hydropolitics and geopolitics within the overall context of the conflict. Israel and Syria looked at the issue through the prism of power politics, ultimately transforming it into a strategic matter, a matter of national security and foreign policy. Still, the water issue was not isolated from broader regional influences such as the strategic hydro-logical position that Turkey occupies in the region especially vis-à-vis Syria (and by implication Israel).

The Jordan River basin is an elongated valley in the central Middle East joining four riparian states, Israel and the Occupied Territories (Golan Heights, West Bank, and Gaza Strip), Jordan, Syria, and Lebanon. The Jordan river is the main axis of the basin system. Its waters are fed by rainfall, rivers, and springs originating from the four riparian states. Although it covers parts of the four states, the basin is mostly located in Israel, the West Bank, and Jordan. Israel and Jordan depend mainly on the basin's waters. On average, one-third of Israel's water supply and slightly less than one-half of Jordan's come from the Jordan River system.[63]

The Jordan extends from Mount Hermon in the north to the Dead Sea in the south. As it shall be recalled, the Dan, Hasbani, and Banias Rivers consti-tute the main headwaters of the Upper Jordan. The Dan rises in northeast

Israel adjacent to the Israeli-Syrian international boundary. It has an average discharge of 245 million cubic meters per year into the Jordan, and has a relatively steady flow. The Banias originates on the slopes of Mount Hermon in Syria approximately one kilometer east of the international boundary, and has an average discharge of 121 million cubic meters per year. Heavily dependent on precipitation, the river has an unsteady flow, fluctuating between seasons. The Hasbani River rises at the foot of Mount Hermon in Lebanon. It crosses a corner of Syrian territory before entering Israel. The river is also heavily dependent on precipitation, and its flow strongly varies between summer and winter.[64]

These three rivers converge in Israel, forming the Upper Jordan about twenty-five kilometers north of Lake Tiberias. The Jordan flows through northern Israel into Lake Huleh before entering Lake Tiberias. Lake Tiberias is wholly located inside Israel. As it shall be recalled, its northeastern part is ten meters from the Israeli-Syrian international boundary. Under mandatory agreements, Syrians had obtained fishing and navigation rights there (see Chapter 1). Until June 1967, about one-half of the lake's eastern bank was demilitarized. The lake constitutes the only natural freshwater reservoir in the basin. Over its course from the confluence of the rivers to the northern tip of Lake Tiberias, the Upper Jordan receives an additional amount of water (averaging 150 million cubic meters per year). It then reemerges from the southern tip of the lake to flow less than ten kilometers through Israel before being joined by the Yarmouk River from the east.

The Yarmouk, which has an average discharge of 400–500 million cubic meters per year, rises in the Hauran plain in Syria and flows along the Syrian-Jordanian border before joining the Jordan River in Israel. From the confluence of the Yarmouk River with the Jordan River, the Lower Jordan flows about forty kilometers, demarcating (forming) the Israeli-Jordanian border. The Yarmouk then flows along the boundary between Jordan and the West Bank, entering into in a deep gorge, known as Zhor, on either side of which are steeply rising terraces, referred to as Ghor. The Lower Jordan ends its meandering by discharging into the Dead Sea, the deepest depression below sea level in the world. Over its course, the Lower Jordan receives an additional amount of water mainly from springs and seasonal streams (wadis) on both its sides. While the quality of water in the Lower Jordan is mostly saline and, as it approaches the Dead Sea, is hardly usable, water quality in the Upper Jordan is very high.[65]

The basin is also characterized by a varying climatological feature. The riparian states, especially Israel and Jordan, share an arid to semiarid Mediterranean climate. Not only are the sources of water limited and qualitatively usable, but they are also subject to significant climatic changes. On the one hand, the climate of the basin's riparian states experiences a largely varying seasonal rainfall. Two distinct seasons predominate the basin: a rainy period from November through March, and a dry period throughout the remainder of the year. On the other hand, there is a marked variance in the distribution of precipitation over the basin. This is well pronounced in Israel. For example, annual precipitation in some parts of southern Israel averages about 27 millimeters, while precipitation in the north averages between 900 and 1,500 millimeters around the Upper Jordan and Huleh Valley. This variance in precipitation is exacerbated by unpredictable yearly rainfall. Consecutive years of drought are not unknown in the basin.[66] The hydrological and climatological features of the basin have made water in Israel extremely limited and unevenly distributed. In addition, while the north provides most of Israel's exploitable water resources, most of its agricultural land and population centers lie in the south.

Since the founding of the state, water took on a significant strategic dimension. Israel had to develop its water resources in order to accommodate an expected growing number of immigrants, to build settlements, and to reclaim land for agriculture. Water was ideologically, demographically, politically, and economically significant. Because of the Arab-Israeli conflict, the Arab states, especially the upstream state of Syria, perceived Israel's development of water resources as a threat. Arab waters were sources upon which their enemy depended to strengthen its state. Suddenly, water became a national security issue. As we have seen in Chapter 1, water issues were at the center of the conflict in the DMZ, which contributed to the eruption of the June 1967 war.

It shall be recalled that after the armistice agreement in 1949, Israel's strategy was to extend its sovereignty to the DMZ (up to the 1923 international boundary) in order to drain the Lake Huleh marshes, win exclusive control of Lake Tiberias, and complete its National Water Carrier. Syria, on the other hand, tried to check Israel's advances and secure its riparian rights with respect to the Jordan River and Lake Tiberias. At issue was control over the waters of the Jordan basin. The northernmost DMZ was adjacent to the Banias River and its springs, located on the lower slopes of the Golan Heights. The Banias and Dan Rivers, the latter of which rises west of the Banias in Israel (along with the Hasbani River, rising in Lebanon), feed the Jordan River. The Jordan itself ran through the DMZ north of Lake Tiberias, into the lake. The southernmost DMZ lay directly beneath a towering part of the Golan overlooking Lake Tiberias. So from the beginning of the Israeli-Syrian conflict, water issues were inseparable from border and thus national security issues. In addition, the fact that the northern Golan, especially the area of Mount Hermon, contains the headwaters of the Jordan River and hence Lake Tiberias, enhanced the strategic importance of the DMZ.

Before the war, some efforts were exerted to reach a multilateral accord on water allocation between the riparian states. The most sustained efforts were undertaken by U.S. Ambassador Eric Johnston between 1953 and 1955, following heightened tensions between Israel and Syria over Israel's attempts to construct a canal at Jisr Banat Ya'qub in the DMZ along the Jordan River, to divert the river's waters. In fact, this plan constituted the first stage of Israel's National Water Carrier. Significantly enough, this plan was drawn largely from an Israeli study prepared by James B. Hays in 1948 to develop the water resources of the Jordan basin.[67] The Johnston Plan, based originally on studies carried out by the U.S. Tennessee Valley Authority, established water allocation quotas for the riparian states using Lake Tiberias as the principal storage reservoir. The plan recommended the building of dams on all tributaries of the Jordan River. Initially, the plan was poorly received by the riparian states. However, counterplans were offered, the Cotton Plan by Israel and the Arab Plan by the Arab states.

Ambassador Johnston avoided discussing water rights and succeeded in reaching an agreement on a fixed apportionment among the technical committees of the Arab states and Israel regarding waters of the Jordan River. Israel was part of the agreement, but it received the residual flow while the other states were allocated a fixed amount of water each year. At times of drought, Israel might receive no water from the Jordan River. This final version of the plan, known as the Revised Unified Plan of October 1955, allocated to Jordan 480 million cubic meters per year (mcm/yr), to Syria 132 mcm/yr (42 from the Banias and 90 from the Yarmouk), to Lebanon 35 mcm/yr, and to Israel 466 mcm/yr, for a total of 1,113 mcm/yr.[68] Although it was accepted by Israel and the official Arab representatives at the technical level, the plan was not approved by the Arab League. Different interpretations were given. One of them "maintained that the Arab 'non-adoption' of the plan 'was not total rejection.'" Another interpretation maintained that the plan was rejected on political grounds. Syria led the opposition to the plan in large measure, fearing that cooperation in a water scheme would imply indirect recognition of the Jewish state and pave the way for normalization of relations. After all, pan-Arabism was at its apex and many Arab leaders were reluctant to cooperate with Israelis or endorse a plan that could enhance the power of the Jewish state. Another interpretation maintained that the Arabs broke off the water negotiations because they did not have serious water needs and thought that they had more to lose politically than to gain economically.[69]

Interestingly enough, although the plan was never implemented, the quotas provided a working arrangement, especially between Jordan and Israel, the two countries most dependent on the Jordan River's waters. Indeed, Jordan and Israel tacitly abided by the quotas until 1967. It was during this time that Israel built its National Water Carrier and Jordan undertook the East Ghor (King Abdallah) canal. For all intents and purposes, the experience with the Johnston Plan showed that political and security-related concerns dominated the issue of reaching an accord between the riparian states.

Notwithstanding the heightened tension in the DMZ, Israel was able to complete its National Water Carrier in June 1964. With the backing of the Arab League, Lebanon and Syria initiated their own plans in 1965 to divert the headwaters of the Jordan River in order to prevent Israel from unilaterally utilizing its waters. As mentioned before, the Arab diversionary plan was mainly politically motivated. The water carrier posed a threat to the Arab states and Palestinians by potentially strengthening the Jewish state. Israel responded by launching several air strikes that brought the Lebanese and then the Syrian works to a halt in 1966.

The 1967 war completely changed the hydropolitics of the Jordan basin because Israel took control of all the tributaries and springs of the Jordan River. This condition allowed Israel to increase its use of water from the Jordan far above the Johnston Plan's allocation. Syria, for its part, increased its use of water from the Yarmouk River by building dams on its tributaries, affecting mainly Jordan.

Throughout the years and until the Madrid peace conference, Israel's consumption of water incrementally increased as its population multiplied and its irrigation land expanded. The country's demand for water exceeded its supply while at the same time its climatic and hydrological features further compounded the problem.[70] Israel never wavered in its attitude of controlling the sources of the Jordan River, as it constitutes the only surface water in the country. While the Jordan River supplies Israel with one-third of its water supply, the country relies mainly on groundwater sources to cover the rest. The principal aquifers are the Coastal Aquifer and the Mountain or Yarkon-Tanim Aquifer, which lies in the western highlands of the West Bank.

Over the years, Israel tried to save on its water consumption by reducing its economic dependence on agriculture, which consumes water in great amounts. In fact, the agricultural sector of the economy employed less than 5 percent of the Jewish labor force and made up on average about 3 percent of the gross national product of the country in the 1990s.[71] But despite its efficient national planning and exploitation of water resources, Israel still faced annual water deficits. The country overpumped the Coastal Aquifer while it used the waters of the Mountain Aquifer, which drains naturally westward. Overpumping caused seawater to enter the Coastal Aquifer, a key freshwater source. On the one hand, this degradation is deepening Israel's dependence on the aquifers underlying the West Bank.[72] On the other hand, the overpopulated Gaza Strip, which derives the bulk of its water supply from the Coastal Aquifer, is experiencing increasing water shortages, thereby putting additional pressure on Israel's water resources.[73]

All this has a direct bearing on Israel with regard to its peacemaking negotiations with Syria. The country potentially needs every drop of water and can ill afford any possible Syrian risks to its water resources, especially in light of the important role agriculture plays in the country's national identity and ideology. This is all the more pressing in light of the Palestinians' attempt to claim their right to the water of the West Bank within the context of their peacemaking negotiations with the Israelis. Consequently, Israel's critical water condition accounts for the importance of protecting the headwaters of the Jordan, making the country extremely reserved and cautious with respect to relinquishing the Golan to Syria.

There are several risks pending Israel's withdrawal from the Golan to the cease-fire lines that existed prior to the June 1967 war. First, Syria might attempt to divert the waters of the Banias as in 1965. Second, Syria could divert or block some wadis on the Golan that drain westward. Third, given its hegemony in Lebanon, Syria could well convince the Lebanese to divert or make use of the waters of the Hasbani. Finally, Syria could not only renew its claim to fishing and navigating rights in Lake Tiberias, trying to gain a foothold on Israel's only reservoir of freshwater, but also claim riparian rights to the Jordan River itself. These risks loom large in Israel's security perceptions, particularly as Syria has refused to join any multilateral negotiations dealing with water issues.

Undoubtedly, Israeli water concerns not only add urgency to security concerns, but also are intertwined with them. In other words, if Israel were to return the Golan Heights to Syria and protect, let alone maintain, the usage level of its water sources, it would need to draw up water security borders with Syria that would ensure the country's control of its current resources. In fact, a study of possible alternative borders with Syria to keep Israel in control over its water resources was conducted at the Jaffee Center for Strategic Studies of Tel Aviv University in conjunction with Tahal Water Planning for Israel, a leading quasigovernmental planning agency. A fairly detailed report about the study that contained a water security map, published by *Ha'aretz*, revealed that from a water security point of view the country could return most of the Golan, keeping the tributaries of the Jordan, some side wadis of the Golan Heights, and the entire area contiguous to Lake Tiberias.[74] This roughly conforms with the areas Israel would keep if it were to withdraw to the 1923 international border.

With some slight variations, this position had been embraced by the Labor governments that sought a peace treaty with Syria. One of the main reasons that led to the failure of the Israeli-Syrian negotiations in 2000 revolved around water security borders (and by implication, Israel's insistence to keep exclusive control over Lake Tiberias; see details in Chapters 7 and 8). Questioning why the Syrians would need access to Lake Tiberias, dovish Labor leader Shimon Perez stressed that Israel has two lakes, one of which is dead (referring to the Dead Sea), the other of which the Syrians cannot kill. He stated: "The problem is not over acquiring a minimal access to the Lake. The minute the Syrians touch the Lake, they would become partners in it. This is international law and this is the problem."[75]

At this juncture, one may wonder why water-related concerns involving the Golan should be hard to work out between Israel and Syria, given the latter's insignificant dependence on the Jordan River basin and generally sufficient water resources at present. On the one hand, and most important, the water issue for Syria is inseparable from the border issue with Israel, which is a matter of national interest. In its peace negotiations with Israel, Syria has been adamant about returning to the cease-fire lines that existed prior to the 1967 war, which would allow the country to claim a riparian right to the Jordan basin. On the other hand, even when discounting the weight of history and enmity between the two countries, Syria still has to worry about its future water supplies, which injects a factor of uncertainty into the calculus of water concerns between Syria and Israel.

Syria's water position is situated between the Jordan basin and the Euphrates-Tigris basin. Syria depends minimally on the waters of the Jordan basin (mainly on the Yarmouk River), and has considerable water resources. But this supply of water is based on its ensured share of the Euphrates River and to a much lesser extent the Tigris River. Syria's other rivers and streams, though not unimportant, are of little relative significance (a small exception is the Orontes River, which rises in Lebanon). The Euphrates rises in Turkey and traverses 680 kilometers in Syria before entering Iraq. The Balikh, Sajur, and Khabour Rivers in Syria, all tributaries to the main stream, derive most of their flow from springs whose catchments are in Turkey. Consequently, about 98 percent of the Euphrates flow is subject to upstream withdrawals. Approximately half of the Tigris originates in Turkey and it flows for only 39 kilometers in northeastern Syria. In 1987, Turkey and Syria reached a bilateral agreement whereby the latter would receive 500 cubic meters per second from the Euphrates.[76]

Agriculture plays an important role in the Syrian economy. The Ba'thi regime still views the expansion of irrigated agricultural land and domestic food production as economic priorities. Indeed, agriculture contributed 26 percent to GDP in 1996 and employed almost 29 percent of the total work force in 1995. About 50 percent of the manufacturing work force depend indirectly on agriculture for employment.[77] Simply stated, the country has a growing need for water since agriculture consumes a big chunk of the supply, let alone the fact that Syria has one of the highest population growth rates in the world. The country saw its water consumption increase dramatically from 4.8 billion cubic meters in 1970 to 13.6 billion cubic meters in 1995.[78] One could assume that this trend will continue, since agriculture remains the mainstay of the economy as well as a national priority for the regime.

Given its Mediterranean climate, and to satisfy this growing need for water, Syria undertook ambitious plans to build dams in order to increase the water available for land reclamation projects, to expand cultivated areas, and to conserve water. The Euphrates basin was the main development region, where three significant storage dams have been built: the Tabqa or Al-Thawra dam, the Al-Ba'th dam, and the Tishrin dam, with the first being the centerpiece. Other dams were built on the Asi (Orontes) and the Yarmouk Rivers. Since 1975, Syria has augmented its water use of the Yarmouk, a tributary of the Jordan River on which Jordan depends. Meanwhile, Turkey launched its huge and ambitious project (expected to be completed in 2010), the Southeast Anatolia Project (GAP), to restructure the course of the Euphrates and to a lesser extent the Tigris by building storage dams on them. The project was designed to harness the waters of the rivers for hydroelectric power and irrigation. Most important, the GAP was undertaken as a domestic project to develop the relatively poor and mainly Kurdish region of southeast Anatolia within the framework of fighting Kurdish separatism.[79]

However, this project had negative consequences for the downstream countries of Syria and Iraq. The project threatened to significantly reduce the water flow of the Euphrates into Syria. Indeed, when the Attaturk dam was filled in 1990, Syria experienced a shortage of water. Despite the Syrian-Turkish agreement of 1987, the Syrians angrily insisted that the project will not only reduce Syria's share of the Euphrates, but also pollute it, further harming Syrian agriculture. Inevitably, the use of pesticides and fertilizers for the agricultural development of southeast Anatolia will negatively affect the quality of the water. Already, Syrian farmers along the border with Turkey complain to their government about the negative effects of water reduction and the pollution of the Euphrates.[80] In turn, Turkey complained about Syria building dams on the Asi restricting the flow of water into Hatay.[81]

The GAP has been an additional source of tension between the two countries, let alone between Iraq and Turkey. Syria has been trying to turn the 1987 agreement into a treaty as well as increase its quota. Turkey has been adamant about its position, to the effect that the waters of the Euphrates are solely Turkish since they rise in the country and no one has any right to dictate any terms concerning them. Turkey declared that it is free to exploit its water resources as it sees fit, and added that Arabs have oil while it has water and it does not interfere with the Arabs over how they use their oil.[82] This Turkish interpretation of the question of how to use the water of a riparian river was naturally rejected by Syria, and heightened tensions between them. International law, which has different interpretations on the subject, offered no helpful recourse. However, on May 21, 1997, the UN General Assembly adopted the Convention on the Law of Non-Navigational Use of International Watercourses. The document gave priority to downstream users and affirmed that upstream users should not harm the former. Turkey voted against the convention and gave no sign that it would abide by it.[83]

Turkey's GAP made Syria's supply of water uncertain and by implication affected Israel. It indirectly but inextricably tied Turkey to hydrological problems between the Arabs and the Israelis. As Syria faces an uncertain water supply compounded by a high population growth, it becomes hardly possible to predict the country's plans to exploit its water. Without a regional accord on the water issue, this condition undoubtedly unnerves Israel.[84] Tensions raised by hydrological problems often tend to compel some sort of cooperation between the antagonists (Jordan and Israel). But with the hydrological problems in the Jordan basin so politicized, they intensify anxieties and fears rather than mitigate the harshness of the situation. This situation could prompt the parties to press for greater access to water at a time when the water supply in the area is shrinking, let alone harden their nationalist/ideological positions.

Notes

1. For excellent topographic details, see Aryeh Shalev, *Israel and Syria: Peace and Security on the Golan* (Boulder: Westview Press, 1994), pp. 101–115. See also Ze'ev Schiff, *Peace with Security: Israel's Minimal Security Requirements in Negotiations with Syria* (Washington, D.C.: Washington Institute for Near East Policy, 1993), pp. 31–33.

2. Ibid. (both sources).

3. Much has been written about Israel's military doctrine. Among the best sources, see Michael Handel, "The Evolution of Israeli Strategy: The Psychology of Insecurity and the Quest for Absolute Security," in Williamson Murray, MacGregor Knox, and Alvin Bernstein (eds.), *The Making of Strategy: Rulers, States, and War* (New York: Cambridge University Press, 1994), pp. 534–578; Yoav Ben-Horin and Barry Posen, *Israel's Strategic Doctrine* (Santa Monica: Rand, 1981); and Ariel Levite, *Offense and Defense in Israeli Military Doctrine* (Boulder: Westview Press, 1989).

4. Hirsh Goodman, "The Golan Heights Security Myth," *Jerusalem Report,* October 20, 1994, p. 56.

5. Yoash Tsiddon-Chatto, "The Golan Security Reality," *Jerusalem Report,* December 1, 1994, p. 54.

6. On extension of the front to Lebanon, see Shalev, *Israel and Syria,* pp. 152–155.

7. Aharon Levran, *Israeli Strategy After Desert Storm: Lessons of the Second Gulf War* (London: Frank Cass, 1997), p. 150.

8. Ibid., p. 151.

9. Ibid., p. 154.

10. Ibid., pp. 154–155.

11. Ibid., pp. 106–108; Schiff, *Peace with Security,* p. 55; and Hearings Before the Subcommittees on Arms Control, International Security and Science, Europe and the Middle East of the Committee on Foreign Affairs, House of Representatives, *Conventional Arms Sales Policy in the Middle East* (Washington, D.C.: U.S. Government Printing Office, 1992), p. 64.

12. The government of Prime Minister Barak, who was a former chief of staff, included Amnon Lipkin-Shahak, also a former chief of staff, Matan Vilnai, a deputy chief of staff, and Yitzhak Mordechai, Benjamin Ben-Eliezer, and Ran Cohen.

13. See Shlomo Brom and Yiftah Shapir (eds.), *The Middle East Military Balance, 1999–2000* (Cambridge: MIT Press, 2000); and Lee Hockstader, "Golan No Longer Vital to Israel, Analysts Say," *Washington Post,* January 6, 2000.

14. Ariel Sharon, "Why Should Israel Reward Syria?" *New York Times,* December 28, 1999.

15. For a detailed study, see Eliot A. Cohen, Michael J. Eisenstadt, and Andrew J. Bacevich, *Knives, Tanks, and Missiles: Israel's Security Revolution* (Washington, D.C.: Washington Institute for Near East Policy, 1998). See also David Rodman, "Doctrine and Strategy: Regime-Targeting: A Strategy for Israel," in Efraim Karsh (ed.), *Between War and Peace: Dilemmas of Israeli Security* (London: Frank Cass, 1996), pp. 153–167; Shimon Naveh, "The Cult of the Offensive Preemption and the

Future Challenges for Israeli Operational Thought," in Karsh, *Between War and Peace,* pp. 168–187; and Avi Kober, "A Paradigm in Crisis? Israel's Doctrine of Military Decision," in Karsh, *Between War and Peace,* pp. 188–211.

16. See Chapter 2 in this volume. See also Michael Eisenstadt, *Arming for Peace? Syria's Elusive Quest for "Strategic Parity"* (Washington, D.C.: Washington Institute for Near East Policy, 1992), pp. 2–3.

17. For details on strategic parity, see Chapter 2.

18. Patrick Seale and Linda Butler, "Asad's Regional Strategy and the Challenge from Netanyahu," *Journal of Palestine Studies* 26, no. 1 (Autumn 1996), pp. 30–31.

19. Shalev, *Israel and Syria,* pp. 13–14.

20. Schiff, *Peace with Security,* p. 68.

21. *Al-Anba',* June 30, 1989, pp. 22–23, in *Foreign Broadcast Information Service–Near East and South Asia (FBIS-NES),* July 13, 1989, p. 43.

22. Reacting to U.S. attempts to restrict the flow of missiles to Syria while Israel is allowed to produce all types of weapons, Asad lashed out: "That is not international legitimacy. That is the law of the jungle, the law of wild animals. They are trying to impose surrender on us." *Mideast Mirror,* March 12, 1992, quoted from Muhammad Faour, *The Arab World After Desert Storm* (Washington, D.C.: U.S. Institute of Peace Press, 1993), p. 86. The United States has also been successful in persuading South Africa not to deliver any arms transfers to Syria.

23. See Eisenstadt, *Arming for Peace?* pp. xi, 88.

24. Syria has organized its army for faster mobility while at the same time fielding a large ground force. It shall be recalled that the Syrian armed forces are concentrated in the Beka Valley and around Damascus, especially in the barracks of Qatanah and Kisweh.

25. General Ali Kudr Maksoud, "Al-Stratigiyah al-Israiliya fi al-Tis'inat" (Israel's Strategy in the Nineties), *Al-Fikr al-Askari,* May–June 1996, p. 80.

26. Israel had pursued an alliance with Iran, a peripheral non-Arab state, and has maintained conventional capabilities equal to if not greater than those of the whole region.

27. For details on the Kurdish issue, see Jonathan C. Randal, *After Such Knowledge, What Forgiveness? My Encounters with Kurdistan* (New York: Farrar, Straus, and Giroux, 1997).

28. Internally, Turkey has a chronic problem in the form of a standoff between its military establishment and its religious elements. Externally, Turkey is surrounded by crises involving Greece and the Greek Cypriots, Syria, Iraqi Kurds, Russia, Armenia, and some countries in the Caucasus. For a detailed picture of Turkey, see Cengiz Candar, "Soura li-Turkeya Mina al-Dakhel" (A Picture of Turkey from the Inside), *Shu'un al-Wasat* no. 64 (August 1997), pp. 10–21.

29. See Necmetin Erbakan's interview with *Al-Wasat,* "Erbakan: Liha-dhihi al-Asbab Ata'awan Ma'a Israil" (Erbakan: For These Reasons I Cooperate with Israel), December 30, 1996, pp. 16–17.

30. See Amikam Nachmani, "The Remarkable Turkish-Israeli Tie," *Middle East Quarterly* 5, no. 2 (June 1998), pp. 24–25.

31. For an analytic assessment of Turkish-Israeli cooperation, see Michael Eisenstadt, "Turkish-Israeli Cooperation: An Assessment," *Policy Watch* no. 262 (Washington, D.C.: Washington Institute for Near East Policy, 1997).

32. Chris Hedges, "Iran May Be Able to Build an Atomic Bomb in Five Years, U.S. and Israeli Officials Fear," *New York Times,* January 5, 1995, p. A10. See also Richard Falken and Michael Eisenstadt, "Iran and Weapons of Mass Destruction," *Special Policy Forum Report* (Washington, D.C.: Washington Institute for Near East Policy, 1998).

33. Shai Feldman, *Nuclear Weapons and Arms Control in the Middle East* (Cambridge: MIT Press, 1997), p. 10.

34. Ibid., p. 15.

35. Deborah Sontag, "Israeli Lawmakers Hold Quick Debate on Nuclear Arms," *New York Times,* February 3, 2000, p. A3.

36. The GCC was established in 1981 and included Saudi Arabia, Kuwait, Bahrain, Qatar, the United Arab Emirates, and Oman.

37. See test of the final agreement in *Al-Nahar,* August 7, 1991.

38. See *Mideast Mirror,* September 18, 1991, p. 19, and October 28, 1991, p. 24. See also *Washington Post,* June 23, 1992, p. 15.

39. Quoted in "Damascus' Ungratefulness," *ABRAR,* December 30, 1995, p. 1, in *FBIS-NES,* January 11, 1996, pp. 75–76.

40. Quoted in "Velayati Comments on Relations with Syria," *Al-Wasat,* January 15–21, 1996, pp. 29–31, in *FBIS-NES,* January 18, 1996, p. 69.

41. On the issue, see various Iranian statements in *FBIS-NES,* December 29, 1995, p. 78, and January 3, 1996, p. 84.

42. Hamid Haidar, "Itisalat Awkafat Mawjat al-Intiqadat" (Contacts Stopped the Wave of Criticism), *Al-Wasat,* January 1, 1996, p. 15.

43. Ibrahim Hamidi, "Suriya Tastaghreb al-Hamla al-Iraniya: Al-E'laqat al-Jayida La Ta'ni al-Tatabuk" (Syria Finds Strange the Iranian Campaign: Good Relations Do Not Mean Complete Agreement), *Al-Wasat,* January 1, 1996, p. 16.

44. Bahrain thought that Iran was behind the recent unrest in the country, as many of its Shia citizens staged rowdy demonstrations against the Sunni government. See *Tehran Times,* July 4, 1996, p. 2, in *FBIS-NES,* July 17, 1996, p. 55.

45. Maksoud, "Al-Stratigiyah al-Israiliya fi al-Tis'inat," p. 79.

46. See Philip S. Khoury, *Syria and the French Mandate: The Politics of Arab Nationalism, 1920–1945* (Princeton: Princeton University Press, 1987), pp. 499–514.

47. Even Asad himself followed this line. See *Al-Thawra,* September 19, 1997.

48. Damascus refused to extradite Ocalan at Turkey's official request in early 1996.

49. Erbakan and his Refah Party encouraged the promotion of Turkey's relations with its Muslim neighbors. In a symbolic statement, Erbakan told *Al-Wasat* that he shall remove the Turkish-Syrian border. See Erbakan's interview with *Al-Wasat,* January 1, 1996, pp. 10–12.

50. See *Al-Hayat,* June 10, 1996.

51. See Abd al-Halim Khaddam's interview with *Al-Wasat,* November 20, 1995, pp. 12–14.

52. See statements of Syria's assistant foreign minister, Adnan Umran, on the Turkish-Israeli military agreement in *Al-Thawra,* April 11, 1996.

53. Author interview with Martin Kramer, director of the Moshe Dayan Center for Middle Eastern and African Studies, Tel Aviv University, November 18, 1998.

54. See *Tishrin,* June 25, 1997, and June 17, 1998.

55. *Al-Hayat,* June 20, 1996.

56. See text of the declaration in *Tishrin,* August 2, 1997.

57. The Treaty of Lausanne of July 1923 did not deal with the future of the province of Mosul, integrated de facto by Iraq but claimed by Turkey. However, in a separate accord between Great Britain, Turkey, and Iraq in June 1926, the three states agreed that the province would remain under the sovereignty of Iraq.

58. Khaddam bluntly repeated his accusation that the Turkish-Israeli alliance threatened the security and stability of the region and was directed against the Arabs. He asserted that Syria would oppose all schemes to dismantle Iraq. He also affirmed that there was no reason for Syria to strain its relations with Turkey and that the coun-

try's crisis with the Kurds should be resolved internally. See Khaddam's interview with *Al-Quds al-Arabi* produced in *Tishrin,* June 15, 1997.

59. See press conference in *Tishrin,* May 2, 1997.

60. *Al-Ba'th,* October 2, 1998, quoted from *Middle East Economic Survey (MEES),* October 5, 1998, p. C2. Israel signaled that it was not involved in the Turkey-Syria border standoff by stepping down its military activities close to the Syrian border at the time.

61. *MEES,* October 5, 1998, pp. C2–C3.

62. See *Middle East International,* October 30, 1998, p. 9. For the text of the agreement, see *Middle East Quarterly* 6, no. 2 (June 1999), p. 24.

63. The Jordan River system has been extensively studied. There exist some discrepancies in data concerning its hydrological and topographical features. However, these discrepancies do not affect the analysis of this section of the study. See Miriam R. Lowi, *Water and Power: The Politics of a Scarce Resource in the Jordan River Basin* (Cambridge: Cambridge University Press, 1993), pp. 20–32; Natasha Beschorner, *Water and Instability in the Middle East,* Adelphi Paper no. 273 (London: International Institute for Strategic Studies, 1992), pp. 8–18; Thomas Naff and Ruth C. Matson (eds.), *Water in the Middle East: Conflict or Cooperation?* (Boulder: Westview Press, 1984), pp. 17–23; Nurit Kliot, *Water Resources and Conflict in the Middle East* (London: Routledge, 1994), pp. 175–185; Shalev, *Israel and Syria,* pp. 156–157; and Efraim Orni and Elisha Efrat, *Geography in Israel* (Jerusalem: Israel Universities Press, 1971).

64. Ibid.

65. Ibid., especially Lowi, *Water and Power,* and Naff and Matson, *Water in the Middle East.*

66. For climatic details, see, among others, Lowi, *Water and Power,* pp. 20–32; Asit K. Biswas, John Kolars, Masahiro Murakami, John Waterbury, and Aaron Wolf, *Core and Periphery: A Comprehensive Approach to Middle Eastern Water* (Oxford: Oxford University Press, Middle East Water Commission Sasakawa Peace Foundation, 1997), pp. 9–12; and Masahiro Murakami and Katsumi Musiake, "The Jordan River and the Litani," in Asit K. Biswas (ed.), *International Waters of the Middle East: From Euphrates-Tigris to Nile* (Oxford: Oxford University Press, 1994), p. 118.

67. James B. Hays, *TVA on the Jordan: Proposals for Irrigation and Hydro-Electric Development in Palestine* (Washington, D.C.: PublicAffairs Press, 1948).

68. Georgiana G. Stevens, *Jordan Water Partition* (Stanford: Stanford University Press, 1965), p. 16. The residual flow is Israel's share of the total flow given that the above-listed amounts were claimed as necessary by the other states. Israel's share would vary according to the flow conditions in the river system.

69. See respectively, Naff and Matson, *Water in the Middle East,* p. 41; Lowi, *Water and Power,* pp. 79–105; and David M. Wishart, "The Breakdown of the Johnston Negotiations over the Jordan Waters," *Middle Eastern Studies* 26, no. 4 (October 1990), pp. 45–53.

70. For details and figures on supply and demand, see Kliot, *Water Resources and Conflict,* pp. 222–248; Naff and Matson, *Water in the Middle East,* p. 47; Biswas, Kolars, Murakami, Waterbury, and Wolf, *Core and Periphery,* pp. 13–14.

71. Data compiled by Elie Rekhess in a paper delivered at the Moshe Dayan Center, Tel Aviv University, December 1998, "The Arab and Druze Minority in Israel: Statistical Data," quoted from *Israel Statistical Abstract, 1998.* See also Bank of Israel, *Annual Report,* 1993.

72. Kliot, *Water Resources and Conflict,* pp. 232–248; and Biswas, Kolars, Murakami, Waterbury, and Wolf, *Core and Periphery,* pp. 13–14.

73. Beschorner, *Water and Instability*, pp. 14–15. For an overview of Palestinian conditions in the Gaza Strip and the West Bank, see Sara M. Roy, *The Gaza Strip: A Demographic, Economic, Social, and Legal Survey* (Boulder: Westview Press, 1986); Sara M. Roy, *The Gaza Strip: The Political Economy of De-Development* (Washington, D.C.: Institute for Palestine Studies, 1995); and Sara M. Roy, *The Palestinian Economy and the Oslo Process: Decline and Fragmentation* (Abu Dhabi: Emirates Center for Strategic Studies and Research, 1998). For Palestinian claims on water, see Committee on the Exercise of the Inalienable Rights of the Palestinian People, *Water Resources of the Occupied Palestinian Territory* (New York: United Nations, 1992). See also Leslie Schmida, *Keys to Control: Israel's Pursuit of Arab Water Resources* (Washington, D.C.: American Educational Trust, 1983).

74. Ze'ev Schiff, "The Censored Report Revealed" (in Hebrew), *Ha'aretz,* October 8, 1992; and Hillel I. Shuval, "Water and Security in the Middle East: The Israeli-Syrian Water Confrontations as a Case Study," in Lenore G. Martin (ed.), *New Frontiers in Middle East Security* (New York: Palgrave, 2001).

75. See Shimon Peres's interview with Patrick Seale in *Al-Hayat,* March 29, 2000. For details, see Chapter 8 in this volume.

76. Beschorner, *Water and Instability*, pp. 27–34; and Biswas, Kolars, Murakami, Waterbury, and Wolf, *Core and Periphery*, pp. 15–16. See also Ibrahim Hamidi, "Mi'yah al-Sarf al-Turkiyeh Touhadid 7 Malayin Souri" (Turkish "Discharge" Waters Threaten Seven Million Syrians), *Al-Wasat,* March 25, 1996, pp. 14–20.

77. *Economist Intelligence Unit,* "Country Profile: Syria 1998–1999," p. 23.

78. See Fahd Diyab, "Syria: Water Resource Management Efforts Reported," *Al-Thawra,* July 7, 1996, quoted from *FBIS-NES,* July 24, 1996, pp. 26–27.

79. For details on the project, see John F. Kolars and William A. Mitchell, *The Euphrates River and the Southeast Anatolia Development Project* (Carbondale: Southern Illinois University Press, 1991).

80. Hamidi, "Mi'yah al-Sarf al-Turkiyeh Touhadid 7 Malayin Souri," pp. 16–19.

81. Istanbul SHOW Television, January 30, 1996, quoted from *FBIS-NES,* January 31, 1996, pp. 37–38.

82. See interview with the Turkish minister of state and overseer of the GAP in *Al-Sha'b al-Arabi,* August 25, 1997, pp. 12–13.

83. UN General Assembly, UN Document GA/9248, May 21, 1997. For more information on the water issue, see Murhaf Jouejati, "Water Politics as High Politics: The Case of Turkey and Syria," in Henri J. Barkey (ed.), *Reluctant Neighbor: Turkey's Role in the Middle East* (Washington, D.C.: U.S. Institute of Peace Press, 1996). For legal and commercial details, see J. A. Allan and Chibli Mallat (eds.), *Water in the Middle East: Legal, Political, and Commercial Implications* (London: I. B. Tauris, 1995).

84. For proposals on how to deal with the Israeli-Syrian water issue, see Shuval, "Water and Security."

7

Elusive Peace: The
Israeli-Syrian Negotiations

In spite of a decade of intermittent, intensive negotiations between Syria and
Israel, a peace treaty continues to elude the two embattled neighbors. Thus it
seems appropriate to present an account of the sequence of the negotiations
they have been engaged in, starting with the Madrid peace conference, a
sequence that shows how every time the two countries appeared to be "on the
brink" of a breakthrough, peace became even more elusive than before.

Sequence of Negotiations

The peace conference, convened in Madrid on October 30, 1991, was cospon-
sored by the United States and the former Soviet Union to advance the
prospects for genuine peace between the Arab states, the Palestinians, and
Israel. It was attended by representatives of the UN, the European Union, the
Gulf Cooperation Council, and Egypt. The principal parties to the conference
were Syria, Lebanon, Israel, and a joint Jordanian-Palestinian delegation. The
aim of the cosponsors was to assist the parties in achieving a just, lasting, and
comprehensive peace through direct negotiations, based on UN Security
Council Resolutions 242 and 338 and the principle of "land for peace." The
conference paved the way for bilateral negotiations, as well as laid the ground
for multilateral negotiations to discuss regional issues such as arms control,
security, water, refugees, and economic development.

The framework of the Madrid peace conference was drawn by the U.S.
letters of assurances sent to the Arab states and Israel. The United States
devised its letters to Syria and Israel to fit their own separate understandings
of how to resolve the Arab-Israeli conflict. The letters were a classic case of
"constructive ambiguity," used ingeniously by the Bush administration to
bring the two embattled neighbors together under one roof. In the letter of
assurances to Syria, the Bush administration, among other points, stated that

the "peace conference and the talks that follow must be based on Security
Council Resolutions 242 and 338," and that the "U.S. will throughout these
negotiations continue to be committed to the fact that Security Council Resolution 242 and the land-for-peace principle are applicable to all fronts, including the Golan Heights."[1]

In the letter addressed to Israel, the Bush administration, among other
points, affirmed that "Israel holds its own interpretation of Security Council
Resolution 242, alongside other interpretations," and that the "U.S. recon-
firms ex-president Gerald Ford's written commitment to ex-premier Yitzhak
Rabin of September 1975 regarding the importance of the Golan Heights to
Israel's security."[2] While these letters succeeded in bringing the two embattled neighbors to Madrid on October 30, 1991, they kept the opening positions
of the two sides far apart. In his address to the conference, the head of the Syrian delegation, Foreign Minister Farouk al-Shara, emphasized that Syria was
seeking a just and honorable peace that comprehensively covered all aspects
and all fronts of the Arab-Israeli conflict. He confirmed that Syria's stand was
based on the principles of international legitimacy and the UN resolutions,
and mandated Israel's total withdrawal from the occupied Syrian Golan, the
West Bank, Jerusalem, the Gaza Strip, and southern Lebanon. He added that
Syria would not join the multilateral talks until a concrete achievement in the
bilateral talks ensured the removal of the major obstacles to peace.[3]

Israel, on its part, dismissed most of Syria's stand on the peace process.
The head of the Israeli delegation, Prime Minister Yitzhak Shamir, unequivocally held to his country's interpretation of UN Security Council Resolution
242, to the effect that Israel withdraw from some of the occupied territories
only. Indeed, this position reflected Likud's and the Shamir government's
"peace for peace" policy. Shamir maintained that the resolution called on the
Arabs to make peace with Israel within the context of "secure and recognized"
boundaries in return for withdrawal from some of the occupied territories.
Since Israel had already met its obligations when it withdrew from the bulk of
the territories (the Sinai), it was now entitled to peace with its Arab neighbors
without offering any additional territorial concessions.[4]

The gap between the two positions was wide and deep, and the two
embattled neighbors exchanged sharp recriminations over the past. However,
the fact that the two of them sat together under one roof after so many years
of shunning and demonizing each other was by itself a great historic achievement. Muwaffaq Allaf, a Syrian diplomat who had served at the United
Nations, and Yossi Ben-Aharon, the director-general of the Israeli prime minister's office, led the two negotiating teams. The negotiations expectedly led
nowhere, while the political parties in Israel prepared for the upcoming elections in summer 1992. Shamir's government showed no sign either of accommodating the Syrian position on the peace process or of stopping the expansion of settlement activity in the territories. Consequently, the Syrians lost
whatever little faith they may have had in that government. As it turned out,

Shamir later admitted, after his failed bid for reelection, that had he been reelected he would have strung out negotiations for at least ten years.[5]

The Israelis went to the polls in June 1992 and handed the Labor Party and its leader, Yitzhak Rabin, an election victory. In addition to the premiership, Rabin kept for himself the Ministry of Defense. He appointed Shimon Peres as foreign minister, and Itamar Rabinovich, the academic and expert on Syria, as ambassador to the United States and chief of the Israeli negotiating team with Syria. Rabin gave priority to the Jewish character of Israel and agreed in principle to the ruling idea of land for peace so long as Israel's security was guaranteed. This new tone, sending a positive signal to Syria, was confirmed when Rabinovich emphasized to the Syrian negotiators in late August 1992 that "Israel accepts Security Council Resolution [242] in all its parts and provisions as a basis for the current peace talks and views it as applicable also to the peace negotiations with Syria."[6]

Syria acknowledged positively Israel's new policy, but insisted on hearing a more explicit statement committing Israel to full withdrawal from the Golan. At the time, Walid Muallem, the Syrian ambassador to the United States, was assisting Allaf. As Syria failed to extract this statement, it prepared a document titled "Draft Declaration of Principles," which would serve as a guide to the next rounds of negotiations. According to Allaf, the document was created taking into account the legitimate demands of both sides:

> The Syrian document includes all the requirements for the establishment of a comprehensive and just peace. And it talks about the complete withdrawal, without which no peace can be established. It also talks about acceptable security arrangements, provided these arrangements are equal on both sides.[7]

According to Rabinovich, the Israeli side found the Syrian document unsatisfactory on account of several problems. The first was that the Syrians had insisted on a full Israeli withdrawal from the Golan Heights. The second was that there were only vague references to the issues of peace, security, and the relationship of a prospective Israeli-Syrian agreement to the other bilateral tracks. Rabinovich interpreted the draft as a glorified nonbelligerency agreement in return for full withdrawal. In addition, the Syrians were setting preconditions for the security arrangements as well as creating a deliberate ambiguity over the issue of linkage to the other tracks.[8]

Apparently, Asad was serious about a settlement but remained determined to obtain from Israel a commitment to full withdrawal from the Golan before any discussion on the nature of peace. He based his position on a "legalistic" interpretation of Resolutions 242 and 338. This was plainly reflected by Allaf's remark that "when Israel says it will not discuss withdrawal until Syria explains the meaning of peace, it is imposing prior conditions not stipulated in Resolutions 242 and 338."[9] Equally significant, the ambiguity over the linkage of tracks suggested that Asad was beginning either to wiggle out of or to show greater flexibility in his initial hard-line position concerning the return of all Arab occupied territories.

Around this time in August 1992, the Bush administration began to pay significant attention to the U.S. election campaign. Secretary of State Baker left the State Department and returned to the White House as chief of staff in order to handle Bush's bid for reelection. Undersecretary of State Lawrence Eagleburger replaced Baker and took charge of the peace process, assisted by former U.S. ambassador to Damascus Edward Djerejian. Not surprisingly, the Bush administration's preoccupation with the election campaign began to cast a pall over the negotiations.

In early September, Asad, addressing a visiting Druze delegation from the Golan, spoke of the need for a "peace of the brave." He stated: "We want the peace of the brave, the peace of the knights, a true durable peace that protects everybody's interests."[10] Apparently, by speaking publicly, Asad was trying to nudge the negotiations along by showing his seriousness. In response to these developments on the Syrian side, the Israelis prepared their own document, in which they included the term "territorial dimension" (and later "territory"). Then, in late October, the Israeli delegation mentioned for the first time the term "withdrawal," but without any reference to its extent. Although the Syrian delegation was delighted with this new approach, it resented the fact that Israel linked withdrawal to establishing "secure and recognized boundaries."[11]

During fall 1992, the Israeli-Syrian negotiations in Washington revolved around Syria's consistent demand for a full Israeli withdrawal from the Golan, on the one hand, and Israel's counterdemand that Syria explain the nature of the peace it is offering, on the other. Israel wanted to hear principally about normalization and security issues. It also tried to persuade the Syrians of the great benefit to the peace process that could accrue from public diplomacy. According to Rabinovich, Rabin reached a formula that remained the hallmark of his Syrian policy for a long time: "The depth of withdrawal will reflect the depth of peace."[12] While this Israeli-Syrian give and take did not yield a result, it made the Palestinians nervous about the possibility of Syria concluding a separate peace, since they were achieving no progress in their own negotiations with Israel. In the meantime, President Bush failed in his bid for reelection in November and Governor William Jefferson Clinton of Arkansas was elected president.

President Clinton appointed Warren Christopher secretary of state and put him in complete charge of the peace process. Subsequently, Dennis Ross, the former Bush administration official, was recalled to the State Department to assist Christopher. With the new Clinton administration settling in, the thrust of the Israeli-Syrian negotiations was parried by lack of progress. Meanwhile, Hamas began a campaign of terror against Israelis in Gaza and the West Bank in order to derail the peace process. In a show of resolve in December 1992, Rabin deported to Lebanon 400 Muslim activists suspected of instigating trouble. Beirut refused to take them in, and the Palestinians ended up in what was referred to as "no-man's land."

Objecting to Rabin's action, the Palestinians and the Syrians suspended their talks with the Israelis. This hurdle in the path of the peace process became only one of many to prompt Christopher to travel to the region in order to try to mediate the outstanding issues. Christopher met Asad and his counterpart Shara in Damascus in late February 1993 and talked them into resuming the negotiations. During a news conference on February 21, Christopher, joined by Shara, stated: "We talked about the desirability of an early resumption of the negotiations and the need to make substantive progress. To that end I conveyed to President Asad President Clinton's commitment to have the U.S. play the role of a full partner in the negotiating process."[13]

Consequently, the bilateral negotiations resumed in April 1993, after a few months' hiatus. Again the Israeli-Syrian talks were bogged down by the same core issues of withdrawal, security, and normalization. On April 28, Edward Djerejian, assistant secretary for Near Eastern affairs, remarked before the Subcommittee on Europe and the Middle East of the House Committee on Foreign Affairs: "The Syrians and Israelis have been addressing the core issues of territory, security and peace. . . . But continued commitment and hard work are needed from both parties to narrow the substantive gaps in their position."[14] In mid-March, Rabin traveled to Washington to meet Clinton. The two hit it off very well and both seemed interested in concluding an Israeli-Syrian peace agreement, which in principle would be easier to deal with than an Israeli-Palestinian one. During this meeting, given his position during the elections of 1992 and his feeling that he did not have a mandate to make a decision on his own concerning the Golan, Rabin told Clinton that any major agreement with Syria would have to be approved by a referendum.[15]

Apparently, to break the stalemate, Asad gave a long interview to Patrick Seale, published in full in the London-based Arabic weekly *Al-Wasat* and in the form of an op-ed by Seale himself in the *New York Times* in May 1993. This came in the wake of Asad's political gesture of allowing Syrian Jews to freely emigrate.[16] In the interview, Asad declared that the Arabs by virtue of accepting the UN resolutions had agreed, de facto, that both the Israelis and the Arabs have their place in Palestine. More important, the president of Syria announced a formula for resolving the conflict with Israel: "Full peace for full withdrawal."[17] Obviously, this Syrian formula was a developed counteroffer to Rabin's earlier position that the Israeli withdrawal be proportional to the depth of the peace with Syria. With this new and more flexible formula, Damascus obviously departed from its original position of "establishing a comprehensive, just and lasting peace in the Middle East," to that of "full peace for full withdrawal." The underlying assumption was that while the first position meant the return of all Arab occupied territories in order to resolve the Israeli-Syrian conflict, the second applied to the Golan Heights only.

However, Asad did not want to convey to Israel the idea that he had completely severed his negotiating track from the others, especially that of the Palestinian. He emphatically expressed in the interview that "any peace which is not comprehensive will not last."[18] It seems as if Asad had begun to emulate the United States by using its own diplomatic language of "constructive ambiguity." Seemingly, he was trying to maintain coordination among the different Arab-Israeli negotiating tracks, while at the same time offering Israel a separate settlement that would "stand on its own two feet," as the Israelis frequently like to describe it. As we shall see later, this position did not sit well with the Palestinians. During this time, Damascus continued to reject the proposal of establishing a secret negotiating channel with Israel. Actually, Israel was pressing Syria to exercise public diplomacy in the negotiations and to open a very secret negotiating channel at the same time. In the meantime, Dennis Ross and Martin Indyk became the inner core of the U.S. team dealing with the peace process, with the former becoming the special Middle East coordinator.

Before long, the Israeli response to Asad's proposal was spelled out by Rabinovich. Writing in the *New York Times,* he welcomed Asad's interview as "one of the most important developments of the round of the Arab-Israeli peace talks that ended last Thursday."[19] However, he added that "Mr. Asad's positive but partial response to some of Israel's fundamental concerns may point to the prospect of a breakthrough in these negotiations in the coming months, but offers the lingering threat of a stalemate."[20] While Rabinovich considered Asad's interview as "the single most impressive act yet of public diplomacy performed by Syria's President in the context of the peace talks with Israel," he perceived it as a far cry from Anwar Sadat's spectacular public diplomacy, as not signifying what "full peace" meant with regard to normalization, and as still retaining some ambiguity with regard to the linkage to the other tracks.[21] In short, Rabinovich declined to fully endorse the new Syrian position since it did not clearly respond to Israel's concerns over security, public diplomacy, and the nature of the peace on offer.

Meanwhile, Hizbollah intensified the tension on the Lebanese-Israeli border by firing Katyousha rockets at the Galilee. Apparently, Asad was combining his diplomacy with military pressure, something that became a staple in Syria's relations with Israel. Rabin did not take this lightly and responded by launching Operation Accountability in summer 1993. The main objective of the operation was to provoke a Lebanese mass exodus from the south of the country to the capital, thereby putting pressure on the Lebanese government and in turn on its Syrian patron. At this point, one could not fail to notice that these two statesmen and former military officials never shucked military pressure as a political option and were eyeing each other through the prism of power politics while engaged in peace negotiations.

Soon enough the operation triggered worldwide criticism of Israel, given the sight of thousands of Lebanese fleeing their homes and becoming refugees in their own country. Secretary Christopher applied himself hard to obtain a cease-fire. He worked out an oral agreement between Asad, Rabin, and Rafiq Harriri, the prime minister of Lebanon, that set the rules of engagement in Israel's occupied security zone in the south of Lebanon. According to Rabinovich, Hizbollah would not launch rockets against Israel while alternately Israel would not fire into villages north of the security zone unless fired upon from within a village.[22]

In the meantime, on August 3, 1993, knowing that Asad would not budge before hearing the magic "withdrawal" word, Rabin met with Christopher and made his historic opening to Syria. He asked the secretary of state to convey to Asad that he was prepared in principle to make the full withdrawal from the Golan Heights, provided Syria would satisfy Israel's concerns mainly in the realms of security and normalization and within the context of a separate peace agreement.[23] According to Rabinovich, Rabin's gambit was a "hypothetical approach," leaving the door wide open for Asad. Equally significant, Rabin told Christopher that he could only proceed on one track of negotiations at a time, with preference given to the Israeli-Syrian track.[24]

After meeting with Asad, Christopher returned to Israel and revealed what he considered a positive response from the Syrian president. But for Rabin the response seemed disappointing. According to William Quandt, while Asad appreciated the opening, he wanted to know first and foremost what Rabin had in mind for withdrawal: Was it to the 1923 international boundary or to the June 4, 1967, lines?[25] Rabin was so annoyed by Asad's response that he shifted attention from the Israeli-Syrian to the Palestinian track. As a result, the Israeli-Syrian negotiations stalled and soon after the Syrians were flabbergasted to learn in late August that the Palestinians and the Israelis had reached a separate agreement. This development immediately turned the Israeli-Palestinian track into the cornerstone of the whole peace process. Asad was furious, but had to contain his anger. He even sent Walid Muallem, his ambassador to the United States, to attend the signing ceremony of Oslo's Declaration of Principles on the lawn of the White House, most likely in a gesture of goodwill to President Clinton.

Rabinovich gave a more detailed account, expounding that while Asad had agreed to a full-fledged peace, he refused to engage in public diplomacy, rejected a five-year time withdrawal period, and rejected the idea of a large measure of normalization in return for a limited Israeli withdrawal at the outset. In short, Asad's response entailed a long list of conditions, making prospective bargaining disadvantageous to Israel. Consequently, Rabin gave Peres the green light to try to clinch a deal with the Palestinians, who a few months earlier had agreed to join the Israelis in a secret channel of negotiations in Oslo.[26]

Clinton presided over the ceremony and the historic handshake between Rabin and Yasser Arafat. He saw in the agreement a precursor of those to follow, particularly between Israel and Syria. Shortly before the ceremony, in an interview with Thomas Friedman, Clinton appeared to reflect his preference for a potential Israeli-Syrian breakthrough.[27] Rabin, on the other hand, began to attach greater importance to fulfilling the Oslo Accords and moving forward on the Jordanian track. The complex issues relating to peace, withdrawal, and security continued to separate the Israelis and Syrians.[28] Given the U.S. preference for a breakthrough with Syria, preparations began for a Clinton-Asad summit meeting, while Christopher went to the region in December 1993 in an effort to move the Israeli-Syrian negotiations forward. In Damascus, after meeting with Asad for several hours, Christopher announced on December 5 that Syria had agreed to invite a team of U.S. congressional staffers to help resolve the problem of Israelis missing in action and to allow Syrian Jews to leave the country.[29] Apparently, Christopher was sending a message to Israel accentuating Syria's desire to proceed with the peace process, as well as paving the way for President Clinton's meeting with his Syrian counterpart.

The year 1994 opened with an optimistic note concerning the Israeli-Syrian peace negotiations. Clinton met Asad in Geneva in January and the two focused on how to move the peace process forward. Interestingly enough, Asad in his lengthy opening statement at a joint press conference with President Clinton said that "Syria seeks a just and comprehensive peace with Israel as a strategic choice that secures Arab rights, ends the Israeli occupation, and enables all people in the region to live in peace, security and dignity." He then added that "we want the peace of the brave . . . a peace which secures the interests of each side. . . . If the leaders of Israel have sufficient courage to respond to this kind of peace, a new era of security and stability in which normal peaceful relations among all shall dawn."[30] This constituted an important turning point in Asad's approach to negotiations with Israel. By committing himself to establishing normal relations within the context of peace, Asad was sending Israel a message of his readiness, unlike before, to discuss normalization.

Rabin was cautious in his response, speculating about what kind of concessions Syria was ready to make. According to Rabinovich, Rabin was not pleased. Asad had agreed to peace and normalization but remained adamant about Syria's position on equal security arrangements on both sides of the border. In addition, Rabin saw the summit as producing very little in public diplomacy that could help him with the Israeli public. So he preferred to move on with Jordan.[31] In any event, the Israelis and Syrians met in Washington and returned to the same familiar pattern. The former would not address withdrawal before discussing security arrangements, a time frame, and phases, while the latter would discuss only withdrawal.

The course of the peace negotiations then took an ominously sharp twist and the optimistic mood of the beginning of the year swiftly vanished. On February 25, 1994, an Israeli fanatic, Baruch Goldstein, vented his hatred of Arabs in the Hebron Mosque in the West Bank. With his automatic assault rifle, he riddled to death twenty-nine Palestinian worshippers celebrating the

Muslim holy month of Ramadan. Consequently, the Syrian and Palestinian talks were temporarily derailed. The United States was quick to intervene to remedy the situation, and before long President Clinton met with Rabin in March in Washington. The president discussed ways to put the Israeli-Palestinian negotiations back on track and emphasized the importance of an Israeli-Syrian breakthrough in 1994. Rabin recognized the importance of Syria to a comprehensive peace in the area and confirmed to Clinton that peace with Syria had always been Israel's strategic choice. But Rabin was careful to indicate that he would not compromise on security and that he would do what was required of him if the Syrians were ready to do what was required of them.[32]

Rabin's statements suggested that while he remained in principle committed to peace negotiations with Syria, he was aware of the security obstacles that lay ahead on that track. At this point, it became clear also that he was concentrating his peace efforts on the Palestinian and Jordanian tracks. So while no progress on the Syrian-Israeli front took place in spring, the Israeli-Palestinian talks resumed and some progress was achieved. In late April, Christopher went to the region to witness this progress, which took the form of the Jericho-Ghaza Agreement. At the same time, he had in mind the reviving of the Israeli-Syrian talks. His first stop was in Israel, where he discussed principally the time frame, the phasing, and the security arrangements, the three components of a peace package that Israel was by now insisting upon.

Then he traveled to Damascus to probe the Syrian response. According to Rabinovich, Asad informed Christopher that withdrawal had to be to the June 4, 1967, lines and that the time frame was about six months. In addition, Asad questioned some of Israel's proposals regarding security arrangements, continuing to insist that they be on an "equal footing" and "on both sides" of the border.[33] It was against this background in May 1994 that Christopher further augmented his mediating efforts, paving the way for what came to be referred to as the "ambassadors' channel." This channel intended to bring Rabinovich, the Israeli ambassador to the United States, together with his Syrian counterpart, Muallem, to discuss privately what is known in Israel's negotiations parlance as the "four legs" of peace, i.e., normalization, security arrangements, withdrawal, and the time frame. Correspondingly, in July 1994, Muallem became the head of the Syrian delegation to the peace talks.

Reportedly, what brought about this Syrian change was Israel's unambiguous admission at the time that full withdrawal meant to the June 4, 1967, lines. Muallem explained what had happened leading to this phase of the negotiations:

> After Rabin became prime minister in June 1992, we still insisted on discussing withdrawal only. When Rabin finally realized that the Syrians would not move a step ahead in discussing any of the other elements of a peace settlement before being convinced of Israel's intention of full withdrawal, he made the opening.

That was in August 1993, and we negotiated the details of the withdrawal element for almost a year, until July 1994, when we finalized the
agreement on full withdrawal to the 4 June 1967 lines. This opened the way
for negotiations on the other elements of a peace agreement—what Prime
Minister Rabin used to call the "four legs of the table." Besides withdrawal,
these elements are normalization, security arrangements, and the timetable
of fulfillment.[34]

Another Syrian governmental source (anonymous) confirmed later on
that Rabin's understanding of withdrawal remained ambiguous until July
1994, at which time it became clear that it would be to the June 4, 1967,
lines.[35] These explanations were rebutted by Rabinovich, who insisted that
there was no such commitment. He added that the opening peace gambit was
hypothetical only.[36] In the meantime, progress was taking place on the Israeli-
Jordanian track. On July 25, 1994, the two countries signed the Washington
Declaration, ending the state of belligerency between them. Again, the Syrians thought that Rabin was giving them short shrift by bypassing them. Nevertheless, the ambassadors' channel began in late July, and Rabinovich and
Muallem discussed in general all issues relating to a peace settlement.

In September, Asad spoke at the opening session of the Syrian parliament, reiterating Syria's strategic choice for a just peace, and took the opportunity to criticize Jordan and the Palestinians for their separate deals with
Israel. He affirmed that Syria wanted a just peace because it wanted stability
in the region, a peace that would return the land. He also indicated that his discussions with President Clinton involved regional issues and that both of them
had emphasized their desire to push the peace process forward. Although his
speech was generally rigid, he ended it on an optimistic note, emphasizing that
despite the obstacles and the lack of progress there still remained some hope
for achieving peace.[37] One could deduce from this speech that Asad was conditioning his people for the probability of peace, on the one hand, and stressing that U.S. involvement was at the center of the negotiations, on the other.

Indeed, it is possible that U.S. involvement and/or pressure prompted
Asad to attempt to reinvigorate the negotiations. For example, he allowed his
foreign minister, Farouk al-Shara, to engage in some public diplomacy by
meeting in late September with a group of Jewish leaders in Washington and
granting in early October an interview to Israeli television. Israelis were not
impressed with Shara's interview, which was characterized by the usual stiff-
ness and lack of warmth. About this time, Shara also delivered a speech at the
UN General Assembly criticizing Israel for not signing the Non-Proliferation
Treaty, bringing his country's position in line with that of Egypt. Apparently,
these acts of public diplomacy accomplished little of what they were intended
for originally in Israeli eyes.[38]

In a show of resolve and support for the peace process, President Clinton
made a foray into shuttle diplomacy in the region in late October with the
objective of mediating the Israeli-Syrian talks. This came also within the con-

text of witnessing the signing of the Israeli-Jordanian peace treaty at a desert outpost along their border. At a joint news conference after Clinton's meeting with Asad at the presidential palace in Damascus, the Syrian president made his opening statement:

> I have reaffirmed to President Clinton the continued commitment of Syria to the peace process and her serious pursuit of a comprehensive and just peace as a strategic choice that secures Arab rights, ends the Israeli occupation of the Arab land in conformity with the Security Council Resolutions 242, 338 and 425. . . . I also stressed to President Clinton—emanating from the principle of full withdrawal for full peace— . . . the readiness of Syria to commit itself to the objective requirements of peace through the establishment of peaceful, normal relations with Israel in return for Israel's full withdrawal from the Golan to the line of June 4, 1967, and from the south of Lebanon.[39]

This was an important development in the peace process. Asad had not only confirmed his readiness to establish normal relations with Israel, but also clarified his new perspective on comprehensive peace, which had come to mean withdrawal from the Golan Heights and Lebanon only. However, Asad's message to Israel was dampened by his reluctance to criticize in public the recent bombing attacks in Israel, something that the United States had hoped he might do to soothe an anxious Israeli public. Although Asad denied any Syrian involvement in terrorism, his reluctance to denounce the attacks most likely reflected his perception of such acts inside Israel as legitimate forms of resistance, a sign that he was still bound by the older dogmas of the Arab-Israeli conflict. For all intents and purposes, the direct impact of the summit was the elevation of the bilateral talks to a higher plane. Rabinovich and Muallem continued their contacts and Asad readied himself to send his military chief of staff to the negotiations in Washington.

From November 1994, security talks began to dominate the agenda of the negotiations, and the two chiefs of staff, Ehud Barak of Israel and Hikmat Shihabi of Syria, met in Washington on December 21. According to Rabinovich, Rabin kept a measure of openness and ambiguity with regard to security arrangements by adopting a tactical decision not to announce his line of withdrawal. To Rabin the Golan was first and foremost a security issue, and he was principally concerned with reducing the danger of a surprise attack. With this in mind, Israel devised a security regime that integrated five elements: "one, the depth of the demilitarized area and area of limited deployment; two, the size and deployment of Syrian armed forces; three, at least one Israeli early-warning station on the Golan; four, monitoring by a non-UN international force with U.S. participation; and five, a system of verification and transparency."[40]

It goes without saying that these elements were far from what Syria could accept. Syria was extremely sensitive about the size and deployment of its forces and the early-warning station. Muallem conceded that the meeting between the two chiefs of staff failed. In early January 1995, Amnon Shahak replaced Barak as chief of staff. Later in the month, the climate of the negotiations became gloomy when on January 22, two bombs exploded at Beit Lid junction, killing twenty-one Israelis. What made this tragic event all the more glaring in the eyes of the Israelis was that Fathi Shikaki, the head of Islamic Jihad, claimed responsibility for the suicide attack right from the Syrian capital. He even boasted: "It gives satisfaction to our people."[41] No wonder many Israelis doubted whether their country was on the right path in pursuing peace with Syria.

For the next two months no progress was noted in the negotiations. During that time President Clinton tried to convince the two parties to renew the talks between the two chiefs of staff. Finally, all parties agreed on setting a framework for security arrangements so that neither party would make impractical security demands. It was agreed that the two ambassadors, with the help of the United States, would work out this framework before the chiefs of staff met. After much effort, all parties reached an agreement on the aims and principles of the security arrangements in May 1995. The final version of the agreement was referred to as the "Non-Paper on the Aims and Principles of the Security Arrangements" (see Appendix 7.1). This paper paved the way for the next meeting of the two chiefs of staff.

The importance of the non-paper lies in the fact that the two parties had agreed on a resolution of the issue of "equality" and "mutuality" in the security arrangements. This materialized with Syria's concession to forego geographic symmetry.[42] Here, it is interesting to point to some ironies about the two parties' positions concerning the Golan. Rabin was still emphasizing that his opening to Syria concerning the withdrawal to the June 4 lines was hypothetical, while at the same time Asad continued insisting that Syria's position was known and clear concerning the Israeli withdrawal to the June 4 lines. In a joint news conference with President Husni Mubarak of Egypt in Damascus on June 1, 1995, Asad emphasized that "Syria adheres strongly to its position . . . and all who deal with the peace process have the conviction that Syria will not accept less than that, for this issue is settled at least as far as we are concerned."[43] In any event, in late June, Shihabi and Shahak met in Washington, and before long the Syrian-Israeli military talks again reached an impasse.

While the two parties disagreed on some issues (size and deployment of Syrian army units and demilitarized zones), the bone of contention was Syria's refusal to accept an Israeli warning station on the Golan. The Syrian defense minister subsequently remarked that the "Israelis do not want peace but want to trick us," and added that "we shall not accept a warning station because we consider it as a spying one."[44] Asad was not happy with the results of the military talks and Rabin conveyed to the United States that Asad behaved this way because he "felt free from pressure and it was a pity that one could not talk to Iraq."[45] This, of course, did not register well with the United States. What Rabin was saying was that only pressure and power politics could work with Asad. It is not far from conceivable that Rabin indeed had toyed with the idea of talking to Iraq.[46]

In the meantime, opposition to the peace process, led by Likud, intensified following several suicide bombings in Israel.[47] Rabin remained adamant about continuing the peace talks, but focused more on the Palestinian and Jordanian fronts.[48] Apparently, he gave priority to concluding Oslo II, which was signed in Washington on September 28, 1995, infuriating Asad anew. Nevertheless, during this period, some flexibility crept into the Israeli-Syrian negotiations. The gap between the two got narrower, but remained wide enough to preclude an agreement with the issue of security at the center of the rift.[49] Shortly thereafter, Asad granted a lengthy and detailed interview to *Al-Ahram* in October in which he revealed his disappointment with the course of the negotiations and conceded that nothing had been decided between the two parties.[50]

In addition, the preparation for the upcoming election campaigns in the United States (November 1996) and in Israel (expected October 1996) began to preoccupy the two countries. Still, progress was not ruled out and the ongoing negotiations by themselves could not but keep the hope that a breakthrough was in the realm of the possible. Tragically, on November 4, 1995, Rabin was assassinated by a fanatic orthodox Jew, Yigal Amir, who believed in putting a stop to the peace process by killing the prime minister. This event betrayed the depth of resistance to the peace process in some segments of Israeli society and the deadly risks associated with it. Peres replaced Rabin as prime minister and defense minister and appointed Ehud Barak as foreign minister. Uri Savir, the director-general of the foreign ministry and a principal architect of the Oslo Accords, soon emerged as Peres's point man for the Syrian track. Peres, unlike Rabin, had a vision for a new Middle East based on economic development. He believed that an economy of peace could well provide the basis for security in the region. He entertained the idea that economic development and cooperation and financial aid provided better incentives for a new relationship with Syria.[51]

Peres was quick to ascertain his ambition for an Israeli-Syrian peace agreement. If Rabin was cautious, slow, and suspicious, Peres was bold, fast, and creative. His famous expression "to fly fast and high" characterized his readiness to take a giant leap in the peace process. Still, Peres needed the springboard from which to catapult his takeoff. He insisted on engaging in public diplomacy by seeking an early meeting with Asad, a deeper U.S. involvement in the Israeli-Syrian negotiations, plus an all-embracing regional plan carrying the signature of the U.S. president. While Asad and Clinton balked at Peres's ideas, they both showed a keen interest in advancing the peace negotiations. The three parties agreed on resuming the talks at the Wye Plantation near the Chesapeake in Maryland, which began in late December 1995. Knowing that security issues had been the main culprit in impeding a breakthrough, Peres chose to deal simultaneously with several issues, thereby demoting the primacy of security for Israel. Given his opinion about the merits of economic development and cooperation, he even signaled his readiness to effect a swift withdrawal from the Golan measured in months not years.[52]

The first phase of the Wye negotiations discussed the issues of quality of peace, normalization, economic cooperation, and comprehensiveness. Asad had already accepted the notion of "normal peaceful relations" in 1994 in the areas of diplomatic relations, termination of boycotts, and movement of people and goods.[53] But what was encouraging now was the fact that Asad had agreed to what Rabinovich explained as the principle of "interface," meaning that the Syrian president would accept some normalization before a meaningful Israeli withdrawal.[54] Also, shortly before the Wye negotiations began, Asad spoke of comprehensive peace at a joint press conference with Mubarak in Cairo:

> Comprehensiveness from our point of view now means Syria and Lebanon . . . of course peace is the peace for all Arabs . . . but things have always started, took off and finished from the surrounding or the surrounding states . . . and from those states only Syria and Lebanon have not concluded agreements with Israel. Comprehensive peace will be achieved when Syria and Lebanon sign a peace agreement. Naturally, I never mean that an Arab will abandon the other Arabs. The issue of the Arabs, no matter how they look and how some of the Arabs view them, will remain Arab issues. Assistance and feelings of pan-Arab responsibility will remain the basis.[55]

While these two developments augured well for the negotiations, they still contained subtle and nuanced conditions. What kind of normalization measures would Asad agree to? And would Asad try to reassociate himself with the Palestinian track? As it turned out, the issue of normalization became a stumbling block. Israel drew out a long list of measures to build a sound infrastructure for normal relations, while Syria followed the line that once the occupation was terminated, the state of war would end, security issues would be worked out, and then normal relations could be established. Eventually, Muallem became very sensitive about bilateral economic ties. According to Rabinovich, Muallem cited three reasons for trepidation: history and sensibility; the gap between the economic position of the two countries; and the Syrian fear of Israeli economic hegemony.[56]

At the time, Hizbollah intensified its attacks on the IDF and its Lebanese proxy militia, the South Lebanese Army, in the security zone. It shall be recalled that in this period Iran was worried about a potential Israeli-Syrian deal (see Chapter 6). As such, one could give Asad the benefit of the doubt that this time Iran, not Syria, was behind the escalating tension. Syrian media, the mouthpieces of the regime, trumpeted the charge that the success of the Syrian-Israeli peace talks depended on Israel. They uniformly emphasized that there must be an "unambiguous, public commitment to the requirements for peace, especially with regard to the full withdrawal of Israeli forces from the Golan and southern Lebanon and accepting parallel *[mutawaziyah]* and equal *[mutasawiyah]* security arrangements that do not give any side advantages over the other side."[57]

It seems that the negotiators were still at square one, with each party focusing on the issues most relevant to it. In the meantime, the Israeli prime minister did not extinguish his hope for an Asad-Peres meeting that could help him with his public. Yossi Beilin, an Israeli cabinet minister and a close associate of Peres, stressed that a summit meeting was very important for the pace of the negotiations.[58] Equally significant, the election campaign in Israel began to weigh heavily on the mind of Peres during his negotiations with the Syrians. He had to make a decision of whether to keep the original date of the elections on October 29, 1996, or move it up to May 29 of that year. Whether a deal with Syria was feasible was at the heart of his decision. Indeed, he made it publicly clear that early elections depended on the outcome of the negotiations with Syria.[59]

The second Wye Plantation round of talks opened on January 24, 1996. Security issues became the focus of difficult and tense discussions. The two parties haggled over the scope and extent of demilitarized zones and limited deployment of troops, as well as over the deployment and size of Syria's strike forces inside the country. Eventually, the atmosphere of the negotiations became charged and a stalemate loomed on the horizon. With the prospects of concluding a peace deal dwindling before May, Peres apparently decided to move up the elections to May 29.[60]

Syria was unhappy with Peres's decision to move up the elections but did not discontinue the talks.[61] In fact, the final round of Maryland talks resumed in late February. At this juncture, a wave of suicide bombs engulfed Israel, shaking Peres's government and the public faith in the peace process, let alone fueling the opposition's strident attacks on the Labor-led government. On February 25, the lull in terror attacks was shattered when Islamist militants exploded bombs in Ashkelon and Jerusalem, killing twenty-five people. Reportedly, the attacks were an act of revenge for the assassination of Yahya Ayyash, a Palestinian Hamas leader known as "the Engineer," by Israel in early January.[62] Ayyash had designed and helped set off bomb attacks against Israel in recent years.

Other attacks were to follow in early March, raising the death toll to fifty-nine.[63] Obviously, the assaults, this time, were clearly both an act of vengeance and a means to derail the peace process. According to Rabinovich, the Syrian refusal to condemn the terrorist attacks made the Israeli delegation's stay at Wye untenable, and led Peres to suspend the negotiations on March 4.[64] This brought about the end of the Peres talks with Syria.

In addition to these dramatic and tragic events, other incidents further alienated the two parties. During and after the negotiations, the cycle of terror was not confined only to suicide bombings in Israel. Hizbollah, in a familiar pattern by now, escalated its attacks on the Israeli army and the SLA in south-

ern Lebanon in addition to firing Katyousha rockets into the Galilee. This violence began to bear heavily on Peres and contributed to sharpening his image
as "weak on security," an image pointedly projected by the opposition, which
had "peace with security" as its election campaign slogan. Apparently, Peres
was cornered and had to react with a show of resolve if this violence were to
continue. Meanwhile, the United States organized an international summit in
Sharm al-Shaykh in Egypt to deal with combating terrorism. European, Russian, Palestinian, and Arab heads of state attended the summit to lend their
support to the peace process and signal their joint dedication to fight against
terrorism. The Syrians refused to attend. While this summit was held to some
extent to help Peres domestically, the Syrians took exception, interpreting it
as a concerted campaign against Damascus and Tehran. In addition, the Syrians saw in the summit a U.S. and Israeli scheme to shift the focus from the
peace process to combating terrorism.[65]

This time it appeared that Syria and Iran had pushed Hizbollah to
heighten the tension in the south of Lebanon, as fighting continued unabated.
Apparently, Syria was using its Lebanese leverage against Israel in an act of
defiance. Peres, like Rabin before him, decided to launch an operation, Grapes
of Wrath, against Lebanon on April 2, in an effort both to strike at Hizbollah
and to put pressure on the Lebanese government and in turn on its Syrian
patron. The thinking behind the operation carried the hallmarks of the previous operation, Accountability. Israel's raw power demonstrated time and
again its limitations. Grapes of Wrath, conducted among innocent and help-
less civilians, resulted in the unintended consequence of shelling a large group
of civilians taking refuge at the headquarters of the United Nations in Kafar
Qana, killing more than a hundred.

World public opinion heaped its opprobrium on Israel for the Kafar Qana
tragedy. Peres brought the operation to a swift end without achieving anything
to help rehabilitate his image at home. Secretary of State Christopher helped
bring about a cease-fire. He also managed to organize a committee drawn
from Lebanese, Syrian, Israeli, and French diplomats to monitor the cease-fire
between Israel and the Hizbollah guerrillas. The parties worked out an agreement, in fact an extension of the 1993 agreement, which called on Hizbollah
not to fire Katyousha rockets into Israel and on Israel not to target civilians in
Lebanon.[66] This agreement became known as the April Understanding.
Against this background, the Israelis went to the polls on May 29, 1996, and
gave Likud and its leader, Benjamin Netanyahu, a victory. At this point, one
could not dismiss the fact that the campaign of terror led by Hamas, Islamic
Jihad, and Hizbollah contributed to the defeat of Peres and therefore to the
long hiatus that followed in the Israeli-Syrian negotiations.

The election of Netanyahu cast a pall over the whole peace process. The
Arab world watched closely the Israeli election campaign and frowned upon
Netanyahu's famous three no's: no to withdrawal from the Golan, no to divid-
ing Jerusalem, and no to a Palestinian state. Insights into Netanyahu's policy

on Syria could be gathered early on in his term from his meetings with Secretary of State Christopher at the end of June and with President Clinton in July. At the June meeting, he branded Damascus in the same breath as Iran as a terrorist state, while at his July meetings he tried to persuade the president to adopt a policy of "triple containment." In this way, Netanyahu hoped to add Syria to the existing U.S. policy of "dual containment" and therefore isolate it.[67]

Netanyahu's thoughts and hopes seemed to be based on his book *A Place Among Nations,* in which he called for a policy of peace deterrence, that is, a strengthening of the democracies and a weakening of the dictatorships.[68] As far as Syria was concerned, this policy would bring international pressure to bear on Damascus to force a change in the country's concept of peace. According to Netanyahu, peace had to be resumed with no preconditions, a position he publicly declared from the podium of the Israeli Knesset following his election.[69] Indeed, in his meeting with Christopher, he emphasized his line of policy reflecting his "peace or terror" formula, a formula harking back to Shamir's "peace for peace."[70] In addition, he made clear that he would not be held responsible for the "hypothetical formula" made by the former Labor government concerning full withdrawal from the Golan.

Netanyahu's statements galvanized the Arab world into organizing a summit, the first in six years, in Egypt in a show of collective unity and support for Syria. President Mubarak, sending an indirect message to Netanyahu, said that he "hoped that the display of unity would help to guard against attempts to stray from the path toward peace in the Middle East."[71] As it turned out, Arab fears of Netanyahu's desire to rob the peace process of its significance were confirmed, as he proved to be an obstructionist with the Palestinians (albeit he affirmed that he would respect the Oslo Accords and work toward their implementation). More specifically, he tried to outmaneuver Syria into agreeing to a resumption of the negotiations without any preconditions, something Damascus was bent on not doing.

Early on in his term, Netanyahu spoke of a "Lebanon First" option, a proposal to enter into negotiations with Lebanon over Israel's withdrawal from the security zone. The proposal was immediately and expectedly rejected by the Lebanese and their Syrian patrons, who shunned any separate solution.[72] He then declared, through his defense minister, Yitzhak Mordechai, his readiness to implement Security Council Resolution 425. The bottom line was that Israel would not talk about peace or normalization; the pullout price would be security arrangements only.[73] Immediately, Vice President Khaddam and Foreign Minister Shara argued that the initiative was part of a plot to isolate Syria, an initiative to evade negotiations over the Golan Heights.[74]

Syria took a firm position regarding the resumption of the negotiations. It made any return to the talks conditional on Israel resuming them from the point at which they were interrupted, thus holding on and protecting the legacy of the previous promises. In an interview with *Al-Majalla,* Shara stressed that the fundamental principle for building a just peace was to resume the negotiations from where they had stopped. He added that substituting the formula of "peace for peace" for "land for peace" as the principle of the peace process was a Likud stratagem violating international legitimacy and the logic of a just peace.[75]

Against a background where one party predicated the peace process on the principle of "land for peace" and the demand of full withdrawal from the Golan, while the other championed the formula of "peace for peace" along with some withdrawals only, the Israeli-Syrian negotiations plunged into an inauspicious hiatus.

The Last Summit

During his short term in office as Israel's prime minister (1996–1999), Benjamin Netanyahu's controversial personality and confrontational politics managed to alienate almost all parties across the country's political spectrum and to sour the U.S.-Israeli relationship. Many Israelis were tormented by the famous nagging question, "Can Netanyahu be trusted?" He was alternately attacked by the right, who charged him with abandoning their ideology and political agenda, and by the left, who impugned him for trying to kill the spirit and letter of the peace process. This, among other things, brought about a difficult, if not impossible, political situation for Israel to contend with, prompting early elections in May 1999. On May 17, Israelis overwhelmingly elected Ehud Barak, the Labor Party leader, as their prime minister. The results of the elections fitted the trend of reducing the strength of the two large parties, but by withering the right wing this time and significantly empowering the center, and adding to it four new parties. While Labor (One Israel) received 27 Knesset seats and Likud received a depressing 19 seats, Shas wound up with an astonishing 17 seats, making it the third biggest party in the parliament.[76]

The newly elected prime minister immediately worked for building a broad-based coalition government in an effort to bring unity to the country and support his policy of moving forward on the peace process. Barak indeed tried to wed left and right, secular and religious, dove and hawk, by forming a coalition government including such disparate parties as Shas, Meretz, the NRP, and Yisrael ba-Aliya. Upon assuming office in July 1999, he set as his goal reaching a comprehensive peace settlement embracing Israel, the Palestinians, Syria, and Lebanon. He also reaffirmed his campaign pledge to withdraw Israeli troops from the security zone in Lebanon by July 2000 regardless of whether an agreement with Syria was reached or not. Barak felt that time and momentum were of the essence and this is partly why he set a deadline of fifteen months to achieve peace on all fronts. He set out to do what his predecessors refrained from, that is, juggling more than one negotiating track at the same time.

Barak was quick in sending signals to Asad, which were immediately seized upon. Indeed, an exchange of praise took place between the two leaders, with Asad describing Barak as a "strong and honest man," while Barak credited Asad with creating a "strong, independent, and self-confident" country.[77] A feeling of euphoria swept the region, as many were taken by surprise with this first ever flirtation between the two leaders of Israel and Syria. Apparently, this flirtation indicated a new concern on the part of Asad as to whether Labor or Likud was ruling Israel. Asad appeared to begin to pay a different kind of attention to Israeli domestic politics after the election defeat of former prime minister Shimon Peres. Most likely, this was part of a pattern that began to develop following the visit of a delegation of Israeli Arabs to Syria in 1994. While Asad was reluctant to engage Israel in public diplomacy, he showed an interest in improving his relationship with Arab-Israelis, whom he referred to as the "Palestinians of 1948." Apparently, a channel of communication was opened between the two sides, as other visits from Arab-Israelis to Syria were to follow.[78]

In July, Barak traveled to the United States to see President Clinton. After several meetings, the two seemed to hit it off very well. Both appeared eager to show that the U.S.-Israeli relationship had been reinvigorated after some deterioration during Netanyahu's term. Clinton promised Barak that the U.S. administration would help strengthen Israel's security. He also promised him to ask Congress to speed the approval of economic assistance to the Jewish state. However, what was first and foremost on their agenda was the peace process. Barak publicly declared that it was his intention to "move the process forward simultaneously on all tracks: The bilateral, the Palestinian, the Syrians and the Lebanese, as well as the multilateral."[79] Clinton pledged that he "would get in touch with President Asad to emphasize that a 'golden opportunity' lay before him to complete a peace deal with Israel."[80]

In this summit, an agreement was also reached to diminish the degree of Washington's intervention in the coming Israeli-Syrian negotiations. In other words, the United States would not serve as full-time intermediary and referee in the future Israeli-Syrian peace negotiations, as it did during the recent Israeli-Palestinian Wye Plantation talks (culminating in the Wye River Agreement of October 1998). Not only had the United States tried to draft the language of that agreement, but it had also provided CIA officers to enforce the deal.[81] This showed that Barak was taking precautionary measures based on the expectation that Israeli-Syrian negotiations would resume soon. He, like Rabin before him, was apparently concerned about any U.S. intermediary role that would erode some of Israel's peace requirements from Syria. Not surprisingly, Washington's speedy approval of such an arrangement fitted its well-established policy pattern toward Israel and Syria. At the time, Syria indicated its readiness for peace talks by instructing the militant Palestinian groups based in Damascus that were opposing the peace accords signed by the PLO and Israel to end their struggle against the Jewish state.[82]

Immediately after the summit, U.S. efforts led by President Clinton and Secretary of State Madeleine K. Albright (who had replaced former Secretary of State Warren Christopher) were undertaken to bring the two parties to resume the negotiations. Although dedicated to the peace process, Albright felt that her legacy as secretary of state and as the first woman ever to hold this position should not depend on the successful conclusion of a comprehensive peace in the region. At one time, she publicly described her role as the handmaiden of the peace process in contrast to former secretary of state Warren Christopher, who seemed like a tireless intermediary. In any event, those efforts paid off when Israel and Syria agreed to President Clinton's proposed formula for resuming the negotiations on the basis of the by now famous "constructive ambiguity" approach. On December 8, 1999, President Clinton announced that the two countries would begin top-level peace talks the following week in Washington. He emphasized that both sides had agreed to resume negotiations "from the point they were left off," without further elaboration on the terms for resumption.[83] This phrasing appeared to allow the two parties to save face, with the understanding that each side would underscore different points about the past. But this also revealed that Syria's seemingly absolute condition for resuming the talks—that Israel agree to withdraw from the Golan to the June 4, 1967, lines—had become negotiable.

The atmosphere among the actors seemed propitious for a breakthrough. Each leader of the three countries appeared to have significant incentives on his own to help bring about a peace deal. All in all, it seemed that Asad's illness and his desire to pass the reins of power smoothly to his son, Barak's campaign vows, and Clinton's hope for a peace legacy drove these leaders to focus on the peace process. Asad appointed his foreign minister, Farouk al-Shara, to represent him in the upcoming negotiations with Barak, a move that raised some eyebrows in Israel given the asymmetrical official positions of the two negotiators.

Before proceeding to Washington, Barak delivered an impassionate speech before the Knesset. From the podium, he declared that "from Israel's perspective, real peace with Syria and the Palestinians, if it can be achieved, is the pinnacle of the Zionist vision."[84] Despite Barak's eagerness for peace, the parliament tepidly endorsed his quest for a comprehensive peace. This gave him a foretaste of the problems that a strategy predicated on a broadly based coalition would generate. This became evident when members of his coalition did not support him. For example, members of the NRP and Yisrael ba-Aliya voted against his initiative, while Shas unexpectedly abstained.[85]

On December 15, 1999, Israel and Syria resumed talks in Washington after a hiatus of almost four years. The face-to-face encounter of the two leaders raised hopeful expectations. However, the euphoric mood soon soured when Shara in his address in the Rose Garden of the White House maintained his country's traditional posture by reiterating grievances against Israel. He argued that Israel's occupation was the root of all misery, Syrian as well as

Israeli. He also made it clear that Syria wanted nothing less than what Rabin had promised: a full Israeli withdrawal down to the June 4, 1967, lines. At the same time, however, he emphasized the value of peace in the region, as it would "usher in a dialogue of civilizations and honorable competition in various domains—the political, cultural, scientific and economic."[86] Shara's statements and stiff behavior—avoiding eye contact as well as shaking hands with Barak—expectedly unnerved many Israelis. However, as it turned out, Shara did not behave in private in a way consistent with his tough public posturing. Commenting on the atmosphere of the negotiations, an Israeli official said that they were "not friendly, not hostile, just businesslike."[87] Shara's tough political posturing did not come as a surprise to many. In fact, it fitted an old pattern in Arab-Israeli negotiations where each side would try to wear an implacable face in order to appear tough for its audience at home to show that a battle was being waged over every issue under discussion. Thus, on the one hand, there seemed to exist on the part of each party a willingness to concede behind the hard-line public talk. On the other hand, playing for the home gallery could undermine the other party's support at home. In this instance, Rabinovich remarked that "when you are catering to your home gallery, like Shara did, you are undermining the other leader's support at home."[88]

The talks in Washington had a narrow goal, namely to set a time and the ground rules for more formal negotiations on the sensitive issues that divided Israel and Syria, namely security, borders, bilateral relations, and water. The parties agreed to meet on January 3, 2000, to begin intensive peace talks. The U.S. State Department chose a fairly secluded and tranquil town on the Potomac River, Shepherdstown, in order to provide a climate of privacy and isolation to the peace talks reminiscent of that at Camp David. Prime Minister Barak headed his country's delegation, which consisted of a retinue of about fifty-five officials including Foreign Minister David Levy, Attorney General Eliyakim Rubenstein, and tourism minister and former chief of staff Amnon Lipkin-Shahak. Syrian foreign minister Farouk al-Shara headed his country's delegation, which included about thirty officials, among whom were two deputy foreign ministers, Yusuf Shakkur and Majeed Abusaleh, and former ambassador to the United States Walid Muallem. According to the Department of State's spokesman, James P. Rubin, President Asad assured President Clinton that Shara carried "plenipotentiary powers" to conclude an agreement with Israel.[89] Although the U.S. team included familiar figures such as Dennis Ross, the administration's special Middle East envoy, and his deputy, Aaron Miller, the U.S. president and the secretary of state closely oversaw the negotiations.

The parties agreed to structure the talks by setting up four committees to discuss the specific issues of bilateral relations, security, access to water, and drawing borders. Keeping to its old pattern, Syria insisted on discussing the issue of borders first, while Israel insisted on discussing security and bilateral relations before all other issues. President Clinton was quick in intervening and breaking the procedural impasse, after which Israel and Syria agreed to discuss both border and security simultaneously. However, no substantive progress took place, as each delegation contrarily expected to achieve some progress on the issues that mattered most to it, prompting again the intervention of the U.S. president.[90]

On January 7, President Clinton presented to the leaders of the two delegations a seven-page "working paper" defining their agreements and differences. The paper was more in the form of a draft treaty, with the points of dispute bracketed. At the same time, the paper reflected the president's private conversations with both sides. Although Rubin stated that the paper indeed had been constantly revised to reflect the president's private conversations with both sides, the fact that none of the issues involved were new greatly helped the president and his staff to define the differences between the positions of each side.[91] After their last meeting with the president, both sides suspended the talks for twenty-four hours for religious observances. But as it turned out, this temporary suspension was prolonged as no progress had taken place, and each party prepared to go home, supposedly to return to resume the negotiations in about two weeks.

The Syrian delegation left Washington feeling apparently angry with Barak, whom they believed was sidestepping the key component of peace. They felt that Barak kept evading discussing the demarcation of the June 4, 1967, lines. Indeed, unlike other committees, the border committee barely met. In the meantime, the Syrians leaked a partial and distorted version of the working paper in the form of excerpts to *Al-Hayat*, which published it on January 9. This upset the Israelis, who pointed out that the published text was inaccurate and biased, and then proceeded to leak the whole working paper to *Ha'aretz*, which published it on January 13. The revelation of the whole text was received with indignation in Damascus. Its publication made clear where each side stood, and revealed before the Syrian public that the text was not just a working paper but the draft of a treaty. It also showed that the Israelis had wrung concessions from the Syrians without getting Israel to declare its commitment to a withdrawal from the Golan to the June 4 lines.[92] It seems that the Syrian attempt to leak a partial text of the paper in order to prepare their public for peace and show their tough bargaining stand backfired on them.

A collation of the two texts reveals that Syria had made three concessions concerning the border, security arrangements, and bilateral relations, while Israel kept using the term "relocate" instead of "withdrawal."[93] On the first issue, Syria admitted that the June 4 lines were not a (delineated) border and that it was ready to cooperate with military experts and surveyors to draw the border. In the draft peace treaty, Syria maintained that the location of the border would be based on the June 4 lines, while Israel maintained that demarcation of the border was to take "into account security and other vital interests of the Parties as well as legal considerations of both sides." The delineation of the exact location of the border would decide whether Syria could have access to Lake Tiberias. For example, if the border was less than ten meters from the Lake, Syria could obtain under international law the right to access the lake's waters. In this respect, Syria maintained in the draft treaty that the resolution of all water issues would be based on relevant international principles.

Regarding security, Syria accepted an early-warning station on Mount Hermon, "operated by the United States and France under their total auspices and responsibilities." This left open the possibility that some Israeli soldiers wearing a French or U.S. military uniform be present at the station. In addition, the two countries agreed to some security arrangements that bore the hallmark of the security treaty between Syria and Lebanon (see Chapter 5). Each party undertook to refrain not only from organizing, assisting, or participating in any acts of violence against the other party, but also from preventing the entry, presence, and operation in its territory of any group or organization that would threaten the security of the other party by the "use of, or incitement to the use of, violent means." The implication of this is twofold. On the one hand, given the military superiority of Israel, Syria could well become the junior partner in the relationship, especially in the geostrategic realm of the region (the way Lebanon has become to Syria). On the other hand, Syria would be expected to sever all relations with Israeli-opposed parties on territories under Syrian control and to curb their activities, including Iran's activities in Lebanon, something that would have the potential of souring the strategic cooperation between Damascus and Tehran.

On the issue of bilateral relations, Syria agreed to a large measure of normalization of relations covering a wide range of matters, from promoting economic and trade relations to establishing postal, telephone, and cable communications between the two countries. Even connecting the electricity grids was mentioned. In this normalization section of the draft treaty, Israel suggested in a bracketed phrase (points of dispute) that Israeli settlers might remain on the Golan Heights even after a peace deal.

Because of these revelations, the Syrians apparently felt humiliated and in mid-January 2000 (before the next scheduled round of negotiations was to begin) they voiced their reservations about resuming the talks, emphasizing that the policy of "constructive ambiguity" had run its course.[94] Obviously, this episode showed that Asad was frustrated by the fact that he could not obtain a face-saving deal, that is, in Syrian parlance, a "dignified" deal, symbolized by an Israeli commitment to withdraw to the June 4 lines, which could be well defended in Syria. This was literally spelled out by Foreign Minister Shara when he stated to the Lebanese newspaper *Al-Mustaqbal:* "Lieutenant Colonel Bashar Asad informed me more than once that President Asad does not accept to leave behind for him a dishonorable peace and that Bashar also will not accept such a deal."[95] Shara's statement also implied that Bashar was the heir apparent and that a flawed peace could jeopardize his succession chances.[96]

Barak's reluctance to discuss the issue of the June 4 lines at the Shepherdstown meetings could be explained on the grounds that this was a highly emotional matter in Israel. He had to contend not only with the opposition but also with the skeptical mood of the nation toward Syria having a foothold on the edge of Lake Tiberias (Sea of Galilee), a mood best described by the common expression "we cannot tolerate Asad dipping his toe into the Sea of Galilee." Also, one cannot dismiss the possibility that Barak had underestimated Asad by thinking that he might be able to get from the Syrian president what his predecessors had failed to obtain. In addition, one may argue, as some U.S. analysts have, that Barak would make such a highly sensitive concession concerning the border issue only to Asad himself in an effort to win Israeli public opinion.

Shortly after the initial suspension of the talks in Shepherdstown, an opposition rally in Tel Aviv protesting any withdrawal from the Golan attracted thousands of participants, with estimates ranging from 100,000 to 200,000. This large rally propelled Barak upon his return from the United States to give a television interview, in which he said that "no in-depth discussion of borders had taken place and that the Israelis had made no political commitment to Syria about a withdrawal from the Golan Heights."[97] In addition, Barak faced right-wing charges that he was overly eager to make concessions, although the draft treaty showed that Israel had wrung concessions from Syria. Moshe Arens, a former hawkish defense minister, wrote about Barak in *Ha'aretz* that "in his quest for an agreement with the Syrian dictator, he seems prepared to do anything, to say anything and even to give away everything."[98]

Keeping with the tradition of a past pattern, the Syrian-Israeli negotiations affected those between Israel and the Palestinians, although Barak tried to adhere to his commitment of juggling simultaneously the two tracks.[99] At the same time and most likely following Syrian orders, Hizbollah heightened the tension in the security zone in southern Lebanon by escalating its attacks on Israeli troops and their Lebanese allies, the South Lebanese Army. This development did not augur well for Barak, as segments of Israel's civil society, ranging from the army to the news media to ordinary citizens, clamored for retaliation against Hizbollah. The Party of God had inflicted heavy human losses on Israeli troops. Graphic television images showing bloodied soldiers shocked many Israelis and jarred their sense of security. What made Hizbollah attacks even more incomprehensible to the Israelis was the fact that Barak remained determined about withdrawing Israeli troops from Lebanon whether a peace deal with Syria was signed or not. Acknowledging that sentiment, Barak threatened Hizbollah but refrained from pointing a finger of blame or responsibility at Syria, though knowing full well that the latter wielded much influence over the Islamic militants.

On February 8, 2000, Barak made good on his threat and ordered a harsh air force reprisal attack. However, the air raid targeted not only guerrilla strongholds but also civilians. The Israeli air force plunged Beirut and other areas of Lebanon into a total blackout as they hit and severely damaged three power stations, one of them in Jamhur, a Beirut suburb. In fact, the raid on Jamhur's power station was the second in little more than seven months.[100] Barak defended his decision to order the attack on civilian targets, which claimed a number of casualties, on the grounds that Hizbollah had systematically violated the April Understanding.[101] But this justification made little sense to the innocent Lebanese who ultimately ended up paying the price. In addition, what made the raid in the eyes of many Lebanese egregious was the fact that it was directed against the country's infrastructure at a time when it was still recovering from a long civil war.

The Israeli raid on Lebanon elicited strong condemnations especially from Arab countries and triggered a wave of protests in Lebanon and elsewhere in the Arab world. In a show of solidarity with Lebanon, the foreign ministers of the Arab League decided to hold their biannual meeting, scheduled in March, in Beirut instead of Cairo. Furthermore, many Arab dignitaries and heads of state traveled to Lebanon to express their support. Prominent among them was President Husni Mubarak of Egypt. His unexpected visit to the country on February 20 was the first by an Egyptian president since 1952.

Seemingly, the heightened tension in the area was not helpful to the already disturbed atmosphere of the peace process. Further ominous developments loomed in the horizon as many expected that Hizbollah would respond to Israel's raids by firing Katyousha missiles into the Galilee. This, however, did not happen, a sign indicating Syria's desire to contain the precarious situation in an apparent effort to pave the way for resuming the peace talks. In addition, although Hizbollah's offensives in southern Lebanon helped to broaden its political base of support (as reflected in a significant parliamentary contingent), many Lebanese seemed convinced, despite their newly elevated respect for Hizbollah, that any attack on Israel was not worth the heavy destructive price the Jewish state would inflict on Lebanon by way of retribution, especially considering Israel's pledge to withdraw anyway. In fact, although Hizbollah had not ceased confronting Israeli troops and the SLA, it reduced the density of its attacks, which were confined to the security zone. In the meantime, the United States failed to work out a cease-fire on account of recriminations among the members of the monitoring committee created by the April Understanding. Following the death of an Israeli soldier, Barak decided against attending the meetings of the monitoring committee until Hizbollah ceased its activities.

The events of February brought forward some pathological reactions on the part of Syria and Israel, emanating from anachronistic and ugly attitudes seemingly still rooted in segments of both societies. This was reflected by the Syrian regime's mouthpiece, *Tishrin*, which called the Holocaust a "myth," and by Israel's foreign minister, David Levy, who warned against any attack on northern Israel by using Saddam Hussein–style threats: "If Kiryat Shmona burns, Lebanese soil will burn. . . . One thing turns on the other, blood against blood, a life against life, a child against child."[102] Still, Syria and Israel appeared to retain the desire to resume the peace negotiations by alternately signaling in some way or another their readiness.

This time it was Israel's turn, as Prime Minister Barak threw his bomb-shell revelation when he told his cabinet that former prime minister Yitzhak Rabin "had given guarantees that Israel would fully withdraw from the Golan Heights in exchange for security commitments by Syria," apparently confirming what Syria had long maintained.[103] Barak added that he would not "erase the past," hinting that "he, too, would be prepared to meet Syria's demand and withdraw down to, or close to, the shores of the Sea of Galilee if Israel's security needs were met."[104] Israeli media perceived Barak's words as indeed a revelation, with Channel 2 News reporting that "'it was the first time that an Israeli prime minister has ever admitted' that Israel had agreed—conditionally—to a complete withdrawal."[105]

A few days later, Barak's apparent overture to Syria acquired a sense of urgency when the Israeli cabinet endorsed the prime minister's vow to withdraw from Lebanon in July, making an official government policy of what had been previously a campaign pledge. The cabinet adopted unanimously a resolution to withdraw Israeli troops from Lebanon in July, preferably, but not necessarily, in the context of an accord with Syria.[106] Being an official statement, the resolution not only gave teeth to Barak's promise of withdrawal, but also presented an unequivocal challenge to Syria. Israel appeared determined to strip Syria of its Lebanese card, forcing the former's hand. Damascus would no longer be able to use Hizbollah as a source of leverage against Tel Aviv. Nor could it justify either its military presence in Lebanon or its desire to keep wedding the Lebanese to the Syrian track of negotiations. Simultaneously, Barak was inviting Asad back to the negotiating table, by indicating his readiness to withdraw from the Golan, and twisting his arm, by depriving him of a bargaining chip in the negotiations over the Heights.

Barak's revelation followed by his cabinet's vow of unilateral withdrawal from Lebanon set the stage for fast-paced U.S. efforts to try to break the impasse between the two countries. These efforts culminated in a decision to hold a summit meeting in Geneva between President Asad and President Clinton on March 26, 2000. Apparently, Asad's embarrassment over the Shepherdstown talks compelled him to sound out beforehand and through the United States what Barak was prepared to offer. In the meantime, opposition to a potential peace deal with Syria grew in Israel. Three coalition partners of Barak's government (Yisrael ba-Aliya, the NRP, and Shas) joined forces with the opposition (Likud) to pass a preliminary bill that would make the success of a future referendum on peace with Syria almost impossible. The bill would require an absolute majority of all eligible voters to approve the withdrawal from the Golan in the referendum, thus counting those who did not report to the polls as a vote against peace. In fact, on the one hand, this bill was an attempt to send a message to Asad that Barak might not be able to make good on his promises because of domestic opposition. On the other hand, it was most likely a thinly disguised attempt to nullify Israel's Arab propeace votes.[107]

Syria seemed flustered by and ambivalent about Israel's decision to unilaterally withdraw from Lebanon. This ambivalence was best illustrated by Syria's protégé, President Emile Lahoud of Lebanon, when he said in an interview with *Al-Hayat* that "an Israeli unilateral withdrawal will not work . . . it will lead to another war."[108] He appeared to warn Israel that a unilateral withdrawal without prior negotiations with Beirut and Damascus could lead to a new conflict, as Palestinian refugees in Lebanon would resume their attacks on Israel, a condition that precipitated Israel's 1978 invasion of Lebanon in the first place. As is well known, Lebanon refused to grant citizenship to the Palestinian refugees, estimated at about 300,000, who came to Lebanon mainly during the wars of 1948 and 1967. Lebanon always demanded that the Palestinian refugees be repatriated. Lahoud critically questioned: "How would it be possible to guarantee Israel's borders when thousands of armed refugees are present in the Palestinian camps, demanding the right to return amid a total absence of any answers about their fate and future."[109]

Lahoud's statement was echoed by the Arab League, which had just convened in Beirut. In addition to supporting Lebanese resistance and condemning Israel for its aggression in Lebanon, a communiqué released by the league's foreign ministers emphasized that if the Palestinians were not assured of repatriation they "will remain a time bomb threatening peace in Lebanon and the threatening [*sic*] the peace process."[110] The Israeli reaction to both Lahoud's and the league's statements was a combination of sarcastic bewilderment and anger. While Barak regarded these declarations as harmful to the peace process and his justice minister, Yossi Beilin, called the league's demands "surreal," former prime minister Shimon Peres ironically stated: "In all my life, I've never heard of a country which wants to put an end to an occupation being threatened."[111] However, it appeared that Israel's real response came in the form of air strikes against two Palestinian refugee camps in Lebanon close to the border, sending a clear message that Israel would not tolerate any armed Palestinian activity.[112]

On March 26, 2000, Clinton and Asad met, their first meeting in more than five years. Clinton transmitted what Barak had to offer, but as it appeared, he failed to persuade Asad to resume the negotiations. Although several issues were on the agenda, one stuck out and proved to be the culprit of the summit's failure. According to different sources, Clinton informed Asad that Barak was indeed ready to fully withdraw from the Golan Heights, but on condition that the northeastern edge of Lake Tiberias (which was under Syrian control before the 1967 war) remain under Israel's sovereignty. Barak also wanted Asad to agree to confidence-building measures that mostly dealt with public diplomacy to allow the Israeli leader to win the support of public opinion. Within the context of his offer, Barak appeared to come up with a pro-

posal to the effect that Syria would have free access to the northeastern edge
of the lake while remaining under Israeli sovereignty; at the same time, Syria
would be compensated by having sovereignty over the hot springs resort of
Al-Hamma while Israel would have free access to it.[113]

Reportedly, Asad was adamant about his long-held view that Israel withdraw to the Israeli-Syrian frontier that existed before the June 4, 1967, lines.
The *New York Times* described Asad as the most implacable person in his delegation.[114] Not surprisingly, the two presidents felt disappointed with the
summit and left for home. Shortly thereafter, Clinton remarked that the "ball's
in his [Asad's] court now, and I'm going to look forward to hearing from
him," a remark that did not sit well with the Syrians.[115]

The immediate Syrian reaction to the failure of the summit was ambivalent, not unlike Syria's reaction to Israel's decision to unilaterally withdraw
from Lebanon. On the one hand, during the summit, when Clinton relayed on
behalf of Barak to the Syrian delegation that the window of opportunities was
narrowing, the Syrians spoke about their readiness to wait for the future generations to retrieve the whole land.[116] While this attitude could be explained
as an attempt to display a position of negotiating strength and to play tough
for the home gallery, it could not be dismissed as a form of willingness on the
part of the Syrian leadership to forego peace if their demands were not met.
In his address to the G-77 countries convening in Havana in mid-April, Shara
reaffirmed that the June 4 lines lay on the northeastern border of Lake Tiberias
and nowhere else.[117]

On the other hand, the Syrians appeared not to give up the hope that the
negotiations would resume and a solution would be found with regard to the
issue of borders. This was reflected by several actions and "trial balloons" signaling Syrian intentions to break the deadlock. Immediately after the summit,
a Lebanese high official declared that "the failure of the summit had not fully
closed the door before resuming American-Syrian talks, in the hope that they
will contribute to rescuing the peace process so that the Israeli withdrawal
from Lebanon comes within the context of a comprehensive peace."[118] In
addition, when the defense minister of Lebanon, Ghazi Zuaiter, spoke of the
possibility that his government might ask the Syrian army to accompany the
Lebanese army while entering the areas to be vacated by Israeli troops (meaning that Tel Aviv would directly become within the range of Syrian missiles),
Shara was quick to respond and put a stop to all such Lebanese interpretations
and speculations. After meeting with the Lebanese president, Shara, in a stern
message directed at the Lebanese defense minister, said that "what is required
is negotiations and peace and not war."[119] Equally significant, Bashar, in an
interview with the London-based Arabic weekly *Al-Wasat,* commented on the
possibility of resuming the negotiations by stating: "The time is not too late
and it has not run out. . . . The positions that need to be achieved and worked
on are known in detail. There is a need to make a decision and enough time
to make such a decision."[120]

Significantly enough, the Syrians appeared to float a "trial balloon" via Patrick Seale regarding a compromise formula over Lake Tiberias. Using *Al-Hayat* again as a medium for conveying his (and by implication Syria's) views, Seale introduced a proposal, in fact more in the form of a draft treaty with provisions, that could resolve the sticking issue of the Lake Tiberias border between the two states. His proposal provided, among another things, that Israel exercises full sovereignty over Lake Tiberias while Syria obtain full sovereignty over the northeastern shore line of the lake, and that Syria pledge neither to pump water out of the lake nor to pollute or divert the waters nourishing it, nor to cause any ecological harm. At the same time, Israel was to pledge access to the lake to Syria for fishing, swimming, and other related activities. Seale concluded his proposal with the question: "Does not this effort deserve a peace prize?"[121]

The Impact of Multilateral and Bilateral Talks on the Israeli-Syrian Negotiations

In this section I will discuss the multilateral and bilateral negotiations between Israel and the Arabs on account of their decidedly negative impact on the Syrian-Israeli negotiating track, thus rendering a peace deal between them even more difficult and elusive than anticipated.

The multilateral negotiations were meant to be an essential complement to the bilateral negotiations. The former were designed at Madrid to address key problems that affect the entire Middle East, namely economic development and environment, water resources, refugees, arms control, and security. The United States was keen on promoting the multilateral talks, seeing them as a means to bring all parties together to work on common problems and to help dissipate years of tension and antagonism. Indeed, the multilateral negotiations worked indirectly to get Israelis to meet face to face with many Arabs, helping in the process of trying to normalize Arab-Israeli relations in general and of ending the Arab boycott of the Jewish state. While the bilateral talks brought Israelis face to face with the Syrians, Lebanese, Jordanians, and the Palestinians, the multilateral negotiations brought Israel in contact with additional Arab states such as the Gulf Cooperation Council countries, Morocco, Algeria, Tunisia, and Yemen. The assistant secretary for Near Eastern affairs, Edward Djerejian, asserted that because "the countries of the Middle East share many problems, all would gain from economic cooperation. The first step toward this end must be an end to the Arab boycott."[122]

Syria made its position clear concerning the multilateral negotiations early on at Madrid. As it shall be recalled, Syria refused to join them before seeing substantive progress in the bilateral negotiations. In addition, while Syria agreed to join the bilateral talks, breaking with its past practice, it strove to maintain some coherence and coordination among the Arab negotiating parties. This effort dovetailed nicely with Syria's earlier perspective on the peace process as based on the return of all Arab occupied territories. Syria argued that each Arab negotiator was weak on his own vis-à-vis Israel, and that a position of strength could be made possible only through a united Arab front. In a way, the bilateral talks were a necessary evil for Syria undertaken as a concession to the United States to show the country's cooperativeness and readiness for peace. But as long as the Arab parties stuck together, Syria's concession was more a tactical move than a setback.

When the Syrians heard of Oslo in August 1993, they were surprised and stunned. They saw immediately that the Palestinians had shattered this presumed Arab unity, giving Israel a strategic advantage in the negotiations and legitimizing future separate agreements. No doubt, the Palestinians undermined the concept of the "comprehensiveness" of the peace as understood by Syria as well as their own negotiating position.[123] Indeed, this is what happened when Jordan signed its own separate peace treaty with Israel in October 1994. Asad regarded these separate deals as high-powered pressure tactics engineered by Israel to force Syria into submission. As indicated above, Asad continued his negotiations, but soon enough showed some of his pent-up anger by commenting critically on the separate Palestinian and Jordanian deals in September 1994 while addressing the Syrian parliament:

> We wanted the Arab parties to go [to Madrid] drawing strength from Syria's strength. We realized that by any criteria, separate negotiations can never be in the interest of separate Arab parties, given the fact that that party is weak in the first place and has no opportunities other than submitting to pressure and offering concessions.
>
> This was our point of view. We wanted to be a support to the Arab parties but we were taken by surprise first by the Israeli-Palestinian and then by the Israeli-Jordanian agreements.
>
> I don't want to discuss what they had arrived at but the course of events revealed unambiguously the great harm that isolated deals have done to the essence of the causes for which we had fought and struggled for such a long time.[124]

On another occasion, Asad's spokesman, Jibran Kourieh, said in Asad's name: "There are attempts and pressures to influence the morale of our nation and disfigure our history and heritage. But if our nation maintains its soberness and spirit of struggle, it is capable of confronting these pressures." He added by way of a new criticism of Jordan and the Palestinians: "If someone has fallen, he will not be able to lead the others to capitulate."[125]

In Asad's eyes the enormity of what happened lay in the fact that these separate deals were flawed, incomplete, and above all harmful. Signing Oslo, the Palestinians seemed to him as if they had signed their own death warrant. How could they commit this strategic mistake of agreeing to interim arrangements that deferred to a later stage the fundamental issues of East Jerusalem, refugees, Jewish settlements, and Palestinian statehood, issues that Syria took to heart. They placed themselves in a situation that stripped them of whatever leverage they had, that legitimized Israel's highhanded policies and subverted the very idea of an equitable peace process. How could they use the threat of resuming the intifada to put pressure on Israel when their only means to get their rights had become a flawed Oslo? They preordained their future actions to failure. They reduced themselves to guardians of Israel's security. Apparently, the implication of the "land for peace" formula underlying the peace process was, for the Syrians, "no land, no peace." In other words, the Palestinians maligned the formula by undermining the option of terror lurking beneath it. All this was reflected at length by Radio Damascus after the Palestinians signed the Taba Agreement:

> Given the fact that the Oslo accord produced an ugly, limited self-rule in Gaza and Jericho, what can the capitulatory agreement initialed between Israel and the self-rule authority in Taba yesterday produce . . . ? Peres might have had the right to express jubilation over the outcome achieved; namely, the consecration of the Israeli domination of the West Bank and the explicit recognition of Israel's right to protect and expand its military bases on the territory falsely called settlement areas. Moreover, Peres might have had the right to express jubilation, particularly since Israel has been relieved of the task of confronting the Palestinian people in the West Bank, as happened in Gaza before. Now, the forces of the self-rule authority will have to confront the Palestinians, coerce them, and liquidate their intifada. By so doing, Israel will spare itself the condemnation and denunciation of the world public opinion, which it has had to contend with due to the oppressive practices and methods it has used to squash the Palestinian intifada. From now on, the self-rule forces will be carrying out this task instead.[126]

On close examination the Jordanian-Israeli peace treaty had far-reaching implications for Syria's own potential treaty, setting precedents vehemently opposed by Asad. The Jordanian-Israeli treaty allowed Israeli farmers to continue to cultivate lands on territory that was being returned to Jordanian sovereignty (in Arava and near the confluence of the Jordan and Yarmouk Rivers), something even Sadat strongly rejected in his peace treaty with Israel. In addition, although the parties agreed on the international boundary, they amended it so that Israel would retain sovereignty over some fields (in Arava) on the Jordanian side of the boundary (Jordan was compensated with land south of the Dead Sea).[127] The implication was that boundary lines were not sacred and situations on the ground were relevant to determining borders. This went against the grain of what Syria had been adamant about, namely Israel's withdrawal to the June 4, 1967, lines.

In light of these developments, the multilateral talks took a dangerous dimension, in Syrian eyes, not only by seeming to reinforce the results of the bilateral talks but also by destroying the psycho-political barrier preventing Israel from widening its link with the rich Arab Gulf states. Syria suddenly found itself facing a situation in which Israel could isolate or bypass it to deal with other Arab countries, while at the same time possessing some legitimate political ground for trying to normalize its relations with them. If the Palestinians, the core of the Arab-Israeli conflict, were normalizing their relations with their former enemy, then why not the Gulf states? This was doubly upsetting to the Syrians.

The first developments in this direction occurred when the Gulf Cooperation Council in September 1994 ended almost half a century of boycotting companies that traded with Israel. Immediately, Syrian foreign minister Farouk al-Shara expressed his reservations about this untimely lifting of the Arab (secondary) boycott, emphasizing that it would be a card in Israel's hands to use to pressure Syria.[128] The boycott affair was followed by the Casablanca economic summit, sponsored by President Clinton and Russian leader Boris Yeltsin. Senior Arab, Israeli, and U.S. political figures met there in October 1994 to discuss joint development plans and to set a framework for business investment in the region.[129] Before long, Rabin visited Oman in December, the first visit by an Israeli leader to a Persian Gulf State, to widen his contacts and try to normalize his country's relations with the Persian Gulf states.[130]

All this, on the one hand, marked a high point in the process of normalization of relations between the Arabs and the Israelis, but on the other hand sent Asad scurrying to Egypt to attend the Alexandria summit. Asad's fears of Israel trying to bypass, isolate, and pressure him were being confirmed. He appealed to President Mubarak of Egypt and King Fahd Bin Abd al-Aziz of Saudi Arabia for help. Correspondingly, the three leaders met in Alexandria on December 28–29, where they reaffirmed their commitment to Israel's withdrawal from the Golan to the June 4, 1967, lines, the south of Lebanon, and the West Bank, including East Jerusalem. What was most importunate on their agenda was what Asad described as postponing the Arab *harwala* ("trot") toward Israel in order not to negatively affect the Syrian negotiating position.[131]

Other economic summits took place, in Amman in 1995, in Cairo in 1996, and in Doha in 1997, and as before, Syria decidedly boycotted and criticized all of them. The Syrians argued that Israel was trying to impose its hegemony on the Arab economies and to stake a claim for regional leadership undermining Arab identity. Syrian vice president Abd al-Halim Khaddam, when asked why Syria had boycotted the Amman conference while it attended the Barcelona summit when Israel has attended both, replied:

> There is a great difference between the Amman and Barcelona summits. The first, like the Casablanca one, aims at a) conceding to Israel an advanced position and a leadership role in the region, b) introducing Israel to this region, c) surpassing the existing state of war between Israel and the Arab states and d) paving the way before Israel to lead the whole area. This project is basically an Israeli one, and the proposal is also an Israeli proposal. The aim is to legitimize Israel in the region . . . and to deprive the area of its

Arab identity, which means saying we are Middle Eastern states instead of
Arab states in the Arab fatherland while Israel holds unto its racist Jewish
being.[132]

This perspective was further elaborated by Asad himself when he
attacked these same Middle Eastern economic conferences as well as Israel's
(Peres's) vision of a "new Middle East." In an interview with Egypt's *Al-
Ahram* published on October 11, 1995, Asad said:

> I believe that they want a dark future for us. . . . I believe that the long-term
> goal of the others is to cancel what is called the Arabs, what is called Ara-
> bism. . . . I mean canceling Arab feelings, canceling pan-Arab identity.
> . . . I wonder about this notion in the far Arab future and what its values and
> role at present and in the future will be. . . .
>   This is the objective they are seeking. . . . Why is the Middle East being
> established? The Middle East does exist. The strange thing is that the Mid-
> dle East is being presented as an alternative to Arabism. . . . We as Arabs cer-
> tainly reject this because this is not the hands of individuals. Arabism is not
> a commodity to trade in.[133]

As it appears, Syria's anger over the multilateral and bilateral negotiations reinforced its deep-seated suspicions of Israel, as well as its negative
perception of what Israel had in store for the region. At this point, I could
safely argue that the direct impact of the bilateral and multilateral talks on
Syria had three results. First, they impelled Syria to seek a direct and substantive U.S. involvement in the peace process. In so doing, not only could
Syria improve its relations with the United States, but it also could try to
extract concessions from Israel under U.S. pressure. This is why Syria
adamantly rejected a secret negotiating channel à la Oslo and made sure the
United States was present in the negotiations at all times. Actually, it frequently seemed as if the United States instead of Israel was Syria's negotiating partner. Second, the talks heightened Syria's sense of frustration with the
peace process, which seemed to purposely sidestep or relegate Syria to the
end of the operation. And third, the talks made Syria see Israel as playing one
Arab party against another to further its interests and agenda at Syria's
expense. These factors hardened the Syrian negotiating position and led Asad
to seek Arab support to block Israel's attempts at normalizing its relations
with the Gulf and North African states. This also led Syria into greater
reliance on Hizbollah attacks against Israeli troops in southern Lebanon as a
means of influencing the negotiating process and as a reminder that no peace
in the region would be possible without Damascus. In a nutshell, Syria made
good on its understanding of the underlying implication of the peace process:
no land, no peace.

The impact of the bilateral and multilateral negotiations on Israel was less
nuanced but no less important. As indicated above, Israel was able to meet

with representatives of most Arab countries and participate in joint Israeli-Arab economic conferences. But Israel early on knew that it could not move forward on two tracks simultaneously and therefore progress in the peace process had to be sequentialized. This was so partly because the Israeli public needed time to digest the concessions it was asked to make in the peace process, and partly because the Israeli leaders appeared to feel that they lacked the mandate to decide on their own what sacrifices the country was prepared to make for the sake of a peace deal with Syria. This had two immediate consequences for the negotiations: On the one hand, Israel had to decide on a track, and by implication this track would become the cornerstone of the peace process. As we all know, Israel's choice fell on the Palestinian track, which represented to a large measure the core of the Arab-Israeli conflict anyway. On the other hand, Israel decided that a peace treaty with Syria entailing a full withdrawal from the Golan could not be finalized without a referendum.

Underlying these consequences was the Israeli assumption that such peaceful measures as public diplomacy, normalization, and security guarantees had to precede the withdrawal. In other words, for Israel: no peace, no land.

Appendix 7.1: Non-Paper on the Aims and Principles of the Security Arrangements, May 1995

Israel agreed to limit its demands with regards to the security arrangements in the Golan Heights to the areas that are close to the border only—this is what is understood from the draft of the agreement made between Israel and Syria last month, and which cleared the way for the current meeting between the two chiefs of staff in Washington. Israel also agreed to Syria's demand, that when a geographic parity in the security arrangements cannot be achieved, Syria will be compensated in other ways.

The understandings include two parts—goals and principles—with regard to the security arrangements between Israel and Syria.

Goals:

1) To lessen if not to prevent completely the possibility of a surprise attack. 2) To prevent or minimize daily altercations along the border. 3) To lessen the probability of a wide-ranging offensive, an invasion or general war.

Principles:

1) It is the legitimate need of both sides that the security demands of one, or the guarantee thereof, would not come at the expense of the other. 2) Security arrangements on both sides will be equal and reciprocal. If, during the negotiations it becomes clear, that implementation of geographic reciprocity is impossible or too difficult, experts from both sides will discuss the problematics of the specific arrangement and solve it by either changing and redefining it (including adding or subtracting from it), or by addressing it in a

mutually agreed manner. 3) Security arrangement must be consistent with the sovereignty and territorial integrity of each side. 4) Security arrangements will be confined to the relevant areas on both sides of the border.

Upon a rereading of this document it appears, that both the Israelis and the Syrians were right in maintaining that the other side yielded in the negotiations of the understandings. The goals are consistent with Israel's stances, and the principles are consistent for the most part with the Syrian demands. However, the document is phrased vaguely, allowing both sides to interpret its articles differently.

Syria gave up its demand for a specific definition of "geographic parity" in the security arrangements. This matter was controversial for a long time and prevented the resumption of negotiations between the sides.

In compensation, Israel adopted the compromise suggested by Syria's ambassador to the United States, Walid Muallem, which stipulated different depths of demilitarization zones on both sides of the border in exchange for a "mechanism of compensation" that Syria would receive in other security matters. Muallem explained a few months ago, that in the Kineret, for instance, demilitarization is meaningless, and a unique solution is needed. This version was included in the final understandings.

The assumption in Israel, before the meeting between the two chiefs of staff, was that both sides would rely on these principles to justify their positions. The agreement that the security arrangements would provide security parity for both sides would enable the Syrians to raise their demands to limit U.S. military aid to Israel and downsize the Israeli air force and nuclear capabilities. Israel would be able to rely on it in order to raise the issue of the Arabic defense alliances in which Syria is a member. Israel would be able to rely on the mutually agreed security goals to justify its demands for demilitarizing the area it withdraws from and for deploying means of monitoring and supervision.

Israel gave up its original demand for demilitarization deep on the Syrian side under Israeli or international supervision and monitoring. It was evaluated in Israel that, following these understandings, the limitations on security arrangements along the border, delivered by Prime Minister Rabin to U.S. President Clinton during their meeting last month, would make it easy for the Syrians to justify their demand for a complete Israeli withdrawal from the Golan.[134]

Notes

1. See U.S. Letter of Assurances to Syria in *Journal of Palestine Studies* 21, no. 2 (Winter 1992), pp. 119–120.
2. See U.S. Letter of Assurances to Israel in ibid., pp. 120–121.
3. See Shara's address in ibid., pp. 139–140.

4. See Shamir's address in ibid., pp. 128–131. See also Itamar Rabinovich, *The Brink of Peace: The Israeli-Syrian Negotiations* (Princeton: Princeton University Press, 1998), p. 41.

5. Clyde Haberman, "Shamir Is Said to Admit Plan to Stall Talks," *New York Times,* June 27, 1992, p. A1.

6. Rabinovich, *Brink of Peace,* p. 57.

7. See Muwaffaq Allaf's interview with *Al-Sharq al-Awsat,* July 15, 1993, in "Chief Negotiator Interviewed on Peace Process," *Foreign Broadcast Information Service–Near East and South Asia (FBIS-NES),* July 20, 1993, p. 35.

8. Rabinovich, *Brink of Peace,* pp. 60–62.

9. "Chief Negotiator Interviewed on Peace Process," p. 35.

10. "Al Asad Meets with Golan Heights Delegation," *FBIS-NES,* September 9, 1992, p. 41.

11. Rabinovich, *Brink of Peace,* p. 76.

12. Ibid., p. 83.

13. "Damascus, Syria," *U.S. Department of State Dispatch* 4, no. 9 (March 1, 1993), p. 125.

14. "U.S. Aid and Assistance to the Middle East," *U.S. Department of State Dispatch,* 4, no. 19 (May 10, 1993), p. 328.

15. Rabinovich, *Brink of Peace,* pp. 92, 118.

16. "Bilateral Relations," *U.S. Department of State Dispatch* 4, no. 11 (March 15, 1993), p. 150.

17. See Asad's interview with Patrick Seale, "Hadith al-Salam Ma'a al-Ra'is al-Suri" (Peace Talk with the Syrian President), *Al-Wasat,* May 10, 1993, pp. 12–20; and Patrick Seale, "Full Peace for Full Withdrawal," *New York Times,* May 11, 1993.

18. Ibid.

19. Itamar Rabinovich, "Smile When You Say Peace," *New York Times,* May 19, 1993.

20. Ibid.

21. Ibid.

22. Rabinovich, *Brink of Peace,* p. 103.

23. William B. Quandt, "Will Clinton's Legacy Include Middle East Peace?" lecture delivered at the Center for International Studies, Massachusetts Institute of Technology, March 14, 2000.

24. Ibid.; and Rabinovich, *Brink of Peace,* pp. 104–105.

25. Quandt, "Clinton's Legacy." Here, clarification of the distinction between the 1949 armistice lines, the 1923 international boundary lines, and the June 4, 1967, lines is in order. The 1923 lines, delineated by the French and British mandates, kept the Jordan River and Lake Tiberias within Israel (Palestine). The armistice lines passed through the Demilitarized Zone (DMZ, an area of less than 100 square miles), which was actually composed of the three sectors conquered by Syria in the 1948 war west of the international boundary. The northern sector consisted of an area next to Tel Dan along the Israeli-Syrian frontier. The central sector straddled the Jordan River between Lake Huleh and Lake Tiberias. The southern sector consisted of an area that ran from the northeastern shore of Lake Tiberias to its southeastern shore, extending to the international boundary lines. The area southeast of Lake Tiberias constituted the bulk of the southern sector. It should also be recalled that the question of sovereignty over the DMZ was never resolved between Israel and Syria. During the period before the eruption of the 1967 war, the DMZ was partitioned de facto by both countries. Most important, Syria remained along the northeastern shore of Lake Tiberias and in the Al-Hamma area, southeast of the lake. These constitute the June 4, 1967, lines, meaning the lines that existed on the eve of the 1967 war. See Chapter 1.

26. Rabinovich, *Brink of Peace,* pp. 106–107.

27. See Clinton's interview with Thomas Friedman, "Clinton Says Support of Israel Will Not Waver," *New York Times,* September 11, 1993.

28. "The Middle East," *U.S. Department of State Dispatch* 4, no. 47 (November 22, 1993), p. 800.

29. "Secretary Christopher," *U.S. Department of State Dispatch* 4, no. 50 (December 13, 1993), pp. 863–864.

30. Mary Curtius, "Assad Calls for 'Normal' Relations with Israel," *Boston Globe,* January 17, 1994.

31. Rabinovich, *Brink of Peace,* pp. 129–130.

32. See "The President's News Conference with Prime Minister Yitzhak Rabin of Israel," *Presidential Documents* 30, no. 11 (March 21, 1994), pp. 544–545.

33. For details, see Rabinovich, *Brink of Peace,* pp. 139–147.

34. See Walid Muallem's interview, "Fresh Light on the Syrian-Israeli Peace Negotiations," *Journal of Palestine Studies* 26, no. 2 (Winter 1997), p. 84.

35. See *Al-Hayat,* November 27, 1999.

36. Author interview with Itamar Rabinovich, November 12, 1998. See also "Rabinovich Yarud 'Ala al-Hayat" (Rabinovich Replies to *Al-Hayat), Al-Hayat,* November 22, 1999.

37. See Asad's address to the Syrian parliament in *Al-Ba'th,* September 11, 1994.

38. For details, see Rabinovich, *Brink of Peace,* pp. 159–160.

39. See excerpts from remarks by President Clinton and President Hafiz al-Asad, "Asad and Clinton Speak: Shared Quest for Peace," *New York Times,* October 28, 1994, p. A21.

40. Rabinovich, *Brink of Peace,* pp. 169–170.

41. Lara Marlow, "Interview with a Fanatic," *Time,* February 6, 1995, p. 34. See also *New York Times,* January 24, 1995.

42. For Muallem's remarks on the agreement, see his interview, "Fresh Light," p. 92. For Rabinovich's remarks, see Rabinovich, *Brink of Peace,* pp. 178 ff. Author interview with Itamar Rabinovich, November 12, 1998, thanks to whom I have a copy of the agreement. See also text of the agreement in *Al-Hayat,* November 22, 1999.

43. See Asad's and Mubarak's remarks during the joint press conference in *Tishrin,* June 3, 1995.

44. See *Al-Hayat,* August 3, 1995.

45. Rabinovich, *Brink of Peace,* p. 188.

46. Tariq Aziz, Iraqi deputy prime minister, affirmed in November 1994 that his country's condition of war with Israel had ended, and that he no longer considered himself among the "confrontational states." At the time, reports circulated that Israeli-Iraqi talks were taking place. Shimon Perez denied any contact, direct or indirect, with Iraq. See Raghida Dargham, "Tarik Aziz Yu'akked Inha' Hal al-Harb Ma'a Israil" (Tarik Aziz Affirms Ending Condition of War with Israel), *Al-Hayat,* November 7, 1994.

47. There were several suicide bombings in Israel, on April 6 and April 13, 1994; October 11 and October 19, 1994; and July 24, 1995. See *Jerusalem Report,* February 23, 1995, p. 14.

48. See Serge Schmemann, "Rabin Declares Blast Will Not Stop Talks," *New York Times,* July 25, 1995.

49. For excellent details, see Rabinovich, *Brink of Peace,* pp. 188–195. See also Muallem's interview, "Fresh Light," pp. 86–87; and Daniel Pipes, "Just Kidding," *New Republic,* January 8 and 15, 1996, pp. 18–19.

50. See Asad's interview with *Al-Ahram,* October 11, 1995.

51. For Peres's vision of a new Middle East, see Shimon Peres and Arye Naor, *The New Middle East* (New York: Henry Holt, 1993). See also Rabinovich, *Brink of Peace,* pp. 196, 202; and Uri Savir, *The Process: 1,100 Days That Changed the Middle East* (New York: Random House, 1998), p. 274.

52. Savir, *Process,* pp. 273–280.

53. According to Abd al-Wahhab Darawshe, an Arab Israeli Knesset, Asad informed him during his visit to Damascus in 1994 that he was ready to offer Israel full normal relations if Israel withdrew to the June 4, 1967, lines. Author interview with Darawshe, November 23, 1998.

54. Rabinovich, *Brink of Peace,* pp. 210–211.

55. See Asad's and Mubarak's remarks during joint press conference in *Tishrin,* December 24, 1995.

56. Rabinovich, *Brink of Peace,* pp. 212–213.

57. Damascus Syrian Arab Republic Radio, "Press Views Hopes for Talks," in *FBIS-NES,* January 4, 1996, p. 50. See also Damascus Syrian Arab Republic Radio, "Syrian Press: Israeli Commitment to Full Withdrawal Still Awaited," in *FBIS-NES,* January 23, 1996, p. 41.

58. Jerusalem Qol Yisra'el, "Al-Asad-Peres Summit Very Important," in *FBIS-NES,* January 4, 1996, p. 33.

59. Jerusalem Israel Television Channel 1, "Peres: Early Elections If No Progress in Talks," in *FBIS-NES,* January 4, 1996, p. 33.

60. For details, see Rabinovich, *Brink of Peace,* pp. 219–222. See also Savir, *Process,* pp. 281–282.

61. See Muallem's interview, "Fresh Light," p. 81.

62. See Serge Schmemann, "Revenge Is Claimed for the Killing of a Hamas Bomber," *New York Times,* February 26, 1996.

63. See Serge Schmemann, "Fourth Terror Blast in Israel Kills Twelve at Mall in Tel Aviv: Nine-Day Toll Grows to Fifty-Nine," *New York Times,* March 5, 1996.

64. Rabinovich, *Brink of Peace,* p. 226; and Savir, *Process,* pp. 284–285.

65. On the Sharm al-Shaykh summit, see Kasem Mohammed Jaafar, "Al-Salam wa al-Intihariyoun: Al-Muwajaha al-Quatila" (Peace and Suicide Bombers: The Deadly Confrontation), *Al-Wasat,* March 18, 1996, pp. 10–19; and Muallem's interview, "Fresh Light," pp. 81–82.

66. Associated Press, "U.S. Arranges Talks on Lebanon Truce," *Boston Globe,* May 9, 1996, p. 11.

67. For details on Netanyahu's policy guidelines, see Leslie Susser, "Where Is Netanyahu Leading Israel?" *Jerusalem Report,* July 25, 1996, pp. 12–16.

68. Benjamin Netanyahu, *A Place Among Nations: Israel and the World* (New York: Bantam Books, 1993). See also Chapter 6 in this volume.

69. Douglas Jehl, "'Struggle for Peace,' Egyptian Urges Arab," *New York Times,* June 23, 1996, p. 8. See also *Al-Hayat,* June 3, 1996.

70. Susser, "Where Is Netanyahu Leading Israel?" p. 12.

71. Jehl, "Struggle for Peace," p. 8.

72. For details, see Joseph Matar (Beirut), "A Diplomatic Babel," *Jerusalem Report,* May 15, 1997, pp. 26–27.

73. For details, see Leslie Susser, "New Approach to a Deal in Lebanon," *Jerusalem Report,* February 19, 1998, p. 22.

74. Ibid.

75. See Farouk al-Shara's interview with *Al-Majalla,* November 11, 1998, pp. 28–29.

76. Ehud Barak won 56 percent of the vote. The breakdown of Knesset seats is as follows: Labor 27, Likud 19, Shas 17, Meretz 9, Yisrael ba-Aliya 7, Shinui 6, Center

6, NRP 5, United Torah Judaism (UTJ) 5, Arab Democratic Party 5, Yisrael Beiteinu 4, National Union 3, Hadash 3, National Democratic Alliance 2, and Am Echad 2. See Elli Sinclair, "Barak Victorious," *Jewish Press,* May 21, 1999.

77. See Lisa Beyer, "Israel's New Syrian View," *Time,* July 5, 1999, p. 44.

78. The first visit ever by a delegation of Israeli Arabs to Syria took place after Asad's elder son, Basil, died in a car accident in March 1994. The delegates, headed by Knesset member Abd al-Wahhab Darawshe, went there to offer their condolences while at the same time using the sad occasion as an opportunity to exchange views on the peace process. A similar delegation, including Knesset members as well, visited Syria in August 1997, with the objective of improving relations with the Syrian regime. Before long, Syrian vice president Abd al-Halim Khaddam invited Azmi Beshara, the outspoken Arab-Israeli Knesset member, to Damascus to hold discussions on two issues of deep concern to Syria: ways to improve Syria's relations with the Arab-Israelis, who constitute almost 18 percent of the population; and how to seek better understanding of Israel's domestic politics. See respectively, *Tishrin,* March 10, 1994; *Tishrin,* August 13, 1997; *Al-Ba'th,* August 13, 1997; Azmi Beshara's interview with *Al-Wasat,* January 5, 1998, pp. 20–21; and author interview with Arab-Israeli Knesset member Abd al-Wahhab Darawshe, November 23, 1998.

79. Joint news conference in the Old Executive Office Building by President Clinton and Prime Minister Barak, *New York Times,* July 20, 1999, p. A8.

80. Ibid., pp. A1, A8.

81. See John M. Broder, "The Empty U.S. Seat at Mideast Talks: A Boon for All," *New York Times,* July 21, 1999, p. A10.

82. Reuters, "Syrian Approach to Militants," *New York Times,* July 20, 1999, p. A8.

83. Jane Perlez, "Israel and Syria to Reopen Talks, Clinton Reports," *New York Times,* December 9, 1999, p. A1.

84. William A. Orme Jr., "Israel Lawmakers Closely Approve Talks with Syria," *New York Times,* December 14, 1999, p. A1.

85. Ibid.

86. Deborah Sontag, "Syria and Israel Begin Peace Talks After Four-Year Halt," *New York Times,* December 16, 1999, pp. A1, A10.

87. Deborah Sontag, "Behind Hard-Line Talk: Willingness to Concede," *New York Times,* December 17, 1999, p. A18.

88. Ibid.

89. John M. Broder, "Israel and Syria Return to Search for Major Accord," *New York Times,* January 4, 2000, p. A8.

90. David E. Sanger, "Clinton Breaks an Impasse at the Israel-Syria Talks," *New York Times,* January 5, 2000; Ibrahim Hamidi and Rafiq Khalil al-Maalouf, "Clinton Yatadakhal Ba'd Tajmid al-Lijane" (Clinton Intervenes After Freezing the Committees), *Al-Hayat,* January 7, 2000; and David E. Sanger, "Clinton Appears to Pick Up Pace of Israel-Syria Meetings," *New York Times,* January 7, 2000.

91. David E. Sanger, "Clinton Offers Israel and Syria Seven-Page 'Working Paper' to Study Golan Heights Contract," *New York Times,* January 8, 2000, p. A6.

92. For more details, see Susan Sachs, "What Syria Wants," *New York Times,* January 18, 2000; and Deborah Sontag, "Dust Settles: Israel-Syria Peace Effort Is Set Back," *New York Times,* February 10, 2000.

93. See the Syrian-produced text of the working paper in *Al-Hayat,* January 9, 2000, and the entire draft peace treaty in *Ha'aretz,* January 13, 2000.

94. Jane Perlez, "Israel and Syria Postponing Talks, the U.S. Reports," *New York Times,* January 18, 2000; and Rafiq Khalil al-Maalouf, "I'lan Ta'jile Mufawadat Shep-

herdstown" (Announcing the Postponement of Shepherdstown Negotiations), *Al-Hayat*, January 18, 2000.

95. See "America: Al-Fajwa Bayn Suriya wa Israil 'Ghayr Wasi'a'" (America: The Gap Between Syria and Israel "Not Wide"), *Al-Hayat*, April 1, 2000, p. 4.

96. Bashar has been given a visible role in Syrian domestic politics going far beyond his intervention in Lebanon. Reflecting this, Bashar told *Al-Hayat* that the Ba'th Party congress would meet in 2000 and that he had recommended some people with merit to be appointed in the new government. The importance of his statement lay in the fact that he touched upon highly sensitive issues dealt with by the president only. Significantly enough, the Ba'th Party congress has not met for over ten years, most likely in order to avoid the possibility of any kind of ideological or personnel reorganization. In addition, the government to be changed has been in office for almost thirteen years. See Patrick Seale, "Bashar al-Asad li-al-Hayat: Mu'tamar al-Ba'th Hadha al-Am wa Zakayt Ba'd al-Akfiya' Lil-Hukuma al-Jadida" (Bashar al-Asad to Al-Hayat: Al-Ba'th Congress This Year and I Recommended Some Meritorious People to the New Government), *Al-Hayat*, March 7, 2000.

97. Deborah Sontag, "Barak Says Talks with Syria Have Reached Critical Juncture," *New York Times*, January 12, 2000.

98. Ibid.

99. See Deborah Sontag, "Barak Delays Third West Bank Transfer, Angering Palestinians," *New York Times*, January 17, 2000; and Deborah Sontag, "Juggling the Mideast," *New York Times*, January 19, 2000.

100. Ibrahim Hamidi, "Darbat Israiliya Tudamer Thalath Mahattate Kahraba," *Al-Hayat*, February 9, 2000; and John F. Burns, "After Raids, Beirut Turns to Trusty Generators," *New York Times*, February 9, 2000.

101. Deborah Sontag, "Attacks Renewed in Lebanon Strife," *New York Times*, February 9, 2000.

102. See respectively, Thomas Friedman, "Dear Ehud, Hafez and Yasir," *New York Times*, February 22, 2000; and Deborah Sontag, "Israel Minister Warns Arabs of Retaliation If Attacked," *New York Times*, February 24, 2000.

103. Deborah Sontag, "Rabin Vowed to Pull Back from Golan, Barak Says," *New York Times*, February 28, 2000, p. A6.

104. Ibid.

105. Ibid.

106. Susan Sachs, "Israeli Cabinet Vows July Lebanon Pullout," *New York Times*, March 6, 2000.

107. Deborah Sontag, "Israeli Bill May Hobble Barak Efforts with Syria," *New York Times*, March 2, 2000.

108. See Lahoud's interview with *Al-Hayat*, March 11, 2000.

109. Ibid. See also John F. Burns, "Beirut Seeks to Use Pullout by Israelis as Leverage," *New York Times*, March 12, 2000.

110. John F. Burns, "Arab League Hotly Attacks Israeli Stand on Lebanon," *New York Times*, March 13, 2000.

111. Ibid.

112. John F. Burns, "Israeli Jets Pound Targets in Lebanon for Second Day," *New York Times*, March 15, 2000.

113. See "Israil Tuaked Niyat al-Insihab Ahadiyan Min Janub Lubnan Ba'd Fashal Qumat Clinton-Asad" (Israel Confirms Its Intention of Unilateral Withdrawal from Lebanon After the Failure of the Clinton-Asad Summit), *Al-Hayat*, March 28, 2000; and "Fashal Qumat Geneve Yuthir al-Shukuk Hawla Qudrat Rais al-Hukuma Ala Quira't al-Kharita al-Siyasiyah" (The Failure of the Geneva Summit Raises Doubts About the Ability of the Prime Minister to Read the Political Map), *Al-Quds*

al-Arabi, April 3, 2000, quoted from *Ha'aretz,* April 2, 2000. See also Ibrahim Hamidi, "Ijra'at Bina' al-Thiqa Tufashel Qumat Geneve" (Confidence-Building Measures Led to Failure of Geneva Summit), *Al-Hayat,* March 28, 2000; and "Ha'aretz: Fursat Iqamat al-Salam Ma'a Suriya Madat" (Ha'aretz: The Opportunity of Making Peace with Syria Passed), *Al-Hayat,* March 31, 2000.

114. Jane Perlez, "In Geneva, Clinton Bet That Assad Would Bend, and Lost," *New York Times,* March 28, 2000.

115. Jane Perlez, "Clinton Says Next Move for Peace Is Assad's," *New York Times,* March 29, 2000.

116. Hamidi, "Ijra'at Bina' al-Thiqa."

117. Samar Azmashali, "Al-Shara: Hududina 'Ala al-Dafa al-Shemaliya al-Sharqiya li-Tiberias" (Al-Shara: Our Borders Are on the Northeastern Shore of Tiberias), *Al-Hayat,* April 16, 2000. The G-77, or Group of 77, is the largest third-world coalition of states. Its number increased to 133, but the name was retained.

118. Muhammad Shuqeir, "Lubnan: Fashal Qumat Geneve Lam Yuqfel al-Bab" (Lebanon: Failure of Geneva Summit Did Not Shut the Door), *Al-Hayat,* April 1, 2000.

119. "Al-Shara Yurid 'Ala Wazir al-Difa' al-lubnani: Al-Matlub Tafawud wa Salame wa Laysa Harban" (Al-Shara Replies to Lebanese Defense Minister: What Is Required Is Negotiations and Peace and Not War), *Al-Hayat,* April 3, 2000.

120. Susan Sachs, "Israeli Accord Still Possible, Son of Assad Tells Paper," *New York Times,* April 18, 2000.

121. For the complete proposal, see *Al-Hayat,* April 8, 2000.

122. Edward P. Djerejian, *Current Developments in the Middle East* (Washington, D.C.: U.S. Government Printing Office, October 15, 1993), p. 9.

123. For a critical analysis of the misapplication of conflict resolution methods to the peace process, see Amr G. E. Sabet, "The Peace Process and the Politics of Conflict Resolution," *Journal of Palestine Studies* 27, no. 4 (Summer 1998).

124. See Asad's address to the Syrian parliament in *Al-Ba'th,* September 11, 1994.

125. See Ibrahim Hamidi, "Al-Asad Yujaddid Intiqadih al-Ittifaqat al-Munfarida" (Asad Repeats His Criticism of Separate Agreements), *Al-Hayat,* December 20, 1994, p. 3.

126. Damascus Syrian Arab Republic Radio, "Radio Commentary: Taba Agreement 'Regrettable,'" in *FBIS-NES,* September 26, 1995, p. 56.

127. See David Horovitz and Ehud Ya'ari, "Syria Looks on in Anger," *Jerusalem Report,* November 17, 1994, pp. 10–12. See also excerpts from the text of the treaty in *New York Times,* October 27, 1994, p. A13.

128. Haysam Bashir, "Dimashq: Al-Tawqit Laysa Munasiban" (Damascus: Timing Is Not Appropriate), *Al-Hawadeth,* October 7, 1994, p. 10.

129. See Jonathan Broder, "Casablanca, the Conference," *Jerusalem Report,* November 3, 1994, p. 33.

130. Joel Greenberg, "Rabin Visits Oman, Taking Step to Widen Link to Gulf Region," *New York Times,* December 28, 1994, p. A2.

131. For details on the Alexandria summit and the leaders' joint declaration, see Muhammad Alam and Ashraf al-Faqi, "Quma Thulathia fi al-Iskandaria Taftah al-Bab Limusalaha Arabia" (A Threesome Summit in Alexandria Opens the Door for Arab Reconciliation), *Al-Wasat,* January 2, 1995, pp. 10–13.

132. See Abd al-Halim Khaddam's interview with *Al-Wasat,* November 20, 1995, p. 14.

133. This translated quote was taken in its entirety from Rabinovich, *Brink of Peace,* p. 195. See Asad's interview with *Al-Ahram,* October 11, 1995.

134. Translated from the Hebrew by Yaron Peleg and Robert G. Rabil.

8

Missed Opportunities and Perspectives on Peace

The most important factor contributing to the elusiveness of the Syrian-Israeli peace likely concerns the very different perceptions each side has of the substantive meaning of the peace and the significance of the opportunities that were supposedly missed along the way on account of those antithetical perceptions.

Nothing illustrates better these differing views than Itamar Rabinovich's dual assertion that "at no time during this period (August 1992–March 1996) were Israel and Syria on the verge of a breakthrough," and that "the potential of getting to that point existed twice—in August 1993 and during the first weeks of Shimon Peres's tenure as prime minister in November–December 1995."[1] Rabinovich explained that in early August, Yitzhak Rabin "authorized Secretary of State Christopher to use the 'hypothetical question' technique in order to find out whether Asad was ready for the very specific package that he regarded as acceptable to him and, ultimately, to the Israeli public."[2]

Rabinovich maintained that although Asad's response was positive in principle, in that he was willing to offer contractual peace in return for the withdrawal, it was disappointing to Rabin's specific peace package. Asad refused two core elements: normalization and interface. Rabin insisted on "applying the Israeli-Egyptian model whereby a limited withdrawal would be matched by a comparatively long period of normalization so as to 'test' the new relationship before a large-scale withdrawal was undertaken."[3] Asad also rejected Rabin's procedural demands: to engage in public diplomacy and to establish a secret channel.

Rabinovich expounded that "Rabin's package reflected his principal consideration: peace with Syria was important in itself and as an indispensable component of an eventual comprehensive settlement. But Asad would not make peace unless offered a full withdrawal. This was a price Rabin was most reluctant to pay." He added that even if Rabin "personally overcame his own feelings he would find it difficult to rally a majority of Israelis to endorse it unless Asad was willing to make an investment in converting the Israeli public."[4] Rabinovich also emphasized that the gap between the two sides could have been bridged by the United States. Rabin believed that this should have been done by pressuring Asad to accept the basic premises of his position. However, he also emphasized that given the history of Washington's relations with Syria, it could hardly be expected that the Clinton administration would pressure Asad into accepting Rabin's position. Rabinovich justified that under the "combined impact of Asad's response and the administration's attitude, Rabin chose to make his move on the Palestinian track."[5]

Rabinovich found it difficult to understand why Asad, "despite his suspicions, reservations and inhibitions, failed to take the steps that would have produced an agreement on terms that should have been quite acceptable to him." According to him, this was poignantly the case with regard to the second potential of achieving a breakthrough during the period from November 1995 to January 1996. During this period, Shimon Peres showed his readiness to negotiate a peace treaty with Asad. He was ready to discuss simultaneous issues and "to fly high and fast or low and slow," depending on Asad's own decision. Against the backdrop of his vision of a "new Middle East," Peres explored the possibility of engaging Syria in joint economic ventures partly centered on the Golan. Peres looked forward to a summit meeting with Asad to help his election prospects as well as advance the negotiations. Rabinovich, explaining the course of events, remarked that "Asad's response was cautiously positive but very guarded."[6] As it turned out, the negotiations proved to be difficult, leading to Peres's decision to move up the elections. While the United States preoccupied itself with Asad's reaction to Peres's decision, Rabinovich felt that Asad had no "cause for being angry." He emphasized that Asad "had not met Peres's terms and had not provided him with real prospects of a good agreement in good time."[7]

In an interview with *Ha'aretz,* published on October 24, 1997, former secretary of state Warren Christopher contributed his own judgment on the question of missed opportunities. When asked whether Asad had missed such an opportunity or whether he saw peace as a long-term threat to his regime, Christopher replied:

> My own view is that he missed an opportunity, an historic opportunity to achieve the return of the Golan, or return of territory. I account for it not by his fear, but his mistrust and suspicion of what was being offered. He examined it so extensively and exhaustively that he missed the opportunity. If he had been responsive and done the public things that we urged and also responded substantively I think much more progress would have been done. Rabin had the strength and the conviction that Syria was and is a threat and it would be a great service to Israel if that threat were removed. One of Asad's miscalculations was that time is and was on his side.[8]

Christopher excluded the possibility that an agreement was feasible during Peres's brief tenure as prime minister after the assassination of Rabin. He argued:

> I really respected that when Prime Minister Peres felt that he needed a mandate for himself . . . and I think that pushed him to the early election decision. . . . They were supposed to conclude a deal in the midst of an election campaign when there had been [a] kind of historic event like an assassination and then a change of government. That would have been very, very short, very tight.[9]

William B. Quandt gave another interpretation of these missed opportunities, emphasizing the U.S. role in the negotiations. He saw the U.S. administration as partly responsible for the failure of the negotiations. His thoughts rested on the analysis that President Clinton was cautious and did not know what to do when Rabin was so annoyed with Asad's response to his opening gambit in August 1993. Quandt emphasized that Clinton held back and did not pick up the phone to talk Asad and Rabin into resuming the negotiations, given the high momentum at the time.[10] Analyzing Clinton's Middle East peace legacy, Quandt scrutinized four issues: presidential character, the role of Congress, some underlying assumptions behind U.S. policy, and reasons for the stalemate.

On the first issue, Quandt emphasized that although President Clinton was skillful and could reach over barriers, he was slow, unfocused, and reluctant to take a stand. On the second issue, Quandt highlighted the fact that the U.S. Congress was pro-Israel, thus raising the stakes for Clinton on the front of domestic politics, which made him reluctant to interfere more forcefully in the successive Israeli-Syrian stalemates. Regarding the third issue, Quandt saw that the U.S. administration was satisfied with the soundness and plausibility of the peace policies it has been pursuing so far. The government's intervention in the peace process mostly as a facilitator involved manageable and modest domestic political stakes. However, Quandt pointed out that when Benjamin Netanyahu became Israel's prime minister, Clinton was confounded by how to deal with the new situation. He then considered a forceful intervention in the peace process, but still he did not act on it. On the final issue, Quandt thought that the U.S. administration had no qualms about putting the blame of the stalemate in the negotiations on the parties of the conflict. Summarizing his views with a touch of irony, the former official and current professor wondered what had happened to former secretary of state James Baker's approach, meaning being tough and resolute.[11]

Patrick Seale, Asad's biographer and semiofficial spokesman, addressed the issue of missed opportunities in a different light. Seale's intention was to defend Asad against these charges of missing the aforementioned opportunities. In an article published by the *Journal of Palestine Studies* in 1996, "Asad's Regional Strategy and the Challenge from Netanyahu," Seale referred to the argument "that Asad missed the chance of peace with Israel . . . when Rabin was alive and then when Peres inherited the prime minister's mantle following the assassination. Peace was there for the taking, it is said, if only Asad had made some gesture such as agreeing to meet Peres, or allowing Israeli journalists to visit Syria, or even expressing grief at Rabin's passing, or addressing himself directly in one form or another to the Israeli public to overcome its deep-seated skepticism of his intentions."[12]

Seale responded to this argument by emphasizing first that Asad "has always been extremely cautious in negotiation, insisting on proceeding step by careful step, seeing a trap in Israel's repeated probing for 'back channels.' . . . Asad seems unable to set aside his deep conviction that Israel is not ready for an honorable peace . . . but conspires instead to hold sway over the whole region 'from the Nile to the Euphrates' with the aim of reducing the Arabs to a subject people."[13] Seale added that "Asad saw Peres's last assault on Lebanon as revealing his and Israel's true nature. Operation Grapes of Wrath elbowed aside the cant of Peres's so-called 'New Middle East.'" Within this context, Seale quoted Asad's interview with *Al-Ahram* in December 1995, in which Asad admitted that the true aim of Peres's "Middle Easternism" was "to eliminate the concept of Arabism, and by extension the Arabs . . . our inner feeling of being a nation, and our national and social identity."[14]

Seale then commented on the Wye Plantation negotiations. He maintained that "while Syria proposed 'total peace for total withdrawal,' total withdrawal from the Golan by Israel was always hedged around by numerous preconditions. First, it was to be subject to an Israeli national referendum, then it was to be accompanied by such draconian conditions as the thinning out and restructuring of the Syrian armed forces; the placement inside Syrian territory of an Israeli-warning station; only token Israeli withdrawal pending proof of Syrian good behavior; and full 'normalization,' in the sense not just of diplomatic relations but of the free movement of goods and people, joint projects. . . . At one of the last sessions at Wye Plantation, the Israelis apparently submitted more than a score of projects for integrating the two economies." Seale emphasized, "Most Syrians would have seen any such settlement as exposing their society, nascent industries, culture, traditions, and national security to hostile Israeli penetration. For Asad, it would have made a mockery of his entire career."

Seale concluded his response by stating that underlying the differences on the key issues of the final boundary, security measures, the timetable of withdrawal, and normalization, issues upon which no agreement was reached, "was a fundamental conflict about what peace was intended to achieve."[15] There existed two different, opposite visions of peace. Seale maintained that for Asad, "the essence of any settlement is not the recovery of this or that piece of occupied territory, but the 'containment' of Israel, just as his notion of a 'comprehensive peace' is not about normalization but, on the contrary, about holding the line against Israel." He added that in Asad's view, "the overall objective of a negotiation should be to reduce Israel to what Sadat once described as 'its natural dimension,' to shrink its influence to more modest and less aggressive proportions, which the Arab players in the Middle East system could accept and live with."[16]

Seale then contrasted Syria's vision to that of Israel. He underscored that "Israel's vision of peace is the very opposite: It sees peace as a means to extend its influence to every corner of the Arab world; to gain access to the money and raw materials of the Gulf; to restructure the region in such a way as to prevent the emergence of any hostile Arab combination." While Seale perceived that it was these "conflicting visions of peace which very probably doomed the talks to failure," he squarely put the blame for missing the opportunity to make peace on Israel. "Could one not argue that it was Israel rather than Syria that missed the boat of peace? Peace was within Israel's grasp, yet it wanted more than that: It wanted hegemony."[17]

A more thorough response to the argument of missed opportunities was presented by Walid Muallem in a lengthy interview published in the *Journal of Palestine Studies* in 1997. What made this response important was the fact that it was the most detailed account of the Israeli-Syrian negotiations given by an official Syrian source. Muallem excluded the possibility of a breakthrough in 1993 by indicating that the two parties had negotiated the details of withdrawal for almost a year, until 1994. Indeed, as Rabinovich stated, the Syrians would not budge until they heard the words "full withdrawal." Muallem also remarked that the major stumbling blocks to reaching an agreement were Israeli exaggerations in two fields: security arrangements and normalization. He stated that "the Israelis have military superiority over any combination of Arab states. They have nuclear bombs, the most advanced arms and technology. . . . Yet despite all this, they used to tell us they are afraid of Syria."[18] Muallem added that the "Israelis wanted an early-warning station on the Golan after their withdrawal, which we considered an infringement of our sovereignty. . . . They already have the technology—including satellites, their own and American—that can do the job far more effective on the ground than early-warning stations." Muallem said that the Israelis spoke also "of the size of the Syrian army, as if what was important was numbers rather than the quality and type of equipment and armaments and such things as the possession of a nuclear arsenal. Finally, they insisted that the demilitarized zones reach just south of Damascus. This means you open the capital to them. We refused all these demands."[19]

Concerning normalization, Muallem emphasized that "Israel believed that you can push a button to make peace warm, to direct Syrian popular attitudes from a state of war to a state of peace." He then stressed that the Israelis "wanted open borders, open markets for their goods, and so on. This would have an obvious effect on our own economy . . . how can you integrate two economies when one has per capita income of $900 per year and the other has per capita income of $15,000 per year?"[20]

Commenting on the second missed opportunity to make peace during Peres's tenure as prime minister, Muallem indicated that progress was taking place as "things were moving." He emphasized that the heads of the three delegations (Dennis Ross, Uri Savir, and himself) had decided to hold continuous talks "to finalize the structure of an agreement on all issues."[21] He stated that "we set a deadline for ourselves, agreeing to close the remaining gaps and finalize all the elements of an agreement by June 1996. . . . The expectation was that by September 1996 the final document would be ready." Muallem added, "So we were very surprised when, soon afterward, Mr. [Shimon] Peres called early elections."[22] Muallem also implied that Peres was in such a hurry that the Syrian government could not sell an agreement to its public and get them to accept it in due time.

Muallem attributed Peres's call for early elections to internal pressures from his own party, because "the margin between Labor and Likud had started to narrow in the polls."[23] He implied that an agreement was beyond reach, since Peres was not sure about the results, and then emphasized that the Israelis had anyway suspended the talks unilaterally in February due to their belief that their public opinion would not support them in continuing the negotiations after the Palestinian suicide bombings. With regard to a summit meeting, Muallem stressed that in order for such an undertaking to be successful, "the gaps between the two positions must be narrow," and there must be a knowledge beforehand that the meeting was "truly the final stage of the agreement." Accordingly, Muallem explained, Asad perceived a summit meeting as premature.[24] Concerning public diplomacy, Muallem felt that this was a problem with the negotiations all along. He explained:

> We always felt that the Israelis wanted Syria to do their work for them. They wanted us to convince their public that peace was in their interests. We prepared our public for peace with Israel. Many things changed in our media. But they wanted us to speak in the Israeli media to prepare Israeli public opinion. They wanted us to allow Israelis to visit Syria. We considered such insistence a negative sign: When you do not prepare your own public for peace with your neighbor, this means you do not really have the intention to make peace.[25]

In his argument that Peres himself was responsible for missing the opportunity to make peace with Syria, Muallem was in fact close to some Israeli sources who supported the same argument. For example, in a story published by *Ma'ariv* in December 1997 under the headline "This Is How We Missed the Peace with Syria," the newspaper, quoting sources close to Uri Savir, argued in line with Muallem's claim that indeed Ross, Muallem, and Savir had brought the negotiations to the verge of agreement. However, the newspaper added that once Savir had presented Peres with the general contours of the peace agreement, "Peres equivocated." The story continued: Peres "knew that he would have to make difficult decisions; to moderate the army demands, to give up the Golan Heights. He knew that Rabin could have done it; he was not certain that he could. Peres decided to move up the elections. . . . This is how the opportunity was missed for a peace agreement between Israel, Syria, and the rest of the Arab world."[26]

In addition, Israeli negotiator Uri Savir wrote in his book *The Process: 1,100 Days That Changed the Middle East,* that he was increasingly convinced that the two sides could negotiate a peace treaty based on compatible strategic interests.[27] In a major television interview, Savir also argued that Syria and Israel had accomplished much at the Wye Plantation and had come to the verge of concluding an agreement, while at the same time attributing no blame for the missed opportunities to either side.[28]

In an effort to fully absolve Syria from the charges and the implication that Syria missed the opportunity to make peace with Israel, Patrick Seale gave the most comprehensive and detailed account of the Israeli-Syrian negotiations, in the form of three major articles published in November 1999 by *Al-Hayat.* In the first article, he examined three issues in the negotiations that led him to conclude that Rabin's opening gambit in 1993 was no more than a political maneuver and a war ruse.

First, Seale emphasized that Rabin's message of commitment to withdraw, known as the "deposit," was transmitted orally by Secretary of State Christopher, who insisted on keeping it secret. The United States asked the Syrians not to disclose the deposit, so as not to expose Rabin to domestic political foes. However, every time the United States suggested that the message be written down, Rabin evaded the request. Second, the deposit came with a long list, namely stringent security arrangements and a peace treaty with complete normalization. In addition, no settlements were to be dismantled, and there was to be a "test" period of five years to verify Syria's good intentions. Finally, the opening gambit took place days before the Palestinians and Israelis reached agreement on the Oslo Accords. So the importance of the gambit lay in its timing.

It was not true that Rabin had left the Oslo negotiations to Peres; his office was well informed. Rabin was under pressure to reach an accord with the Palestinians. Whereas the Golan front has been quiet, the intifada shook Israel. The urgency lay with the Palestinians. Rabin knew that Asad would be angered by Oslo and might frustrate the deal, while at the same time he recognized that the Palestinians were worried about the possibility that Israel and Syria might conclude an agreement. So Rabin's gambit was an attempt to preemptively blunt Asad's attack on Oslo while pressuring the Palestinians into

making concessions. Correspondingly, these three issues led in one direction—that Rabin's opening gambit was a political maneuver produced to
serve other goals.[29]

In the second article, Seale tried to justify Syria's stand in the negotiations by stressing the idea that Asad had every reason to doubt that Rabin was
serious about concluding a peace treaty with Syria. Seale began his article by
noting that Asad had asked Christopher two questions on August 4, 1993, the
day the "deposit" was transmitted: What does Rabin mean by full withdrawal,
does this mean to the June 4, 1967, lines? And, Does Israel have any claim on
the land it occupied on the Syrian front in June 1967? To the first, Christopher
replied that he had a commitment to withdrawal, but without a specification
regarding the lines, while to the second, he answered that to his knowledge
Israel had no such claim.

Seale explained that from this time Asad began to doubt Rabin's seriousness. Asad remained adamant about his position that there would be no
progress in the peace process until Israel clarified its position and committed
itself to a full withdrawal from the Golan to the June 4, 1967, lines. This happened in July 1994, when Christopher informed Asad that Rabin had committed himself to full withdrawal to the June 4 lines, but on condition that
Syria meet Israel's peace requirements. Again Christopher asked Asad to keep
this secret.

At this point Seale observed that Rabinovich had another account of what
happened in July when Christopher wanted to know from Rabin if he could
clarify to Asad the June 4 issue. Seale quoted Rabinovich, who wrote that "by
now Rabin had clearly decided that he could actually fit the issue into the paradigm built on August 3 as long as it was a 'clarification' and not a 'commitment,' and told Christopher that he could tell Asad that this was his 'impression.'"[30] In addition, Seale further tried to cast doubt on Rabin's commitment
to an agreement with Syria by depicting him as needlessly prolonging the
negotiations. Bolstering his argument, Seale again quoted Rabinovich, who
wrote that Rabin was ready to "keep Asad engaged in the negotiations even if
that required occasional verbal concessions."[31]

Seale went on, saying that security was a principal issue in the negotiations discussed from April 1994 to early November 1995. Israel wanted an
early-warning station on Mount Hermon, and equally significant, Rabin—as
transmitted through Christopher—suggested that all of Syria be divided into
four zones: a demilitarized zone, a zone of limited armaments, a zone in
which only two Syrian divisions and a military airport would be allowed, and
a final zone with unlimited armament. According to Seale, Asad received the
suggestion with extreme anger. Asad's view was that Rabin, instead of withdrawing from the Golan, was seemingly seeking to occupy Syria. Asad interpreted Rabin's intent as wanting to strip the country of its arms and deprive it
of its ability to defend itself.

Asad's principal demand, then, was to confine security arrangements to the engagement areas, that is, along both sides of the June 4 lines, which came to be known as "relevant areas." Against this background the "Non-Paper on the Aims and Principles of the Security Arrangements" of May 1995 (see Appendix 7.1) was negotiated with the objective of placing Israel's security requirements within a reasonable framework. When the two countries' chiefs of staff met and disagreed over the relevant areas and the early-warning station, Asad was convinced that Rabin was wasting time. Asad believed that Rabin's obsession with security was no more than a reflection of his irresolution, meaning that Rabin did not take the final decision regarding making peace with Syria. Asad also believed that Christopher and Ross did not pressure Israel to move forward on the peace process but were supporting Israel's "game" of negotiating on superficial instead of essential issues. The United States had just relinquished its leadership position in the negotiations and allowed Rabin to impose his will.[32]

Going along with Muallem's explanation regarding the second missed opportunity, Seale in his final article put the blame squarely on Peres. He began by noting that Peres, upon assuming the premiership, did not know about the "deposit." On December 11, 1995, after meeting with Peres, Clinton called Asad and informed him that the new Israeli prime minister had adopted Rabin's commitment and was looking forward to a summit meeting. But again, said Seale, Peres, like Rabin before him, conditioned Israel's withdrawal on meeting Israel's needs. In addition, Peres focused on a "new Middle East," making the Golan an entrepreneurial hub for the two countries. Asad refused Peres's joint Israeli-Syrian plans for the Golan on account that the Syrian public would look at them as symbols of Israel's hegemony.

Significantly enough, Seale observed that when Peres asked for Syrian guarantees concerning Lake Tiberias's inflowing waters, Asad replied that he never thought of diverting or polluting the Golan's waters, indicating that in any event Syria had a share in the lake. Seale added that Asad declined to see Peres until a substantive progress was achieved in the talks. However, Seale explained that progress was taking place between the two countries at the Wye Plantation talks. At this juncture, Peres authorized the assassination of Yahya Ayyash on January 5, 1996, in spite of the fact that this Hamas operative had suspended all activity a year earlier, thereby triggering the Islamist suicide bombings that compelled him to suspend the peace talks. At the same time, Asad was deeply disappointed when Peres decided on February 7 to move up the elections. Everything began collapsing, there was the wave of terror that struck Israel, and thereafter came operation Grapes of Wrath, followed by Peres's loss of the Israeli elections. Seale added that during this time Syria was concerned about the Israeli-Turkish agreement and the attempts at bringing Jordan into this alliance, let alone trying to topple Saddam Hussein and bring post-Saddam Iraq into the alliance as well.[33]

This debate on missed opportunities and perspectives on peace acquired a new dimension when it was taken up by Peres in a resentful and detailed interview with none other than Seale himself. Seale interviewed Peres for *Al-Hayat* in the latter's office in Tel Aviv. Not surprisingly, the interview itself turned into a debate between the two as they dealt with the most crucial and controversial issues concerning the question of peace between Syria and Israel. Replying to Seale's question about whether he regretted that he was unable to reach an agreement with Asad in 1996, Peres grimly and deploringly said:

> Asad is the only Arab leader who refuses to look at us, we Israelis, as human beings. . . . Sadat came to the Knesset. . . . Had Asad agreed to a meeting with me in 1996, I would not have called for early elections and we would have reached an agreement. Why was he so concerned about meeting me? I begged him repeatedly to meet me. I said let us meet. Let me know what you want to say and hear what I have to say. He said that the meeting was a card he did not want to play. But there is no meaning for a single card. Can you play cards without two players?
>
> I lost the 1996 elections because of Hizbollah and Hamas suicide bombings. . . . I asked Asad to stop them. I sent him a letter, but he said: Who gets elected in Israel is no concern of mine.
>
> We are concerned with what happens in Syria because they are the party we have to negotiate with. You cannot negotiate if you don't understand your counterpart. And they have to try that as well. Let us try to understand what is going on in his mind and let him understand what is going on in our mind.
>
> We cannot reach an agreement . . . via Walid Muallem or someone else. They are not authorized to negotiate . . . not even Shara himself. From here I would like Asad to hear me himself. I would like to clarify to him how I see the world. I don't say he has to agree to my vision.[34]

Then Seale asked Peres what he had in mind when he agreed to a withdrawal to the June 4, 1967, lines in December 1996. Peres answered:

> President Clinton informed me in a definitive way that Rabin gave him this promise or that. I immediately answered him that I will respect one hundred per cent what Rabin had promised. But I added: Mr. President, when Rabin mentioned the June 4 line he was pointing to a situation not to a map. Because we never had a map for the June 4 line.[35]

In the course of the interview, Peres questioned why the Syrians demanded the June 4 lines when in Lebanon they wanted the 1923 international border. To that Seale remarked that the June 4 lines were their defensive border before the 1967 war. Britain and France had delineated the 1923 boundary, in which independent Syria had not participated. At this point, Peres revealed Israel's principal concern over the June 4 lines by questioning Seale why the Syrians needed access to Lake Tiberias. He then stressed that

Israel had two lakes, one of which was dead (referring to the Dead Sea), the other of which the Syrians could not kill. Peres stated: "The problem is not over acquiring a minimal access to the Lake. The minute the Syrians touch the Lake, they would become partners in it. This is international law and this is the problem."[36]

On Israel's security doctrine, nuclear weapons, and whether the country needed more weapons, Peres had this to say:

> There is nothing stronger than peace. If I had to choose between the nuclear option and that of peace it would not take me more than five minutes to decide on peace. I did not want Hiroshima when I created the nuclear option! I created it to arrive to Oslo! If you ask me about my personal belief I could say that my march from Dimona . . . to Oslo took forty years. And I never got lost on the way.
>
> We are not spellbound by military power. This was never among our qualities. We want to be superior in education, morality and spirituality. But do not misunderstand me, we will use force if we have to.[37]

Given the fact that the interview occurred after the Davos international economic conference, in which Peres had angered the Arab participants by stating that he did not want Israel to be an island of affluence in a sea of misery, Seale asked Peres about the significance of his statements. The former Israeli prime minister took the occasion to vent haughtily and candidly his pent-up anger with the Arabs' misconception of his Middle East economic vision:

> I meant that we have to help the Palestinians build a modern economy. . . . There should be also an economic peace. They misunderstood me. . . .
>
> Egyptians and others accused me of the desire to control the Arab economy. And I would like to tell them: Don't be stupid Gentlemen! Who wants to control your poverty? Have you gone mad? We can barely control what we have by way of poverty. . . .
>
> You have no national economies but national poverty! And you shall not have rich economies unless they become global. You cannot postpone.[38]

Peres then detailed his vision of the new Middle East accompanied with dire warnings to the Arabs. He sarcastically pointed out to the Arabs that either the world had to become old like the Middle East or the Middle East had to become new like the world. He emphasized that the new world comprised three economies: global, regional, and national. "The global economy is the economy of brains and not land. It recognizes no borders. . . . The regional economy deals with geography. In the Middle East the fear of war disfigured and corrupted the economic infrastructure. . . . The Middle East wastes 50 billion dollars a year on weapons. . . . The Gulf War cost 100 billion [dollars], an amount [large] enough to resolve all regional problems. . . . If the Middle East does not join the . . . global high-technical economy," said

Peres, "it will become a part of Africa. . . . May God help the Arabs if they don't understand that." Concerning the national economy, Peres explained that it was "the economy of instruction and education. . . . It is your heritage, language, religion and children." He added that "the Arabs feel insulted when we say we are ready to help in the science, agriculture and tourism fields. But China itself comes to Israel, India as well. We want nothing in return. I think the Arabs have a wrong conception of Israel. They do not try to understand us, and probably we do not try to understand them either. Tell this to Hafiz al-Asad if he wants to hear."[39]

Additional insights into the missed opportunities of peace came into the open in 2000 when Muallem wrote an unpublished paper, "Beyond the Brink of Peace," dealing with Rabinovich's account of the Israeli-Syrian negotiations.[40] Muallem contends that the most important points in Rabinovich's book, that there was no Israeli commitment to withdraw from the Golan Heights, that anything that was said was "hypothetical," and that Syria missed two opportunities for peace, contained omissions and misrepresentations.

Muallem emphasizes that there was nothing "hypothetical" regarding the Israeli commitment to withdraw from the Golan. Rabin's commitment to withdraw, conveyed to Asad by Secretary Christopher in August 1993, was not hypothetical. Consistent with his earlier account and that by Seale, Muallem explains that Asad could not have been more explicit about Syria's position that Israel must withdraw to the lines of June 4, 1967. Asad would not budge until the line was defined. Muallem adds that, contrary to Rabinovich's claim, there was no Syrian "counterpackage" at the August meeting between Rabin and Christopher. However, Asad's initial position that Israel's time frame for withdrawal be six months changed to twelve months when in July 1994 Asad received the "deposit." After that, Muallem recounts, Asad "wanted the Americans present as witnesses and as partners . . . no one could accuse the United States of favoring Syria over Israel, which made it all the more important that the Americans should witness our positions and judge for themselves whether our position was fair."[41]

According to Muallem, Asad made another concession regarding the withdrawal timetable when he met with President Clinton in Damascus in October 1994. Asad extended the period "from 12 to 16 months, and, conditional on Rabin's acceptance of the 16-month timetable, agreed to have some kind of diplomatic representation three months before the final withdrawal."[42] Muallem stresses the importance of the "Non-Paper on the Aims and Principles of the Security Arrangements." The need of the non-paper came in the wake of the failed first meeting of the chiefs of staff (December 1994), in which Barak evaded discussing specifics. While the first obstacle over "equality" was resolved, the formulation of security arrangements snagged the negotiations. Muallem wanted the "formulation to read that the security arrangements should be established equally 'on both sides of the line of 4 June 1967,'" a formulation that Rabinovich rejected. The impasse ended when

Ross presented the idea that the word "line" be replaced by the word "border," explaining in a side letter to President Asad that "border" means "line." The letter, signed by Secretary Christopher, was not given to Asad, on account of Rabin's objections. Rabin was furious, because he did not want the "deposit" (the commitment to withdraw) to be delivered in written form to the Syrians. In spite of all of this, Muallem continues, Asad, to everyone's surprise, said to Ross, "As long as it is known to all of us—to you, to us, and to Israel—that withdrawal is to the line of 4 June 1967, I will not hold things up on this issue."[43] The non-paper was signed in May 1995.

Muallem wonders why the first document signed by Israel and Syria is taken so lightly by both Israel and the United States. He asks why Rabinovich seems to imply that the non-paper was a waste of time, and in his long narrative never really tells what the paper says. Muallem continues: "Indeed, both the Israelis and Americans refer to it as the 'Non-Paper on Aims and Principles of the Security Arrangements,' though its is difficult to understand why something that is written, that is deposited with the State department, that took three months of negotiations and several trips to the region to finalize would qualify as a 'Non-Paper.'" Muallem cites the side letter and the non-paper as proof that Rabinovich knew very well that Rabin's commitment to withdraw was not the "hypothetical exercise" he repeatedly mentioned in his book.

Regarding the missed opportunities (August 1993 and Winter 1995–1996), Muallem explains that although Rabin made a promising offer, he knew that it fell below Syria's level of acceptability. While Asad showed a willingness to negotiate, Rabin did not. According to Rabinovich, when Rabin did not find Asad's response sufficiently forthcoming, he decided to pursue the Palestinian track. In other words, Muallem continues, Asad was given some forty-eight hours to accept the deal virtually as it was presented, which Rabin knew very well could not happen. On the second missed opportunity, Muallem emphasizes that the Syrians were of course aware of the possibility of early elections. President Asad specifically raised the issue when Secretary Christopher came to Damascus in December 1995. President Asad asked Christopher to convey to Prime Minister Peres that "if the talks were to resume, he did not want to be surprised by early elections: If the two sides were to go to talks, they must continue until reaching an agreement. If Peres wanted early elections, on the other hand, let him call them now, President Asad said, and the Syrians would wait."[44]

Muallem says that although the first rounds of the Wye talks went very well, Secretary Christopher informed him that Peres "was under great pressure from within his party to go for early elections." Although Asad was disappointed, he agreed to resume the negotiations. Uri Savir, according to Muallem, expressed his gratitude to President Asad for agreeing to continue the talks. Savir then suggested that "we plan to have continuous talks at Wye in the aim of wrapping up all the elements of our agreement by June."[45] Following the suicide bombings in Israel, Ross informed Muallem that the

Israelis had suspended the Wye talks and were returning to Israel. That was the end of the negotiations.

Muallem explains that "the Wye talks began as they were scheduled by the Americans and were going well in the apparent view of the Israeli as well as the American and Syrian participants. Yet Mr. Peres called early elections; one can speculate as to whether opinion polls showing that the Syrian negotiations were not popular with the Israeli public influenced his decision."[46]

Rabinovich, Muallem continues, said that Peres called early elections because the Syrians were not moving fast enough. Muallem adds, "If Syria is guilty of 'delays,' such 'delays' come from its insistence on a fair deal, from President's Asad cardinal rule that there can be no 'ambiguity' in any agreement with Israel. We did not think it unreasonable, in negotiating a settlement with the greatest military and economic power in the region—a country with a nuclear capability and which had occupied land of all its neighbors—to insist that Damascus be protected or that the security arrangements be equal on both sides of the border."[47]

With a new administration in the White House after the election of George W. Bush as president, former Clinton administration officials began to break the taboo and discuss their own opinions and views on the peace process, especially the failure to conclude an Israeli-Syrian peace deal. Leading them was none other than Dennis Ross, the veteran go-between with the Arabs and Israelis, who granted an interview to the *New York Times Magazine* in March 2001.

Ross believes that he did not fail in his role in what some consider the failure of the United States to conclude an Israeli-Syrian treaty and a final settlement of the Israeli-Palestinian conflict. This is so, he explains, "because the United States is never going to impose an agreement. What we can do is make it easier for them to make really hard decisions. In the end, the failure can never be our failure. It may be their inability to get to where they want to go. But it's much more their doing than ours."[48] He adds, "That was true on both the Syrian and Palestinian fronts. . . . Syria, under the despotic Hafez al-Assad, would never even have talked peace with Israel without Washington serving as a broker." Regarding the Israeli-Syrian track, Ross continues, "An agreement was achingly close last March [Geneva Summit]. . . . We were down to a couple of hundred meters basically. Disagreements remained on security arrangements and on a timetable for Israel's withdrawal from the Golan. But those were technical issues, and there were different creative formulas we could have come up with."[49]

The sticking point, however, according to Ross, was that "we [Americans] basically ran out of time with Assad." He adds, "The Syrian ruler simply wasn't prepared to close the deal. He was also in poor health and may have been more concerned at that point with the question of who would succeed him." Says Ross, "Assad approached negotiations like a man who was absolutely not in a hurry, as a way to show he wouldn't pay more than he had to pay—and I think he genuinely wasn't in a hurry. . . . Barak at that point was ready to go. But Barak himself got caught by moving too quickly, because he saw there was more resistance at home to doing this deal than he had anticipated." Ross explains "There's so much gamesmanship in negotiations, where if one side suddenly signals it's going to go slower, you have to show you don't need it more. Because if you show that something you need it more, they'll think you'll give away more. We got into that."[50]

This U.S. perspective was further expanded when another senior official and frequent participant in the negotiations offered his view to me in April 2001.[51] Explaining the root causes that doomed the Israeli-Syrian negotiations, this official began by emphasizing that from the start of the talks, the United States started with a derivative role because the Israelis and the Syrians dictated the pace and content of the negotiations. At the same time, the negotiations proceeded in the shadow of the Israeli-Palestinian talks. This condition made it close to impossible to undertake two simultaneous channels entailing serious and sensitive implications for both parties. In addition, this official continued, there must exist essential ingredients for the talks to succeed, namely secret diplomacy, public diplomacy, and direct diplomacy including the U.S. role.

Diplomacy to the Syrians, the official maintained, was somehow close to a reactive role in that the Syrians relied heavily on the United States. This was compounded by Asad's personality and idiosyncrasies. The inconsequential result was that the Syrians, especially Asad, wanted to hear from the United States exactly what they expected to hear; anything less than that could, and did, doom the negotiations. This was highlighted at the March summit. In addition, the Syrians did not try to engage in any creative formula to apply to the peace talks. So they, and to some extent the Israelis, pinned their hopes solely on U.S. efforts to achieve a breakthrough. This constituted a flawed thinking on the part of Syria, particularly on the part of Asad.

There is also, according to this official, a certain law of gravity to the ongoing peace process. While the process needed confidence-building measures to bring the two parties closer together, Syria's support of Hizbollah constituted confidence-breaking measures. Asad also never envisioned that he was going to be last in the peace negotiations. He disliked the very idea of subordinating the Syrian track to another. This transformed into a situation whereby his deal ought to have been the best for being the last. He refused to stand in the shadow of Arafat, Sadat, or Hussein. So the process that was supposed to be easy became dysfunctional, in contrast to the Palestinian-Israeli process, which was difficult in substance but functional at the time.

All of this was exacerbated by Asad's refusal to hold secret channels and engage in public diplomacy. Had he allowed some room for maneuvering or been forthcoming in his public diplomacy with Israel, Israel could have given him what he wanted. This official ended his interview on a pessimistic note, stating that it is difficult now to create the situation that existed during the peace negotiations. The challenges lying ahead are formidable.[52]

An Analysis: "Dignity" Versus "Insecurity"

From Peres's final observation, "They do not try to understand us, and probably we do not try to understand them either," I would like to begin by saying how right he was when he said that neither Israel nor Syria tried to understand each other. They acted like one-eyed negotiators looking at each other with their blind eyes. Peacemaking did not emerge as part of a comprehensive reorientation of their domestic and foreign policies. Rather, the cataclysmic events in the region and the world (the Gulf War, the intifada, and the collapse of the Soviet Union) brought the two embattled neighbors together at an unexpected time when they were neither fully prepared nor ready for peace. Consequently, most obstacles to peace, ranging from the ideological to the domestic, had a negative cumulative effect on both Syria and Israel. Inadvertently, this effect underscored Israel's and Syria's vulnerabilities. Importantly, the Syrian regime feared the implications of peacemaking for its political legitimacy, while Israeli governments feared the political cost involved in peacemaking. So from the beginning, the negotiations took the form of Syria insisting on principles while Israel emphasized the established facts.

The subsequent negotiations between them went against the known norm of successful negotiations in that they did not acquire a momentum of their own. This was so because the common denominator between the two countries was a choice in favor of peace, but peace had different substantive meanings for each party. These meanings conformed more with politico-military and sociocultural interpretations steeped in the history of the Arab-Israeli conflict than in a new future for the two countries. They waged a new kind of war in the name of peace, and this was particularly true with Rabin and Asad. These two leaders wanted to settle through the peace process what they could not settle on the battlefield.

At this point, one could safely argue that there existed a very dim chance for a breakthrough during Rabin's tenure of office. I disagree with Seale's analysis that Rabin's opening gambit was no more than a political ruse in the form of a "take it or leave it deal" that Asad could not but refuse. Rabin undoubtedly knew from the beginning that once he presented his offer, hypothetical or not, he committed himself to an irreversible path. The offer not only conformed with the land for peace formula and Asad's full peace for full withdrawal, but also opened the door for options that Rabin could not have controlled had Asad and especially the United States played their hands more diplomatically and forcefully. Although I disagree with Rabinovich about the missed opportunity then, he seemingly was more on the mark when he explained that Rabin sought to find out whether he had a viable option for a settlement with Syria as the cornerstone in his peacemaking strategy.

Even if we take for granted that Rabin was aware and in control of the Palestinian-Israeli negotiations, he must have known that this situation involved painful, costly, and risky decisions to be made in the near and distant future. Helping to bring about the end of the intifada was one thing, but the risks in helping to create an embryonic Palestinian state with all its attendant consequences was something else. I am sure that on account of these lurking difficult and painful decisions, the thought of concluding a deal with Syria must have crossed Rabin's mind if only because this would take the most dangerous ideological and military threats out of the equation of the Arab-Israeli conflict.[53] As a result, the Palestinians would have to moderate not only their position on the peace process, but also their vision of it. In addition, instead of Rabin feeling the urgency to negotiate with the Palestinians, it would be Arafat who would be compelled to seek a deal with Israel under the threat of an Israeli-Syrian deal. But we should also remember that there was no real urgency on the part of Rabin, given his ability to play the two tracks against each other. After all, let us not forget that the Palestinians, in general, emerged from the Gulf War in pitiful shape after their support of Saddam Hussein. So using Seale's argument, one could reach other analytical conclusions as well.

A good part of the difficulty of reaching a breakthrough on the Israeli-Syrian front had to do with the personalities of the two leaders and their concepts of peace. What Rabinovich characterized as Rabin's reluctance was matched by Asad's ambiguity. This represents only a tiny fraction of what each leader stood for. The two deeply suspected each other and believed so much in using power politics against each other. This was reflected, on the one hand, in Rabin's loaded peace offer, which was indeed hedged by many conditions (as Seale noted), and in Asad's response to it, and on the other hand, in Asad's remorseless willingness to unleash Hizbollah's attacks on Israel during the ongoing negotiations, and in Rabin's readiness to negotiate an alliance with Turkey, let alone his toying with the idea of opening a channel to Iraq, both in order to bring pressure to bear on Syria. Apparently, the two leaders believed that only in this way could they extract concessions from each other. How could Rabin expect Asad to agree to such stringent security arrangements, some of them affecting the security of the Syrian capital and thus the internal security of the country? And how could Asad expect Rabin to agree to counterarrangements, some of them bringing the Syrians down to the shore of Lake Tiberias?

In addition, what made an agreement between them hardly possible at the time was the U.S. position. I agree with Quandt that Clinton was overly cautious (on this issue also with Christopher) and did not know what to do to capitalize on the momentum created by Rabin's opening withdrawal gambit. But

I would like to stretch this argument further. Against the background of my analysis of the U.S.-Syrian-Israeli relationship, I can safely add that the U.S. administrations, especially the Clinton administration, lacked the will to use their political coercive power with either Syria or Israel, due on the one hand to conflicting political perceptions of the two countries by the U.S. executive and legislative branches of government, and on the other hand to the high political domestic stakes. Consequently, the two countries felt receptive to U.S. help (including financial and security), but not to U.S. pressure. This was strongly manifested when on one occasion Christopher had to wait endlessly in Damascus to see Asad, and when Netanyahu blundered by threatening to "set fire to Washington."

So in my assessment, what made a deal far from possible at the time was the cumulative effect of the personalities of the two leaders, the impracticality of Rabin's offer and Asad's reply to it, and the overly hesitant U.S. approach to the peace process. This was less the case during Peres's tenure as prime minister, mainly during November–December 1995. For one thing, Peres was not Rabin and the two leaders had a recent history of negotiations. In addition, of course, the U.S. president had become familiar with the nature of the negotiations and acquired a good grasp of the sensitive issues separating the two countries. Significantly enough, the two sides (Savir and Muallem) admitted in their own way that an agreement was in the realm of the possible. But then, what went wrong to preclude such an agreement?

I believe there existed a good chance for a breakthrough at the time. Peres, unlike Rabin, was a visionary ready to take bold steps as well as reach over barriers. Furthermore, he was a man that undoubtedly saw Israel's "guts," to use an Arabic expression, as connected to those of the Arabs. He was eager to find common solutions to common problems in the region affecting both Israel and its neighbors. He really saw Israel as part of the Middle East. His record shows that he made possible what was unimaginable only a few years earlier, when he negotiated with the PLO and paved the way for Arafat to come to Gaza. People tend to forget rather quickly that events of such magnitude took place. So his immediate readiness to adopt Rabin's "deposit" and then attempt to concentrate on the Syrian front not only was serious but also contained the inherent mechanics of not getting snagged in the process. This explains his effort to conduct negotiations on simultaneous channels. But his bold effort to attach grand economic plans to his negotiations when it came to discussing normalization of relations while at the same time dealing with worst-case scenarios when it came to security issues apparently frightened the ever cautious and "principled" Syrians.

What did not help was Asad's reluctance to engage in even minimal public diplomacy to help Peres to fight his way through the maze of Israeli domestic obstacles. Taking into consideration both sides of the story, I think that Peres's apparent feeling of a lack of a mandate to make significant concessions on the Golan was counteracted by his eagerness to overcome obstacles and conclude an agreement with the Syrians. What was needed was an injection of some balance in the calculus of this disparity. Herein came the role of Asad, who not only blunted Peres's thrust but also contributed to his downfall by his "dogmatic" silence on terrorism. At this point, I disagree in principle with Seale, who implied that Peres's decision to assassinate the Hamas operative triggered the suicide bombings that compelled him to suspend the Wye Plantation talks. While some terrorist acts could be undertaken for revenge purposes, the motivation of terror in this instance is definitively strategic and not for the sake of vengeance. However, the assassination was ill-timed, and in retrospect Israel's assassination policy has accomplished little to curb suicide bombings.[54] Reportedly, Peres's appeals to Asad to try to stop the wave of terror engulfing Israel went unheeded.

On a deeper level, there is more to my assessment than the above analysis, as I would like to explain why peace was and remains "elusive" for the time being. Several reasons account for this. First, analyses of both Syria's domestic situation and Syria's conduct in the negotiations lead to the conclusion that the Syrian regime simply cannot afford a flawed peace. Apparently, the old charge of treason loomed large in Asad's mind and still haunts the regime. Only as recently as 1995, Issam al-Attar, a former superintendent of the Syrian Muslim Brotherhood, denounced the Arab-Israeli negotiations as a capitulation rather than a peace process.[55] The Asad family's main concern is not only to absolve itself of this charge but also to make sure that the family, clan, and sect are not stamped by it in the future. The regime's strategic peace appears to be predicated on the premise that it is achievable only within a particular context whereby it could show that it took from Israel as much as, if not more than, Sadat did, while at the same time putting to rest the charge and by implication the blame that Asad as defense minister in 1967 lost the Golan. This explains the inextricable link Asad consciously made between his commitment to Arab nationalism as related to Ba'thi ideology (and Syria's territorial integrity) and his adamant attitude about the June 4, 1967, lines as a matter of national honor. What confirms this point is the premium an Arab, especially an Alawi Arab of peasant origins such as Asad, would put on the issue of "dignity," the dignity of retrieving in full what was lost in defeat.

Second, Syria is in a state of transition. As I have tried to show, the country had been gripped by two immediate concerns: the political economy and the question of succession. A peace treaty that is somehow flawed or indefensible in the corridors of power in Damascus could have far-reaching implications for the stability of the regime. At this point, I could argue that strategic peace for Syria could mean the safeguarding of its national interests as measured against the price it can pay for peace. In other words, how to protect the privileged status of the military, especially the Alawi dominant faction, and at the same time pass the reins of power to Bashar, when peace may have negative effects on these two processes. Under these circumstances, the lines between domestic and foreign policy become blurred.

It should be no surprise, then, that peace for Syria hinges on a certain order of priorities: first, terminate the state of war; second, end the state of occupation; third, work out security arrangements; and finally, agree on a minimum level of normalization that does not affect Syria's domestic and regional policies (mainly in Lebanon). The underlying assumption is that peace should take more the form of a settlement excluding conspicuous normalization of relations. Indeed, this was implied by Syrian negotiator Walid Muallem, the mufti of Syria Kaftaro, and Muhammad Aziz Shukri, a professor of law at Damascus University, who met on several occasions with some Israelis and who are close to the upper echelons of the regime.[56]

When peace is closer to a settlement than a real peace, Syria could transform the conflict from a military to a cultural and economic confrontation, modulating the stakes of the struggle with Israel only to keep some continuity in its own domestic and foreign policy. In so doing, the country could try to obviate or diminish the impact of the peace process on its ideology and raison d'être. This is particularly consistent with Asad's concept of settlement and vision of peace with Israel, as expounded by Seale. The essence of any settlement is not just the recovery of this or that piece of occupied territory, but the "containment" of Israel, just as Asad's notion of a "comprehensive peace" is not about normalization, but on the contrary, about holding the line against Israel (on this issue I am at one with Seale). Consequently, peace could not be separated from taking into consideration Syria's geostrategic rivalry with Israel, making security concerns weigh heavily on Syria.

Finally, the Arab-Israeli conflict still echoes clamorously in the minds of many Syrians, especially the rejectionists—who oppose the peace process—of the country that has been the cradle of Arab nationalism. Asad's Syria, regarding itself as the vanguard of Arab nationalism, fits well the pattern of a country that prides itself on carrying the weight of its history. One could not ascertain that Asad stopped identifying with the rejectionists simply because he joined the peace process. Sadek al-Azm pointed out in an article, "The View from Damascus," that Syria certainly has its deep rejectionists.[57] Although they are in the minority now, under the right circumstances they could rebound, strike a chord with the mainstream, and become a decisive force in its life, culture, and politics. Prominent among them, al-Azm continued, are the Islamist currents in civil society who now rally around a Muslim version of the doctrine of Palestine as the Promised Land. The doctrine teaches that Palestine is a waqf (religious endowment) that the Almighty has reserved permanently and eternally for the Muslim ummah (nation or community). This logic turns Palestine into an endowment made by God to the Muslim ummah, and like all such endowments it may not be alienated, tampered with, or squandered by any one person, government, generation, or even age.

The other type of deep rejectionists, al-Azm continued, are hard-line nationalists who rally around a watered-down and secularized version of the waqf doctrine. They argue that Palestine does not belong to their generation only—or to any one Arab generation, for that matter—so they can proceed to sign it away both de facto and de jure. According to them, Palestine belongs to the entire Arab and/or Syrian nation and to all its generations, past, present, and future. This means that the best course of action at present is to keep both the conflict and the struggle open toward the future and its manifold possibilities, thus securing for the new and unborn generations the chance to continue the just fight against the usurper under a hopefully improved balance of power.

Most likely, one factor keeping these deep rejectionists in the minority is the regime's domestic policy of co-opting or liquidating its threatening political forces. However, there are other types of rejectionists within Syrian civil society. Although they are not radical rejectionists, they surely reflect to a great extent the depth of their nation's disenchantment with and unreadiness for the peace process. They partly reflect a significant aspect of the mood of the nation that the Syrian regime has to paradoxically identify and contend with at one and the same time. They are some of Syria's "silent" intellectuals, whose silence suddenly exploded into a deep and impassionate cry reflecting the mixed mood of fear, apprehension, resentment, defeat, and stoic resignation gripping their society.

What sparked this explosive debate and by implication its cathartic effects was an article by Hisham Dajani, a Damascus-based Palestinian commentator, published in *Al-Hayat*. This debate took place against the background of the failed Shepherdstown Israeli-Syrian talks in January 2000. Dajani took Syrian intellectuals to task for what he described as their "astonishing silence" on the momentous issue of peace with Israel and their reluctance, bordering on a groundless fear, to engage in a dialogue with their Israeli counterparts. He challenged them to spell out their position boldly on an issue affecting them as well as future generations.[58] The article evoked several responses, among which three were from Syrian intellectuals. The common denominator of the three responses was animosity not only against a comprehensive peace but also against the whole process of negotiations. Two articles by major Syrian intellectuals, Mahmoud Salameh and Mamdouh Adwan, especially the latter, stand out by their poignant and pointed criticism.

Mahmoud Salameh answered Dajani by pointing out that the Syrian intellectuals indeed present their opinions, which are heard and respected, but that there is a great difference between silence and screaming:

> There is confusion between the concept of comprehensive and just peace and the concept of settlement. Comprehensive peace fundamentally takes off from the recognition of Arab historical rights, whereby geographic borders coincide with political ones. But a settlement is an attempt to contain a certain condition and control it taking off from the balance of power and other considerations and interests. On the basis of this understanding it is the Israeli side which is destroying the peace process and attempting to impose on the Arabs a settlement and the signing of their defeat warrant.[59]

Salameh went on to stress that the Arab cause was a matter of neither optimism nor pessimism, as Dajani saw it, but rather a matter of a political and nationalist vision: Dajani's article should have been directed at Israeli writers in general and at all Israeli intellectuals in particular, primarily to persuade them of the urgency of peace. Salameh added that these Israelis should comprehend that there is no future for them without recognizing Arab historical rights and integrating themselves in the region and its culture, relinquishing the project based on hostility, expansion, evacuation, and hegemony.[60]

Mamdouh Adwan's response was an impassioned, bitter cry from the heart that vented all his pent-up emotions, destroying whatever pretensions existed about "silent intellectuals" regarding peace with Israel:

> I understand peace but I am against normalization. This is not just because I do not want to deal with the historic enemy "so we can face a new era," but because I do not know how to deal with this enemy. I do not know how to deal with murderers and murderers they are. And they (even those of them who now appear supportive of peace) have never dealt with us other than as second-class human beings who had to be killed, or whose killing was not something that warrants concern or discussion. When they discovered it was impossible to kill us all, they said "we would allow those survivors to remain, in the name of peace, in congregations (sometimes called states and at other times called autonomous enclaves). So let us stop the bloodbath now. Let us rest a little. We are tired of killing, tired of killing you.[61]

Adwan continued:

> I want to say with a full mouth that I will not shake hands with those who have my blood on their hands, even if I recover my land from them. I will not normalize with those who are not shamed by my blood which stains the same hand they extend for me to shake. . . . I do not know how I can sit down with thieves, hashish addicts and hooligans to discuss poetry and culture merely so that I can be accepted as "civilized" by those whose memories suffer from immune deficiency. . . .
>
> Let us say it frankly. This peace ends a problem for those who ever since the Palestine catastrophe have considered the conflict to be about showing pity for those "miserable refugees," poor things, who have become homeless and are living in the open. . . .
>
> Land? Let whoever wants it to take it. And let them pay the price imposed on them. My problem is not about land. My problem is about justice. For this I insist on saying that Palestine is Arab. Let the rulers of Palestine and the Arab world recover whatever territory they can, and let them make the concessions which political and international circumstances force them to. . . . But I am the one painfully sitting with my pains, ambitions and identity, I do not want to forget that the whole of Palestine is Arab. In addition to that, I would like to declare, at least in my literature, that Palestine is that Arab dream, which I do not want, and no one has the right to want, to give up. And I declare in a poetic courageous moment that whoever squanders this is the traitor of the Arab dream and human honor.

Is this a throwback to the rhetoric of the 1950s or the 1960s? Let it be a throwback to the stone age. This is what I believe in from the bottom of my heart.[62]

Suffice it to say that this long response speaks for itself. In addition, underlying this response is the assumption that even the return of the Golan does not warrant the loss of a single handspan from Palestine. What makes it also increasingly significant is that the author is well known, respected, and an Alawi. If this serves as only a mere reflection of the mood of the intelligentsia and by implication sectors of the Syrian public, it is undoubtedly enough to further confirm my analysis that peace beyond a "dignified" settlement in the near future is elusive. Syria is not ready yet for the peace Israel is calling for. Old habits die hard in the Middle East, especially in Syria. Part of the problem lies in the readiness of many Arabs to lay claim to "Palestine." Let us hope that the next generation will be less shackled by the past.

Is Israel ready for peace? Israel is also in a state of transition. Segments of Israel's public are eager for peace, but the whole country is neither ready nor prepared for the peace it is calling for. For one thing, Israel, like Syria, although trying to go beyond its past, is still allowing its past to be part and parcel of its present and future. The history of the Jews in Europe and the wars that the Israelis fought with the Arabs weigh heavily on their consciousness, creating a profound existential angst. Domestic opposition to peace and security and water concerns are not only reflections of the country's requirements of peace, but also products of that existential angst, which is still gripping the nation. It is this condition that compels Israel to constantly pursue a position of superiority vis-à-vis its neighbors, to keep believing that there is a military solution to every problem, while at the same time yearning for signs of warm acceptance by the Arabs, especially the Syrians. At this point I shall quote Meron Benvinisti, who partly captured the essence of Israel's unpreparedness for peace for the time being. He wrote in *Ha'aretz:*

> Those who believe in peace as a value per se, and in peace arrangements and border demarcations as a foundation for new relations are also making life easy for themselves. They are ignoring the fact that the peace agreements can lead to peace only if Israeli society undergoes a substantive change, which will be no less intense than the change the Arabs have to undergo. It is impossible to expect a diminution of the hostility when one side insists on maintaining a nuclear option (which creates supremacy over all the Arab states combined), economic protectionism, coercion of the Palestinians, discrimination against the Arabs in Israel, cultural arrogance, an educational system that is contemptuous of minority rights and the crass exploitation of the Jewish lobby in the United States.
>
> Those who fear that we will not get peace but only an armistice in return for our concessions are right. But that is in large measure a self-fulfilling prophecy. Those who believe that the prospect exists to build a firm peace are also right. But the condition for that is an integrated, intertwined

system, the price of which is not measured solely by the depth of the withdrawal from the Golan Heights but also by readiness to withdraw from
anachronistic attitudes that have been sanctified by the passions of the century-old conflict.[63]

It is clear to me that the processes of internal and external normalization
are incremental and involve the shedding of deep-seated anxieties and
ingrained habits. To this end, not only Syria but also Israel has a long way to
go. At this point, I feel that my account is by no means complete without taking into consideration what lay behind the failure of the Geneva summit.

Given the importance of the summit, one would wonder why Asad was
so immovable, so implacable with Clinton in Geneva in the first place.
Reportedly, the summit collapsed after a few minutes when Asad realized that
Barak refused to return the northeast quadrant of shoreline on Lake Tiberias
(Sea of Galilee), an area Syria had controlled before the June 1967 war.
Apparently, Asad was adamant about his long-held view that Israel should
withdraw to the Israeli-Syrian frontier that existed before June 4, 1967.[64]
Sadek al-Azm, in a lecture delivered at the Kennedy School of Government,
explained that the cause of Asad's behavior in the summit lay in what happened at the Shepherdstown talks. Asad was so upset with the way the talks
unfolded there, especially after he had given considerable concessions to
Israel, that he went to Geneva simply to even the score.[65] In an op-ed piece
published in the *New York Times,* former secretary of state James Baker commented on the failure of the summit:

> Though his approach at Camp David was creative and proactive, I fear that
> at Geneva President Clinton may simply have presented the Israeli position
> to President Assad and recommended that he accept it, because it offered to
> return practically all of the Golan.
>   A better approach would have been for the United States to make its
> own proposal, recommending the return of all the Golan conditioned on Mr.
> Assad's then agreeing to the firm security and access arrangements on the
> ground that Israel required, including restrictions on the Sea of Galilee and
> on a narrow strip along the shore.
>   This compromise should have satisfied both Israeli and Syrian political
> needs.[66]

Given Asad's peasant origins, I think that all these explanations have a
large measure of truth. I have no doubt that Asad would like to appear before
his people in particular and before the Arab world in general as the only Arab
leader who stood his ground in negotiating with Israel and who, unlike others,
never cried on the U.S. shoulder.[67] Still, other issues undoubtedly figured predominantly in Asad's mind.

By reading the political map of the region one would expect that Asad
would capitalize on the opportunity of meeting Clinton to discuss several

issues of great importance to Syria at the time. Prominent among them: (1) the future of U.S.-Syrian relations and removing Syria from the U.S. terrorism list, (2) the possibility of U.S. economic, financial, and even military aid, particularly to help Syria reform its dilapidated economic structure and smoothly connect with the global economy, (3) the Syrian regional role vis-à-vis U.S. foreign policy in the area, (4) the U.S. position concerning Syrian-Turkish relations, particularly over the issue of the waters of the Euphrates, (5) the future of Syria's presence in Lebanon and U.S. guarantees that nothing would be undertaken on the part of the United States to undermine Syrian influence in the country, particularly after the Israeli withdrawal, and (6) U.S. neutrality and/or a U.S. promise to respect a prospective transfer of power to Asad's heir apparent, Bashar.

I think that what underlay the above points was the sense at the time that Syria's negotiating position vis-à-vis Israel had been slowly eroding. Surely, Israel's promise of withdrawal from Lebanon put this position into sharp relief. What at the time apparently made the Syrians even more indignant had been the unpalatable likelihood that sooner rather than later the Arab states would normalize their relations with Israel with or without an Israeli-Syrian peace deal. Already the Yemenis and Tunisians had begun to establish contacts with Israel, and given U.S. influence with the Gulf states it would be natural to expect that these states would not wait forever for Syria to make its peace with Israel. Herein lies, I believe, a good part of the psychological answer as to why Asad was so implacable in Geneva. It was specifically because of his seemingly weak state that Asad refused to appear weak and thus flexible in Geneva. In addition, according to a prominent Syrian, Asad felt betrayed by Clinton. Not only did Clinton pass Barak's proposal to Asad, but he also appeared as an accomplice to Israel's scheme to set up the context for Israel's withdrawal from Lebanon. The summit was a farce and a balancing act of pressure and deception. This, according to the Syrian, was confirmed by the fact that Israel and the United States ignored Damascus's calls for resuming the negotiations before Tel Aviv's withdrawal.[68] Consequently, flexibility at such a time was tantamount to surrender, maligning Asad's leadership legacy, and putting him in the same light as Arafat, Sadat, and King Hussein, leaders he abhorred. After all, he had showed enough flexibility in Shepherdstown. This dovetails neatly with my earlier explanations about a "dignified" settlement.

At this point, a word of caution is well in order. Syria's eroding position does not mean that it will be a bystander vis-à-vis regional developments. Syria may opt for using the weapons of the weak, which may include terrorism, to frustrate regional plans excluding it. "Normal" relations among Arab and Middle Eastern countries have always included a good dose of tension, confrontation, threats, and attempts at subversion. One need only look at the relationships between Syria and Iraq, Syria and Jordan, Syria and Turkey, Syria and the PLO, Algeria and Morocco, and Egypt and Libya to see what the "norm" is for interstate relations in the region. Under these circumstances, it would be utopian to expect "normal" relations between Israel and Syria to be much better in the long run than, say, "normal" relations between Syria and Turkey.

With all this in mind, I am fairly sure that Barak's admission of Rabin's "deposit" was meant to redress the slight that Syria suffered in Shepherdstown. But there is a limit to what an Israeli leader can offer. It is hardly imaginable at present that any Israeli leader would permit the Syrians to have sovereignty over the northeastern edge of Lake Tiberias. But it is within the realm of the imaginable that an Israeli leader would agree to a compromise formula in the spirit of Seale's proposal were Syrian leaders to engage in public diplomacy with Israel. When all is said and done, the bottom line, the handspan meters of land standing against a settlement, is merely a symptom of both countries' state of quasi-unreadiness for peace, considering that both are going through a phase of transition. It seems as if a settlement is being held hostage to "dignity" and "insecurity," a settlement torn between the need to achieve peace with dignity in large measure to safeguard the legitimacy of the Syrian regime versus the need for a peace with security in large part to protect Israel's government against the political cost of making concessions and to alleviate the collective angst of the nation. Destroying this psychological barrier is only one step among many toward the realization of a full and warm peace, a peace at one time distortedly called the "peace of the brave."

Notes

1. Itamar Rabinovich, *The Brink of Peace: The Israeli-Syrian Negotiations* (Princeton: Princeton University Press, 1998), pp. 235–236.
2. Ibid., pp. 235–236.
3. Ibid., p. 236.
4. Ibid.
5. Ibid., p. 238.
6. Ibid., p. 208.
7. Ibid., p. 222.
8. See Warren Christopher's interview with *Ha'aretz* (English edition), "A Believer in the Road Already Traveled," October 24, 1997, sec. 2, p. 5, first quoted from Rabinovich, *Brink of Peace,* p. 242.
9. Ibid.
10. William B. Quandt, "Will Clinton's Legacy Include Middle East Peace?" lecture delivered at the Center for International Studies, Massachusetts Institute of Technology, March 14, 2000.
11. Ibid.
12. Patrick Seale and Linda Butler, "Asad's Regional Strategy and the Challenge from Netanyahu," *Journal of Palestine Studies* 26, no. 1 (Autumn 1996), p. 35.
13. Ibid., p. 35–36.
14. Ibid., p. 36.

15. Ibid.

16. Ibid., pp. 36–37.

17. Ibid., p. 37.

18. Wallid Muallem, "Fresh Light on the Syrian-Israeli Peace Negotiations," *Journal of Palestine Studies* 26, no. 2 (Winter 1997), p. 86.

19. Ibid.

20. Ibid., pp. 86–87.

21. Ibid., p. 81.

22. Ibid.

23. Ibid., p. 82.

24. Ibid.

25. Ibid., p. 87.

26. "Kakh Fisfasnu et Hashalom im Surya" (This Is How We Missed the Peace with Syria), *Ma'ariv,* December 12, 1997, sec. 2, pp. 1–3, quoted from Rabinovich, *Brink of Peace,* p. 241.

27. Uri Savir, *The Process: 1,100 Days That Changed the Middle East* (New York: Random House, 1998), p. 283.

28. Rabinovich, *Brink of Peace,* p. 241.

29. "Qissat al-Wadia' al-Rabiniya" (The Story of Rabin's Deposit), *Al-Hayat,* November 21, 1999.

30. Ibid., November 22, 1999; and Rabinovich, *Brink of Peace,* p. 147.

31. Rabinovich, *Brink of Peace,* p. 239; and "Qissat al-Wadia' al-Rabiniya," November 22, 1999.

32. "Qissat al-Wadia' al-Rabiniya," November 22, 1999.

33. Ibid., November 23, 1999.

34. See Shimon Peres's interview with Patrick Seale in *Al-Hayat,* March 29, 2000.

35. Ibid.

36. Ibid.

37. Ibid.

38. Ibid.

39. Ibid.

40. Walid Muallem, "Beyond the Brink of Peace: Syria's Chief Negotiator Responds to Itamar Rabinovich's *The Brink of Peace*" (Damascus: N.p., n.d.). This paper was given to me by a senior Lebanese official, who requested that his identity remain anonymous.

41. Ibid.

42. Ibid.

43. Ibid. See Appendix 7.1 for the full text of the non-paper.

44. Ibid.

45. Ibid.

46. Ibid.

47. Ibid.

48. See Dennis Ross's interview with *New York Times Magazine,* March 25, 2001, p. 36. He is currently counselor for the Washington Institute for Near East Policy.

49. Ibid., pp. 36–38.

50. Ibid., p. 38.

51. Author interview with a senior U.S. official who spoke on condition that his identity remain anonymous, April 16, 2001.

52. Ibid.

53. In fact, according to Avi Shlaim, the main reason Rabin agreed to accept Oslo was that he believed it would lead to peace with Syria. See Avi Shlaim, *The Iron Wall: Israel and the Arab World* (New York: W. W. Norton, 2000).

54. For a critical analysis on Israel's assassination policy and the ramifications of Yahya Ayyash's death, see Uzi Benzamin, "Think Again About Assassination Policy," *Ha'aretz,* October 21, 2001.

55. See Issam al-Attar's interview with *Al-Ra'id* (Germany) no. 168, February 1995, pp. 14–19.

56. See Muhammad Aziz Shukri's interview with *Al-Wasat,* March 3, 1997, pp. 28–29.

57. Sadek al-Azm, "The View from Damascus," *New York Review of Books,* June 15, 2000.

58. Hisham Dajani, "Aswat al-Ra'y al-'Am . . . wa al-Samt 'al-Ajib' Tijah Qadiyat al-Salam" (Voices of Syrian Public Opinion . . . and the "Astonishing" Silence Toward the Peace Process), *Al-Hayat,* February 9, 2000.

59. Mahmoud Salameh, "Al-Matlub Ijad Aliyat Tad'um al-Mufawed al-Suri Ma'a Israil" (The Requirement Is to Find Mechanisms to Help the Syrian Negotiator with Israel), *Al-Hayat,* March 1, 2000.

60. Ibid.

61. Mamdouh Adwan, "Al-Musaqaf al-Suri wa Tihmat al-Samt: Al-Haq Huwa al-Mushkila La al-Ard" (The Syrian Intellectual and the Charge of Silence: Right Is the Problem Not Land), *Al-Hayat,* March 2, 2000.

62. Ibid.

63. Meron Benvenisti, "The Mirror Image of Peace," *Ha'aretz,* January 27, 2000.

64. William B. Quandt, "Clinton and the Arab-Israeli Conflict: The Limits of Incrementalism," *Journal of Palestine Studies* 30, no. 2 (Winter 2001), p. 40.

65. Sadek al-Azm, "Two Summits: Shepherdstown and Geneva," lecture delivered at the Kennedy School of Government, Harvard University, April 13, 2000.

66. James A. Baker III, "Peace, One Step at a Time," *New York Times,* July 27, 2000.

67. For the latest and most comprehensive study on the peasant origins of Syria's rulers, see Hanna Batatu, *Syria's Peasantry, the Descendants of Its Lesser Rural Notables, and Their Politics* (Princeton: Princeton University Press, 1999).

68. Author interview with a prominent Syrian who requested that his identity remain anonymous, April 16, 2001. According to the interviewee, Asad felt considerably dejected following the summit and this condition partly caused his death.

9

Conclusion

The failure of both the peace talks in Shepherdstown and the Clinton-Asad summit at Geneva appeared to help energize the Ba'thi regime to attend to its urgent domestic affairs, namely the dismal economy and the succession question. In fact, this had been gathering steam for a few months. In contrast to an earlier pattern where Asad had been grooming his son for succession without publicly confirming him as heir apparent, the president's bold new moves indicated that he was unequivocally passing the reins of government to Bashar. This was revealed in the power Asad vested in his son to wage a campaign against corruption—also a way to elevate Bashar's status in the public eye—and in deciding to hold the ninth convention of the Syrian Ba'th Party, which had not been convened for fifteen years. Obviously, the convention was meant to pave the way for a smooth succession.

Bashar began intervening in high-profile domestic issues once only the sacred domain of his father. After apparently helping to dissolve the government of Prime Minister Mahmoud Zubi for inefficiency and corruption, Bashar confirmed that the Ba'th convention would take place and declared that he recommended people with merit be appointed in the new government.[1] He added that the first mission of the new government would be to modernize the bureaucracy and reduce the level of corruption.[2] These declarations followed frequent public statements about the necessity of introducing changes in all public and private sectors of the Syrian state.

On March 14, 2000, the new prime minister, Muhammad Mustafa Miro, headed a new government, which included twenty-five Ba'thists, five independents, and six representatives of the Progressive National Front.[3] Apparently, the selection process of the members of the new government rested in large part on their professed loyalty to Bashar. One could not dismiss this point, given that the former government was ousted after serving for thirteen years. This unusual change in government was followed by equal and important measures taken by President Asad. Supposedly within the context of the

269

policy of "openness and forgiveness," Asad not only issued a law releasing some political prisoners in the spirit of his recent actions (1998), but also enacted three constitutional decrees, which respectively abrogated Law no. 24, reduced the role of security courts in inconsequential economic infractions, and raised the ceiling of violations in connection with wasting public funds. The abrogation of Law no. 24 was long overdue and was expected especially by the merchant bourgeoisie class, who considered the law a real obstacle to investment and in conflict with Law no. 10.[4]

The timing of the enactment of those laws coincided tidily with Asad's efforts to broaden his son's popular base of support. Not only was Asad easing the bureaucratic red tape for doing business in Syria, but he also appeared indirectly to give credit to his son for his apparent involvement in helping to foster a new propitious business climate. The merchant class had been voicing serious concerns over the state's economic policy along with some members of the parliament and the establishment itself. Rateb Shallah, the president of the Federation of Syrian Chambers of Commerce and Industry, posed the question, "How is Syria going to face European states that are free and open while Syria is the least developed in terms of its industry." He added that "it is not feasible to postpone decision-making because we will lose the chance for reform."[5] Hashem Akkad, a legislator, sarcastically commented on the way business is conducted in Syria: "We have a mentality here that is unique in the world."[6] Not long ago these public admonitions would have been unthinkable.

Regardless of what they think of the implications of the peace process for the Syrian economy, Syria's entrepreneurs worry about their eroding competitiveness in an advanced regional and global economy. So they have been looking at Bashar as a silent ally given his attitude toward introducing needed reforms. Correspondingly, the timing and nature of those new laws preceded by the forming of a new government could only harden the merchants' belief that Bashar is their only natural ally. In turn, Bashar could depend on them as loyal supporters.

Soon enough, domestic considerations were overshadowed by a momentous event. Israeli prime minister Ehud Barak made good on his promise to withdraw his troops from Lebanon by July 2000 by pulling out of the country ahead of schedule on May 24. Israel's withdrawal was swift and was watched by UN observers, who certified Tel Aviv's fulfillment of UN Resolution 425. Interestingly enough, in the immediate run-up to the withdrawal, the U.S. and Israeli governments continued to virtually ignore Syria's frantic signaling that it still wanted to negotiate with Israel (see Chapter 8). In the process, Antoine Lahd's army speedily disintegrated, provoking an exodus of a significant number of Lebanese officers and their families, mainly Christians, into Israel. Other members and affiliates of Israel's proxy army surrendered to the incoming forces of Hizbollah, who claimed victory over the retreating Israelis.[7] Barak objected and reiterated his campaign pledge, which was to end Israel's "misguided" involvement in Lebanon. At the same time, he held Damascus and Beirut directly responsible for attacks on Israeli territory launched from Lebanon. Israeli army officials bolstered Barak's warning by suggesting that future retaliatory strikes from Israel "would not exclude" Syrian military installations in Lebanon.[8]

In addition, Israel's ambassador to the United Nations, Yehuda Lancry, delivered a letter from Barak to Secretary-General Kofi Annan warning Syria and Iran. An excerpt from the letter read:

> I [Barak] am referring particularly to Syria's cynical exploitation of the Palestinians in Lebanon to commit terrorist acts against Israel after the withdrawal and the fact that it provides a free hand to Iran, its messengers and protégés— Primarily the Hezbollah—to build infrastructures which would undermine regional stability to the point of a possible outbreak of hostilities.[9]

Israel's withdrawal without a peace deal with Syria set in sharp relief Tel Aviv's intentions and Damascus's premonitions. No longer could Syria use Hizbollah to militarily pressure Israel with impunity. Nor could Syria any longer hope to wrest concessions from Israel during peace talks. Most important, Tel Aviv appeared not only to be pulling the rug of legitimacy out from under Syrian feet in Lebanon, but also to be severing any future connection between Lebanon's and Syria's peace negotiations tracks. Why should Syria keep its supposedly protective heavy military presence in Lebanon when Israel's military threat to the sovereignty of the country no longer existed? Why should the Lebanese track remain wedded to that of Syria? Suddenly, the configuration of the Israeli-Syrian conflict appeared to change at the expense of Syria's role. Out of this fluid situation, a new one emerged centering on Shebaa Farms.

Shebaa Farms is an area on the southwestern slopes of Mount Hermon, which the Lebanese government and Hizbollah claim is occupied Lebanese territory, while the UN, after the Israeli withdrawal from Lebanon, considers it a land captured by Israel from Syria in the 1967 Middle East war. In fact, during the run-up to Israel's withdrawal, the speaker of parliament, Nabih Berri, raised the question of Shebaa Farms, obviously at the instigation of Syria. When the issue first arose, few Lebanese, including even senior Hizbollah officials, knew of the case. Syria acknowledged Lebanon's claims to the territory. In addition, when the UN rejected Lebanon's claims, arguing that Shebaa Farms was not covered by Resolution 425 but by Resolution 242, and was therefore subject to Israeli-Syrian negotiations, Lebanon and Syria refused to acknowledge this UN position. They have been arguing that Israel has not completed its withdrawal from Lebanon and thus resistance will continue until all Lebanese territories are liberated.

Given Syrian hegemony in Lebanon, it is clear that Damascus will create any situation in the country whereby it could retain the option of military pressure against Israel as well as thwart attempts to separate Lebanon from Israeli-Syrian negotiations (other potential cases similar to Shebaa include several villages such as Nkhaile, al-Ghajar, and the "seven villages"). Until Syria retrieves its Golan Heights, this condition will most likely persist. Following some Lebanese calls for Syria to withdraw from Lebanon (see below), Defense Minister Mustafa Tlas emphasized Lebanon's centrality to Syria: "We made sacrifices in Lebanon and gave many martyrs in order for Lebanon to achieve victory. . . . And we are still ready to give all support until the last Lebanese occupied hand-span is liberated. We have the right to demand support from Lebanon in order for us to liberate our occupied land in the Golan."[10]

Significantly enough, Hizbollah took over all border area positions and filled the vacuum left by Israel's withdrawal, which the Lebanese government refused to acknowledge as its responsibility on account that it will not play the role of a policeman to secure Israel's borders. With Syria's blessing, Hizbollah has maintained its resistance role, keeping the card of Shebaa Farms up its sleeve to restart hostilities.

In the meantime, Bashar's orchestrated campaign against corruption along with preparations for the Ba'th convention proceeded smoothly. The campaign resulted in the suicide of former primer minister Mahmoud Zubi and the flight to the United States of former chief of staff Hikmat Shihabi (who later returned home). Apparently, the ulterior motives behind the corruption campaign were succeeding by continuing to purge some members of the old guard deemed as potential challengers to Bashar's presidential candidacy.

Other momentous events took Syria and the region by surprise. On June 10, 2000, President Asad passed away after thirty years in power. Immediately after his death, Vice President Abd al-Halim Khaddam issued legislation promoting Bashar from colonel to lieutenant-general—the rank of his father—and appointing him commander in chief of the Syrian armed forces.[11] This was followed by a series of actions that made Bashar the uncontested new leader of Syria. The Ba'th Regional Ninth Congress convened as scheduled, and on its second day, July 18, the ruling Ba'th Party unanimously elected Bashar as its secretary-general. In addition, Bashar headed a committee of six whose responsibility included overseeing the congress in general and appointing the new ruling Regional Command Council of the Ba'th Party in particular.[12] The council wields much power in the party and state. Interestingly enough, the political report of the congress included two points: "Islam is a dogma and a heritage and part of our political life," and "the peace process is the strategic choice" for Syria.[13]

Shortly thereafter, Bashar was elected head of the Regional Command Council and approved unanimously by the parliament as the sole candidate for president in a referendum, in which he eventually won 97.27 percent of the votes. At this point, it is important to elaborate on the appointments, especially to the Regional Command Council, since they indicate the shifting political alliances and by implication the locus of political power in Syria. Out of twenty-one members, twelve new members were inducted into the council. They included Bashar, Prime Minister Mustafa Miro, Deputy Prime Minister Muhammad Naji Atri, Foreign Minister Farouk al-Shara, Ghiath Barakat, Ibrahim Huneidi, Faruq abu al-Shamat, Majed Shadud, Salam al-Yasin, Muhammad al-Hussein, Walid al-Bouz, and Said Bakhtian. Vice Presidents Abd al-Halim Khaddam and Muhammad Zuhair Mashariqa, deputy secretaries of the Ba'th Party Suleiman Qadah and Abd allah al-Ahmar, parliament speaker Abd al-Qader Qadura, Defense Minister Mustafa Tlas, Ahmad Dargam, Fa'z al-Naser, and Walid Hamdoun all kept their membership in the council.[14]

It appears that an established core of supporters for Bashar included the original and loyal members of the committee of six, supplemented by Shara, Miro, Atri, and Bakhtian. The latter is a close aide of Bashar and is now director of the National Security Bureau, which coordinates party and government bodies.[15] It is significant that the council did not include Ali Aslan, chief of staff, and Asef Shawkat, military intelligence chief and Bashar's brother-in-law, both considered the military muscle of Bashar's new regime. This was more or less countervailed by beefing up the Central Command Council of the Ba'th Party (ninety members), by bringing into it military officers constituting a third of its total number and including Maher al-Asad, Bashar's brother, and Manaf Tlas, the secretary of defense's son.[16] In addition, Ali Duba, the former strongman of military intelligence, was ousted from the Central Command Council.[17] Shortly thereafter, Bashar's attempts to continue to consolidate his power involved promoting several loyal supporters in the military, among whom was none other than his brother, Maher, and discharging several military officers whose loyalty to Bashar is in doubt.[18]

Apparently, the configuration of the new power structure in Syria continued to follow the old pattern institutionalized by the late Asad. No organic change has taken place and it appears that the new regime will rely on an informal core of loyal military officers, mainly Alawi, and on a formal core of high-ranking state officials, mainly Sunni. Most important, Khaddam and Tlas, I believe, will play a significant role in protecting and guiding Bashar, but this might come at the expense of the new president's exclusive power. This could impose limits on what Bashar could do internally and externally until he ensures his survival by totally consolidating his power. In a chilling yet sober remark, Eyal Zisser said that "Bashar will survive only if he shows determination, leadership capabilities, charisma and, finally, the necessary degree of brutality toward his enemies at home."[19]

Hafiz al-Asad departed from life without signing an agreement with Israel and saddled his son not only with an unfinished task but also with a peace process legacy that Bashar could ill afford to deviate from. The configuration of the new power structure in Syria leaves no doubt that for the time being, Bashar will toe the line of the regime's stand on the peace process. In addition, the major development in the region (Israel's withdrawal from Lebanon) and Syria's chronic domestic concerns appear to have the potential to pull Bashar in different directions, forcing him into a predicament. He needs to modernize Syria and introduce reforms to improve the state's economy, while he appears set on protecting and relying on his clan for his own survival. He seems also to want to protect his Lebanese investment without either running the risk of a conflagration with Israel or implying a lack of determination for retrieving the Golan Heights. All this was set into sharp relief when Bashar delivered his presidential inaugural speech before the parliament.

He focused on repairing his country's ailing economy, modernizing the bureaucracy, and enhancing democracy, while at the same time he gave no sign that he will introduce reforms that will threaten the structure his father built. "We are in urgent need of constructive criticism and not destructive one," he said. He continued: "Western democracies are the product of a long history. . . . We should have our own democratic experience springing from our history, education and civilized personality . . . and arising from the needs of our people and reality. . . . Our National Progressive Front is a democratic model developed by our own experience."[20]

Regarding his country's relationship with Lebanon, Bashar said: "We consider the relationship with Brother/Lebanon is a model one between two Arabic states. But this model has not been completed and is in need of a great effort to become exemplary." With respect to the peace process, Bashar gave no indication that he will be less flexible than his father in negotiating a peace treaty with Israel. In much the same formulaic language as his father, Bashar stated: "Liberating our occupied land is a top national priority whose importance matches the total and comprehensive peace we relied upon as our strategic choice . . . but not at the expense of our land and sovereignty." He added: "This land [Golan] is going to remain ours and shall be returned in full sooner or later."[21]

One can only wonder how Bashar is going to pursue and reconcile such inherently incompatible policies without endangering the very system his father built. If his wily and ruthless father was hesitant to introduce significant political and economic reforms and was not able to retrieve the Golan, how can Bashar? This is Bashar's challenge. These doubts became manifested as events unfolded. Bashar's statements and initial actions of political liberalization, such as permitting the publishing of newspapers and releasing political prisoners, fostered an atmosphere of change that was speedily capitalized upon by many Syrians.[22] Prominent among them were intellectuals, writers, independent members of parliament, members of the merchant class, and Muslim Brothers. In a spate of a few months, public forums, emphasizing the need to introduce substantive political and economic reforms, mushroomed in Syria. Intellectuals and writers signed consecutive statements, known as Manifesto 99 and Manifesto 1000, in which they called for ending the state of emergency and abrogating martial laws in effect since 1963, releasing all political prisoners, holding democratic elections, and reviving the country's civil society.[23] Simultaneously, the Muslim Brothers demanded reforms similar to those made by the intellectuals and writers. Importantly, they asked the government to grant their movement a legal status in the country (membership is punishable by death in Syria). The magnitude of this civil society's movement took a far-reaching dimension when parliamentary members and other visible members of Syrian society began to air their criticism of the regime in a tone and openness not yet heard of in Syria.

For example, in a public forum on economic reforms, bearing the title "Syrian Society for Economic Science," parliament member Riad Seif, a prominent figure of the group Friends of Civil Society, which issued Manifesto 1000, railed against the system. He stated: "We have no transparency, no exact monetary figures, no accountability . . . we don't have any development. We don't have dialogue. We don't have strong institutions. We have no anti-corruption campaign."[24]

Paralleling these domestic events, the regime faced a new situation in Lebanon with grave implications for Syria. Discontented with its political, social, and economic situation in the wake of the Taif Accord, and chafing over Syrian hegemony in Lebanon, the Maronite community, led by the Maronite patriarch Nasrallah Boutros Sfeir, called for the redeployment of Syrian troops in Lebanon in preparation for their complete withdrawal.[25] The call acquired a heightened sense of urgency for Syria when, in a surprising shift of alliances, former pro-Syrian Druze leader Walid Jumblat sided with the Maronites and called for a reexamination of Syria's security role, particularly in light of Israel's withdrawal.[26] Coming from a supposed Syrian protégé, this was tantamount to calling into question the Syrian political role and thus its hegemony in Lebanon. Suddenly, a controversial debate erupted over the Syrian presence in Lebanon and polarized the country along confessional/sectarian lines, thereby raising the stakes for Syrian involvement in the country.[27]

All of these evolving developments have been taking place against the background of the second (Al-Aqsa) intifada in the Palestinian occupied territories, which erupted in September 2000 following the failure of Israeli-Palestinian negotiations. Largely in response to escalating violence, Likud leader Ariel Sharon was elected prime minister in February 2001. At the same time, the period of relative calm (four months from the date of Israel's withdrawal) along the Lebanese-Israeli border deteriorated dramatically. Still riding high on its wave of victory against Israel in southern Lebanon and becoming an exemplary militia to many Palestinians, Hizbollah, acting supposedly in solidarity with the Palestinians, launched a raid into Shebaa Farms and kidnapped three Israeli soldiers.[28] This marked the beginning of a dangerous new game between Israel on the one hand, and Hizbollah and Syria on the other, centering on Shebaa Farms. In addition, the issue of Shebaa acquired a legitimate regional cover when the Arab League, convened in Cairo in late October 2000, issued a statement holding Israel responsible for the violence and affirming that Shebaa is Lebanese occupied territory, thereby indirectly giving Hizbollah and by implication Syria the political pretext to attack Israelis there.[29]

In November, Hizbollah raised the stakes of renewed cross-border hostilities when it set off a roadside bomb near an Israeli patrol in Shebaa, killing an Israeli soldier. Immediately, and for the first time since its withdrawal, Israel responded by air and ground artillery attacks on Hizbollah targets and positions in southern Lebanon.[30] Subsequently, on April 16, 2001, Sharon made good on Israel's warning to Damascus and struck at Syrian positions in Lebanon following the death of an Israeli soldier by Hizbollah's fire. According to Israeli officials, the air strike on a Syrian radar installation in Lebanon, in which three Syrian soldiers were killed, was meant as a warning to Syria not to abet Hizbollah and was not an invitation to escalate the conflict. While emphasizing that the rules of the game have changed, Israel's defense minister, Benjamin Ben-Eliezer, asserted that "we cannot just sit and suffer day and night and live under shelling and harassment and say thank you. . . . We have been ignoring this for several months, but finally it couldn't be ignored. We had no choice but to send a clear message to the Syrians: only you can stop Hezbollah. At the same time, we are sending a message saying we have no interest in seeing things get any worse."[31]

Keeping with this new retaliatory policy and brushing aside Lebanese and Syrian warnings, on July 1, Israel launched another air strike, targeting Syrian military sites in Lebanon following a Hizbollah attack on its soldiers.[32] Syria again refrained from any military action and confined its reaction to statements of warning while at the same time, along with Lebanon, justifying Hizbollah's actions. Against a background of escalating violence in the region, one cannot rule out a broad conflagration. While Syria and Lebanon do not wish to fight a war with Israel, in which they could suffer far out of proportion, the foreboding of war could well become a self-fulfilling prophecy. The overall dynamics in the region leading to acts of warfare, having Shebaa Farms as their focal point, could precipitate war by miscalculation.

At this point one needs to ask how Syria has reacted to all of these ongoing grave domestic and regional developments. Syria has so far pursued a contradictory policy, in large measure similar to past policies. It clamped down on the movement of civil society, calling for reforms while at the same time professing that it would continue "on the path of freedom and democracy." It is clear that the swiftness with which the movement spread took the regime off-guard. The regime feared that the trickle of reforms it allowed could cause a flood, sweeping it away in the process. Bashar lashed out at the dissidents, warning them against threatening the stability of Syria.[33] Keeping to its tradition, the regime counteracted first by attacking those standing in the vanguard of the reform campaign, then by enacting laws restricting their movement. No longer could a public forum be held without the approval of the regime, nor could an intellectual, or anyone else, be safe from the threat of arrest on charges ranging from embezzlement to threatening state security.

Significantly enough, the regime has reused the card of Arab-Israeli conflict, which has been simmering in violence, to put reformers on the defensive. The rationale has been that while the regime supports freedom in the spirit of the modernization and evolutionary movement carried forward by Bashar, it rejects a "total freedom" that could rend Syrian society at a time when it needs to be strong to face the challenges of the Arab-Israeli conflict. Correspondingly, why the movement of civil society omitted from its platform and discussions the paramount issue of the Arab-Israeli conflict is a question the regime has asked.[34] The campaign against reformers took a sharp turn when the regime began arresting important political figures. Under the pretext of derailing reform, freedom, and democracy, the regime arrested parliamentary deputies Muhammad Ma'moun al-Homsi and Riad Seif, and president of the Communist Party–Political Bureau (the branch that is not proregime) Riad al-Turk.[35]

The regime's reaction to the developments in Lebanon has been no different in style or substance than that to the developments in Syria. While it professes to look into the predicament of the Christian opposition to Syrian presence in Lebanon, the Syrian regime, through its proxies in the country including Hizbollah, has been trying to discredit the opposition by accusing its leaders of treason as well as trying to further fragment the opposition by arresting some of its members, all under the pretext of collaborating with Israel. In an unprecedented and sweeping campaign targeting the Lebanese Forces and the followers of former general Michael Aoun, the Lebanese security apparatus arrested in August 2001 more than 140 individuals.[36] Arbitrary arrests are becoming the norm in Beirut, sending a clear message that anti-Syrian activities are not tolerated, and that Syria has no intention of leaving the country anytime soon.[37]

It is clear that the regime has reverted to its "time-honored" method of using the Arab-Israeli conflict to suppress opposition. This took a grave dimension when Bashar denounced Israel in anti-Semitic terms never used by his father. Upon welcoming the pope to Syria on May 5, 2001, Bashar delivered a speech in which he accused Israel of torturing and murdering Palestinians and suggested that Christians and Muslims make common cause against those "who try to kill the principles of all religions with the same mentality with which they betrayed Jesus [and] in the same way that they tried to commit treachery against Prophet Muhammad."[38] A few days later and after much world opprobrium was heaped on Bashar, he paradoxically not only denied that he had attacked Judaism but also claimed that the region, including Syria, has an interest in a true peace. He added that "sooner or later . . . the day will come as I believe . . . where there will be peace and stability."[39]

But with the peace process all but presumed dead, and with violence flaring in the occupied territories, the regime has sought not only to silence the opposition at home and in Lebanon, but also to enhance its regional strategic standing. Most important, the regime has begun a process of rapprochement with Iraq based mainly on trade. This has been done in spite of the fact that the regime knows full well that the United States needs Syria's help to put teeth in its Middle East policy (see Chapter 3). Many commercial treaties have been signed between Iraq and Syria, the most recent of which occurred in August 2001, when for the first time in years Syrian prime minister Muhammad Mustafa Miro traveled to Baghdad along with a contingent of Syrian entrepreneurs. During the visit, the vice president of Iraq, Taha Yassin Ramadan, affirmed in a show of support for Syria that Iraq "will offer Syria support 'in all fields including the military one' in the event a confrontation with Israel erupted."[40] Simultaneously, Syria has continued to deepen and improve its relations respectively with Iran, Turkey, Jordan, and the Palestinians, not to mention strengthening its presence in Lebanon.[41]

Taking all of this together, and in view of the regime's history, it becomes clear that the Syrian leadership is blurring anew the lines between domestic and foreign policies in the interest of national security in general and security of the regime in particular. Most of the regime's policies, whether internal or external, are part of Syria's attempts to minimize its vulnerabilities while at the same time sending a clear message to Israel and the United States that Syria's regional role is not to be excluded or reduced. This has become all the more important (and complicated) following the Bush administration's war on terrorism. Significantly enough, President Bush in his 2002 State of the Union address singled out Iran, Iraq, and North Korea as countries making up an "axis of evil." In addition, he mentioned in his address Hizbollah as a terrorist organization. Although President Bush left Syria out from his speech, he put the country into a double bind. He highlighted Syria's regional role but compelled the country to make a choice with respect to any U.S. potential future action against Iran, Iraq, or Hizbollah.[42] This is an immediate challenge for Bashar having serious implications for both Syria and the United States. How Bashar will meet this challenge is exacerbated by his challenge over how to fix the system without breaking it.

As mentioned in Chapter 3, Syria has called for a definition of terrorism with the objective of distinguishing acts of terror from acts toward resisting occupation. Already Syria (along with Arab countries and Iran) has refused the U.S. designation of Hizbollah as a terrorist organization with global reach. In fact, after a meeting between President Asad and Lebanese prime minister Rafiq Harriri, the two decided to object to any "infringement on the movement of resistance under whatever pretext, including that of terrorism."[43] As such, Lebanon declined the U.S. request to freeze the assets of Hizbollah.

What complicated matters was the seizure by Israel in January 2002 in the Red Sea of a ship *(Karina A)* carrying fifty tons of weapons to the Palestinian Authority. According to Israeli and U.S. intelligence sources, Iran supplied the weapons with the logistical help of Hizbollah. This came in the wake of a fiery and defying speech delivered by Hizbollah's leader, Hasan Nasrallah, in which he stated that "Israeli society has no civilians but invaders and occupiers."[44] According to the statement, Hizbollah may extend its operations beyond Shebaa Farms to Israel proper. In addition, after some quiet on the Israeli-Lebanese border, Hizbollah launched an attack on Shebaa Farms on January 23, which Israel accused Iran and Syria of supporting.[45] Taken together, all these events focused attention on what role Syria might play in the region in general and in Lebanon in particular.

Damascus will continue to contribute to the U.S. war efforts on terrorism (which have been significantly expanded to cover nonproliferation of weapons of mass destruction), mainly in the intelligence field. But Damascus will not defang Hizbollah or reduce its cooperation with Iran before settling its conflict with Israel. With the violence in the occupied territories escalating and Arab public opinion resenting the U.S. bias toward Israel, paired with the Bush administration's unwillingness to articulate a well-defined concept for resolving the Arab-Israeli conflict, Syria will be disinclined to completely curb Hizbollah's operations. In addition, Syria will have little incentive to clip the wings of Hizbollah so long as it is ready to defend Syrian presence in Lebanon and put the mainly Maronite opposition on the defensive. Along with other Arab countries, Syria will try to work out a diplomatic solution for the Iraqi crisis. However, it will most likely either cooperate with the United States on enforcing the "smart" sanctions on Iraq or will stand idly by in the event of a U.S. attack on Iraq provided that Washington develops a plan protecting Iraq's territorial integrity and clarifying U.S. objectives in the region, and appears resolute. In all cases, the extent of Syria's cooperation with the United States will depend in no small measure on Damascus's strategic calculation of the implication of this cooperation for its ability to pursue its foreign policy priorities: recovering the Golan Heights, preserving its "special relations" with Lebanon, and enhancing its regional role.

The other challenge facing Bashar, as mentioned earlier, is how he is to reconcile Syria's foreign policy priorities with its domestic priorities, given that the regime has intentionally blurred the lines between the two in the interest of its security. As his past actions reveal, Bashar appears reluctant to introduce significant political reforms. Conversely, he has continued slowly and cautiously on the path of economic reform, relying heavily on tackling institutional incompetence. He recently made changes to his cabinet, appointing several independents to economic positions. As such, he gave a bigger role to the independents in his government. He based the formation of the economic team on merit and experience.[46] With change inevitable in Syria following the death of Asad, the main question is whether Bashar can control the nature and speed of change while remaining in control and weaning himself from the old guard.

This overall Syrian attitude can also be partly understood as a result of Syria's and Israel's experiences during a decade of peace efforts. How did Syria and Israel emerge vis-à-vis each other from the peace process? Syria emerged from the peace process more skeptical about Israel than before. Negative Syrian beliefs and perceptions of Israel previous to the peace negotiations, across the country's political and social spectrum, have been reinforced. Syria believes that Israel is aggressive and bent on dominating the region, considering Tel Aviv's relentless quest for security within and beyond the purview of peace. This is buttressed by Israel's attempts at manipulating Syria, which run the gamut from constantly deferring the Syrian track to another, to waiting for Syria to campaign for peace in Israel, to pressing Syria into unacceptable positions. Correspondingly, Syria is not yet sure about Israel's true intentions concerning relinquishing the Golan Heights.

Central to this belief are three notions that Syria gleaned from the peace process, one of which is that the United States can barely keep Israel in check, despite Washington's open support for the country. In fact, this is why Damascus feels that it must include the United States in all Israeli-Syrian negotiations, if not as a mediator then as a witness, while at the same time trying to involve international interlocutors; and that it must maintain a relationship with the United States decent enough to prevent an Israeli aggression against Damascus. The second notion is that Israel's domestic politics are chaotic. Damascus is bewildered by Israel's pork-barrel and horse-trade politics, which it feels feed Tel Aviv's indetermination and unpredictability. Therefore, a fair negotiated settlement is inadvertently beholden to Israel's labyrinthine politics. Finally, there is the notion that the U.S. presidency is much weaker than is reflected by the position's prestige and prodigiousness. Syria thinks that Israel and its supporters in the United States have undue influence on U.S. foreign policy.

Israel, for its part, believes that Syria has not yet shed its past impulses and attitudes. Syria is more interested in retrieving the Golan Heights and having a warm relationship with the United States than in normal peace with its neighbor. Syria speaks peace and indirectly attacks Israel through Hizbollah. The right wing in Israel believes that were Syria ready for peace it would have capitalized on Labor governments' proposals. The left wing believes that Syria should work for its peace no less than Israel does. Public diplomacy is a must.

When all is said and done, peace between the two embattled neighbors remains elusive at this time. However, a new epoch is beginning in the Middle East that might contain under its wings auspicious events, events of the kind that made possible the once unimaginable handshake between Rabin and Arafat. One should not discard the fact that Bashar has projected an image of modernity and supposedly is still intent on improving Syria's dismal economy. After his consolidation of power, the price Bashar needs to pay for a ticket to the global economy with the blessing of capitalism's guru, the United States, might be a pact with the Israeli "devil."

Notes

1. Patrick Seale, "Bashar al-Asad li-al-Hayat: Mu'tamar al-Ba'th Hadha al-Am wa Zakayt Ba'd al-Akfiya' Lil-Hukuma al-Jadida" (Bashar al-Asad to Al-Hayat: Al-Ba'th Congress This Year and I Recommended Some Meritorious People to the New Government), *Al-Hayat,* March 7, 2000.
2. Ibid.
3. For the names and titles of the members of the new government, see *Al-Hayat,* March 15, 2000.
4. See Chapter 4 in this volume. Law no. 24 decrees a prison term of three to ten years to anyone who deals with foreign exchange outside official channels. Asad substituted Law no. 6 for Law no. 24. Law no. 6 reduced prison punishment from twenty-five to five years as maximum limit for anyone caught smuggling more than 5 million Syrian pounds (U.S.$100,000) and permitted the holding of foreign currencies, including the ability to pay for business procedures in foreign exchange. For more details on the laws, see *Al-Hayat,* April 26, 2000.
5. Rateb Shallah's comments were voiced at a symposium on trade between Syria and the European Union in January 2000. See Susan Sachs, "Syria Businessmen Yearn for Reforms," *New York Times,* January 27, 2000.
6. Ibid.
7. See *New York Times,* May 23, 24, 2000. Almost all members of the South Lebanese Army who remained in Lebanon were taken into the custody of the Lebanese government.
8. See William A. Orme Jr., "Barak Declares End to 'Tragedy' as Last Troops Leave Lebanon," *New York Times,* May 24, 2000.
9. See "Warning from Barak," *New York Times,* May 24, 2000.
10. See Nada Abd al-Samad, "Tlas: Jumblat Ikhtira' Suri" (Tlas: Jumblat Is a Syrian Invention), *Al-Quds al-Arabi,* May 12–13, 2001.
11. See *Al-Hayat,* June 12, 2000.
12. See Ibrahim Hamidi, "Bashar al-Asad Raasa 'Lajna Sudasiya' Li-Edarat Muatamar 'al-Ba'th'" (Bashar al-Asad Heads a "Committee of Six" to Manage the "Ba'th" Congress), *Al-Hayat,* June 20, 2000. The committee of six included Bashar, Vice Presidents Abd al-Halim Khaddam and Muhammad Zuhair Mashariqa, deputy secretaries of the Ba'th Regional and Central Command Councils, respectively Suliman Qadah and Abd allah al-Ahmar, and Defense Minister Mustafa Tlas. Tlas played as pivotal a role as Khaddam by organizing meetings between high-ranking military officials and Bashar and rallying unequivocal support for him.
13. Ibid.
14. Ibrahim Hamidi, "Mu'tamar al-Ba'th Yantakheb Bashar wa Yudkhel 12 'dwan Jadidan" (Ba'th Congress Elects Bashar and Brings in Twelve New Members), *Al-Hayat,* June 21, 2000.
15. Ibid.; and John Kifner, "Assad's Son Designated Sole Candidate for Syrian Presidency," *New York Times,* June 28, 2000.
16. Manaf Tlas, a Sunni, has been a loyal and close friend to Bashar. He has been helping Bashar in forging good relationships with the Damascene merchant bourgeoisie class. Kifner, "Assad's Son."

17. Hamidi, "Mu'tamar al-Ba'th."

18. See Ibrahim Hamidi, "Dimashq: Tarqiyat Maher al-Asad 'Aqidan wa Tasrih 'Adad min Kibar al-Dubat" (Damascus: Promotion of Maher al-Asad to Colonel and Discharging a Number of Senior Officers), *Al-Hayat,* July 3, 2000.

19. Jane Perlez, "Albright Finds Syria's New Leader Willing to Pursue Talks," *New York Times,* June 14, 2000.

20. See the entire inaugural speech in *Tishrin al-Usbu'I* (Tishrin Weekly), July 18, 2000.

21. Ibid.

22. The authorities permitted the publishing of the first privately owned newspaper, *Al-Dumari,* in the country in four decades. They also permitted the proregime branch of the Communist Party to publish its own newspaper. In November 2000, the authorities released 600 political prisoners. See *Al-Hayat,* November 18, 2000.

23. For the texts of Manifestos 99 and 1000, see respectively, *Al-Hayat,* September 27, 2000, and January 12, 2001.

24. Neil MacFarquhar, "Syria Reaches Turning Point, But Which Way Will It Turn?" *New York Times,* March 12, 2001.

25. See Nasrallah Boutros Sfeir's statement (delivered through the Council of Maronite Bishops), in *Al-Safir,* September 21, 2000.

26. See Walid Jumblat's statement in *al-Hayat,* November 4, 2000.

27. For complete details, see Robert G. Rabil, "The Maronites and Syrian Withdrawal: From 'Isolationists' to 'Traitors'?" *Middle East Policy* 8, no. 3 (September 2000).

28. Deborah Sontag, "Conflict Spreads to the Border of Lebanon," *New York Times,* October 8, 2000.

29. See the Arab League's statement in *New York Times,* October 23, 2000.

30. Joel Greenberg, "Israeli Killed at Lebanon Frontier; Airstrike Follows," *New York Times,* November 27, 2000.

31. Deborah Sontag, "Israeli Strike Deep into Lebanon Unsettles Arabs," *New York Times,* April 17, 2001.

32. Joel Greenberg, "Israel Kills Three Militants and Hits Syrian Site in Lebanon," *New York Times,* July 2, 2001.

33. See Bashar's interview with *Al-Sharq al-Awsat,* February 8, 2001.

34. See Vice President Abd al-Halim Khaddam's statements in *Al-Hayat,* February 19, 2001. See also Defense Minister Mustafa Tlas's statements in *Al-Hayat,* April 12, 2001.

35. See *Al-Hayat,* August 10, 2001, and September 8, 2001.

36. See Rabil, "Maronites and Syrian Withdrawal"; and *Al-Hayat,* August 8, 2001.

37. On June 14, 2001, Syrian troops suddenly began to redeploy from primarily Christian sections of the capital and surrounding areas. The redeployment included troops stationed at Yarze, where the Lebanese defense ministry is located, at Baabda, site of the presidential palace, and at Mount Lebanon. The decision to withdraw was widely perceived as an attempt to defuse tension caused by the mounting opposition to the Syrian presence. However, the redeployment was tactical, entailing moving the troops from one area and concentrating them in another to reduce their ubiquity in Christian areas. Commenting on the redeployment, Bashar stated that "the presence of Syrian troops in Lebanon is temporary," but then added that "the timing of withdrawal is linked to internal and regional circumstances." See *Al-Nahar,* June 15, 2001; and *Al-Quds al-Arabi,* June 23–24, 2001.

38. Allessandra Stanley, "Pope, Arriving in Syria, Hears Its Leader Denounce Israel," *New York Times,* May 6, 2001.

39. See Bashar's statement in *Al-Quds al-Arabi,* June 23–24, 2001.

40. See "Ramadan: Unbub al-Naft al-Jadid Yabda' Tanfizahu Qariban Ma' Suria" (Ramadan: The New Oil Pipeline Will Soon Be Implemented with Syria), *Al-Hayat,* August 14, 2001. Miro's visit to Baghdad was shortly followed by Ramadan's visit to Damascus.

41. The two young leaders of Syria and Jordan have intensified their contacts, and Mahmud Abbas (Abu Mazin), the architect of the 1993 Oslo Accords and Arafat's top man, visited Damascus. The visit attests to a real desire to improve Syrian-Palestinian relations. For years, Arafat had been persona non grata in Damascus. See *Al-Hayat,* August 6, 2001.

42. As of this writing, the United States has refrained from confronting Syria over its trade with Iraqi oil, estimated at between 150,000 and 200,000 barrels daily. This makes Syria a crucial source of money to Iraq outside the UN's oil-for-food sanctions program.

43. See *Al-Hayat,* November 8, 2001.

44. See "Nasrallah: Al-'Amliyat al-Istishadiya Khiyar Wahid wa Kulahum Fi Israil Shuraka' Fi al-Majzara" (Nasrallah: Suicidal Operations Are the Only Option and All of Them in Israel Are Partners in the Massacre), *Al-Hayat,* December 15, 2001.

45. See *Al-Hayat,* January 24, 2002.

46. Sa'dallah Agha al-Qala', Ghassan Rifa'I, former expert at the World Bank, Muhammad Bashir al-Munjid, and Muhammad al-Atrash received respectively the portfolios of tourism, economics, transportation, and finance. In addition, in a move considered to strengthen the executive branch, Bashar appointed the former director of general intelligence, Ali Hamoud, as minister of state. See *Al-Hayat,* December 14, 2001.

Selected Bibliography

Official Documents, Autobiographies, and Other Sources by State Officials

Aflaq, Michel. *Al-Nidal Didd Tashwih Harakat al-Thawra al-Arabiya* (The Struggle Against the Disfiguring of the Arab Revolutionary Movement). Beirut: Dar al-Tali'a, 1975.

———. *Fi Sabil al-Ba'th* (For the Sake of the Ba'th). Beirut: Dar al-Tali'a, 1963.

———. *Ma'rakat al-Masir al-Wahid* (The Battle of One Destiny). Beirut: Dar al-Adab, 1958.

al-Asad, Hafiz. *Kadhalika Qala al-Asad* (Thus Asad Said). Compiled by General Mustafa Tlas. Damascus: Tlas Press, 1984.

al-Hindi, Hani, and Abd al-Ilah al-Nasrawi. *Harakat al-Qawmiyyin al-'Arab: Nash'tuha wa Tataworiha 'ibr Wathaiqaha, 1951–1968* (The Arab Nationalist Movement: Its Emergence and Evolution Through Its Documents, 1951–1968). Pts. 1–2. Beirut: Institution of Arab Research, 2001–2002.

Baker, James A., III. *The Politics of Diplomacy: Revolution, War, and Peace 1989–1992.* New York: G. P. Putnam's Sons, 1995.

Ben-Tzur, Abraham, ed. *The Syrian Baath Party and Israel: Documents from the Internal Party Publications.* Givat Haviva: Center for Arab and Afro-Asian Studies, 1968.

Bureau of Public Affairs. U.S. Department of State. *U.S. Policy in the Middle East, December 1973–November 1974.* No. 12. Washington, D.C.: U.S. Government Printing Office, 1975.

———. *U.S. Policy in the Middle East, November 1974–February 1976.* No. 4. Washington, D.C.: U.S. Government Printing Office, 1976.

Central Bank of Syria. *Quarterly Bulletin* 35, nos. 1–2 (1997).

Congressional Information Service. 1992 House Resolution 4546, 102nd Congress; 1997 House Resolution 3080, 105th Congress; 1998 House Resolution 4569, 105th Congress.

Davis, Helen Miller. *Constitutions, Electoral Laws, Treaties of the States in the Near and Middle East.* Durham, N.C.: Duke University Press, 1953.

Dayan, Moshe. *Moshe Dayan: Story of My Life.* New York: William Morrow, 1976.

Djerejian, Edward P. *Current Developments in the Middle East.* Washington, D.C.: U.S. Government Printing Office, October 15, 1993.

Documents of the Arab Ba'th Socialist Party. *Nidal al-Ba'th* (The Struggle of the Ba'th). Vols. 1–6. Beirut: Dar al-Tali'a, 1963.

Economist Intelligence Unit. 1991, 1992, 1993, 1995, 1997, 1998, 1998–1999.

Hearing Before the Committee on Foreign Affairs, House of Representatives, July 22, 1992. *To Consider Release of Dual-Use Export Licenses to Iran and Syria Pursuant to Section 12(c) of the Export Administration Act.* Washington, D.C.: U.S. Government Printing Office, 1992.

Hearing Before the Committee on International Relations, House of Representatives. *Syria: Peace Partner or Rogue Regime?* Washington, D.C.: U.S. Government Printing Office, 1996.

Hearing Before the Subcommittees on Arms Control, International Security and Science, Europe and the Middle East of the Committee on Foreign Affairs, House of Representatives. *Conventional Arms Sales Policy in the Middle East.* Washington, D.C.: U.S. Government Printing Office, 1992.

Hearing Before the Subcommittee on Europe and the Middle East of the Committee on Foreign Affairs, House of Representatives. *The Situation in Lebanon, July 1989.* Washington, D.C.: U.S. Government Printing Office, 1989.

Hearing Before the Subcommittee on International Operations of the Committee on Foreign Affairs, House of Representatives. *American Hostages in Lebanon.* Washington, D.C.: U.S. Government Printing Office, 1990.

Hearing Before the Subcommittee on International Organizations and Movements of the Committee on Foreign Affairs, House of Representatives. *Treatment of Israeli POW's in Syria and Their Status Under the Geneva Conventions.* Washington, D.C.: U.S. Government Printing Office, 1974.

Higher Command of the Islamic Revolution in Syria. *Declaration and Program of the Islamic Revolution in Syria.* Damascus: N.p., 1980.

Hurewitz, J. C. *Diplomacy in the Near and Middle East: A Documentary Record, 1914–1956.* Princeton: D. Van Nostrand, 1956.

Kissinger, Henry. *The White House Years.* Boston: Little, Brown, 1979.

————. *Years of Upheaval.* Boston: Little, Brown, 1982.

Laqueur, Walter, and Barry Rubin, eds. *The Israel-Arab Reader: A Documentary History of the Middle East Conflict.* 5th ed. New York: Penguin Books, 1995.

McGovern, Senator George S. *Realities of the Middle East.* Washington, D.C.: U.S. Government Printing Office, 1975.

Muallem, Walid. "Beyond the Brink of Peace: Syria's Chief Negotiator Responds to Itamar Rabinovich's *The Brink of Peace.*" Damascus: N.p., n.d.

————. "Fresh Light on the Syrian-Israeli Peace Negotiations." *Journal of Palestine Studies* 26, no. 2 (Winter 1997).

Nixon, Richard M. *RN: The Memoirs of Richard Nixon.* New York: Grosset & Dunlap, 1978.

Peres, Shimon. *Battling for Peace.* New York: Random House, 1995.

Prados, Alfred B. "Syrian-U.S. Relations." *Congressional Research Service.* Washington, D.C.: Library of Congress, May 12, 1992.

Rabin, Yitzhak. *The Rabin Memoirs.* Expanded edition with new photographs, speeches, and an afterword by Yoram Eri. Berkeley: University of California Press, 1996.

Rabinovich, Itamar. *The Brink of Peace: The Israeli-Syrian Negotiations.* Princeton: Princeton University Press, 1998.

Reagan, Ronald. *An American Life.* New York: Simon & Schuster, 1990.

Report to the Committee on Foreign Relations, U.S. Senate, by Senator James M. Jeffords and Senator Hank Brown. *Trip to Croatia, Syria, Jordan, Israel, and Egypt.* Washington, D.C.: U.S. Government Printing Office, 1993.

Savir, Uri. *The Process: 1,100 Days That Changed the Middle East.* New York: Random House, 1998.

Staff Report Issued on November 23, 1992, by the Subcommittee on Crime and Criminal Justice of the Committee on the Judiciary. *Syria, President Bush, and Drugs: The Administration's Next Iraqgate.* Washington, D.C.: U.S. Government Printing Office, 1993.

Syrian Arab Republic. *Statistical Abstracts.* Office of the Prime Minister, General Bureau of Statistics, 1993, 1995.

Tomeh, George J., ed. *United Nations Resolutions on Palestine and the Arab-Israeli Conflict.* Vol. 1, *1947–1974.* Washington, D.C.: Institute for Palestine Studies, 1975.

U.S. Department of State. *American Foreign Policy: Basic Documents 1977–1980.* Washington, D.C.: U.S. Government Printing Office, 1983.

———. *American Foreign Policy: Current Documents 1957, 1961, 1964, 1966, 1981, 1982, 1984, 1988, 1990.* Washington, D.C.: U.S. Government Printing Office, (respectively) 1961, 1964, 1967, 1969, 1984, 1985, 1986, 1989, 1991.

———. *American Foreign Policy, 1950–1955: Basic Documents.* Vol. 2. Washington, D.C.: U.S. Government Printing Office, 1957.

———. "Israel Human Rights Practices 1995" and "Syrian Human Rights Practices 1995." *U.S. Foreign Affairs,* March 1996.

———. *Patterns of Global Terrorism 1994, 1995, 1996, 1997.* Washington, D.C.: U.S. Government Printing Office, (respectively) April 1995, April 1996, April 1997, April 1998.

U.S. Department of State Bulletin. 1957, 1964, 1973, 1977, 1979, 1982, 1983, 1984, 1985, 1986.

U.S. Department of State Dispatch. 1989, 1990, 1991, 1992, 1993, 1994, 1995, 1996.

U.S. Letters of Assurances to Syria and Israel, and Farouk al-Shara's and Yitzhak Shamir's addresses to the Madrid peace conference. *Journal of Palestine Studies* 21, no. 2 (Winter 1992).

Weekly Compilation of Presidential Documents (U.S.). 1983, 1984, 1985, 1991, 1992.

Weizman, Ezer. *The Battle for Peace.* New York: Bantam Books, 1981.

World Debt Tables. "External Finance for Developing Countries." *World Bank.* Vol. 2 (1996).

Articles

al-Hafiz, Yasin. "About the Experience of the Ba'th Party." *Fi al-Fikr al-Siyasi.* Vol. 1. Damascus: Dar Dimashq, 1963.

al-Haj, Majid. "The Political Behavior of the Arabs in Israel in the 1992 Elections: Integration Versus Segregation." In Asher Arian and Michal Shamir, eds., *The Elections in Israel, 1992.* New York: State University of New York Press, 1995.

Arian, Asher. "Israel's National Unity Governments and Domestic Politics." In Asher Arian and Michal Shamir, eds., *The Elections in Israel, 1988.* Boulder: Westview Press, 1990.

Arian, Asher, and Michal Shamir. "Two Reversals: Why 1992 Was Not 1977." In Asher Arian and Michal Shamir, eds. *The Elections in Israel, 1992.* New York: State University of New York Press, 1995.

Atasi, Jamal. "Arab Socialism and the Myth of [Its] Special Qualities." *Fi al-Fikr al-Siyasi.* Vol. 1. Damascus: Dar Dimashq, 1963.

Batatu, Hanna. "Some Observations on the Social Roots of Syria's Ruling Military Group and the Causes of Its Dominance." *Middle East Journal* 35, no. 3 (Summer 1981).

Ben-Tzur, Avraham. "The Neo-Ba'th Party of Syria." *Journal of Contemporary History* (Institute of Contemporary History, London) 3, no. 3 (July 1968).

Bick, Etta. "Sectarian Party Politics in Israel: The Case of Yisrael Ba'Aliya, the Russian Immigrant Party." In Daniel J. Elazar and Shmuel Sandler, eds., *Israel at the Polls, 1996.* London: Frank Cass, 1998.

Byrd, Senator Robert. "Senator Byrd on Loan Guarantees and U.S.-Israeli Relations." *Journal of Palestine Studies* 21, no. 4 (Summer 1992).

Caplan, Neil. "A Tale of Two Cities: The Rhodes and Lausanne Conferences, 1949." *Journal of Palestine Studies* 21, no. 3 (Spring 1992).

Cendar, Genkhis. "Sura li-Turkeya Mina al-Dakhel" (A Picture of Turkey from the Inside). *Shu'un al-Wasat* no. 64 (August 1997).

Clarke, Duncan L. "U.S. Security Assistance to Egypt and Israel: Politically Untouchable?" *Middle East Journal* 51, no. 2 (Spring 1997).

Dalila, Aref. "Al-Siyasat al-Iqtisadiya wa al-Ijtimai'ya wa al-Maliya fi Suriya" (Economic, Social, and Fiscal Policies in Syria). *Dirasat Ishtirakia* vol. 169 (Damascus, 1997).

Fein, Aharon. "Voting Trends of Recent Immigrants from the Former Soviet Union." In Asher Arian and Michal Shamir, eds., *The Elections in Israel, 1992.* New York: State University of New York Press, 1995.

Gresh, Alain. "Turkish-Israeli-Syrian Relations and their Impact on the Middle East." *Middle East Journal* 52, no. 2 (Spring 1998).

Hadar, Leon T. "High Noon in Washington: The Shootout over the Loan Guarantees." *Journal of Palestine Studies* 21, no. 2 (Winter 1992).

———. "The Last Days of Likud: The American-Israeli Big Chill." *Journal of Palestine Studies* 21, no. 4 (Summer 1992).

———. "The 1992 Electoral Earthquake and the Fall of the 'Second Israeli Republic.'" *Middle East Journal* 46, no. 4 (Autumn 1992).

Handel, Michael. "The Evolution of Israeli Strategy: The Psychology of Insecurity and the Quest for Absolute Security." In Williamson Murray, MacGregor Knox, and Alvin Bernstein, eds., *The Making of Strategy: Rulers, States, and War.* New York: Cambridge University Press, 1994.

Hazan, Reuven Y. "The Electoral Consequences of Political Reform: In Search of the Center of the Israeli Party System." In Asher Arian and Michal Shamir, eds., *The Elections in Israel, 1996.* Albany: State University of New York Press, 1999.

Heilman, Samuel C. "The Orthodox, the Ultra-Orthodox, and the Elections for the Twelfth Knesset." In Asher Arian and Michal Shamir, eds., *The Elections in Israel, 1988.* Boulder: Westview Press, 1990.

Heller, Peter B. "Document: The Permanent Syrian Constitution of March 13, 1973." *Middle East Journal* 28, no. 1 (Winter 1974).

Heydmann, Steven. "The Political Logic of Economic Rationality: Selective Stabilization in Syria." In Henri Barkey, ed., *The Politics of Economic Reform in the Middle East.* New York: St. Martin's Press, 1992.

Hinnebusch, Raymond A. "State, Civil Society, and Political Change in Syria." In Augustus Richard Norton, ed., *Civil Society in the Middle East.* Leiden: E. J. Brill, 1995.

Hirsch, Abraham M. "Utilization of the International Rivers in the Middle East." *American Journal of International Law* 50, no. 1 (January 1956).

Hof, Frederic C. "Analysis: The Line of June 4, 1967." *Middle East Insight,* September–October 1999.

Horowitz, Tamar. "Determining Factors of the Vote Among Immigrants from the Former Soviet Union." In Arian Asher and Michal Shamir, eds., *The Elections in Israel, 1996*. Albany: State University of New York Press, 1999.

Jones, Nathan. "Skepticism About Israel Accompanies Opposition to Loan Guarantees." *Washington Report on the Middle East Affairs,* April–May 1992.

Jouejati, Murhaf. "Water Politics as High Politics: The Case of Turkey and Syria." In Henri J. Barkey, ed., *Reluctant Neighbor: Turkey's Role in the Middle East*. Washington, D.C.: U.S. Institute of Peace Press, 1996.

Jumayil, Pierre. "Lebanese Nationalism and Its Foundations: The Phalangist Viewpoint." In Kemal H. Karpat, ed., *Political and Social Thought in the Contemporary Middle East*. New York: Praeger, 1970.

Khalidi, Walid. "The American Factor in the Arab-Israeli Conflict." *Middle East International,* January 30, 1998.

Khouri, Fred J. "Friction and Conflict on the Israeli-Syrian Front." *Middle East Journal* 17, nos. 1–2 (Winter–Spring 1963).

Khoury, Philip S. "Divided Loyalties? Syria and the Question of Palestine." *Middle Eastern Studies* 21, no. 3 (July 1985).

Kober, Avi. "A Paradigm in Crisis? Israel's Doctrine of Military Decision." In Efraim Karsh, ed., *Between War and Peace: Dilemmas of Israeli Security*. London: Frank Cass, 1996.

Levy, Avigdor. "The Syrian Communists and the Ba'th Power Struggle, 1966–1970." In Michael Confino and Shimoni Shamir, eds., *The U.S.S.R. and the Middle East*. Jerusalem: Israel Universities Press, 1973.

Little, Douglas. "Cold War and Covert Action: The United States and Syria, 1945–1958." *Middle East Journal* 44, no. 1 (Winter 1990).

Maksoud, General Ali Kudr. "Al-Stratigiyah al-Israiliya fi al-Tis'inat" (Israel's Strategy in the Nineties). *Al-Fikr al-Askari,* May–June 1996.

Ma'oz, Moshe. "Attempts at Creating a Political Community in Modern Syria." *Middle East Journal* 26, no. 4 (Autumn 1972).

Middle East Watch. "Human Rights Watch World Report 1992: 'The Israeli-Occupied West Bank and Gaza Strip.'" *Journal of Palestine Studies* 21, no. 4 (Summer 1992).

Morris, Benny. "A Second Look at the 'Missed Peace,' or Smoothing Out History: A Review Essay." *Journal of Palestine Studies* 24, no. 1 (Autumn 1994).

Murakami, Masahiro, and Katsumi Musiake. "The Jordan River and the Litani." In Asit K. Biswas, ed., *International Waters of the Middle East: From Euphrates-Tigris to Nile*. Oxford: Oxford University Press, 1994.

Murqus, Ilyas. "Collapse of the Parliamentary System." *Fi al-Fikr al-Siyasi*. Vol. 2. Damascus: Dar Dimashq, 1963.

Nachmani, Amikam. "The Remarkable Turkish-Israeli Tie." *Middle East Quarterly* 5, no. 2 (June 1998).

Naveh, Shimon. "The Cult of the Offensive Preemption and the Future Challenges for Israeli Operational Thought." In Efraim Karsh, ed., *Between War and Peace: Dilemmas of Israeli Security*. London: Frank Cass, 1996.

Perthes, Volker. "From Front-Line State to Backyard? Syria and the Economic Risks of Regional Peace." *Beirut Review* no. 8 (Fall 1994).

———. "The Private Sector, Economic Liberalization, and the Prospects of Democratization: The Case of Syria and Some Other Arab Countries." In Ghassan Salame, ed., *Democracy Without Democrats? The Renewal of Politics in the Muslim World*. London: I. B. Tauris, 1994.

Polling, Sylvia. "Syria's Private Sector: Economic Liberalization and the Challenges of the 1990s." In Gerd Nonneman, ed., *Political and Economic Liberalization:*

Dynamics and Linkages in Comparative Perspective. Boulder: Lynne Rienner, 1996.

Rabil, Robert G. "The Maronites and Syrian Withdrawal: From 'Isolationists' to 'Traitors'?" *Middle East Policy* 8, no. 3 (September 2001).

Reich, Bernard, Noah Dropkin, and Meyrav Wurmser. "Soviet Jewish Immigration and the 1992 Israeli Knesset Elections." *Middle East Journal* 47, no. 3 (Summer 1993).

Robinson, Glenn E. "Elite Cohesion, Regime Succession, and Political Instability in Syria." *Middle East Policy* 5, no. 4 (January 1998).

Sabet, Amr. G. E. "The Peace Process and the Politics of Conflict Resolution." *Journal of Palestine Studies* 27, no. 4 (Summer 1998).

Safran, Nadav. "Dimension of the Middle East Problem." In Roy Macridis, ed., *Foreign Policy in World Politics.* 8th ed. Englewood Cliffs, N.J.: Prentice Hall, 1992.

Sayigh, Yezid. "Escalation or Containment? Egypt and the Palestine Liberation Army, 1964–67." *International Journal of Middle East Studies* 30, no. 1 (February 1998).

Seale, Patrick, and Linda Butler. "Asad's Regional Strategy and the Challenge from Netanyahu." *Journal of Palestine Studies* 26, no. 1 (Autumn 1996).

Shlaim, Avi. "The Debate About 1948." *International Journal of Middle East Studies* 27, no. 3 (August 1995).

———. "Husni Za'im and the Plan to Resettle Palestinian Refugees in Syria." *Journal of Palestine Studies* 15, no. 4 (Summer 1986).

Shuval, Hillel I. "Water and Security in the Middle East: The Israeli-Syrian Water Confrontations as a Case Study." In Lenore G. Martin, ed., *New Frontiers in Middle East Security.* New York: Palgrave, 2001.

Smooha, Sammy, and Don Peretz. "Israel's 1992 Knesset Elections: Are They Critical?" *Middle East Journal* 47, no. 3 (Summer 1993).

Specter, Arlen, and Daniel Pipes. "Arlen Specter: Invite Asad to the White House." *Middle East Quarterly* 4, no. 1 (March 1997).

Susser, Bernard. "The Direct Election of the Prime Minister: A Balance Sheet." In Daniel J. Elazar and Shmuel Sandler, eds., *Israel at the Polls, 1996.* London: Frank Cass, 1998.

Tinaoui, Simone Ghazi. "An Analysis of the Syrian-Lebanese Economic Agreements." *Beirut Review* no. 8 (Fall 1994).

Torgovnik, Efraim. "Likud 1977–81: The Consolidation of Power." In Robert O. Freedman, ed., *Israel in the Begin Era.* New York: Praeger, 1982.

Willis, Aaron P. "Shas: The Sephardic Torah Guardians: Religious 'Movement' and Political Power." In Asher Arian and Michal Shamir, eds., *The Elections in Israel, 1992.* New York: State University of New York Press, 1995.

Wishart, David M. "The Breakdown of the Johnston Negotiations over the Jordan Waters." *Middle Eastern Studies* 26, no. 4 (October 1990).

Yaniv, Michal. "Peres the Leader, Peres the Politician." In Asher Arian and Michal Shamir, eds., *The Elections in Israel, 1996.* Albany: State University of New York Press, 1999.

Yishai, Yael. "Factionalism in the National Religious Party: The Quiet Revolution." In Asher Arian, ed., *The Elections in Israel, 1977.* Jerusalem: Jerusalem Academic Press, 1980.

Zisser, Eyal. "The Maronites, Lebanon, and the State of Israel: Early Contacts." *Middle Eastern Studies* 31, no. 4 (October 1995).

———. "The Succession Struggle in Damascus." *Middle East Quarterly* 2, no. 3 (September 1995).

Books

Ajami, Fouad. *The Vanished Imam: Musa al Sadr and the Shi'a of Lebanon.* Ithaca: Cornell University Press, 1986.

al-Azm, Khaled. *Mudhakkirat* (Memoirs). Vol. 2. Beirut: Al-Dar al-Taqadumiya lil-Nashr, 1973.

al-Jundi, Sami. *Al-Ba'th.* Beirut: Dar al-Nahar, 1969.

al-Khair, Hani. *Akram Hawrani: Bayna al-Tanaqulat al-Siyasiya wa al-Inqilabat al-Askaria* (Akram Hawrani: Between Political Movements and Military Coup d'É-tats). Damascus: New Orient Press, 1996.

Allan, J. A., and Chibli Mallat, eds. *Water in the Middle East: Legal, Political, and Commercial Implications.* London: I. B. Tauris, 1995.

Anderson, Terry A. *Den of Lions: Memoirs of Seven Years.* New York: Crown, 1993.

Azoury, Negib. *Le Reveil de la Nation Arabe dans l'Asie Turque.* Paris: Plon-Nourrit, 1905.

Bailey, Sydney D. *Four Arab-Israeli Wars and the Peace Process.* London: Macmillan, 1990.

Bar-Simon-Tov, Yaacov. *Israel and the Peace Process, 1977–1982: In Search of Legitimacy for Peace.* Albany: State University of New York Press, 1994.

———. *Peace Policy as Domestic and as Foreign Policy: The Israeli Case.* Jerusalem: Leonard Davis Institute, Hebrew University of Jerusalem, 1998.

Bar-Yaacov, Nissim. *The Israel-Syrian Armistice: Problems of Implementation, 1949–1966.* Jerusalem: Magnes Press, Hebrew University, 1967.

Batatu, Hanna. *Syria's Peasantry, the Descendants of Its Lesser Rural Notables, and Their Politics.* Princeton: Princeton University Press, 1999.

Be'eri Eliezer. *Army Officers in Arab Politics and Society.* New York: Praeger, 1970.

Ben-Horin, Yoav, and Barry Posen. *Israel's Strategic Doctrine.* Santa Monica: Rand, 1981.

Beschorner, Natasha. *Water and Instability in the Middle East.* Adelphi Paper no. 273. London: International Institute for Strategic Studies, 1992.

Biswas, Asit K., John Kolars, Masahiro Murakami, John Waterbury, and Aaron Wolf. *Core and Periphery: A Comprehensive Approach to Middle Eastern Water.* Oxford: Oxford University Press, Middle East Water Commission Sasakawa Peace Foundation, 1997.

Blum, Zvi Yehuda. *Secure Boundaries and Middle East Peace.* Jerusalem: Hebrew University of Jerusalem, Faculty of Law, 1971.

Boogaerde, Pierre Van Den. *Financial Assistance from Arab Countries and Arab Regional Institutions.* Washington, D.C.: International Monetary Fund, 1991.

Bradley, C. Paul. *Parliamentary Elections in Israel: Three Case Studies.* Grantham, N.H.: Tompson and Rutter, 1985.

Brom, Shlomo, and Yiftah Shapir, eds. *The Middle East Military Balance, 1999–2000.* Cambridge: MIT Press, 2000.

Brookings Middle East Study Group. *Toward Peace in the Middle East.* Washington, D.C.: Brookings Institution, 1975.

Brown, Seyom. *The Faces of Power: Constancy and Change in United States Foreign Policy from Truman to Clinton.* New York: Columbia University Press, 1994.

Carter, Jimmy. *The Blood of Abraham.* Boston: Houghton Mifflin, 1985.

Cohen, Eliot A., Michael J. Eisenstadt, and Andrew J. Bacevich. *Knives, Tanks, and Missiles: Israel's Security Revolution.* Washington, D.C.: Washington Institute for Near East Policy, 1998.

Committee on the Exercise of the Inalienable Rights of the Palestinian People. *Water Resources of the Occupied Palestinian Territory.* New York: United Nations, 1992.

Copeland, Miles. *The Game of Nations.* London: Weidenfeld & Nicholson, 1969.

Diab, Iz al-Din. *Akram Hawrani . . . Kama A'ariftahou* (Akram Hawrani . . . How I Knew Him). Beirut: Beisan Press, 1998.

Eisenstadt, Michael. *Arming for Peace? Syria's Elusive Quest for "Strategic Parity."* Washington, D.C.: Washington Institute for Near East Policy, 1992.

el-Shazly, Lieutenant-General Saad. *The Crossing of the Suez.* San Fransisco: American Mideast Research, 1980.

Faour, Muhammad. *The Arab World After Desert Storm.* Washington, D.C.: U.S. Institute of Peace Press, 1993.

Farsoun, Samih K. *Palestine and the Palestinians.* Boulder: Westview Press, 1997.

Feldman, Shai. *The Future of U.S.-Israel Strategic Cooperation.* Washington, D.C.: Washington Institute for Near East Policy, 1996.

———. *Nuclear Weapons and Arms Control in the Middle East.* Cambridge: MIT Press, 1997.

Flapan, Simha. *The Birth of Israel: Myths and Realities.* New York: Pantheon, 1987.

Haig, Alexander M., Jr. *Caveat: Realism, Reagan, and Foreign Policy.* New York: Macmillan, 1984.

Haim, Sylvia G. *Arab Nationalism: An Anthology.* Berkeley: University of California Press, 1962.

Hamizrachi, Beate. *The Emergence of the South Lebanon Security Belt.* New York: Praeger, 1988.

Harkabi, Yehoshafat. *Arab Strategies and Israel's Responses.* New York: Free Press, 1977.

Heikal, Mohamed. *The Road to Ramadan.* London: Williams Collins Sons, 1975.

Hinnebusch, Raymond. *Authoritarian Power and State Formation in Baathist Syria: Army, Party, and Peasant.* Boulder: Westview Press, 1990.

Human Rights Watch. *Israel's Record of Occupation: Violations of Civil and Political Rights.* New York: Human Rights Watch, 1998.

Jumblat, Kamal. *Fi Majra al-Siyasah al-Lubnaniya* (In the Course of Lebanese Politics). Beirut: Dar al-Tali'a, 1962.

———. *Hadhihi Wasiyati* (This Is My Will). Paris: Stok, 1978.

———. *Lubnan wa Harb al-Taswiya* (Lebanon and the War for a Settlement). N.p.: Center of Socialist Studies, Progressive Socialist Party, 1977.

Kelidar, Abbas, and Michael Burrel. *Lebanon: The Collapse of a State.* London: Eastern Press, 1976.

Khoury, Philip S. *Syria and the French Mandate: The Politics of Arab Nationalism, 1920–1945.* Princeton: Princeton University Press, 1987.

———. *Urban Notables and Arab Nationalism.* Cambridge: Cambridge University Press, 1983.

Kliot, Nurit. *Water Resources and Conflict in the Middle East.* London: Routledge, 1994.

Kolars, John F., and William A. Mitchell. *The Euphrates River and the Southeast Anatolia Development Project.* Carbondale: Southern Illinois University Press, 1991.

Levran, Aharon. *Israeli Strategy After Desert Storm: Lessons of the Second Gulf War.* London: Frank Cass, 1997.

Lochery, Neill. *The Israeli Labour Party: In the Shadow of the Likud.* Reading, UK: Ithaca Press, 1997.

Lowi, Miriam R. *Water and Power: The Politics of a Scarce Resource in the Jordan River Basin.* Cambridge: Cambridge University Press, 1993.

Mahler, Gregory S. *The Knesset: Parliament in the Israeli Political System.* Rutherford, N.J.: Fairleigh Dickenson University Press, 1981.

Malik, Habib C. *Between Damascus and Jerusalem: Lebanon and Middle East Peace.* Washington, D.C.: Washington Institute for Near East Policy, 1997.

Ma'oz, Moshe. *Asad: The Sphinx of Damascus, a Political Biography.* New York: Weidenfeld & Nicolson, 1988.

————. *Syria and Israel: From War to Peacemaking.* Oxford: Clarendon Press, 1995.

Middle East Contemporary Survey. Tel Aviv University: Moshe Dayan Center for Middle Eastern and African Studies, 1976–1977, 1989, 1990, 1991, 1992, 1993, 1994, 1995, 1996, 1997, 1998.

Middle East Watch. *Syria Unmasked: The Suppression of Human Rights by the Asad Regime.* New York: Vail-Ballou Press, 1991.

Morris, Benny. *The Birth of the Palestinian Refugee Problem, 1947–1949.* Cambridge: Cambridge University Press, 1988.

————. *1948 and After: Israel and the Palestinians.* Oxford: Oxford University Press, 1990.

————. *Righteous Victims: A History of the Zionist-Arab Conflict.* New York: Knopf, 1999.

Naff, Thomas, and Ruth C. Matson, eds. *Water in the Middle East: Conflict or Cooperation?* Boulder: Westview Press, 1984.

Nasrallah, Fida. *Prospects for Lebanon: The Questions of South Lebanon.* Oxford: Centre for Lebanese Studies, 1992.

Netanyahu, Benjamin. *Fighting Terrorism: How Democracies Can Defeat Domestic and International Terrorists.* New York: Farrar, Straus, and Giroux, 1995.

————. *A Place Among Nations: Israel and the World.* New York: Bantam Books, 1993.

Pakradouni, Karim. *La' nat Watan: Min Harb Lubnan ila Harb al-Khalij* (Curse of a Fatherland: From the Lebanese War to the Gulf War). Beirut: Trans-Orient Press, 1992.

Pappe, Ilan. *Britain and the Arab-Israeli Conflict, 1948–51.* London: Macmillan, 1988.

Peres, Shimon, and Arye Naor. *The New Middle East.* New York: Henry Holt, 1993.

Perthes, Volker. *The Political Economy of Syria Under Asad.* London: I. B. Tauris, 1995.

Pipes, Daniel. *Greater Syria: The History of an Ambition.* Oxford: Oxford University Press, 1990.

————. *Syria Beyond the Peace Process.* Washington, D.C.: Washington Institute for Near East Policy, 1996.

Puschel, Karen L. *U.S.-Israel Strategic Cooperation in the Post–Cold War Era: An American Perspective.* Tel Aviv: Jaffee Center for Strategic Studies, 1992.

Quandt, William B. *Camp David: Peacemaking and Politics.* Washington, D.C.: Brookings Institution, 1986.

————. *Decade of Decisions: American Policy Toward the Arab-Israeli Conflict, 1967–1976.* Berkeley: University of California Press, 1977.

————. *Peace Process: American Diplomacy and the Arab-Israeli Conflict Since 1967.* Berkeley: University of California Press, 1993.

Rabinovich, Itamar. *The Road Not Taken: Early Arab-Israeli Negotiations.* New York: Oxford University Press, 1991.

————. *Syria Under the Ba'th, 1963–1966: The Army-Party Symbiosis.* Jerusalem: Israel Universities Press, 1972.

————. *Waging Peace: Israel and the Arabs at the End of the Century.* New York: Farrar, Straus, and Giroux, 1999.

————. *The War for Lebanon, 1970–1985.* Ithaca: Cornell University Press, 1985.

Roy, Sara M. *The Gaza Strip: A Demographic, Economic, Social, and Legal Survey.* Boulder: Westview Press, 1986.

————. *The Gaza Strip: The Political Economy of De-Development.* Washington, D.C.: Institute for Palestine Studies, 1995.

————. *The Palestinian Economy and the Oslo Process: Decline and Fragmentation.* Abu Dhabi: Emirates Center for Strategic Studies and Research, 1998.

Safran, Nadav. *Israel: The Embattled Ally.* Cambridge: Belknap Press of Harvard University Press, 1981.

————. *Reforming Israel's Political System: What Needs to Be Done?* Cambridge: Harvard University Press, 1991.

Schiff, Ze'ev. *Peace with Security: Israel's Minimal Security Requirements in Negotiations with Syria.* Washington, D.C.: Washington Institute for Near East Policy, 1993.

Schmida, Leslie. *Keys to Control: Israel's Pursuit of Arab Water Resources.* Washington, D.C.: American Educational Trust, 1983.

Seale, Patrick. *Asad of Syria: The Struggle for the Middle East.* Berkeley: University of California Press, 1988.

————. *The Struggle for Syria: A Study of Post-War Arab Politics, 1945–1958.* London: Oxford University Press, 1965.

Shalev, Aryeh. *The Intifada: Causes and Effects.* Boulder: Westview Press, 1991.

————. *Israel and Syria: Peace and Security on the Golan.* Boulder: Westview Press, 1994.

Shimoni, Gideon. *The Zionist Ideology.* Hanover: Brandeis University Press, 1995.

Shlaim, Avi. *Collusion Across the Jordan: King Abdullah, the Zionist Movement, and the Partition of Palestine.* Oxford: Clarendon Press, 1988.

————. *The Iron Wall: Israel and the Arab World.* New York: W. W. Norton, 2000.

Tessler, Mark. *A History of the Israeli-Palestinian Conflict.* Bloomington: Indiana University Press, 1994.

Tibi, Bassam. *Arab Nationalism: A Critical Enquiry.* 2nd ed. New York: St. Martin's Press, 1990.

Tlas, General Mustafa. *Mar'at Hayati: Al-Aqd al-Awal, 1948–1958* (Mirror of My Life: The First Decade, 1948–1958). 2nd ed. Damascus: Tlas Press, 1997.

Tlas, General Mustafa, et al. *Al-Ghazu al-Israili li-Lubnan* (The Israeli Invasion of Lebanon). Damascus: Tlas Press, 1985.

Van Dam, Nikolaos. *The Struggle for Power in Syria: Politics and Society Under Asad and the Ba'th Party.* London: I. B. Tauris, 1996.

Wedeen, Lisa. *Ambiguities of Domination: Politics, Rhetoric, and Symbols in Contemporary Syria.* Chicago: University of Chicago Press, 1999.

Wolffson, Michael. *Israel, Polity, Society and Economy, 1882–1986.* Atlantic Highlands, N.J.: Humanities Press International, 1987.

Yariv, Aharon. *War in the Gulf: Implications for Israel.* Boulder: Westview Press, 1992.

Index

Abou Ghudda, Abd al-Fatah, 137
Abu Nidal, 66
Accountability, Operation, 204–205
Adwan, Mamdouh, 261–262
Aflaq, Michel, 27–29
Agriculture: agrarian reform, 16; cultivation
 of land within the DMZ, 14; hydropolitics,
 190, 192–193; Israeli-Jordanian peace
 treaty, 229
al-Ahmar, Abd allah, 273
AIPAC. *See* American Israel Public Affairs
 Committee
Airborne warning and command systems
 (AWACs), 63
Ajami, Fouad, 57
Akkad, Hashem, 270
Alawi sect, 32, 34, 50, 119–127
Albright, Madeleine K., 218
Alexandria summit, 230
Algeria, 227
Allaf, Muwaffaq, 200
All-Arab Ba'th Congress, 17–18
Allison, Graham, 106
Allon, Yigal, 36
Alpher, Joseph, 104
Amal militia, 56–57, 70, 73–74, 77–78
Ambassadors' channel, 207–208
American Israel Public Affairs Committee
 (AIPAC), 91–92, 99
Amir, Yigal, 211
Amman summit, 230–231
Anderson, Terry, 89
ANM. *See* Arab Nationalist Movement
Annan, Kofi, 271
Aoun, Michael, 78–80, 83(n64), 277
April Understanding, 214, 223
Arab anti-Iraq coalition, 181
Arab League, 189, 225, 276

Arab Legion, 6
Arab nationalism: molding the Middle East
 situation, 1, 5; as obstacle to peace
 negotiations, 260; as tenet of Ba'th Party,
 27–28; weakening under Asad, 33
Arab Nationalist Movement (ANM), 28,
 41(n69). *See also* National Movement
Arab summit (Cairo, 1964), 17
Arab unity, 27–34, 231
Arad, Uzi, 106
Arafat, Yasser: formation of guerrilla groups,
 21; George W. Bush's view of, 111;
 improving Syrian-Palestinian relations,
 283(n41); Israeli invasion of West Beirut,
 67; Israeli-Palestinian peace agreement,
 205–206; Lebanese civil war, 51; PLO
 founding, 17
Arens, Moshe, 75, 109, 222
Argov, Shlomo, 66
Armistice agreements, 6–10, 14–20,
 234(n25). *See also* Cease-fire agreements
Armistice Demarcation line, 9
Arms control, 179
Arms Control and Regional Security (ACRS),
 179
Arslan, Emir Majid, 69
Arslan, Emir Talal, 69
al-Asad, Bashar, 238(n96); balancing
 economic and political reform with
 national security, 277–279; election as
 president, 272–274; as potential successor
 to Asad, 139–141, 148(n92), 269;
 repositioning Syrian troops in Christian
 Lebanon, 282(n37); response to
 Shepherdstown talks, 221–222; on
 resuming Syrian-Israeli peace talks, 226
al-Asad, Basil, 139, 237(n78)
al-Asad, Dorid, 141

About the Book

Israel's ongoing dispute with Syria and Lebanon gravely undermines the potential for peace in the Middle East. Charting the course of this triangular relationship since 1948, Robert G. Rabil successfully integrates the domestic and international dynamics of the key players to reveal the complexities of this seemingly intractable conflict.

Robert G. Rabil served with the Red Cross in Lebanon, taught at Suffolk University, Boston, and currently is the project manager of the Iraq Research and Documentation Project at the Iraq Foundation, Washington, D.C.